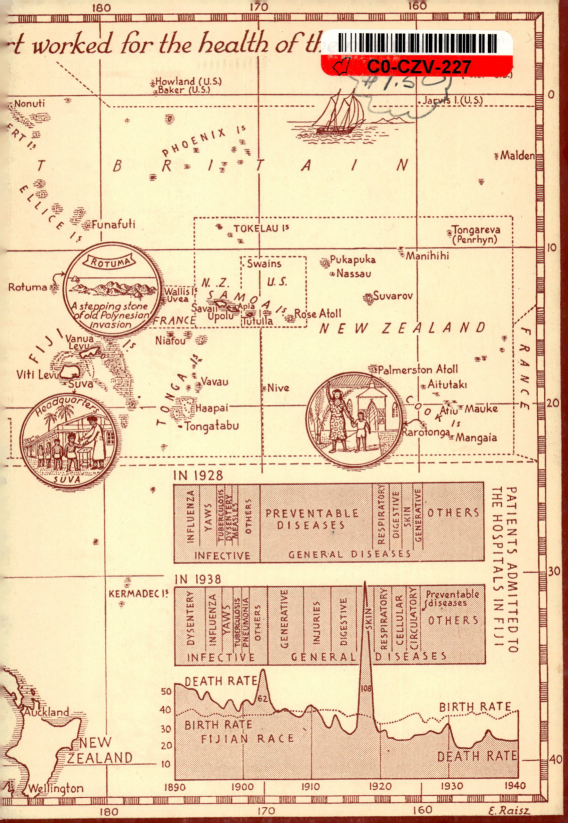

...t worked for the health of th...

PATIENTS ADMITTED TO THE HOSPITALS IN FIJI

IN 1928

INFECTIVE					GENERAL DISEASES				
INFLUENZA	YAWS	TUBERCULOSIS	DYSENTERY MEASLES	OTHERS	PREVENTABLE DISEASES	RESPIRATORY	DIGESTIVE	SKIN GENERATIVE	OTHERS

IN 1938

INFECTIVE						GENERAL		DISEASES				
DYSENTERY	INFLUENZA	YAWS	TUBERCULOSIS PNEUMONIA	OTHERS	GENERATIVE	INJURIES	DIGESTIVE	SKIN	RESPIRATORY	CELLULAR	CIRCULATORY	Preventable diseases OTHERS

DEATH RATE 50 62 108
BIRTH RATE 40
BIRTH RATE 30
FIJIAN RACE 20
10
DEATH RATE

1890 1900 1910 1920 1930 1940

E. Raisz

A YANKEE DOCTOR
IN PARADISE

THE AUTHOR

A YANKEE DOCTOR
IN PARADISE

BY S. M. LAMBERT, M.D.

BOSTON
LITTLE, BROWN AND COMPANY
1946

Published May 1941
Reprinted May 1941 (twice)
Reprinted July 1941
Reprinted December 1946

DEDICATION

To my father, William Walter Lambert, who made sacrifices for my education, who never harassed me with advice; I did the things he would have liked to do.

AND TO

Eloisa Tays Lambert, my wife, who has packed and unpacked in a hundred homes, nursed me when I was sick, made me go on when I wanted to quit; there wouldn't be any story without Eloisa.

FOREWORD

In 1927 there were two plump New York-Californians vacationing in Fiji: Martin Egan and Wallace Irwin. It thrilled me to meet the creator of my boyhood's admiration, "Hashimura Togo," and I was pleased if unprepared when he wanted me to put my adventures — then half completed — into a book. I remember our three days' trip to Mbengga to see the fire-walkers; all the way I was enthralled with his experiences as a writer on the other side of the world; he could talk two hundred words to the minute, a record that surpasses mine. Our meeting resulted in a desultory correspondence that covered several years. When I came home with a trunkful of my own data I naturally turned to him for help; and I want to thank him for the patient editorial advice through which I have been able to assemble a quantity of rather mixed material, and to put it into some form.

I have so many to thank besides those mentioned in the text — few have been other than helpful. Probably I am the most grateful to the British in the South Pacific colonies, officials and laymen. If a Britisher had come to an American colony and assumed the critical role to which my job compelled me, he would have been tarred and feathered and ridden out of bounds. Their long tolerance reminds me of the Arizona saloon motto: "Don't Shoot the Pianist. He's Doing His Damndest."

We were made to feel welcome in the various communities as we moved along. My daughter, Sara Celia, was born in Suva, Fiji; I owned a house there, and on momentous occasions had my vote solicited by Henry Marks, Alport Barker and Pat Costello. I belonged to the Fiji Club. Uncle Bill Paley and I settled mine and the world's affairs in a few minutes every morning. What more has the future to offer?

Space did not permit me to emphasize the admiration I have for New Zealand's high conduct in native affairs. I had the best advice and cooperation, from the Permanent Head of the Prime Minister's Department and the Director General of Health down through the Civil Service.

If I had the privilege of making out my Personal Honor Role I should certainly put Fiji's Colonial Sugar Refining Company close to the head of it. Without their W. P. Dixon and F. C. T. Lord I could not have progressed far in my Fijian endeavors; for in 1922 the island communications were next to nothing, and almost every hookworm district was over the cane lands they controlled, and opened up for me. We lived in their quarters, used their track-cars and railroad, had the assistance of the managers and underofficials of this whacking big Australian concern, operating in both Fiji and North Queensland.

And I want to thank my Field Inspectors, young fellows who knew how to do about anything — except complain; men like Chris Kendrick, Kenny Fooks and Bill Tully, — whose Irish mother said, "Doctor, you'll take care of Willie, won't you?" — and the wild American lad, Byron Beach.

And Malakai, the Fijian practitioner with an inflexible medical conscience. In jungle, swamp or canoe, nobody would wish for a stronger heart or a better brain.

I was just an item in the Rockefeller Foundation's globe-circling humanitarianism. Dr. Victor Heiser gave me my first job in the South Pacific; Dr. Sawyer, now Director for the International Health Division, turned the tide for me when my favorite plan seemed about to fail. With Dr. Heiser I have tramped over Fiji and Samoa, agreeing or disagreeing on various questions of tropical health. Once or twice he turned to me and asked, "Lambert, why don't you write a book?"

Well, this is the book.

S. M. L.

Walnut Creek, California

CONTENTS

PART ONE

PART TWO

PART THREE

I	Old Brandy and New Eggs	279
II	Another Island Night's Entertainment	284
III	Through the Solomons to Rennell	315
IV	The Fate of a Race	335
V	Such a Little School	357
VI	In Retrospect	377
	Index	387

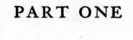

PART ONE

PART ONE

CHAPTER I

SHORT NOTICE FOR A LONG CHORE

"Lambert, I've got a good one for you this time. I'm sending you to Papua."

Dr. Victor G. Heiser, the Rockefeller Foundation's famous Director of the East, made this announcement as if Papua were across the street.

"That's fine, Doctor," I said, "perfectly fine."

Papua? Where was Papua? Vainly I fished for scraps of geography and pulled up impressions of palmy islands where black warriors asked guests how they liked their missionary, rare or well done.

Dr. Heiser sat behind a modest desk in one of the smallest rooms at 61 Broadway, delivering a sort of curtain speech to an act that had taken longer than a Chinese play, an act which had played through the war summer of 1918. I had finally found a successor and resigned my superintendency of the United Fruit Company's hospital in Costa Rica; I was in New York to offer my services. But Uncle Sam wasn't looking for medical officers with weak eyes.

Now Dr. Heiser's kindly voice was praising and instructing one of the family, for at last I had joined up with the Foundation. There he was, kneeing his desk, telling me nothing about Papua, saying that my Costa Rican and Mexican experience had particularly fitted me for work with the International Health Board, not mentioning that war had taken away many of their physicians. He dwelt on the preparatory three months' hookworm training I had already taken, under the Foundation's auspices, among the hillbillies of Mississippi . . . kept me moving, didn't it, canvassing from door to door? . . . Lambert, you can work a lot faster down in the South Pacific, where you'll lecture and treat in batches of from fifty to five hundred. . . . You'll have to cover a lot of ground down there. . . . Take along plenty of khaki, and no evening clothes. . . . Get your family ready and start day after tomorrow.

"And on your way to Papua, Lambert, you'd better report to Waite, who's in charge of our work in Australia. There's quite a hookworm campaign going on in North Queensland. Good place to brush up on what you'll need in Papua. You'll find the Australians good fellows, like our Westerners, rough and generous and tolerant — they haven't had to jam together in big cities and get small-minded."

During our argumentative stage, I had told Dr. Heiser about a mining syndicate's offer to take me down to Peru. I didn't bring that up again, or mention General Gorgas' half-promise to forgive my blinky eyes and commission me in the venereal section of the Medical Corps.

When I left that morning I was under the spell of the Heiser charm; a charm that has sent armies of scientific men, great and small, to follow jungle trails all over this planet, and work until they drop. In later years I walked with him along some of those trails, and my admiration for him increased every step of the way. There is a godlike something about Heiser that will never let him fall from the pedestal he deserves. Grant him clay toes if you wish, he is still a colossus who has bestridden the field of public health for twenty years — and been the target of much professional jealousy. In 1937 when I was at a League Conference in Java I heard an envious Yankee voice say, "Yes, I've read his *American Doctor's Odyssey,* and I wonder why he didn't call it *Alone in the Orient.*" Which gave me the luxury of a reply: "Did you watch him inaugurate public health work in the Philippines? *Alone in the Orient* describes it rather well."

I found an atlas and looked up Papua. Rather dully I was informed that Papua lay on the southeastern edge of New Guinea, the second largest island in the world — the Australian Continent's hottest neighbor, no doubt, since its northern shoulder jogged the equator. The extremely savage names of its numerous tribes, the aimless fertility of its soil, its wealth of gold, copper and pearls, struck only dull fire on my imagination. I was going to a place called Papua, not to flirt with rubber-bellied brunettes in grass skirts, but to search sensibly for yaws, malaria, dysentery, tuberculosis and intestinal parasites. And to rout out the hookworm as tamely as I had poked him up in polluted Mississippi.

That was 1918, when a trip to Paris and back was something to talk about. The armistice hadn't yet sent back a million doughboys with a smattering of obscene French. The world cruise hadn't risen as a major industry. Today any debutante who has sauntered around the globe can tell you more about Fiji fire-walking and Arabian sword-swallowers than anybody but a professional explorer knew then.

No, the hereditary Lambert is not a geographer. We are a home-body family, and I often wonder how the colonial Lamberts ever found courage to cross over from England to seventeenth-century New Jersey. They certainly stayed put when they got here; nothing but hunger and Indian raids could budge them. My father, who was a tanner and often used his best leather trying to teach me civility, was looked upon as something of a sea rover because he once drove mules along the Delaware and Hudson Canal towpath. Relatives in Ellenville, New York, where I was born, paled when they learned that Father was moving us to Little Falls.

Our pious Methodists always regarded Father as a freethinker; and wasn't it like him to want Sylvester to be a doctor? Mr. Babcock, head of our Free Academy in West Winfield, was even more radical. A boy ought to have a college education before he started studying medicine. I had worked with the tannery gang long enough, and had learned too many of the rich, brown oaths they spat out with their chewing tobacco. Hamilton College was the place to smooth me out for medical school. Hamilton College! My mother's hands went up at the spectral idea of a place so remote that Sylvester would have to go overnight, by train.

I entered with the class of 1903, and the thought of all my father sacrificed to send me there made me a rather earnest student — that, and his threat of more tannery, if I didn't make good. I am thankful that Hamilton and the Syracuse Medical, which I later attended, were both small, for in small classes the instructor knows the needs and failings of every student. I was a hard worker, but not a grind. I found time for football, which toughened the tannery boy for harder years to come. Trips with the team to rival colleges were early adventures in foreign travel. Colgate, swollen with toothpaste money, was easy fruit for us then. Williams rubbed our noses in the mud to the tune of 4-0 — and I wept, limping off the field.

Sometimes in my late middle age I awake from sleep swearing. I have been dreaming of a game with the Carlisle Indians. That big Injun, Red Water, is on the line opposite me, tall as a church, never losing his grin. The ball is snapped and his long arm reaches tenderly over me, gets the seat of my britches . . .

In 1904 I was prepared for Johns Hopkins, but Mother wanted to know what I'd be doing with myself, 'way over in Maryland. Syracuse was in New York State, anyhow, and that was far enough for anybody.

Syracuse had a faculty disproportionately large and able for so small an enrollment. The ideal of scholarship was Spartan; if a student's nose roved from the grindstone it was pushed back again. The quizzes were little inquisitions, the recitations no place for a sleepwalker. To study under Elsner, Jacobson and Levy was to appreciate Jewish respect for scholarship. Dr. Steenson, of the Department of Pathology, had a time-keeper's complex and you missed his eight-thirty bell at your own risk. We called him "Johnnie Cockeye," for his devotion to the gonococcus germ. I stared through the microscope for interminable hours, seeing but little on the slides. My eyes were already going, but I could read easily. Before I came to class I knew, theoretically, what I was sup-posed to see under the glass — and that's how I coped with Steenson's sudden quizzes.

The very distinguished Dr. Frank William Marlow, graduate of the Royal College of Surgeons, is dead now, but he crowned his career with a book called *The Relative Position of Rest of the Eyes*. A course un-der him put my eyesight, quite literally, on the blink. And this is how it came about.

Toward the end of my third year my brother became seriously ill, and I had to take him to Arizona. There I discovered, to my bald aston-ishment, that this Lambert had a wandering foot. In Tucson I obeyed a mad impulse and joined the crazy medical unit of a construction gang, working down the West Coast of Mexico. I had time to grow romantic when I came to the fine old hacienda of Mr. Eugene Tays, an American mining engineer. The dark eyes of his pretty daughter, Eloisa, melted my every ambition to go home and plug again at a stiff medical course. She was half Spanish, one of the influential Vegas around San Blas; but she had enough Scotch common sense to tell me to go home and graduate. When I had a practice of my own, she said, I could come back and marry her. She had to wait five years, but she kept her promise.

So I went back to Syracuse, weeks behind in my work and facing the final examination in ophthalmology. There were only three days and nights to make up lost time. I had nothing but a photographic memory to help me out. With a shrewdness born of despair I cracked the book at Marlow's pet subjects. When I finally blinked my way into the classroom I had committed to memory a half-dozen picked pages. I was in luck; iritis, conjunctivitis, glaucoma and myopia were all there to be dealt with. I wrote the answers almost word for word from the pages my mind had photographed. Doctor Marlow was so impressed that he showed my paper around the faculty; it was fairly well decided that I had been cribbing. I might just as well have been, for after a long, tired sleep I found that I had forgotten half the stuff I had crammed. And my eyes were never the same after that ordeal.

No use going so early into the technicalities of my half-ruined sight. Microscopy became all-important to me over twenty-five years of service. I have been very fortunate in the assistants I found or trained to operate the lens for me. With glasses, my middle vision and far vision remained fairly good. And this was fortunate, too, for in my wanderings I have been required to look on many beautiful and horrible things.

Photographic memory-plates are apt to fade rapidly. Several years later, I was admitted to the Costa Rica Medical Faculty, after another feat of intensive cramming. Costa Rican professional standards are high, and not too friendly to Yankee doctors. Though I passed the very severe examination, I am not sure it was my learning that won my degree; my initiation included many cocktails with a great many influential medical officers. Those things help in Central America.

That was in the calmer period, following four years in Mexico, where I practised medicine between raids by Carranzistas, Villistas, Yaquis. Twice I established myself with my wife and baby on the West Coast, near Eloisa's home. Twice, because the United States Navy ordered us to escape with our lives, we left the country as refugees.

Those years were heavy with adventure. There was the time when smallpox broke over the helpless people like a cloud of poison gas; I worked alone among hundreds of peons who were anti-vaccinationists to a man and died in their own stench, hidden under dirty clothes. Time and time again I performed emergency amputations on kitchen tables, my Chinese cook giving the anesthetic. I diagnosed malaria on myself, and found my mistake when I came down with a bug of an atypical typhoid group. I lost forty pounds from dysentery and Donna Angela nourished my convalescence with iguana stew. I brought an hysteria-stricken girl back from a state like death by scaring her with a sharp knife. One day I gasped with horror, seeing a native midwife promoting childbirth by tying a woman to high rafters and jerking her legs. One afternoon I barricaded my wife and baby behind sacked beans, and performed a tonsilectomy while the Yaquis broke into a liquor warehouse. Still, there were sweet, mild months under a benevolent Aztec sun; then there came a night when I smelled burning houses and heard the wild-horse squeal of women being raped by Indians.

One adventure I might record, if briefly. The dreaded Yaquis had joined forces with General Obregón. Colonel Antunez, like a good fellow, was bossing the Indians. They had been letting us alone at Mochis, but danger was always brooding in a place that never knew which side it was on. One day, to my discomfiture, this Colonel Antunez came limping in. He complained of pain in his groin, and a large swelling indicated an operation. He urged me to be quick; he had to be at the front, he was the only man whom Obregón trusted with the wild Yaquis.

When I got in with the knife I found a tumor that extended into the big blood vessels. Removing it was a serious major operation. As soon as he was out from under the anesthetic the war horse snorted again. He must be up and back at the front. I told him that his condition necessitated three weeks of complete rest; he got so excited that his temperature shot up and I had to stop arguing. As he recovered, his officers and their Yaquis were always around.

One morning I found his bed empty. They had smuggled him away in a jolting truck, through a cold rain. He died at Navajoa, of peritonitis or phlebitis, one of the inevitable results.

Next day I was called to the office of His Honor, the *Síndico* of Mochis, and was surprised by a captain's tap on my shoulder. I was under arrest. It was a long trip toward the death-house. They jailed me first at Mochis, where I managed to have three words with Meade Lewis, a little red-headed friend of mine who was American consul. I told him what I guessed: I was booked to be shot because one of Obregón's most valued officers had died after my operation.

My tumbrel to Topolobampo was a track car, bristling with rifles; half the population and their dogs tagged along for a look at the gringo who was going to be tried — which was a synonym for being executed. I had been allowed one glance at Eloisa and our baby. The cell in which I spent ten days was a Yaqui butcher shop when it wasn't occupied by the condemned. Into a fragrance of spoiled meat my jailor came at last to inform me that the trial and shooting were set for Saturday morning. And here it was Friday.

On Saturday morning I had prepared my sinful Methodist-born soul for a stern hereafter, when the officer in command swung wide the door, saluted deferentially and proclaimed, "Doctor, you are free!"

Not until I had rejoined my family did I learn what this, or anything else, was about. I had become an international affair, they said. Consul Meade Lewis had fairly pulled the cables loose between Topolobampo and Washington. William Jennings Bryan had sent a cruiser down from San Diego. The captain of that cruiser burned the wires to Mexico City with a Richard Harding Davis sort of message: "Release Lambert at once or I'm coming to get him."

It made a ripping newspaper story. Away up in Newark my brother Fred had been visiting some Mexican friends who told him how wonderfully I was doing in Mochis. After the party Fred passed a subway newsstand and saw the black headline, "JAIL DOOR SWINGS WIDE FOR LAMBERT." He was proud of the family when he read how William Jennings Bryan had taken steps.

I have jotted down these few facts about myself so that my readers may try to decide how well experience had equipped me to be an international health physician. I hope they're not as unsure as I was that day in September, 1918, when I put my family aboard the train for our first long pull toward Papua.

CHAPTER II

BY THE RAM'S HORN ROUTE

It was early May, 1920, before I saw the sterile hills and corrugated iron roofs of Papua's capital, Port Moresby. As they traveled in those days it would have taken the ordinary voyager six weeks from San Francisco. I was no ordinary voyager, it turned out. The little stopover in North Queensland, which Dr. Heiser had suggested for me, held me there a year and a half in one of the most strenuous hookworm campaigns in the history of the parasite. The minute I saw Dr. Waite, who was our chief worker there, I was shocked by the picture of what the tropics can do to a man engaged in the benevolent business of public health. Malaria had yellowed his skin, and a horrid fungus called "sprue" had ravaged him so that he was going home to die. He didn't die; but I did very nearly, of the same foul blight that lays bare a man's intestinal tract from mouth to anus.

Fieldworkers for the Foundation don't go about bragging of the bugs they pick up along the way. In twenty-one years I think I caught everything the tropics have to offer, with the exception of yaws, venereal and leprosy. I'm not sure about leprosy. It's so slow to develop you can't be sure you haven't got it until you've died of something else.

We were leaving North Queensland at last, in the seagoing washtub *Morinda*, Papua bound. In the Australian hot country I had been the Buffalo Bill and the Jim Farley of a whirlwind campaign. I had acted as director there until October, 1919, when Dr. W. A. Sawyer came out to take charge of Australasia. Then there were six months of it, helping him organize.

The North Queensland campaign had offered the combined excitement of a *Blitzkrieg* and a Methodist revival. I had shouted my sprue-sore mouth raw. I had ballyhooed a Yankee's message to Australasia — privies and more privies! Our greatest popular hygienist, Mr. Chic Sale, could never have been prouder of his Temple of Necessity than

I of my fly-proof, worm-tight w.c. when it was accepted as a model by the committees of North Queensland. I was preaching a crusade, and I was heeded. At Shire Council meetings, soil-pollution questions flamed like torches; labor unions called strikes on and off, excited by thousands of feet of lumber to be hauled and nailed together into latrines; commercial travelers took up the cause and were asking their customers, "Have you got one of those things the Yankees are peddling up and down the coast?"

Now it was May, 1920, and that was over. The little *Morinda* was off Cairns; we would be moving, maybe, when the tide rose. I laughed wickedly, remembering what the shattered Dr. Waite said when he left North Queensland to my tender care. "Lambert, if you stick, you'll probably go out feet-first." Well, my feet were still under the deck chair where I loafed and totaled up eighteen months of hard campaigning.

We had supervised the building of 4,000 model latrines and repaired 4,000 more up to the standard. We had treated thousands and thousands of hookworm cases; from Proserpine to Cooktown we had examined 98 per cent of the population for intestinal parasites. We hadn't found infection heavy, but I gloated over the change wrought in many people by the humble expedient of a decent privy behind every house. Brightness was coming back to eyes and skin. Healthy children were playing.

Yes, the Australians are like our Westerners. When there is work to be done they go at it wholeheartedly. Subsequent improvement in North Queensland's health shows what these people can do.

The story of the hookworm disease and its cure is a twice-told tale, or a thousand times told in the medical libraries. But because the subject is pertinent to my years of work, let me say a little about a scourge which was so widespread in 1918 that it had but one rival — malaria. Just as Dr. Heiser said, one third of our planet's inhabitants had hookworm.

It is one of the oldest diseases recorded in history. The Ebers papyrus, dating back to 1500 B.C., speaks of "worms in the abdomen" and makes the hieroglyphic guess that the trouble was caused by "much handling of sand." It is more likely that the infection came from the sacred scarab, a creature so unclean that it is commonly called the "dung beetle." Moses said to his wanderers in the wilderness, "And thou shalt have a paddle upon thy weapon; and it shall be, when thou wilt ease thyself abroad, thou shalt dig therewith, and shalt turn back and cover that which cometh from thee." Without that wise precaution against the infesting parasite, the Children of Israel might never have seen their Promised Land.

The Greeks probably had a name for it; ages later an Italian doctor called it *Ankylostoma*, which is fairly good Greek for "hookmouth." Caesar's legions carried it from Africa into Italy. In 1838 Dr. Dubini of Milan found 105 infected post mortems, and a year later it was discovered that Italian laborers had conveyed hookworm into the Alps. Australia got her dose of it when she imported Orientals and Islanders to work her plantations.

Hookworm and his wife came to America with Africa's compliments to slavery. No worm travels far on its own belly; it is the human belly, to mix a metaphor, that gives wings to the pest. During the Spanish American War Colonel Bailey K. Ashford of our Medical Corps studied "coffee picker's anemia" in Puerto Rico; he segregated the hookworm in these cases and wired the news to Dr. Charles W. Stiles of the United States Health Service. Stiles became our pioneer investigator in the South, something of a martyr to science. He called this variety of worm *Necator americanus* (American murderer), although he might more properly have named it *Necator africanus*. The Negro's habitation of our soil could be proved by the infection he has left behind, even though the race should disappear. Scientific investigators like Darling have studied hookworm-content to trace great racial migrations.

Investigation and treatment of the hookworm disease is no job for a florist. Much of the work has to do with microscopic examination of human excreta. But the physician is a realist, and every function of the body has, for him, the equal rights of a true democracy.

Here is the life cycle of this dreadful little bloodsucker: Its eggs cannot hatch in the intestine, where the hungry mother clings and lays them by thousands. They must pass out with the bowel movement and lie exposed to moist, warm, shady air; under these conditions, they hatch in from twenty-four to thirty-six hours, and begin their progress as tiny larvae in search of human flesh. They infest the soil for several feet around the filth in which they have incubated. Enterprising ones crawl up weeds and will even bore their way into ankles under thin stockings.

Once inside the skin the embryo finds the blood stream and makes its long pilgrimage — through the heart, through the lungs, up the throat; then down into its destined home, the upper intestine, where it fastens its teeth and grows by what it feeds on, human blood. On one drop of blood a day it grows almost to the size of a pin and develops jaws as steely strong as wire-cutters. Multiply these blood-drops by a hundred, by a thousand, and watch the pale anemia that lays the sufferer open to the first epidemic that comes along.

In infected districts the health physician's job was routine diagnosis and routine treatment. When we had to treat and survey whole villages and tribes within a limited time we gathered as many as we could into an audience and lectured them in whatever language they happened to speak. After the lecture we would hand them out small tin containers, each marked with a person's name. We told them carefully how to put a small portion of each individual's next bowel movement into the tin with his name. We urged that all tins be returned next morning. These specimens we usually examined by the "Willis salt flotation" method. This routine was invented by a brilliant young Dr. Willis, an Australian whom I broke in during the campaign in 1919. In the Willis test a specimen of excreta the size of a small filbert is mixed in a tin container with saturated salt solution. The solution comes level with the top of the container, and a glass slide is laid over it. The eggs concentrate by floating to the surface and are lifted with the salt solution when the glass is raised. Under the microscope the floating eggs can be seen. When the Willis test proved positive the patients were set aside for treatment — if we had the time and the drugs to finish the job. Those were the days of "the awful oil of chenopodium," as it was often called. It was regarded as a specific; it was relatively ineffective, and dangerous to use with large groups. I shall go into that later.

Much of the work planned for Papua was the making of "surveys," which means a medical census of vast areas as remote from our usual earthly experience as so many lunar landscapes. Perhaps I am running a little ahead of my story and putting too much stress on ankylostomiasis, the hookworm disease. Our later work carried us into investigations of every tropical malady, from ringworm to leprosy.

At last Papua and novel adventures lay ahead of me, if we ever got there. The *Morinda* was poking her distracted snub nose into blue water, doing her darnedest. It was Sunday morning and our skipper was an old-fashioned practical joker. Captain Teddy Hillman, brief of bone and round of belly, solemnly invited me to his cabin to hear his phonograph play "Shall We Gather at the River?" Sadly he asked me how I liked it, and when I said, "Fine, you old so-and-so," it was somehow the perfect reply, for he spatted my knee and crowed, "Then we'll make you a member of the Gin Club!" Gin Club initiates ordered drinks by pushing buttons that had needles concealed in them. The drinks came in the sort of glasses you order at trick-stores; lift one and it squirts gin over your shirt-front. All very adolescent, but anything went on slow-going junks like the *Morinda*.

The job ahead was much on my mind. We had been given seven months to cover a Territory which, to a large part, had defied explorers, where the census had been little more than guesswork, where estimates placed a thousand natives for every two Europeans. The inspectors I brought with me were four of the six men I had planned to put in charge of separate surveys or use for laboratory work. They were Australian boys, except Chris Kendrick, a tropics-seasoned Englishman and one of the ablest helpers I have ever sent into the field; with a sort of planned recklessness he used his head so well that he might have gone through hell and brought back the Devil's hookworms. With few exceptions all my inspectors had that sporting spirit — "Tomorrow, by the living God, we'll try the game again." The youngest of the ones who came with me on the *Morinda* was Bill Tully, only eighteen; the oldest was thirty. A terrific shortage in tropical physicians had made helpers like these an absolute necessity. They had been trained to diagnose and treat a limited number of native diseases and to lead our dark safaris wherever the work called them, from gloomy swamp to savage mountaintop. A man's job, and they were men.

We stood on a Port Moresby dock and blinked at a collection of hot tin roofs, the white man's gift to the tropics. Sweltering, steaming. The town was on the dry fringe of an island famous for moisture; the merciless sun seemed to dry up everything but sweat. A crew of Papuans came to our relief, thunderously pushing along small flat cars to carry our freight and baggage. They were big blacks with oiled skins and nothing on but *lavalavas*. Their bushes of hair were two or three feet in diameter; jolly smiles relieved the savage look. These were the first Papuans I had seen, and already I was learning a word of their language. Glancing respectfully toward me they repeated it, *"Bogabada, Bogabada!"* This, I thought, was some native honorific. I took the salute gracefully. "Just what does *Bogabada* mean?" I asked the Irish customs inspector. "Big belly," he said.

Some of my 235 pounds I dropped in the strenuous months that were to follow. However, I knew that *Bogabada* would still stick by me.

My Papuans rolled the luggage up a corrugated iron street to the corrugated iron hotel. Ryan's Hotel became my headquarters. The bedroom walls ran about seven feet high; above them to the ceiling was a great open space which let in breezes, bats and mosquitoes. If elephants could fly they would have made it, too. These ventilation holes breathed the very breath of scandal, for you could hear every whisper, and wonder who were paired off now. Like most tropical hotels it was the home of dissatisfied customers; they drank excessively, they said, to drown the taste of Ryan's food.

Almost at once I assumed the role of lobbyist for human health. Financial details had been arranged. Papua, Australia and the Foundation were to share expenses equally. When I saw Governor Murray I found him polite but vague, with a smile that let me know that our work had been thrust upon him, and that every hookworm we might find would be an added insult to his administration, something that would lead to trouble with the overlords in Melbourne.

He quoted discouraging figures, and said that census-taking in Papua couldn't be much more than an estimate. When you put the population figure at 300,000 you always had to say "more or less." There were so many places that white men seldom or never saw. How could you be accurate about a Territory that covered 87,786 square miles on the mainland alone, and 90,540 when you counted in the outlying islands? You had to tackle mountains that were practically unclimbable, streams that were unnavigable and tribes that even explorers couldn't dig out. He stroked a graying mustache over a withering mouth. . . . Yes, his own medical service was quite adequate, he thought. (Fading eyes strayed a little, peering to see which way Parliament was going to jump.) Yes, Lambert, this Rockefeller idea might do some good here. . . . When could we dine?

I have had time to reverse my first opinion of Governor Murray, who lived to be over eighty and died with a fine administrative record. He didn't happen to like us, that was all. So I had to go to the very competent Chief Medical Officer, who understood the situation exactly and gave us the most generous help. The planters backed us all the way.

I decided to begin with short surveys of plantations lying around Port Moresby. Heiser and Waite had told me I needn't fool with the villages; all the parasites were on the plantations. I hadn't been out a week before I realized they had reached this conclusion only because they hadn't gone beyond Papua's freakish little dry belt, where the Ankylostoma cannot thrive. I found the villages in the moist area alive with hookworm.

After our short tour was finished, we were to push into the wild interior. We had decided to give mass treatments where we could; otherwise we must leave medicine and instructions with planters and missionaries along the way. It was talk, talk, talk these first few days, and I was like a wild horse, rarin' to go. I got plenty of going before my seven months were up.

There was a touch of madness in this little hot-spot of semi-civilization where Queenslanders had come to build up another Australia. The superintendent of the hospital, Dr. Mathews — ("Dr. Mathews, one *t* in the name, please") halted operations to quote a Biblical passage proving, to him, that the world would end in 1925. He had worked it out mathematically; exactly 144,000 souls would be spared from fire by a race-conscious Creator. These would be mostly Papuans, who would rise and inherit the earth from England. He hated England. His prophecy of destruction, he told me, had come to him when a boy of fifteen, in the midst of a football scrimmage.

Port Moresby, during the war scare of 1914, earnestly believed that German New Guinea might at any minute cross the border to burn and loot. At the Papuan Club they could laugh it off after the third whisky-soda. They told about native sentries posted around town, instructed to shoot at sight. One gray dawn a sentry spied an excessively smelly scavenger's wagon rolling up, and took it for the enemy. The password was "*Vailala*." The guard leveled his rifle nervously and said, "You no talkim *Vailala* me shoot." The baffled Motu driver replied, "Me no sabe *Vailala*. This no shoot-cart. This shit-cart," — and rolled away into the mist.

The Motu is a tamed and pleasant savage who only murders when it is conscientiously necessary. In the Port he is quite a city fellow, wearing his great bush of hair with style, but not aggressively. His kind brown eyes hold no reproach for the white folks who set him to minor household drudgeries. He is inclined to be timid; but in Papua you mustn't put too much faith in kind brown eyes. Even the butcherous Koiaris and the cannibal Goaribaris can look at you with winning gentleness when you visit their villages.

Viewed from all angles, — geographical, political, medical, — our situation was not easy.

Here were three thousand miles of coast, with mountains massed so near that roads by the sea were impossible; the nineteen-mile road that ran from Port Moresby to Sapphire Creek was the only one that wasn't a goat path or a postman's trail. The Governor's yacht was out of my reach, and we hired or borrowed the canoes that took us up rivers; therefore, for transportation we were largely at the mercy of recruiters and planters.

We were only there on sufferance, for the Australian Government which ran the Territory chose to snub local authority. The depression of 1920 had set the planters yammering for subsidies to help a Territory which, for the tropics, is strangely unfertile. Governor Murray was at his wits' end to carry on his pinch-penny policy with the aid of ships' engineers and stewards whom he had made into roughly able magistrates and district officers.

The whole medical service was pared down to an excellent Chief Medical Officer with nothing to work with, a Judgment Day prophet in charge of the local hospital, and one physician for each of three far-flung districts. These five, with a couple of nurses and two European dispensers, were supposed to service the 90,000-odd square miles. The officer at Samarai was efficiently modern; the other three were elderly hacks. This was typical of the general medical situation over the South Pacific.

Sometimes I wonder how we ever got our units organized. At last we imported two extra inspectors from Australia and scattered like scalded dogs from a steaming kettle. In my weeks of preparation, I found that I had the Papuan Club behind me. That meant support from the ablest colonials in the South Pacific: Loudon, Bertie, Sefton, Jewel, Tom Nesbitt and a dozen more. I couldn't have moved a finger without the help of these men and their friends. These were the forward-looking ones who wanted native labor restored to health, to revitalize races for whom, at that time, there seemed no future but extinction.

At the Papuan Club I couldn't open my mouth for any fly-blown anecdote without there being wild laughter and shouts of "More! More!" A new man would come in. "Harrigan, have you heard the Doc's latest? Doc, tell it again." I was rather puffed up until I found out what they were laughing at: it was my funny Yankee accent.

CHAPTER III

WHERE THE DEAD MEN TALK

Only a day by motor lorry from the galvanized iron of Port Moresby, and untamed Papua was pressing around us — a brute that could throw sudden tremendous cliffs into tangled drylands that were flat as your hand, a country where the souls of men seemed forever broken between gross materialism and fantastic belief in ghosts and magic. Perhaps the black man's mystic spirit imparted to his white conqueror a shuddering faith in the walking dead.

Papua isn't rich in the things that man needs. Either it is parched with drought or reeking with wetness that produces giant weedy growths with no nourishment in them. A hemp plantation, big as a Texas ranch, was one of a certain development company's failures; almost every enterprise in Papua seemed to be on the downgrade. Over yonder, a closed and battered factory revealed the company's vain attempt to manufacture a trade tobacco that would be foul enough to suit the native taste.

Everywhere in the Pacific trade tobacco is native coin and currency. A few sticks of it will buy a man's labor for the week, a woman's virtue for the night. Government regulations have set a standard ration: two sticks a week. But the natives will accept only the stinking twist that traders import from Virginia. The development company had a bright idea: they would make a trade tobacco of their own and corner the business. They spent £50,000 trying to reproduce that exquisite dung flavor. The black boys put it in their pipes, but couldn't be fooled. "Me want tabac!" they yelled. So the company imported an expert from Virginia. That didn't work either. Maybe the local tobacco was a grade too good. The factory shut down and more shillings dropped out of the pockets of hopeful stockholders.

*   *   *

On one trip to these regions I went with Inspector Chris Kendrick, a planter named Sefton, and Archie McAlpin, who was chief inspector for the big development. There was also my "boy," Ahuia.

In Port Moresby I had designed a uniform for my native interpreters. It was a jumper and skirt in gaudy blue edged with bright yellow braid, and on the breast was a large yellow **H**. The **H**, of course, stood for HOOKWORM; but it made boys throw out their chests and strut as if it meant HARVARD at least.

Down there they call every male native a "boy"; Ahuia was my chief boy. Splendid in his new uniform, he had the look of a Malay pirate coming over the side with a big knife in his teeth. He wore more hair than I had ever seen on anything, living or dead. On special occasions he loved to decorate it with lilies. To the natives he was an oppressor, to me a tender guardian. He could wash clothes, hookworm specimens, camp dishes. He could cook and sew. He could put the fear of devils into the gang of carriers who bore our equipment. He spoke Motu fluently when he interpreted. Motu is the *lingua franca* along the dry belt. In remoter villages they didn't understand Motu. But in every settlement under government control Ahuia would engage the services of the village constable, usually a murderer who had graduated with honors from Port Moresby jail. Jail was the native's university, where he could learn more in three years than the home folks could teach him in a lifetime. The authorities always had a job waiting for a good jailbird. Ahuia, who was a great traveler, knew that any constable with a Port Moresby jail degree could speak Motu. A handy boy was Ahuia, and, like most natives, as afraid of ghosts and magic as a rabbit of a hound-dog.

At the big hemp plantation, field hands thronged around our lorry to help us with our load — queer fellows with sloping foreheads crowned with tight Negro wool. Long beaked noses gave them an ironic look; they had the appealing eyes of beaten hunting dogs, and were not healthy men. Some of them showed the dreadful ulcers of that false syphilis we call "yaws." Others were too pallid for brown men — hookworm infection and malaria.

"What name dis fellow?" I asked Ahuia.

"Him Goaribari." Ahuia spat contemptuously.

Goaribaris! I had heard bloodcurdling stories of these savages. It must have been a long haul for them — seven hundred miles or so from the Delta country which they terrorized. Here they labored along with downcast eyes, or looked up almost fawningly.

The plantation manager arrived and invited me to his comfortable, balconied house. These planters have the generous hearts of all good Australians. "And it's a God's blessing that you Yankees are jogging the Government up a bit. Half a million natives, maybe, and not half of 'em fit to lift a bloody hand." When I asked about the Goaribaris who had so sedately helped us with our gear, the manager said: "Cannibals? Well, just a bit. When they're home they'll eat anything, from maggots to raw eels."

I inquired into hygienic conditions. He said, "When the recruiters bring these boys in they're lousy with the diseases they've caught in their blighted villages. The ones you saw are newcomers. Six months on a good plantation and they'll pick up."

He looked at me studiously. "The plantation's a bit seedy now, but we have two sanitary features we're proud of."

Back of the cabins he led me into one of those latrines designed by Dr. Strong, the Papuan Chief Medical Officer, who strove so well for the people and never got a breath of credit. It was built with a rough wooden rail and the pit was some twenty-five feet deep. Darkness below was unattractive to the dysentery-carrying fly, the sides too steep and high for the hookworm larvae to climb.

That was admirable, I said. And what was the second sanitary improvement in which he took so much pride?

Beyond the hemp fields untidy black women loafed in the shade, revealing their baggy breasts; they were spitting bloody streams of betel-juice or smoking short clay pipes. "We have fourteen now," the planter said. "We've sent some away — gonorrhea, you know. Bring a few more in this week. Yes, they have the ration of trade tobacco, rice and tinned food. They're all married, so it's just a matter of seeing the husband."

Admirable. But what had that to do with sanitation?

The manager held me with clean gray eyes, and said: "Do you know what happens to men without women? These natives are only animals. You've seen how animals behave, when they can't get what they want naturally? Indenturing men, taking them in herds away from the wives and the whores, teaches them a lot of tomfoolery. Europeans don't think that the primitive man goes homosexual. Humbug! The missionaries think the savages will live like Christ, and they've made it illegal to have prostitutes on plantations. Well, these ladies here are just good hard-working wives. Ask any of the big planters — and they're he-men if ever there were any — ask 'em about the native boys that weave their hips and ogle at the work-gangs going by. We call 'em 'queens,' and they're a nuisance we've jolly well got to get rid of."

The planter's idea was brutal, like Papua. But his object was kindly, and, in its way, scientific. Since then I have seen much of the turning of simple people to the ways of perversion. The hard-hitting Queenslander, manly as a frontiersman can be, was doing his best to square the vicious circle.

That night I saw my first ghost. We had sat up rather late with the manager, who mumbled in a corner with Archie McAlpin. Once I heard him ask, "Is it still around?" Heads were together, voices lowered. Finally Archie McAlpin, who had finished his share of whisky, and mine, rambled upstairs. I rambled up too, for I was tired. That evening there had been a long lecture before an audience of sedate cannibals, earnestly attentive to what I told Ahuia to say in Motu to a Goaribari interpreter.

The Papuan servant never wakes you harshly, because when you sleep your soul has left your body to wander among dreams. Wake the body suddenly, and where is the soul? Still loitering with a dream. Therefore you die. When Ahuia wished to rouse me he would move a chair or give a polite cough. His cough woke me and I saw him, shadowy in a patch of moonlight. His jittery voice was imploring the *taubada* to "Look along veranda. . . . Devil-devil belong him outside."

A voice was yammering somewhere. I looked out and saw a white figure that appeared to float as it gestured. I hadn't many hairs to stand up, but they all stood. Yammering, yammering, the voice of the pale apparition beat out a long speech in Motu, then in English. "*No, don't come here again!*"

The specter turned. It was Archie McAlpin. The voice hadn't been that of a drunken man; under the white moon his look was sober. He shook his head, the debate was over. He didn't see me, he appeared not to see anything as he went back to bed.

"Ahuia, what was he seeing?" I whispered, because the natives know

so much of devils. Dark eyes were expressionless in the white night.
"Maybe he see nothing, Taubada," he whispered.

In three days I finished dosing two hundred Goaribaris. I had found
that newcomers bore the heaviest load of worms, reversing a prevalent
medical theory that plantations were infected and villages clean. Labor
was bringing disease from the towns to the farms.

The plantation that was sanitated by prostitutes and model latrines,
worked by tame cannibals and haunted by invisible things, disappeared
in a dust cloud as our lorry rumbled away toward the unbelievable
cliffs of Hombrom Bluff. When I spoke of ghosts to Archie McAlpin
he turned his steel-gray eyes the other way.

We slept at the little inn at Sapphire Creek, where the specters
wailed again, if only in the imagination of the English landlady whom
I treated for a slight attack of alcoholism. Poor woman, she had raised
two husbands and fourteen children, and had been a rough Florence
Nightingale to the sick miners in the last flu epidemic. She stared up
from her pillow and said, "No, Doctor, I'm not seeing things — only
what's all around us, all the time. Strange things happen in Papua." She
closed her eyes to shut them away.

Hombrom Bluff hangs over the seared scrub of flatlands below. All
Papua is like that, a vast bear-rug, shaggy and tumbled in a hundred
folds; man is the louse that must crawl up and down, down and up,
to cross these endless entanglements. Craning my neck to look up
Hombrom's forehead I saw the change in vegetation from strangling
tropic vines at the base to temperate evergreens that shagged its top.
Blinking at three thousand feet of it, I said to Archie McAlpin, "How
do we get around to the Sogari District?"

Archie said, "We don't get around. We go over."

They brought us horses and I mounted clumsily, being thirty pounds
too heavy for the little shaggy animal. Then it was up, four breakneck
miles of cliffside trail that was seldom more than a yard wide. It would
have been a hard scramble for a man, but my Papuan horse must have
been bred of a goat. On the one side we were elbowed by monstrous
vines; on the other side loosened pebbles flew into empty air. At one
high twist the forests were sliding down to Port Moresby harbor,
where the reefs were fine spun lace, tattered over the expanse of lapis
lazuli sea. Another turn and one of the world's great waterfalls, Rona,

joined diamond necklace to diamond necklace as it met the wild
Laloki River, slicing through savage green.

Now at the top we dismounted on a narrow ridge. "What's that
lake over there?" I asked Archie McAlpin. The lake was a Venus'
mirror, framed in the lips of a dead volcano. Archie's eyes were still
as the lake; he stood silent at the marge of a cliff. Then I heard it
again, heard the queer babble in Motu. I turned and saw that it was
Archie, speaking to the sky. I whispered to Sefton, "Is he a bit off his
head?" Sefton answered gravely: "No. But that lake over there is where
dead men go. Archie's saying the invocation. It keeps ghosts from
following us. You can't get a native to go within a mile of that lake.
They know what's good for them."

Perhaps the lake had put its curse on me too; maybe it didn't like to
be photographed. When I was remounting my horse the saddle slipped
and left me dangling in midair. Two hundred and thirty-odd pounds
of me hung by a creaking stirrup. Quick-thinking Chris Kendrick
caught me in time and shoved me back into the saddle. What I liked
best about Chris was his way with an emergency.

Far away across a vertigo of green depths Mt. Victoria, a tall land-
mark in New Guinea, was in a misty shroud. On this silent trail the
sudden flutter of a bird's wing sounded like a shot.

"The mountain's like a ghost," I said to Archie McAlpin.

The trail had widened, we could ride closer together. "Along here
I like it best in daylight," he said. I asked him if he was afraid of
Koiaris — for they were the killers with long spears. No, he wasn't
afraid of Koiaris. Their country was farther on.

Sefton stared into the pale mountain light. "There's a trail that leads
down from Jawavere where the Koiaris wait for anything that comes
along. You don't linger on the Jawavere trail.

"I have a station on the trail," he said, "and always look for anybody
passing to have a drink with me. It's a bit lonesome. About four one
afternoon, a native runs in and says he saw a *taubada* (white man) who
had been riding along there, taking his time, just staring ahead. His
horse didn't make any noise, the bush didn't flutter. I thought that was
a lot of native humbug, and was annoyed that the man didn't drop in
for a drink. I asked around among the other plantations. Yes, they'd
all seen the rider, and at about four o'clock the same afternoon — in
places miles apart. Finally we searched the bush and found the bones

of a man and a horse, around some smoky stones. The Koiaris had done him in, weeks before we saw him riding."

Archie said thoughtfully, "Yes, and there was the woman dressed in white. I couldn't sleep one night, and there she was in the garden, bending over picking flowers. I spoke to her, but she didn't look up. She was the Englishwoman who married that chap from Cairns. She made a little English garden, but it never suited her. Always wanted to go home; you know how the English are. Her man thought Papua was good enough for her, until she died. Then he shot himself."

"Do you ever see his ghost?" I asked.

"No. He's too deep in hell, I fancy, to get out."

They believed earnestly in the horseman who rode over the bluff. They believed that lights appeared in the deserted house from which another woman had run away with her baby.

We were riding along silently when our horses stopped, snorted and sat on their tails. At first I thought it was a fallen vine, then I saw it wiggle. I slid off and threw a handy stone at eight black feet of snake; which was a diplomatic blunder, for the thing made straight at me. Sefton broke its back with a whip. "Venomous?" I asked. I hate snakes. "Rather," Sefton said, and poked the poison sacs.

We rode on. Ghosts were real, snakes only a nuisance in a country where anything could happen. Except mules. According to the planters there was just one mule in Papua; and his long ears waved over a fence at the Seventh Day Adventist Mission. Natives marveled and fed him votive yams; because he was a member of God's house, locally presided over by a missionary they called "Smiling Charley."

The first time his celebrated animal strayed away, Charley organized his black men to search for it. They hunted until they were tired out. Smiling Charley went on over the brow of the next hill, and there was the mule. Charley thought this was an opportunity to demonstrate the power of prayer, so he went back and said, "Boys, let's pray for guidance." They prayed, and in a few minutes overtook the mule. A week or two later it strayed again, much to the chagrin of the boys who had to do all the carrying when it wasn't there. Smiling Charley tried to organize another search, but the boys were unwilling. He questioned them and they said, "More better you pray first time, Taubada." So Charley had to pray, but it didn't work so well, for it was a week before the mule came home.

Dusk was falling when we left Smiling Charley's Seventh Day joyfulness. After shadows began blackening the hills, Archie McAlpin said, "We're in the Koiari country now, and we'd better push along. On the slope there, you can see the graveyard." Stones were like skulls among the scrub. "Those are planters that the jungle got the best of." Everybody who's been a week in Papua knows how the jungle defeats all but the strongest — malaria, accidents, bites and infections, all take their toll of the pioneering white.

A mountain chill blew from the pale stones. A tall horseman came toward us, and I tried to forget the mounted ghost. But Archie McAlpin sang out, "Hello, Sam!" The horseman stopped. Archie said, "Seems to me, Sam, that you're not giving this graveyard a very wide berth." "Me? Archie, I never see ghosts."

"Then I suppose, Sam, you wouldn't mind sleeping among the graves?"

"I may be crazy," Sam said, "but I'm not a bloody fool. If I see any ghosts there'll be one more horseman riding over the Bluff. He won't be back, either."

He galloped on. No, people don't loiter on the Jawavere trail. I was still thinking of the lonely Englishwoman who couldn't go home; her poor shadow was earth-bound to Papua.

How about the ghosts of indentured natives, confused spirits that can never find their way back to the villages they loved because they were born there? Here's a scrap from my diary, written from a survey which I made a little later: —

> On Saturday P.M. gave lecture to natives. Back of the boys' houses found evidences of gross soil pollution . . . natives must be educated to some idea of sanitation. . . . Seem well fed and contented, save for a lot from the Dutch border, some of whom have died for no apparent cause, other than homesickness. . . .

CHAPTER IV

THEY WALK ALONG DREAMS

On those first short trips our main effort was to count and report the diseased. I often had a deep sense of personal guilt when I left the villages just as I had found them, crying out for the healing I had no time to give. All I could do was lecture them, hand out the tins and gather them up for tests in the next place I stopped. Sometimes the containers were returned in fifteen minutes — such is the celerity of the savage gut. Faces would be wreathed in smiles. They had filled the magic boxes, just as I had ordered, had they not? To them that was all that was needed for the cure; fill the magic boxes, hand them over to the white medicine man who would say an incantation — and lo! sickness would vanish from the tribe.

This was a sort of Heathen Science point of view which would have been funny, had it not been so tragic. I got used to it, and left the people with a smile as cheery as their own. After all, the drug would be coming soon, and I had told the missionary or planter how to administer it.

When we had sufficient oil of chenopodium we did not waste an overnight stop in making diagnoses; in this district wherever there were villages the infection was obviously so heavy that we could call it 100 per cent. Therefore we lined them up and dosed every man, woman and child. With great gusto they swallowed down the nasty oil, in a spoonful of sugar, and smacked their lips. They laughed over the bitter purge that followed. More than once they lingered to steal the leavings of Epsom salts solution, on the principle that the more you take the sooner you get well. Only the children held back. I won't forget the naked four-year-old who knew enough missionary English to yell, "Oh, Jesus, no!" when his elders dragged him forward.

Many of these first trips took us no farther from Port Moresby's tinny orderliness than it would be from New York's city hall to Trenton. Yet with every mile we found some curious or savage twist to the human animal's makeup. There was always the white man,

standing one against five hundred natives, in an urge to develop a re-
sisting wilderness. Keep the tribes alive for another day's work, that
was the problem. My early expeditions were all zigzags. There was a
plunge into the sawmill country along the Laloki River to inspect a
mining company's Kiwais, big jolly fellows like Virginia Negroes; I
stayed there long enough to advise the operators on the use of their
lumber for pit latrines. I won't forget the cleanest native village I ever
saw. The Company had surrounded it with a stockade fence and commanded the people to sweep the streets and throw their rubbish away.
I had only one fault to find: the dark villagers polluted the trash-heaps
they piled on the other side. These people should have been crawling
with hookworms. Actually, the infection was extremely light. Another
medical paradox . . .

I sometimes came upon pathological freaks. There was the paralytic
at Kabadi plantation, who seemed to have lost muscular control of one
side at a time; when he turned he grimaced horribly with the conscious effort. His walk was like pushing forward two sticks of wood.
I wondered why they kept such a monster, then they told me. Oh, he
was very useful. The Koiaris were so afraid of him they didn't dare
raid the place.

In the black belt of the South Pacific dreams are very real things.
When you sleep your soul goes walking into living adventures. If you
love a girl in sleep, then she is no longer a maiden when you meet her
in the morning. A nightmare murder is no mere fancy; you have killed
your enemy dead as dead. When you happen to meet him tomorrow
sauntering down the glen, that is nothing. What you are seeing is
merely a fancy. Your dream has killed the man you hate. And take
care how you treat that frightful paralytic who leers at you in the
hemp-fields. He may "walk along your dreams."

Too many things I saw walked along my dreams. There was that
pageant at Boera . . .

Boera was a dismal beach and supported a London Missionary Society station, presided over by two Samoans. Samoa was a far cry from
that lost spit of sand. Alien to the soil, these imported teachers grow
to be like many white missionaries, muddling along with Christ's work.
Their impulses are as fine as their results are vague in a dingy routine of
bell-ringing, prayer-saying, Sunday school reading and more bell-
ringing. This pair, Mosea and Emma, were meekly discouraged, but

with the beautiful manners of the Polynesian aristocrat. Mosea was already heavy-legged with elephantiasis. His cousin Samueli dropped in to report with Christian cheerfulness that conditions were "very bad.". . . Queer how they travel. Years later this same Samueli came to me on an Ellice Island beach far away from Papua, and made me a present of a fresh-killed chicken. When I asked him how conditions were, he said, "Very bad."

At Boera I got my first real look at a yaws-stricken community. This hideous thing was apparent on the bodies and faces of at least a third of the people, men and women with noses reduced to yawning holes in the middle of a flat scar. Fingers and toes curled like withering twigs. Swarms of flies carried the filth-born germ. I looked into baby faces and saw how the process of healing had drawn their lips together into a featureless surface with an opening so small that you could hardly get a lead-pencil through.

Yes, these Papuan specters walk along your dreams. The tropics are dreamlands, released from the balance of Northern things. Life down there moves between poetic loveliness and monstrous disgust. I have since seen many other villages like Boera; and I should have become callous, seeing so much of it. I could get used to the maimed adults, but the children always wrung my heart.

It is quite understandable that the early voyagers should have confused yaws with syphilis. That such confusion still persists is reasonable. For all we know of yaws, it may be syphilis modified by Stone Age conditions. We call it *framboesia tropica* (tropical raspberry). When you speak of yaws you must always speak of syphilis — the two are so alike, with wide differences.

Captain Cook, who first visited the Pacific in 1773, wisely wrote: "Another disease of more mischievous consequences, which is also very frequent, and appears on every part of the body, in large broad ulcers, discharging a thin, clear pus . . . it being certainly known and even acknowledged by themselves that the natives are subject to this disease before they were visited by the English, it cannot be the result of venereal contagion, notwithstanding the similarity of the symptoms. . . ."

So yaws was already in the Pacific, and who brought it?

The enlightened traders and missionaries who followed Cook sketchily jotted down "syphilis." All my work in Papua and my following years of careful research over the whole Pacific failed to find one case of syphilis, although I have run across one or two rather doubtful diagnoses. I have never found the tell-tale chancre scar, which is the sure mark. The manifestations of the two diseases run so parallel that carelessness or ignorance have put a libel on the native races.*

Yaws is not a venereal disease, nor is it hereditary. It is usually acquired in early childhood. Native mothers expose their babies to it in hopes of "getting it out of their systems," much as some Yankee mothers do when measles come around.

Now here's the confusing resemblance. The yaws germ *Treponema pertenue* is so closely related to the syphilis germ *Treponema pallidum* that the two are hard to tell apart. Both diseases progress in three of four stages. The "mother yaw" first appears on any part of the body, and its secondary manifestation is a great number of "daughter yaws" which are widely distributed over the skin and progress into the third stage, which is remarkably syphilitic in appearance. Arterial changes and nerve lesions (as in syphilis) sometimes cause the general paralysis of the insane.

Missionaries have an easy way of accounting for yaws: it's a curse inherited from cannibal ancestors. Certainly it is ugly enough to have come to the world through that black door.

And here's another parallel. The treatment for yaws is exactly the same as the treatment for syphilis — arsenical injections. Framboesia was quite beyond the reach of medicine until Professor Ehrlich produced his salvarsan. There is nothing more dramatic in medicine than the almost visible growth of healthy tissue over a yaws sore after an arsenical injection.

The Pacific is the one place in the world where yaws is in no way complicated by syphilis. I am told that in Tahiti the two diseases thrive, but the same person never has both. On the Islands there seems to be a cross-immunity, so that the two germs cannot prosper in the same host. Certainly the native has been abundantly exposed to syphilis; East Indian labor, when it came to Fiji, brought with it 75 per cent infection. The Chinese and the white sailors fetched their share and did their amatory best to spread it, but nothing happened. Something had made the native immune, and that something is quite apparent.

* Recent Wassermann tests on the Maoris of the Bay Islands, New Zealand, have revealed 13.05 per cent syphilitics. There is no yaws in New Zealand.

The stamping out of yaws is largely a matter of intensive campaigning. But what will happen when the fight is won? Will syphilis slip in to take the place of the spirochete it could never meet — on equal terms? That is another doctor's dilemma.

The morning after we heard the planters' ghost stories I sent Kendrick to ride ahead for preliminary inspection of the rubber plantations. On a rough sea or a jungle trail, Chris was at home. I made short surveys along the trail, resting my raw posterior when I could. Then horseback again, clenching my teeth at every bump on the saddle-sores. Imagine a Coney Island roller coaster magnified a hundred times, and you have our slide and scramble, up and down, down and up, to attain an elevation of 3,000 feet. Down, down would go the coaster on a grade so steep that a fly, if he tried it, would fall over on his nose; and I marveled again at the adhesive footing of my horse. On the final upgrade I spared my buttocks and skinned my heels, for even the horse surrendered.

Now the rubber trees were all around, above and below me, their coarse, hard leaves like green glass that blinded the eyes in afternoon sun. Underneath was a grotto of soft light, upheld by pale trunks like pillars of snakeskin. Naked men worked in silent preoccupation, sharp knives making incisions in the bark; neatly they would rip down paper-thin slices, and the tree's milk-white blood would trickle into cups. Watching, I was thinking: they are natural surgeons. Down the ages they have learned so much, dissecting human flesh with the razor-edges of split bamboo. Train men like these to use the knife to save instead of kill, and what couldn't they accomplish for their people? . . .

The man nearest to me turned. His wooly hair, his sloping brow, his long, hooked nose told me that he was a Goaribari. I looked at his companions. All Goaribaris, with that undeniably Hebrew profile which gave them the name "the Lost Tribes of Israel." But these were different from the scrawny cannibals I had seen on the hemp plantation. They were fatter, better-muscled, and their brown skins were beginning to show silk. They were not newcomers, and the planters had taken care of them. Back home, where they pursued the jolly business of going to war and dining on the enemy, they hadn't eaten very regularly. On the farms the white man had fed them, and done his best to teach them sanitary ways; an uphill job among primitives who were naïve as cattle in their bodily functions. In subsequent surveys all over the Territory I could tell, almost at a sweep of the eye, the men who had been on plantations. They were the upstanding, healthy specimens.

Rubber plantations have a smell of their own, something like the aroma of fried overshoes. It drifts from the factory where the sap is being smoked and reduced to the wide, dirty-gray ribbons that go forward to market. Here my cannibals worked like hiving bees, swarming in and out of the door on the commonplace business of supplying crude material for the raincoat trade. I looked around and saw Chris Kendrick, smiling and self-assured, pushing his way through the throng.

"You missed something yesterday afternoon," Kendrick said. "The Koiaris came down and staged a raid on the Goaribaris. A lot of workmen were loafing in a field, then a naked devil was in the midst of them, poking away with a long spear in either hand. There was just one of him, mind you, and there must have been twenty Goaribaris. They may be tough bastards in their home towns, but here they were taking it like frozen lambs — till somebody ran in with a shovel and a hoe handle. Next you knew the Koiari was making for the woods, naked and howling, shaking his long spears.

"But the Goaribaris caught him and — what do you think? — turned him over to the management! What the hell did he care? He'd got his man." Like so many of the fiercer tribes, Koiaris kill because murder is a proof of manhood, and a warrior who has not bloodied his spear is laughed at, even by the women.

"I got a snapshot of the fellow he left behind," Kendrick said, and showed me the print he had developed. A broken body lay in the scrub. The plantation manager came up just then and grinned, "We buried him deep. His brother Goaribaris might take a notion to eat him, you know. Of course, they're pretty well fed, but . . . Yo-hum, farming's so full of little problems like that!"

Yes, farming in Papua, even at its best, offered many problems never dreamed of in the philosophy of a Secretary of Agriculture. The old hands were far from hookworm-free, although vastly improved in general health. New recruits were coming in with fresh loads of parasites to be hatched from the filth they scattered in spite of managerial watchfulness. Green laborers regarded the well-built privies as queer traps set by the white man for their undoing . . . pretty, but look out!

That night I lectured by the light of hurricane lanterns swung from the beams of a great, empty warehouse. The audience sat cross-legged in a wide crescent, their oily faces gleaming up at us. The front row was solid Goaribari with natives of gentler tribes behind. These, being more nearly civilized, understood Motu, which was so much Greek to the Delta savages. Therefore it had been up to Ahuia to fetch the local constable, a very ugly man in a G-string and a policeman's cap.

Such occasions were Ahuia's hour to shine. Out on the trail he went stripped to the waist, but at lectures the gaudy yellow **H** on his bright blue jumper stretched with every expansion of his chest. And he hadn't forgotten to put lilies in his hair. He had set the stage with our regulation International Health Board chart, loosely bound pages with simple illustrations of the hookworm's course to the intestines; there were drawings, greatly enlarged, of the male and female parasite and the egg their mutual love produced. There were big photographs of a sick boy and a well boy — something like the patent-medicine man's "Before and After Treatment."

Ahuia quelled the Goaribaris with his pirate's scowl, and in impressive silence brought out our prize number, a large bottle of adult hookworms, pickled in alcohol. This was a stage property which we carried for purposes of demonstration. Cannibal eyes popped as the collection was passed from hand to hand.

Ahuia was getting his lesson by heart, but I still felt it safer to prompt him. "Tell them first," I said, "that they must look carefully at what is in the bottle." He spoke Motu, straight into the mouth of the interpreter: "*Tatau bona, memero, umui iboumuiai inai gaigai ba itaia. . . .*" The native constable was saying it after him, in the queer lingo of the Goaribaris: "Men and boys, all of you look at these little snakes."

Education strained through three languages. The row of man-eaters sat very still; their long noses, pointed up, were like the muzzles of wistful hounds. Ahuia was telling them how the lady snake laid very bad eggs that fell out of the black boy and the black "mary"; how the eggs hatched tiny baby snakes that nipped the black boy's foot and crawled back into his belly. Now see the picture of the sick boy and the well boy — they are both the same boy. The well boy took the medicine the *taubada* brings, and the snakes came out of his belly. Now he will keep well, because he is a wise boy. He goes to the clean privy the white man built him, so that the snake cannot come out and crawl into him again.

Patiently drumming simple words into wooly heads, we tried to make simple men understand cause, cure and prevention of a disease they might have brought from Africa, ages ago; a disease so wasting that the mills, rivers, the plantations were calling upon half-invalids to furnish brawn for Europe's driving ambition.

Sometimes in my early lectures as I looked over the stooped dark figures I would have moments of weakening. I would wonder if it was worth while to save these curious beings, so out of touch with anything our Northern civilization knew.

As time went on, I came to realize how very much worth while it was.

The lecture was over and I started alone across an open swathe of dim moonlight that pointed toward the plantation house. I was anxious to get to headquarters where I could write up my notebook and tumble into bed. On both sides of me rubber trees made high black walls, like something built of coal. My conscious mind was concerned only with the day's work and tomorrow's; somewhere in the back of my dreams I may have sensed the danger of another such Koiari spear as had butchered a man yesterday.

I looked up and saw the outline of three men, emerging out of the shadows. Even to my defective eyes they made a grotesque group, all locked together in a shambling stride. There was nothing for me but trust in the white man's prestige. I was unarmed. If I had shouted for help it would have been a sign of fear, and these fellows, I knew, worked in a hurry. When they came closer I saw that they carried no weapons.

Two of them, who had been holding to the third, began jabbering in Goaribari, making friendly sounds. Was this a trap? Fortunately Ahuia and the native constable came swinging up with hurricane lanterns — even in moonlight they carried lanterns to scare away ghosts. Ahuia pointed to the man in the middle. "That fellow broke his hand in a fight. There were not enough women to go around."

All right, let's have a look at it. We led the foiled lover to my quarters where I examined the wrist and found a bad Colles's fracture.

In dim lantern-light I did a careful job of bonesetting, even though the fellow had just scared the living lights out of me. If he had shown up in the dispensary at Rochester with the pick of the faculty looking on, he couldn't have had more meticulous surgical attention. I even took time to give him Doctor Moore's famous dressing, which is fussy, but perfect.

"All right, boy," I said, "run along." He stood there patiently, holding out his unwounded hand. What the devil was he waiting for? "Does he want to thank me?" I asked Ahuia.

"No, master." Ahuia looked fiercely sad. "He is waiting for you to pay him. That fashion belong this fellow."

"What fashion?" My short temper was getting shorter. "What should I pay him for?"

"For mending his sick hand, Taubada."

I growled and Ahuia shoved him out into the night. When I was around Ahuia feared neither ghosts nor Goaribaris. The incident seemed to be closed, but I was aware that the cubicle next to Kendrick's, where I slept, was quite doorless and exposed to pale moonlight.

Next morning I was aroused by softly arguing Motu voices. Ahuia and Quai, who was with Kendrick, had missed something from our bags. Quite likely. For there was a gentleman's agreement among Motuan servants: Never steal from your master — oh, that was very tabu. But you could take a little something from your master's host, or from some stranger *taubada*, sleeping near you, if he happened to leave his bags open. It was honorable to snitch a handkerchief or a pair of new shorts and drop the small loot into your bag. When two white men were bunking adjacently, their boys working with the bags would watch each other as cat watches mouse. It was all right for the good servant to get away with a few of the stranger's cigarettes, for personal smoking.

There were other guests on the plantation, and I was wondering whose boy had gotten by Ahuia's watchfulness when a sleepy glance through the sunlit window awoke me to a real annoyance. There sat the Goaribari with the bandaged hand, serenely chewing betel-nut. "For the love of God, Ahuia, what does he want now?"

Ahuia's funny English informed me, "Taubada, he still wishes to be paid. He has slept all night on the porch."

I jumped out of bed, dragging the mosquito netting with me. Like a fishwife in a bridal veil I exhausted all the arts of profanity. With an amiable smile on his betel-red mouth the cannibal listened — and held out his good hand. Then I checked myself in mid-oath and laughed as I have never laughed before. This was socialized medicine with a reverse English.

"Ahuia," I shouted, "give this cheeky bastard two sticks of trade tobacco."

Quite unemotionally the savage accepted his fee and departed.

I was still laughing when the planter came in, and he grinned. "It's the fashion — that's all a bush fellow will say. They're pretty much confused about money values. To them a white man's a sort of cross between Simon Legree and Santa Claus; when he comes around it's either to send 'em to jail or pay 'em off."

I grumbled: "Next thing they'll expect me to pass around free tobacco before every hookworm lecture."

"Certainly they will," he said. Then he rang the changes the planters had rung all along the line. "Anything can happen in Papua."

CHAPTER V

JUST THIS SIDE OF THE MOON

In July I decided to lead my own expedition as far into the interior as possible and get a proper picture of infestation in districts remote from the influence of white traders and planters. I had worked like a beaver along the coast, up rivers, into plantations, sea villages, hill villages. My inspectors were always away, leading surveys and campaigns that spread out fanwise across the country. Communications were crude. Canoes, whaleboats and jiggery launches plied their precarious way among the infinite shoals, or lost themselves under lush palisades where an all-wise Creator saw fit to turn on the shower at the slightest excuse.

I moved ahead of my inspectors, surveyed the districts, turned them over to my men and passed on to the next. Although the Government was inclined to look on me as a secret agent of John D. Rockefeller, they offered me a sort of mild indulgence. Our main handicap was supplies, as the Foundation's Dr. Sawyer, then my over-director, could not believe that such great quantities of drugs were necessary to treat infected Papua. Where was all the stuff going? In Australia, where treatments had been comparatively few, expenditures had been small. Sawyer simply couldn't grasp the immenseness of that sick population in the Territory. Yet to treat them *en masse* would have been the only answer. At that time mass treatments had been tried among laborers in Java; but a wholesale curative campaign was unheard of.

Our work had been so heavy that we had exhausted Central Office supplies. Even in the following year there weren't enough to go around. We had to carry on with what we had.

On July 21 I was more than glad to be setting out for Yule Island, a splotch of land some sixty miles from Port Moresby. This island is separated by a thin gut of water from the prodigious jungle-covered mountains that stalk beyond Mafulu to the mysterious border some still call "German New Guinea." Again we were jogging along on the little *Morinda*, with Captain Teddy Hillman and his Gin Club in command. With me I had the two boys, Ahuia and Quai. We took with us a quantity of "gear," which was our term for the variety of things we must carry with us into the field.

A white man, bent on an excursion straight into the thick of Papua, requires several swag bags — one for his bed, mattress and mosquito netting; another for scientific equipment; a smaller bag to hold incidentals. The number of tucker boxes for food depends on the time one spends in the field. There will be no chance to replace anything after the start is made. These must be included: frying pan, teapot, billy-cans, a tin opener, a lantern with kerosene, an ax and an assortment of tinned food. Absorbing topics around a Papuan campfire are the relative merits of different brands of tinned meats, and cunning ways to disguise the taste of tin.

The tins for hookworm specimens, packed by hundreds, were little half-ounce cylinders about the diameter of a silver dollar. The gear made a load for many carriers, burdened too with their own food for the whole trip. And don't forget the trade tobacco that must be doled out everywhere as strike insurance. We were prepared for almost anything; the going up to Mafulu would be hard.

Getting carriers for these long pulls was always a part of Papua's labor problem. Ask a Motu boy to pack and follow you into the jungle and he'd begin to shuffle, roll his big eyes and move away. There was *puri-puri*, bad magic, in those hills out there. It was not "our fashion" to go among the Mondo or the Kuni people. They have enchantments, you die under a spell. The same fear lay across every district border; we had to change our carriers as we went along.

Yule Island, flat and green as a dish of parsley, lay separated by a thread of salt water from the distant panorama of tumbled mountains that climbed the wilds of Papua. It was an exotic and frightening beauty over there, peak after peak, their height exaggerated by closeness to shore. The tallest looked taller than Mt. Everest, and more unattainable.

Three white men waited for me on flat Yule Island beach. I recognized two of my inspectors, the Orr brothers, Jack and Ron. Their food supply had been spoiled by surprise tumbles from canoes. They greeted me with unrestrained shouts of joy; they would eat again! The third greeter was Mr. Connelly, the jolly, hard-boiled District Officer. When I mentioned the giant mountains across the stream he said casually: —

"They're a bit of a climb. When you've finished with Yule Island I'll show you up, part of the way. Business and pleasure. I'll have to push beyond Mafulu — after a batch of murderers, you know. Come over to the house and we'll have a spot of tea or something."

I was no sooner in Mr. Connelly's house than I heard a strain of sweet, familiar music. An American accent! It was young Mrs. Connelly saying, "Pleased to meet you." She was a native of New Jersey. How she came here to be the wife of a man who scaled crags to round up murderers was just another in the grab-bag we call marriage. My own wife, after all, was born in Mexico, educated in California — and was now waiting for me in a Port Moresby bungalow.

Connelly knew the ropes, as needs must be when one man combines the duties of sheriff, judge advocate, postmaster, tax collector and justice of the peace in a country where the people are hard to count as wild pigs. After an evening of bridge he told me, casually, that he'd fix me up with the forty-seven carriers I needed. How? Just leave it to him. "I'm Government, you know" — with a dry smile.

During our week's survey of Yule Island the Orr brothers and I were lodged in the patrol officer's house, walls and floors of split bamboo, ceiling of nipa palm thatch. The shower bath was two Standard Oil cans ("petrol tins" over there) hung one below the other. Can Number 1 is filled with fresh water, and when you pull a string a plug comes out and empties it into Can Number 2, which has been drilled full of nail-holes to give a fountain effect. The first time you use this Rube Goldberg invention you soap yourself carefully under the spray — and the water gives out. The next time you try soaping yourself in your own sweat, which can't be done. The third try you just say "Oh, hell," and pull the string.

The Mission of the Sacred Heart has a business name which I have remembered accurately: Company of the Sacred Heart of Jesus, Ltd. Its holdings ran all the way from Yule Island to a point some 130 miles distant across the channel, up into the wild mountain-heart of Papua, and its practical label was a key to its practical Christianity. The Sacred

Heart was, and still is, about the best mission establishment in the Pacific, and should serve as a model for the numerous jarring sects and creeds — Church of England, Calvinist, Wesleyan, Seventh Day Adventist, London Missionary Society and even Mormon — that confused the native mind with conflicting roads to salvation.

I grew to admire these curiously devoted Fathers, thirty-one in all, who usually put aside their priestly robes for the frontiersman's rough khaki. Fierce beards relieved them entirely of the soft ecclesiastical look. In little convents, strewn along the broken trails up to Mafulu and beyond, there were twenty-six nuns living the same rigorous life.

There was almost every European nationality in this French order: French, German, Swiss, Dutch, one Italian, one Spaniard. They were understaffed, hideously overworked; in faces around the luncheon table I could see the look of men who were not going to last much longer. They were short-lived because they followed their incessant work without considering illness or the demands of a difficult climate. They all died in Papua. With them I visited two cases of typhoid which they said had been brought in from Port Moresby, despite their efforts to quarantine against the germ. I operated on one Father for a bad case of hydrocele, and on others for injuries and infections common to their hard life.

They had solved the food problem troubling the rest of Papua, which was stuffed with American and Australian canned goods. Here they had their own truck gardens, bountifully yielding, so that they could feed their 120 pupils wholesomely and at minimum cost. There were nearly a hundred half-castes in this school. The Sacred Heart method of dealing with mixed blood was practical.

The half-caste too often comes into the world with no father willing to attend the baptism. Bishop Boismenu, a fighting priest, carried this question to the Government; his persistence was responsible for a law requiring the registration of every half-caste child's white parent. And, my word, what a hullabaloo! Major Jones-Smith and Judge Brown-White had to do some tall explaining when sons or daughters suddenly materialized at the Mission of the Sacred Heart. One high Government official had a hard time facing his wife and his public; one rich American decided that he had loitered too long and had pressing engagements back in the States.

The half-caste problem is increasing in Papua. When the Melanesian was 100 per cent cannibal his women were chaste; the husband carried an ironwood club, and the tribe was never lax in enforcing blue laws. Poaching lovers were firmly lashed together with vines and laid across the liveliest ant-heap in the neighborhood. Or experienced tormentors would hobble the wandering bride permanently; they would just tie a hot stone under one of her knees. Nevada in the early days was almost as rough with domestic incontinence (if female). And look at Nevada today.

It was a strict mission rule that half-caste children should speak no language but English. Britishers they were; the law had acknowledged them. When they came of age the girls and boys were encouraged to marry each other, or to go into orders. They were to have a respectable place in society, and no handicaps.

I take off my old white helmet to the men and women of the Sacred Heart. There was Sister Magdalena, aged seventy-six. I found her sweet old face bent over a busily clicking typewriter. She had been stone blind for two years. "It was hard at first," she said, "learning the touch system. But it's like playing a musical instrument. I write poetry when I have time, and letters home. I'm useful too. One of the girls dictates to me, and I keep accounts for the mission."

And there was Brother Heinrich, the jolly undertaker. Sallow and malarial, he had the smile of the artist who loves his work and has plenty of orders. Papuan fevers never bothered him so long as he had coffins to build. Bang, bang went his lusty hammer, doing a neat hardwood job. "Don't forget a solid lid," I said, coming up to him. Brother Heinrich chuckled and said, "I try not to forget anything. For instance, Doctor, you'll need lots of brass nails on those shoes, if you're going up to Mafulu. Won't you send that pair to me before you go? I'm a cobbler too."

Mother Ligouri, who presided over the neat little hospital, was another jolly one, round and rosy in spite of hell and high water. Her housekeeping was immaculate; she isolated typhoid cases, and was always in comic despair over sanitary arrangements, primitive latrines, flies and mosquitoes that infected her patients. Brother Heinrich was one of her favorite pests. "I have to shoo him away," she said. "When anybody's sick he gets the measurements somehow. I never knew him to fail to have a coffin ready, and a perfect fit. That man Heinrich!"

The day before we set out for the mountains I let Brother Heinrich have my shoes, and asked him if he had me on his list of measurements. "Oh, I can tell your size from your shoes," he said with a glow of professional pride. That night he presented me with a remarkably fine job of hobnailing.

During the week I had talked to the half-castes, and it gave me pleasure to lecture in English. Already I was looking forward to my surveys in New Guinea Territory, where, I was told, the people understood pidgin English. I carelessly believed that pidgin would be easy to pick up. I little knew.

All I saw of that enterprise on Yule Island, and of its far-flung stations among the peaks and gorges of Mafulu, never failed to remind me of what Herman Melville, who didn't like missionaries as a class, had said of the South Sea Catholics a hundred years ago. They were to him the great missioners. And they are the great missioners still, as long as they live in the purity of self-sacrifice.

Ahuia came to me with the air of a certified cruise conductor; he was wearing his full-dress jumper with the **H**, and had lilies in his hair. Would the Taubada care to see the natives dance tonight? I wanted to know if it would be any good. Ahuia puffed his chest and shrugged away the commonness of all bush natives. Oh, pretty fair, he admitted, but the girls around here didn't do a lot of things they did in the East. We passed between aristocratic trunks of betel-nut palms. With each step the drum-pulse was louder, that jungle beat which can stir the same animal-soul that bares its sensuality before the repetitive chant of a camp-meeting revivalist. A slow cadence, *tum* teetee, *tum* teetee, *tum* teetee *tum*, speeding up to a rapid *tum* tee-*tum* tee-*tum* tee-*tum*. Light shone above oily shoulders, things moved and tossed like shaggy pillows that had been dyed with every color in the rainbow. Musicians were slapping hour-glass drums.

Then with a gasp I realized what those moving pillow-things were. Headdresses . . . Headdresses made of bird of paradise plumes, hundreds of the lovely things flowing and flaming in every bushy ball of hair. Parrot feathers — blue, fire-green and crimson — accentuated the unearthly hues; and cassowary feathers, built up into high crowns like glittering sheaves of wheat. . . .

Men and women danced in two close lines, facing one another. Mouths were red with betel-nut, eyes were fixed, intoxicated. Golden skin flashed through stripes of gaudy paint adorning their hips; golden breasts bubbled through showers of bright shells. Yet this was no blatant exhibition. Each man faced his woman, and if he touched her it was according to the rote and rule of tradition; their passions are never on public show. Bright skins and delicate bodies revealed the Polynesian strain which gives the Motuan his urge to laugh and sin with every change of the moon. Melanesian women drudge at home and let their men wear all the feathers. But the Polynesian wife is nobody's squaw.

Slim-waisted, straight, demi-nude, more handsome than grotesque in their paint, each man had his girl opposite him. Her arms and ankles were bangled with polychrome shells that tinkled with every suggestive movement. It was sensuality expressed in grace and rhythm. Under the least of grass skirts women's buttocks wove with sly languor as couples moved in a curious shuffling gait — her hips quivering in retreat, his in attack: the sex struggle, the male forever in pursuit, the female always in flight, yet drawing him on by every allurement within her power.

A voice said, "It's what Yankees call a Marathon dance. The people of Tsiria are competing with the people of Pinapuka. It'll last until they drop — into each other's arms, a lot of 'em." I looked around to see Ron Orr, my inspector, who had been beating along the coast. "Watch that couple," he said. A man and girl vanished under the shadowy palms. "They'll be back after a while, maybe. During the Marathons here it's the fashion for a man to take the one he picks. But only during this set period. If they forget and break the rule it's just too bad. Sometimes a married man loses his head and takes his 'mary' away for a week end that lasts a month. Then there's more trouble for the District Officer."

"What sort of trouble?"

"Well, Connelly's going up in the hills tomorrow after a bunch of murderers," Ron said. "That's the sort of trouble."

There were no priests hovering about to give the pagan spectacle a disapproving eye. Protestant missionaries, Wesleyans or Church of England, might have broken up the performance, clothed the ladies in Mother Hubbards and sent them home to brood in sanctity — and secrete their vices. The people of Tsiria, possibly, were not among the Sacred Heart's 8,000 converts; and if not, the Church of Rome, with its balanced system of discipline and tolerance, would bide its time before gathering them in. The people would still dance, maybe with a churchly curb on their orgiac moments — but they would still dance.

Night wore on, drums grew wilder. Everybody was chewing the betel-nut that natives can go drunk on. My good boy Ahuia was chewing, and his eyes were like live coals as he slavered red and gazed hungrily at the dancers. I smacked him on the arm and brought him to his senses. We were starting for the mountains tomorrow, and I didn't want Ahuia to go native on me.

Next afternoon, as a floundering whaleboat took us across the narrow channel toward the looming mainland, I had a comfortable feeling that Brother Heinrich had secretly measured me for a coffin which he'd have to use on somebody else of my size and weight. I might as well say here and now that I have been the undertaker's disappointment in twenty-one years of knocking about down there. I'm afraid that I offer pretty poor material for Hollywood.

Connelly and I, perched in our whaleboat, were off on a murder hunt; his quarry would be the human type of killer, mine the assassin-worm that yearly laid low more natives than cannibal wars could demolish in a generation. The looming mainland melted to a lace of Papuan bayous; we went on nosing up Ethel River, searching for Bioto Creek, a needle in a haystack of house-high tropical grass. Bloodthirsty mosquitoes welcomed us; we could find the miserable town of Bioto, if we could see it through that buzzing cloud.

Connelly had elaborated on a number of gruesome things which the Fathers had told me. Somewhere along this coast was the Pacific's only native educational institution, a School of Poisoners, in the remarkably stinking village of Mou. *Puri-puri* men graduated with honors and knew about arsenic and strychnine to the last dying gasp. They were accomplished in "dead-man's-poison," which was a spear-head dipped into a rotting corpse; they made toxic applications by sticking spears through a floor to pierce the sleeper on his mat. If the natives built their houses on stilts to keep out evil spirits, the *puri-puri* men would crawl under and prong them from below; if they built on the ground, the first malevolent ghost that came along would walk in and do his dirtiest. They were between the devil and the deep blue spear.

Postgraduates of the Mou school had a specialty which required much study, and they prided themselves on it accordingly. It was the snake-in-bamboo trick, worked like this: First get on the confidential side of a certain venomous yellow-striped wriggler, and train him to lie inside a hollow bamboo wand; then look around for a client who wants somebody killed. When the time comes, drop your poison pet into an uncomfortably heated earthen jar; work him up to a frenzy; throw in scraps of clothes or bodily material from the chosen victim. The striking, tormented snake confuses these things with the cause of his pain; so he is ready, he has the scent. Pop him back in the bamboo and turn him loose in the accustomed path of the man who is about to die. The snake, like the elephant, never forgets, according to Connelly and Father Gerbout. By scent he can pick his man from a long file on the trail.

As we fought our way through the mosquitoes defending Bioto Creek the District Officer gestured toward the mountains. The Kuni people were up there — bloody little dwarfs, rather cook a man than fry an egg. The Government holds 'em down a bit, Connelly said, and the priests have tamed a few. But never trust a Kuni behind your back.

Bioto, when we found it, was a tumbledown huddle of huts. At first we couldn't see a living thing but mosquitoes, then crocodiles, wallowing in the stream or basking on the mudbanks. All the way up the Ethel River we had counted them by half-dozens, too bold and too lazy to roll off the sandspits when we came within thirty feet. Bioto was almost a deserted village because of the mosquitoes. D'Albertis, an early Italian explorer, was the first white man to sleep here; after one night he told his father confessor that he wasn't afraid to go to hell.

At last a few scrawny natives, naked except for a coating of mud, came ambling in. Their chief made a melancholy speech, but the message was cheery enough. We shouldn't worry, we'd have our forty-seven carriers in the morning. He repeated this sententiously, as though announcing bad news. The energetic anopheles pecked their way through the netting when we crawled under for protection. Even Ahuia as he cooked our supper looked reduced and crestfallen. He vented his spite by throwing a billycan at a baby crocodile under our house.

Morning blossomed hot and bright; the chief was back with a motley collection of nudes. I saw Connelly marching up and down and telling the interpreter dirty words to say to the chief. "Call him a pig's tit — no, better go easy on that — but ask him if he can't count. I said forty-seven and he's only brought twenty-three. Where's the rest of 'em?" There was some mysterious form of native strike. Connelly ordered his police to beat the grass for the absentees. When we got up to Kubuna Mission Station, he said, he'd hold court and sentence those bloody runaways to work for me. And at Kubuna that was what he did. The thirteen or so he sentenced might or might not have been the deserters, but they were with me for the balance of that strange month.

We left the bulk of our gear with the corporal's policeman and went on through reed-grass so tall that it arched over our heads. It was suffocating between those swishing walls, but we were well quit of Bioto. I don't know whether Ahuia or I was gladder to get away. The priests of Yule had filled me with crocodile stories. The beasts were bolder at nightfall, they said, and they had a bad habit of putting their front paws over the sides of a canoe and grabbing the first native who fell into the water. Once a fifteen-footer, basking in the sun, had challenged Brother George, who was riding a bicycle. Brother George turned his wheel just in time, and for a long span felt the monster's breath puffing behind. Saint George and the dragon in modern clothes, only this time the dragon had the saint on the run.

Two hours in sweltering grass, then because it was Papua we had to climb 800 feet of ridge and climb down again before we could reach the knoll which was Father Rossier's mission, all scattered wooden houses around the chapel's simple cross. Father Rossier, kind, bearded and khaki clad, showed us a little stream down the glen which they had dammed to make a swimming pool. Connelly, Ron Orr and I undressed, cackling that the last one in was a nigger. Then plop! Ron Orr dove into crystal water — and was out again in record time, swearing under his breath. Some bloody fool had left a log in there. Just look at the way it had skinned his wrist. Yes, the wrist was certainly skinned. . . .

Slowly, languidly, a crocodile rose and appraised us with cold green eyes. We decided to go to dinner a little dirty.

Around the mission table with its bare boards and coarse crockery we were gratefully aware of being among Frenchmen; they could have broiled the crocodile out of their pool and given it the flavor of filet mignon. In the kitchen were two Sisters who worked Parisian marvels with taro and yams and a surprisingly good native asparagus. No canned goods here, everything fresh, and that included heart of palm salad pepped up with lime juice. There was some sort of idealized pork, two kinds of birds, a rich, sound claret, and black coffee far too good to come out of a French kitchen. The mission grew its own coffee, and the berries were ground hot from the oven every morning. Incidentally, chicory doesn't thrive in Papua.

Sipping my share of Australian wine — and it can be good — I was thinking irreverently, "The Fathers manage to do themselves pretty well up here," when I noticed that Father Rossier had watered his glass to a thin, pale ghost of what every Frenchman must have with his meals or starve. They drank sparingly because wine cost money. They ate well — it cost only labor to raise good crops. On their penny-saving system they smoked trade tobacco, and had learned to love its rank kick. They refused our cigarettes politely.

Father Rossier gathered in the people, and to a scanty audience I gave a lantern-light lecture which Ahuia interpreted to an interpreter. When I lectured the priests on their own infections and commented on the sparsity of the population Father Rossier told me that they were slowly increasing. "And that's because we have discouraged cannibalism, infanticide and abortions."

I had heard many stories of some magic weed which the native women used to promote race suicide. I suppose now I wore a cynical smile. "Oh, but it's so," he said solemnly. "I have seen it happen too often." He showed me curled dry leaves powdered in his hand. "Fortunately European women don't know about this."

I asked him if he knew the relation between yaws and syphilis. These closely related diseases affect the procreative functions so that abortions are apt to occur. Now these dry leaves that the witch doctors supply might or might not have a mild action. Certainly they could not effect an abortion on a normally healthy woman, because modern medicine has never found a non-poisonous drug that can. I was making up my theory as I went along, but my later observations proved that it was sound.

Next morning, the carriers Connelly had sentenced to serve me took on their loads as Ahuia was going through the last motions of packing my bags. "Look, Taubada!" He held up my extra pair of shoes. One of the priests had spent the night hobnailing the soles.

You read of tropic beauty and smile at the flourishes with which a writer attempts to put ecstasy on cold white paper. There are no words in our dictionary too fantastic or farfetched to describe that man-killing climb to the valley of Popo Popo. Milton would have funked it in his blind visions of Paradise, and De Quincey would have given it up for lack of words and opium.

The region takes its name from some jungle-hidden bird that cries "Popo-popo-popo-popo," a bell-like sound that gives a thrill of music. Paradise as we saw it on those days of puffing and scrambling was always joy to the mind and pain to the body. Thousands of feet up, thousands down, with hardly room for a tiny house on any of the razor-sharp ridges. Down in a Valley of Eden the "Popo-popo-popo-popo" sounded, ringing a welcome to the mission's resthouse somewhere in the sky.

Up through the giant mass of lawyer-vine with knotted trunks thick and hard as a walking stick and supple as a morning-glory; from their stems exotic orchids hung so richly that blossoms whipped your face as you struggled through greenish twilight. Tree ferns were fine as cobwebs. The trail was like a slippery stairway running through a tunnel of opalescent gauze. Rain sifted over clothes that were bogged in perspiration. Then a small clearing. An awful shriek — What was that? The air was all trailing plumes and angel wings, flying colors that you can't believe, even when you see them. Birds of paradise, dozens and dozens of them, whirling away to the mysterious nests which no hunter-ornithologist has ever found.

With every hundred feet of climb we seemed to see a new variety, plumed with white and rose and gold. Much higher were the rare blue ones, which they say are worth twenty-five pounds — if a hunter dares shoot protected game. With every flight there was that fierce, dissonant "Caw-caw-caw." My eyes were tired of miracles; I was aware of the oozing blisters on my heels, the miserable wetness of my shirt. "Oh, go along!" I scolded. "You're nothing but a lot of painted crows." We appreciate beauty best from a padded chair.

One afternoon, dead to the world, we flopped down in the resthouse 2,400 feet in air. These resthouses are among the mercies which the priests have scattered for their own long tours and for the comfort of travelers. Little bamboo huts are closed with combination locks; the Fathers give you the combination before you start on a trip. Houses are provided with chairs and beds, and set at distances that measure off a strong man's endurance for the day. No Alpine traveler, coming upon a hospice of St. Bernard, could have been more gratified than we, sitting in real chairs while we opened blisters in our heels and covered them with adhesive plaster. Tea revived us, and we squatted around the door.

We were over the clouds. Far above them was the crazy pattern of zigzag points and ridges. Everything was angled into steeps without even a hand's breadth of level ground. Waterfalls cascaded through the glossy jade and emerald. People go crazy in Papua. Why not? All that journey, we had struggled past cliffs honeycombed with caves that were stuffed with orchids and draped with crimson begonias; birds of paradise flew, arabesques through slanting sun. Now that I am an older man, retired and with time to think it over, I wonder if I really saw it. This was not the land of human beings. When I was a small boy my mother used to scare me, singing: —

> Up the airy mountain,
>   Down the rushy glen,
> We daren't go a-hunting
>   For fear of little men.

We didn't meet the little men until the day we scaled a higher ridge toward Dilava. Dark figures were stealing toward us across a breakneck stretch of open ground. "They're Kunis," Connelly said. This might have caused a shudder, but these tiny people — the tallest was no more than midget-size — were unarmed and mostly women. They carried loads on their backs, suspended by straps across their foreheads; baskets of vegetables, bundles of firewood piled on top, and on top of that a baby. The women were naked except for a G-string. They had chic, pretty little faces; their bodies were curiosities of distortion: powerful thighs, short legs, pigeon breasts, sway backs. Their feet were stranger still, with toes that spread out like the claws of clutching birds. The few men who were with them showed the same anatomical freakishness, the same G-string.

They made gestures toward their fallen loads and let us know that they had come to sell vegetables and not to eat us. I studied them and learned the secret of their odd shapes. The Kuni people never follow the zigzag trails as other tribesmen do. When they cross a ridge they go straight up it, straight down the other side. The continual strain of hillside walking had thrown their whole skeletal structure out of line. When I saw them walking across one of the few level places in the district I was struck by their clumsy waddling gait. Yet give them a mountainside and they speed up like so many goats. They are a study for evolutionists; the effect of environment on physical characteristics. I wonder if their babies are born that way?

During our last day's approach into this incredible Kuni country some of the trails were no more than wrinkles across mountain brows that were all but cliffs; the soil, where there was any on the surface, had a greasy texture in the wet, and the least slip might grow into a skid, then a giddy fall into the milky fog. The mountains had a way of breaking suddenly into gaping ravines, a thousand sheer feet down to the pouring river.

At last we saw Dilava mission station, like a collection of birdhouses nailed to the crags. It perched on a mat of ground which the priests had blasted off the peak. Away up there, when we had panted to the height and our sweating bearers had thrown themselves down beside their loads, we could look over range after range, up through thin air to Mount Yule and Mount St. Mary — maybe 100 miles away, looming 12,000 feet into calm evening like tall queens, with cloaks of mist that foamed from the cavernous valleys.

(Note from my diary: "If I stay here a week longer I'll go stark mad and take to writing poetry.")

Father Chabot had just come from the valley, where they were setting up a sawmill. He pointed down the slopes where small square gardens stuck like colored rugs. Naked Kuni people, forgetful of the days when human flesh was their meat, worked like beavers among their growing vegetables. "It's good for them to work," Father Chabot said; an echo of the old monkish *Laborare est orare*.

It was time to gather them for the lecture, so Father Chabot sent messengers to various high points around the ravines. They yelled from cliff to cliff — high, echoing cries: "Come to the mission station! The Doctor is at the mission station!" Nature's telephone, connected by the shortest way, took hours to bring the people in; they had to go roundabout, because the cliffs were too steep for even Kuni feet to climb.

Father Chabot said much the same thing that Father Rossier had said in the station below. "Before the mission came this district had dwindled to less than two thousand. The Kunis would have disappeared if we had not discouraged cannibalism, infanticide and abortion." I wondered if the good priests were not fooling themselves. Abortion and infanticide may reduce a population, but cannibalism and continual tribal warfare may be blessings in hideous disguise. They keep the tribes apart. Warfare is a sort of rough quarantine. *In times of peace strangers wander in and out, and bring infections with them. Native races die off not through their own suicidal customs, but through diseases introduced from the outside world.*

Lecturing that night, my attention was caught by something that gave my audience a troll-like look: several little pigs followed the women with the affection of lap dogs. When the women sat down the pigs jumped in their laps. And what in the world was that one doing? I stopped talking to look again — one of the women had picked up her pig and was holding it to her breast, nursing it. There was a second woman doing the same thing, and a third. This might have taken a deal of explaining, but its reason was purely economic. A sow had died in pig-birth and left an orphan litter.

Taller, darker people who came in for the second lecture — we gave three that night — were as curious to me as the pig-nursing women. The young bucks were wearing corsets, tight-strapped arrangements of bark that squeezed them to the perfect hour-glass figure. I asked Father Chabot if these were effeminates and he chuckled, "The fellows in this tribe never do a lick of work — the women are the field hands. Well, if a woman sees a man with an especially small belly she says, 'He doesn't eat much. He ought to be easy to support.' But he takes off his corset the day they're married — and she goes on working."

I had to change carriers again before we went on to Deva Deva. No use arguing; these fellows knew that there was very bad sorcery over the mountains. I paid them off with three sticks of trade tobacco per man. But the thirteen who had run away and been rounded up again stayed faithfully by me. They had to. Before Connelly pushed on he said, "Hang on to that bag of salt. From now on trade tobacco's no good." Everywhere I went I found the people stampeding for salt. They would put it in water, rank, and drink it as you would lemonade. When I doled out a spoonful in payment for something there were always children reaching up in hopes that I would spill some. The priests of Yule had warned me not to be too generous with the precious stuff. I might start a high-price epidemic. A Kuni or Mondo or Mafulu man who had his own bag of salt might retire on what we'd call a million dollars. They say that these mountain people drink themselves sick with sea water whenever they get to it. But the Government has forbidden the practice of recruiting them for labor; most of the few who ever reached the coast died of malaria.

The high-price epidemic had already struck Deva Deva. For an assortment of food which included sweet potatoes, yams, taro, pumpkins, bananas, sugar cane, pawpaws and two chickens they unreasonably asked two tablespoonfuls of salt. That wasn't right. Last year the price had been one teaspoonful, and glad to take it. They were getting spoiled. But had they known it, I would have given bushels of solid brine for one of the delicious okari nuts which they usually threw in as a bonus. These things, in the husk, are as large as lemons; crack them open and you have something the size and shape of a cigar, with the flavor of an almond, only twice as good.

All along the tumbled way I tried to investigate recent epidemics of dysentery. The germs were probably fly-borne to a large extent; also one might blame the local habit of eating with dirty fingers. Though soil pollution was common enough to cause a large hookworm infection, there was stream pollution too, because like many other Melanesians the mountain folk stand in water to perform their natural functions; otherwise, they tell you, the *puri-puri* man will get some of their bowel movement for his black magic.

In giving out tins to these villagers I encountered a kind of shyness new to me. They hadn't the least prejudice or tabu against our form of examination, but when Ahuia asked this man or that what name should be written on his specimen he would simper and wriggle and shut up like a clam. Ahuia told me grimly, "He shamed to tell name belong him." Finally he would manage to cajole the reticent one into whispering his name to his neighbor, who passed it on, whispering. In the land of ghosts frightened men will change their names, often two or three times, to fool the evil spirits of their dead relatives who come searching in the dark. Fiend-haunted natives have so many aliases that they can't remember the last one, if asked suddenly. I lost a great deal of time trying to pump the name from one blushing warrior. Finally a mission boy bawled out, "Oh, Joni!" (meaning Johnnie) — and the man stepped up.

I found the Kunis only too anxious to listen and obey instructions. They were firm believers in the "se-nake in bell'" theory, and we were magicians who had come to relieve their bellies. There were old women, they said, who could remove the snake by sucking it from your ears, your nose, your navel. Did anybody ever see the snakes? No, Taubada, such magic only removed "the ghost of a snake" — and the serpent was so very tabu that you would surely die if you even looked at him as he crawled out of you.

Jestingly one of the Sacred Heart priests said that the witches were working in competition with the Rockefeller Foundation. That sounded funny; but I discovered that it was true.

Ahuia told me that a magician was coming to a house "over there" and had asked to have me see him cure a woman of her snake. It was like a call to a medical consultation. The house over there was a leaf-thatched hut, spooky with faint lights through mountain dark. Among the branches queer birds croaked like frogs.

Inside the dirt-floored room, lit by a hurricane lantern, a nude woman lay on her back. Her abdomen was puffed; it looked like a gastric case, superinduced by intestinal parasites. There were other witnesses, men in the all-prevalent G-string, and among them the black local constable whose services I might appreciate. Dead silence reigned, except for the woman's painful breathing.

A wizened little man came in quietly. He wore no paint or feathers, and his air was professional, as if he intended to put on rubber gloves and lecture before a class in surgery. A small boy followed with an earthen pot and a basket; he set these near where the woman lay. The witch doctor was businesslike, striking a trade match and dropping it into the pot, his face lit by the red flame. Daintily he reached into his basket and took out dried leaves, which he scattered over the fire. The room was fragrant with smoke. He crouched and said an incantation. Even though he was speaking in the strangest of strange languages his voice had a thick sound, as if he were talking through a mouthful of yams. Suddenly he sprang to his feet, went over to the patient and put his mouth tightly on her navel. There was a series of sucking sounds. He lifted his head and out of his mouth fell a little brown snake. It wriggled across the swollen abdomen, then glided to the floor.

The wizard rose and turned to me with a professional bow. "How was that, Doctor?" "Very good indeed, Doctor," my eyes replied. The native constable asked the woman how she felt now, and she said, "Oh, so much better!" Even in the dim light it was easy to see what the sorcerer had done. It isn't hard to carry a small snake in your mouth, if you don't mind understudying Bosco.

The next day I was giving my own exhibition of magic. We had lingered here long enough to administer chenopodium and Epsom salts and to wash the specimens for observation. In the throng I recognized my rival physician, and he was a long time studying the slides. At last he turned away with a stony face. Was he convinced that my method was superior to his? I doubt it. It takes a great deal to change the mind of an old-school doctor.

I was surprised to find that Dilava, Deva Deva and Mafulu ran over 90 per cent infections. This upset all my previous convictions, but when I stopped to consider it, this was not so remarkable. One carrier, coming in from the outside world, could easily infect a village, for these settlements were perched on narrow ridges not over twenty feet wide. In Okaka, for example, there was barely elbow room and no attempt at sanitation. Here, when the natives left home, they must all follow the same trail. They lived like animals, and like animals they died.

If I were a sentimentalist I would think of Father Fastre with a smile and a tear. He was the giant priest who presided over Popolo Mission; he was all brawn, with the great red beard of a bush frontiersman. Sometimes a fey look would come into his eyes; for here is tremendous loneliness for a white man, which neither work nor prayer can quite banish from a mind that consorts with spirits and grows more morbid year by year. But Father Fastre had a sense of humor which saved him, I hope.

When he first talked to me he braced his big shoulders against the guest house porch and told me about the sacred G-string. The G-string is not only a stingily concealing garment; in these mountains it is the mark of a "true man." With it he is respected, a tribesman in good standing; without it he is a pariah — he isn't properly dressed, that's all. With Biblical simplicity they say of the G-string wearer, "He is a true man and belongs to the true people."

Now Father Fastre and a colleague were the first white men to penetrate this Kuni country, and they were great curiosities because they came in their priestly robes, to impress their faith upon the savages. At Deva Deva they were shown to a native house which was about as private as a goldfish bowl; they were no sooner in it than the dwarfish Kunis came crowding in, gibbering and peering at the strangers in the long skirts. After a spell of whispering one of them stole up behind the priest, who had just leaned over to tie his shoelace. Slyly the little savage lifted Father Fastre's robe, and went suddenly across the room, propelled by the Frenchman's big fist. The situation was tense. The onlookers were all armed killers. A dread silence fell. Then the crowd burst into a gale of laughter.

"They were trying to find out if I was a man," Father Fastre grinned.

One afternoon he told me to take a good look at an approaching native. "A few years ago he brought his little boy to our school and we dressed him up for mass in clean European clothes. His father saw him and flew into a frenzy. 'I want to take him home,' he said, 'he's not properly dressed.' When I asked what was indecent about a nice white shirt and trousers the man gasped, 'But where's his G-string?' and made a terrible scene. He wasn't going to let neighbors say that his son wasn't of the True People."

The Mafulu folk divide the world into three parts, Missionaries, Belitan (British) and True People. Up here crocodiles have been killed at an altitude of 5,000 feet and the natives "know their name." True People have an annoying way of high-hatting unfamiliar things. They merely say "We do not know its name." They have a name for salt, which is *ama*. Once they ate it the way native traders from the coast palmed it off on them, mixed with sand. When white salt came they "did not know its name" — but brine hunger got the better of them and they learned to love it. In their gardens mere women are not allowed to plant yams because these are "true gardens," and women are considered too dirty either to plant or eat the precious vegetable. They are permitted to plant taro, but yam work and yam eating are for True Men. It's all very confusing, and as ridiculous as some of our civilized conventions.

Ahuia was never quite the man of the world among these stranger tribes. Father Fastre's jolly Mondos were piling lumber, down below Popolo. The first night we stopped there Ahuia and Quai came creeping up to my door. "Taubada," they whimpered, "we scared, we like sleep along you." With no further explanation they curled up on the floor and slept the velvet sleep of the native.

When I asked Father Fastre about this he laughed. "My Mondo boys acted the same way last night. They wouldn't come within a mile of your boys. You know why that is, don't you? Witchcraft. They 'do not know the name' of strange people, and keep away from them for fear they'll cast some evil spell."

Father Fastre could smile at evil spells, but Papua was getting him. One night he stood in front of his mission and looked down over a veil of moonlight. He seemed to be talking to himself. "Ten years ago I could count ten thousand people along those hills. They are gone. Sometimes I hear their voices."

He told me that he often heard voices. The Bishop had better send him home for a while, I thought.

We were a hundred miles inland when I decided that the mountains beyond would offer no new health problems. We had found hookworms enough for ten years. There were plenty of mosquitoes, but no malaria, although conditions were ideal for it. But the *Anopheles punctulatus* of the coast had not penetrated so far inland. There were no enlarged spleens. Only one reasonable conclusion offered itself — malaria must be a recent importation to Papua.

How Father Fastre's big Mondo boys could sing! What a splendid chorus of rich, deep voices, the only really native harmony singing I heard in the South Pacific. In other tribes, and on other islands, too often they chant monotonously in unison; or they borrow syrupy chords from mission hymnals and Tin Pan Alley. Here among the Mondos their ballads and war songs were beautiful, soul-stirring things. One of the priests, Father Morin, who was an able musician and a nobleman in France, tried in vain to set down these songs; he failed because the Mondo has quarter-notes which the European scale does not recognize. But it is true harmony — I say this in the face of many learned anthropologists who have decided that there are no chords in primitive music. A troop of naked Mondos, war dancing, swinging sticks as they used to swing spears, filling the air with their big organ-notes, is a sound and a spectacle that fills the heart with rapturous fear.

They marched with me to their boundary singing and holding both my hands as we swung along. I could have done without the hand-holding, for I had heard of a certain honored custom: two men hold the stranger's hands while a third steals up behind him with a club. Not so these merry fellows, who left me with a cheer and marched away, still singing.

When I left the tuneful Mondos my stride was snappy and sure-footed. The priests had put a brand-new set of hobnails in my shoes.

I have snake stories to remind me of that mountain trail. The last three feet of an anaconda was visible in the slippery mud; my foot missed him by an inch; if I hadn't stopped suddenly with one leg in air, he might have squeezed out my life. Again, when I wandered a little ahead of my carriers — they usually thrashed around so that they scared *gaigais* away — I felt a whirring under my foot, and something like a tack-hammer struck my leg. It was one of those deadly little striped fellows that the *puri-puri* men train to bite. Fortunately I was wearing heavy leather puttees. . . .

A crocodile bade us farewell at dusk as we were swinging down-river in a frail canoe. We were moving philosophically along when a native paddler pushed me flat. A scissor-like snout horned up, a foot from where I had been sitting. He had been attracted by my white shirt, extremely tempting bait. Brother Heinrich might have used my coffin after all.

We didn't go back by way of Bioto. I'd rather die of one crocodile than a million mosquitoes. We went over to the Aropiquina sawmill and picked up a whaleboat for Yule Island.

Among the priests of Yule I found Brother Heinrich grinning away his disappointment. I was a pretty tired doctor when the good men put me to bed. Brother Heinrich managed to get hold of my best heavy shoes, and looked ruefully at the soles when he mentioned pulling out the hobnails. In the morning he brought them back. He hadn't stopped at hobnails. He had resoled them, and beautifully.

All that month of tramping, up to Mafulu and back again, the priests of the Sacred Heart had showered me with these simple kindnesses. They refused all payment and modestly waved aside my thanks. Hereditary Methodist though I am, I honor them as the best missionaries and the best hosts in New Guinea.

CHAPTER VI

A CHAPTER ON CONTRASTS

In Papua the dryest statistician might easily burst into the literary style of Sinbad the Sailor. At the time of year that folks back in Utica call "autumn" I had traversed great areas of ragged mountains and boggy shores, and had done my best to hold on to my statistical mind in a land where census figures were evasive as blowing chaff. Meanwhile my field units had been working all over the Territory, and the inspectors who led them were often lost to me for months at a time. Aside from my fact-finding studies of hookworm I was following the course of malaria, which is Melanesia's deadliest blight.

Field technique may seem monotonous to the reader, for it is just a matter of making the same tests over and over, moving on and continuing the motion in another tribe or village. But it was never monotonous to me.

Compare the mountains of Mafulu with the delightful little village of Gaile, not more than twenty-five miles from Port Moresby. The Gaile folk lived Venetian-style, their houses stilted over tidewater. They were gentle, industrious and generous Motuans, and with no evil history behind them. An invading maritime race, they had built over water to avoid their savage enemies; and the water had always been their blessing, for it carried away the bodily waste that breeds so many worms and germs. Gaile I remember as one of the few truly restful spots I have visited in the Pacific. There were no diseases worth worrying about.

Then, since I'm dwelling on comparisons, let's look at Tepusilia, a few miles away. My whaleboat got stranded there on the way to Gaile, otherwise I should never have seen the row of dirty chicken coops that leaned crazily over the inlet. I hadn't much time to look into their case, but I found the inhabitants covered with tropical ringworm that had turned their skins into a brownish crêpe. But there was no hookworm, because they evacuated into the sea, as the Gaile folk did. A few miles inland, where the people had no access to the water, ankylostomiasis was very prevalent.

I can't pass Tepusilia by without mentioning the lone policeman there. Because his house was the only clean one, I was glad to sleep in it. He sat in a chair not quite wide enough for Shirley Temple, and kept me awake with a constant stream of questions. How had the World War come out? (That, mind you, was 1920.) Sleepily I informed him that Britannia still ruled the waves, and he seemed surprised. He told me that he had served his time in Port Moresby jail, and had come out well-educated. Then he looked wistfully at my chin and asked if I shaved with a razor. "Yes," I said, "and don't you?" "No," he said, "I shave with a shark's tooth." He showed me the shark's tooth and asked me if I wouldn't give him a real razor, a nice sharp one. The subject was growing a bit morbid, so I sat up and asked him what he had gone to jail for. "Oh," he sighed, "I was falsely accused of killing a man. Taubada, don't you think you can give me a razor?" "No," I said softly and turned my face to the wall.

From pleasant Gaile I followed the course of the lakatoi for 700 miles across the Gulf of Papua into the land of the Goaribari savages. The lakatoi was already growing extinct. From time immemorial the watermen in the Motu district had been building these giant vessels, from five to ten long canoes lashed side by side and covered with a platform that would support houseroom for maybe twenty men. Every spring, when the wind blew toward the northwest, Motuan traders would carry a load of pots and jars over to the wretched Purari Delta and exchange them for logs and sago. They would stay until Christmas, when the hot monsoon could blow them home again. During the trading season there was a truce between the peaceful Motuans and the man-eating Goaribaris. The annual voyages in these raft-ships were among the strangest things that charmed a Polynesian wanderer.

Unromantically in a chugging steamer I crossed the Gulf and came upon the terrible land of terrible people. The business of public health called me there; Kenny Fooks had been surveying the Delta region for months, and was so lost to me that he might have been sucked into the prevalent mud. The Delta region is ravaged by rivers that pour mud upon mud or throw up shifting sand banks that wallow and stink like dead sea monsters. As I came ashore with Ahuia, long-nosed faces stared hungrily. These were the type of Goaribaris I had seen on the plantations, but dirtier, skinnier. You think of cannibals as tiger men, fierce-faced and lusty. But these were brothers to the jackal.

I was interested in something curiously inhuman that wagged from the buttocks of the queer fellows. The old men around Port Moresby had told me that Goaribaris grew tails as long as monkeys' tails, and let them hang down through holes bored in their floors; and the way to catch a Goaribari was to sneak under the house, tie a knot in his tail then run up top and grab him at your leisure. This story, unfortunately, is another nature fake. What this Delta savage wears at the stern of his breechclout probably gave rise to the yarn. It is a sort of dangler, not unlike a horse's tail, and, with his long hair done in ringlets stuck together with mud, adds to his mildly demoniac look.

The customary nude policeman, distinguished by a cap and an entirely empty cartridge belt, told Ahuia that his house, where we would sleep, was in Dopima where the famous martyr missionary, James Chalmers, was murdered in 1901. But our policeman gallantly assured us that we needn't be afraid now, because Government took care of everything. The house was stilted very high to keep devil-devils out. A sickly looking native stood at the foot of the ladder, wistfully waiting. In the background were a pack of the most repulsive women I have ever seen. Their breasts hung like empty bags, their greasy black faces were puckered to an animal look — a picture of lost femininity.

Kenny asked the policeman to go tell the fellow that it wasn't the fashion to solicit white men. I looked at Kenny's soiled legs and remarked that he was inviting hookworms. "Inviting them? They accepted the invitation weeks ago, and I'm all fed up with chenopodium and salts. My score was twenty-six good ones — Necators, of course. You've got to go barefoot in this bloody country or you'll be sucked under, feet-first."

The popular name for these Delta people is Goaribari, but there are really several related tribes, many of them of a somewhat higher type. They are named after their principal or central village — like the Kaimares, for instance. The Kaimares are much the better builders, but they get none of the benefits of over-water sanitation and live quite innocent of anything like a latrine. The hookworm infestation

was probably much less general in the old days of unchecked cannibalism and warfare. Even when I inspected various sections and
compared notes with Kenny Fooks I found that some places reeked
with worms, others were comparatively free. It was spreading, I
could venture. The Goaribaris no longer hunt each other openly,
and they do a great deal of visiting around.

A village consists of three houses, one of them 100 to 150 yards
long and 30 yards wide. These are "crocodile houses"; the main entrance is a gaping mouth, the rear narrows to a long tail. A corridor
runs full-length; small cubicles open on either side, in the less pre-
tentious dwellings, and each cubicle suffices for an entire family.
But the largest of the houses is a sort of clubhouse where the men
live and teach pubescent boys the arts of Delta manhood. In this
building there is a smaller door halfway down the passage; beside it
a niche contains an altar painted with the frightful face of a devil-
devil, and in front of it is an offering of human skulls.

I did not quite believe the grisly tales of peddling women's hacked
bodies around the sandspits and offering choice cuts to willing pur-
chasers. They said a lot of things about these miserable creatures. As
to cannibalism, the Government had hanged so many of them for it
that if they ate "long-pig" at all they must have conducted their ban-
quets with Masonic secrecy. Yet I saw the pile of skulls around the
devil-devil altar. The interpreter told me they were "skulls of ancestors." Perhaps. . . . I had a mental picture of Missionary Chalmers,
whose bones had been very hard to recover, according to one eyewitness.

We were quite unarmed. The man with the cap and cartridge belt
seemed to exercise a remarkable control over the other natives. Along
the line of publicity he was another P. T. Barnum. After his fireside
chats the people came slinking in, droves of them, milling around the
imported magician who could take snakes from the belly. We didn't
recover many snakes, for our job was to make microscopic examinations and determine the ratio of infection. However, from a lad named
Komo, I recovered 107, and Kenny Fooks did better still. Now and
then as I looked over my scrawny audience I would see a man with
clean skin and good muscle; and I would know that he had just returned from indentured service on one of the plantations.

Kaimare houses looked more like crocodiles than the Goaribari jumbles. In going through one of their larger buildings I found a sort of sanctum, completely shut off. As I started through the door my guides, who had been pleasant enough, suddenly showed their teeth and attempted to block my entrance. I pushed my way through; perhaps my prestige as a magician saved me from rough handling. Then I jumped back. The room was full of crocodiles, big ones, little ones, on the floor, crawling up the walls. I blinked, and saw what these things really were — woven of some sort of pliable reed, they were artfully modeled; and as I sighed my relief I remembered scraps of what Cushing, who lived among the Zuni Indians, had written: "Primitive peoples generally conceive of everything made . . . as living . . . a still sort of life, but as potent and aware nevertheless and as capable of functioning. . . ."

There were more human skulls. I decided to get out.

In the Bamu country beyond, I saw the most repulsive people in all Papua. The Bamus live in mud, and nature seems to have fitted them for their environment. They are as skinny and long as dead eels, and appear to be split clear to the breastbone in order to give their storklike legs a chance to hoist them out of the muck.

No white man can stay long in this blighted country without a feeling of extreme depression and hopelessness for the ill-favored branches of the human race. It was fortunate for my peace of mind one morning when our canoe swept into a deep estuary and I saw something that blossomed like a flower garden in a city dump: a lakatoi from the Gaile region! A big, seven-canoe one, and a crowd of laughing, gesturing, bargaining Motu men busily trading with the Delta folk. The shore was bright with pots and jars, the water was jammed with loose logs which the savages had floated down from faraway hills, hundreds of miles from Mudland. A curious trading.

There was a carnival air. Even the Goaribaris puckered their jackal faces into a smile. I asked a Motu trader if he wasn't getting tired of it; and didn't he want to go home? He laughed and answered in effect, "And how!" Soon the hot December wind would be blowing homeward to fill their coco sails and take them blundering back to their clean little Venice. Then the long truce would be over and the Goaribari would be his old sweet self again.

I was glad when the Purari Delta and I parted company. If professional work had called me back I would have gone, but not without a secret wish for some cleaner, greener land. This is probably the lousiest place that God ever made and didn't quite finish.

I had been closely watching the principal carrier of malaria, a lady mosquito of the *Anopheles punctulatus* tribe, and the odder varieties of flies and mosquitoes I had been sending to Dr. Francis Root, biologist of Johns Hopkins. Since quinine was malaria's one known specific, I was rather fussy about teaching my inspectors to take their daily dose. I knew what a delirious wreck an attack can make of a white man in the jungle, and I had impressed upon my young inspectors that I would not forgive any carelessness about quinine — five grains a day as a prophylactic, and at the slightest symptom increase the dose until the temperature swings back to normal. Those were written orders.

Then as I worked down the coast on the last leg of my Papuan adventure, I came down with malaria, in spite of large precautionary doses of quinine which swamp and jungle conditions had made necessary. I was too miserable to laugh at myself when I got to the snug little settlement on Samarai, the eastern tip of Papua's tail. I was a bilious wreck; I saw yellow. The neat British town was pretty as a bride, but I was in no bridegroom mood. One of my inspectors, a new one who had already proven shiftless, also showed up with malaria. I had to be restrained from throwing him downstairs. Why? Because he hadn't taken his quinine, and had allowed himself to get sick. At the Widow Henderson's hotel, the town's only meeting place, I invited another fight. A one-armed planter and I sat in the barroom, the only possible place to talk, and were discussing a survey in his district when a dough-faced stranger poked his head between us and asked if the planter was afraid of him, or what? Instead of brushing him off I kicked over my chair and reverted to common Australian: "Open your mouth to say one word and I'm inta you, right now!" The stranger departed. A couple of days later the Widow Gofton, who served the bar, said: "When that man gets tough around here now I just say to him, 'Look out, or I'll call the Doctor.'"

I saw Samarai through jaundiced eyes, and biliousness gave me a sort of malign power when it came to an argument. However, I managed to be diplomatic when I found that Samarai was having a

City Beautiful campaign and didn't want its view spoiled by a row of over-water latrines. To the health officer, of course, that was nonsense; Paradise might be lined with those coquettish little shrines and he would call it perfect — at least, that was what the esthetes implied when I argued.

Swallowing bile, I combined architecture with diplomacy and devised some dainty palm-thatched sanctums to sit over the tide, with rustic bridges running out to them and clumps of croton to act as screens. I became an engineer and sketched out plans for deep pits to be dug into the coral and filled with rubble so that the contents would be sifted gently out to sea. I left too soon to find out whether or not they followed my plan. It was just another quarrel between Hygeia and Mrs. Grundy. In such a fracas Mrs. G. usually comes out the winner.

The two fights in Samarai were more than counterbalanced by two fortunate meetings. One night I came into Bob Whitten's sheet-iron trading store and saw a figure quite out of harmony with the smelly hurricane lamps and piled-up canned goods. His smart dinner suit gave him a clubby look which stirred the old bile, for I had been out in the field and was a mass of dirt and scratches. He turned a wind-hardened business face and a pair of Scotch-gray eyes. "Are you Dr. Lambert?" he asked. I said that I was. "My name's George Fulton," he said. George Fulton was executive head of the powerful Lever Brothers firm, who bought and sold islands, controlled supplies and shipping, over a great watery empire. He began popping keen, intelligent questions at me, and I forgot his evening clothes after one exciting revelation.

"Know anything about Rennell Island, Doctor?" I had heard of it sketchily from a skipper who said that nobody ever went ashore, for fear of the natives, and that there was nothing worth trading for.

George Fulton said: "It's just off the blue-black Solomons, but the people aren't black. Nobody knows what they are. They're primitive as monkeys, but rather superior humans. Sleep in caves, worship an invisible god, have traditions that may be either Polynesian or Caucasian. Since the white man came to the Pacific, there hasn't been a landing party that's penetrated Rennell farther than the beach. They simply won't let strangers get in. Why? Maybe they're protecting themselves against foreign disease, or maybe it's the same old tabu. For ages they've been practically untouched.

"Missionaries tried it not long ago, and three of them got knocked on the head. I know more about this island than most. It's a sort of lost world, terrible cliffs all around it, one small beach protected by a reef. Last year we were short on labor and thought we might recruit some of the men. Fine, strapping fellows — incidentally, the women are very pretty. Well, we picked up a handful of laborers, bribed them with hatchets and jackknives. They're crazy for steel and iron. They do their carving with shells."

I asked what became of the men he took away; I was afraid he'd stop talking and go to somebody's bridge table, but he said:

"Around the Solomons we would put a few of them ashore here and there to work on the plantations. Before we could up-anchor they would plump into the sea and swim back to the ship. Finally we gave them up and took the survivors home. Interesting folk? Rather! They're not castaways or newcomers. They've been there since God made them. They might be worth a scientific man's time."

He moved away but I almost tripped him up. "Mr. Fulton, if they are an untouched people, they must be free from imported diseases. I've pretty well decided that the natives are dying off from the worms and germs that white men, orientals, and friendly tribes bring in." He nodded approvingly, and I plunged on, "It would be very valuable to me, and to the world too, if I could study these Rennellese. Hookworm, for instance . . . If they have it at all it might be a variety we have never seen . . ."

"Well, Doctor — some time when one of our boats swings your way. . . ."

George Fulton was a super-businessman. I decided not to let him forget his offer, and for half a year I showered his Australian office with remindful letters. Finally my insistence bore fruit — of a mixed variety.

The young inspector whom I had found guilty of idleness and malaria and ejected from my staff had been scheduled to survey the Trobriands, two or three days sailing to the north. The shortage of help compelled me to take my headache and a supply of quinine and cover the job myself. But in the South Pacific you don't just buy a ticket and start. You play Micawber until something turns up. In this case the turn-up was the fantastic little cutter *Bomada*, owned in partnership by a professional butterfly collector and a hairy-chested planter-adventurer named Bob Bunting. The butterfly collector had a German name and looked rather Chinese. Bob Bunting was something of a slave driver when he managed plantations; if native laborers lay down to die of witch-doctoring he revived them with a bull-whip. Bob's sort survive in the tropics.

So we were off in the crazy craft, which promptly broke down in a mushy, drizzly rain. And that was where I had the other pleasant meeting. Out of the glazed mist loomed a whaleboat, steadily rowed. A gorgeously American voice yelled, "Hey, can I do anything for you fellows?" A young man sprang aboard; almost before he spoke again I was thinking, "I just kicked out an incompetent, and there's the boy to take his place."

His name, he said, was Byron Beach. Enthusiastically he scrambled into his whaleboat and brought back an outdated pile of *Saturday Evening Post* copies, and Theodore Roosevelt's book on the "River of Doubt." Americanism stuck out all over the boy. He had graduated from one of the better New England preparatory schools, then war broke out and he decided to "travel." Possibly he was a conscientious objector; but Byron Beach was no slacker. His headlong bravery and resourcefulness in a later adventure proved that.

Bob Bunting, who knew everybody, accused him of being too keen for the Milne Bay traders; they were ganging up against him. Beach had been out after copra and had bought so much under competitive noses that local dealers were swearing vengeance. An enterprising lad. When the old engine came to life again I said, "Beach, if they make it too hot for you here, why not join my outfit?" His young face flushed with pleasure. "Golly, Doctor, that would be swell!"

I was afraid that would be the last I'd ever see of him.

Our breakdown at Dobu gave us a view of the geyser field at Seymour Bay which matches the Yellowstone. The greatest spouter is Seo-seo-kuna, which roars like a hundred menageries. Beside one of the boiling pools I saw a group of natives kneeling reverently. Ah, this would be something worth seeing; the primitive heart bowed down to some powerful goddess of fire and water . . . When I came closer I soon found what they were doing. They were cooking yams.

Probably they did say a little heathen prayer — if the missionary was not looking. Unofficial paganism is the custom everywhere in the Christianized Pacific. In choosing my native assistants I usually rejected the mission-trained boys, who were too often slackers, liars and hypocrites. "Him Mission" meant "He's a Christian," and was a scornful term.

I do not underrate the work of missionaries, the best of them; I have known so many who tackled their problems cheerfully on the pittance doled out by Foreign Boards. They had volunteered for a life so bitterly hard and so meagerly paid that it might easily have brought out something more petty than the helpful generosity which the best of them showed me. But the days of the great missioners like Chalmers and Brown, who fought and died in the midst of ferocious savagery, have passed away.

The man of God down there, when he went in for selfish profit, usually made his investments in his wife's name and took advantage of special concessions allotted by the Government for legitimate mission work; or he used the funds from good Christian collection plates at home. Professional traders had a right to complain of unfair competition in the labor market, for the business-missions often secured labor for nothing under a forced system of "donating" work. Among the missions which "came clean" were the Catholics, who were accustomed to look to Europe for their support; but when 1914's war came on that support was cut off. They faced the music manfully, and did their bit toward paying their own way. The fruits of this labor were turned back to the native, in the form of an intelligent attempt to better his condition. But too often the missionaries were wrapped in a dream of heavenly perfection, seeing nothing, hearing nothing, smelling nothing. It was refreshing to meet an honest-minded one, who could be fair enough to rationalize his ideals. . . .

Our cutter *Bomada* had staged her terminal breakdown in one of the Trobriands' divine lagoons which seemed to take its color from the pearls that lay below. The *Bomada*, I felt, had killed every noble impulse in my heart. Especially that rainy day when we tried to hoist sail and saw the rotten thing — which hadn't been looked at for two years — fall to pieces in the first breeze. And now I was taking afternoon tea in the pleasant garden of a pleasant missionary. The prettily

A CHAPTER ON CONTRASTS

formed native girls who served us wore single garments, brief fiber skirts. The only shamed person present was the missionary's wife, who kept chirping, "Isn't it disgusting, Doctor!" Her husband, who had entered the ministry from Oxford, had educated these people in cleanliness and right living. He had taught them many things that natives must know in order to meet the perils of European civilization. On purely scientific grounds he had opposed the missionary custom (encouraged by the traders) of dolling the women up in disease-breeding clothes.

I asked this sensible messenger of Christ, "How many converts, in our sense of the word, have you made here?" He rubbed his tired forehead and replied, "Doctor, not one in twenty years." I honored him for that, and was willing to wager that he had won his way many times over a "civilizer." He was human, and he knew humanity.

He was in refreshing contrast to at least one luxuriously living Christian who had entertained me in Samarai. He "instructed" the natives in collecting nuts, cutting copra and building boats. His fine house and teeming acres revealed how well he had profited by his instructions. If he had made any attempt to civilize the people, the effect was not apparent. Except in the case of the lone missionary who honestly despaired of making converts, there seemed to be no attempt to teach the natives English.

But there must have been another exception once, for on a small Trobriand island a native boy addressed me primly: "Undoubtedly, sir, you will find more clement weather for the remainder of your voyage." Startled, I asked, "Where did you learn to talk like that?" The boy said, "My missionary taught me. Unfortunately he expired in an insane asylum. He had been irrational for quite a long time."

The Trobriands, land of pearls and parrots, were romantic. The fertile soil put the rest of Papua to shame and the delightful lagoons abounded in fish and oysters — also sharks. I shall not compete with ten thousand travelogue-poets in describing lagoons, but I never went in an outrigger over one of these beautiful sheets of crystal without a feeling of complete rest and detachment.

However, when you go on medical inspection you had best leave romance outside. I wish that a crew of Jack London's admirers had followed me through the local hospitals and seen the cases of venereal granuloma, a disease still called "tropical." I wish they had helped

me count the cases of hospitalized gonorrhea, and helped me guess at
the prevalence of that disease in villages and on plantations. I have
heard sentimentalists say that the islanders are morally like ancient
Greeks. Perhaps. But when Greek meets Greek, see what the doctor
sees.

Dr. Bellamy, the District Medical Officer, took me over to look at the
wreck of a sturdy Scot, once a wealthy pearl trader. When hard luck
came with tropical ulcers he had squatted in one position so long that his
joints ankylosed, and he was now unable to move except on all fours. An
un-Scottish generosity had been the cause of his downfall. Because
he had married a native wife and had several children, he thought
of the natives as his own people. When famine came, he gave everything he had to relieve hunger. White friends warned him of native
ingratitude, but it was too late. Sick and useless, he didn't notice how
his wife and children sneered when they passed him. He had taken
to chewing betel-nuts because they were a cheaper anodyne than gin. A
look into his eye-sockets made me ashamed of my race.

In the Trobriands, the pearl was the beautiful breeder of disease
and crime. Every trading store had pearls to sell, and French buyers
from Parisian jewelry firms came every year to bargain. The Government protected native fishers from the traders' rapacity; most of the
stories of greed and treachery had white men or half-castes as principal actors.

There was the one about the Britisher who married an extremely
pretty half-caste and had a collection of pearls ready to show the
Parisians. His little wife, who was French on the white side, was
extremely fond of the short, tight-waisted corsets then in style. After
her husband found that she had flaunted that corset up and down
the beach to the gratification of many, he did what white men too
often do there under strain. He shot himself. His wife disappeared;
so did his pearls. A couple of years later the authorities found her
in Sydney, living rather too well. But oh, what an innocent little
lady! She had inherited the money, and what were they accusing a
poor, sick widow of doing? A Sherlock Holmes could have told her
how she had sneaked into the house right after the suicide, hidden
some rich double handfuls inside her corset, and flitted away. The
case was dropped; after all, she was the man's legitimate widow.

I summed up this trip with a line or two in my notebook: —

Trobriands rich prize for trade. Hence heavily diseased. Am feeling much better, letting up on quinine. If I had not stuck to regular dosage feel sure that I would have died.

To economize on my budget I paid Skipper Billy Carson of the *Ruby* enough fuel to take me back to Samarai. When we came up from the beach the Widow Henderson's barroom piano was thrashing out a music hall ditty, and an American voice in the doorway said, "Hello, Doctor! Gee, it *is* the Doctor! I was just telling the guy in there that you'd forgotten all about me. You *are* going to take me along, aren't you?"

I caught young Byron Beach's enthusiasm. I was well again, resolved that when I got back to Port Moresby I'd go on with the Foundation for another campaign, or a dozen. It was wonderful work after all, and I wasn't going to let the tropics lick me.

After a good supper I asked, "How many of us can sing?" They all could. We were a male quartet with Beach's pleasant voice to carry the air against Carson's sad bass, my raw baritone and the squeaky tenor of the young man at the piano — he was the one Byron Beach called "the guy in there." "Guy" is sufficient name for him. Drink didn't interfere with his fingers on the keys, and he seemed to know the old standard tunes, "I've been working on the railroad," "I was see-eee-ing Nelly home," and "Farewell, my own true love." We were happy as four men can be, making close harmony in the shadow of an admiring bar. It was late when the guy at the piano banged a fist on the keys and muttered, "That's enough." We had been singing about any little girl being a nice little girl.

I asked Beach what was the matter with him. He said, "Back from the war, living on booze. He's really quite a nice guy."

That night the guy shot himself, but his aim was ineffective. I took care of him long enough to tell him that liquor is a poor substitute for quinine. I heard later that he sobered up and married some little girl who was a nice little girl. I like to record one story with a happy ending. But Billy Carson, who sang bass for us, had a grimmer finish. He had married a wealthy half-caste, and when he sent his children to Australia to be educated he had found that they were being set aside as "blackfellows." One morning on Samarai wharf a loiterer found a neat bundle of clothes. Billy was always methodical,

In our tidy Port Moresby bungalow, comforted by my dear wife, whom I had seen too little during my restless months in Papua, I told my senior, Dr. Sawyer of the Foundation, that I would undertake a year's survey of what some still called German New Guinea. Sawyer said, "Lambert, you're certainly a hard man to kill!"

My farewell to Ahuia may supply a good finishing scene. Eloisa, like the perfect housekeeper she is, always packed and unpacked my boxes in his presence. She would give him the keys; when we returned from the field he would hand them over to her for inspection. On this day of parting the boy was proud as a chancellor, delivering the keys. How could anything be missing? Hadn't he served the best doctors in Papua and acted as the Governor's orderly? And when he started out on his expeditions with me hadn't he stopped his ears against the wail of his friends, howling that he'd never come back alive?

Counting the wash, Eloisa giggled. Mine was all there, plus many unidentified shirts, socks, shorts and singlets. It was hardly worth while asking him the names of various hosts he had borrowed them from. Ahuia had conveniently forgotten.

When he was about to depart with my bonus of cash and tobacco he maintained his fierce expression, but there were tears in his eyes. Melanesians weep rather easily. Could he serve the *taubada* again? He would so like to serve the *taubada* if he came back. . . .

I was a little rough, pushing him out of the place. I didn't want him to see that white men can also weep. I would miss Ahuia.

So ended the Papuan chapter, with a few hard figures. I had covered 2,284 miles on foot and horse, in motor cars, canoes, whaleboats, sailing boats, motor launches and steamers. Fourteen miles of it I had done in the quaint vehicles they call "track cars," iron-wheeled bone-breakers pushed by cannibal labor. With my inspectors we had covered 8,461 miles. Nor did my official report include the few miles we swam when our canoes heeled over. In villages and plantations we had examined people by tens of thousands. We had marked down a grand total of 59.2 per cent infection. We had upset an old theory that hookworm is carried from the plantations into the villages; our survey had gone to prove that quite the reverse was true.

The Papuan people by the Government's reckoning of 1920–21 had been roughly estimated at 300,000. More likely, in the light of what a

few explorers had found among the lost mountains, the population figures should have run nearer 500,000. The estimate of 166,721 for New
Guinea Territory was ridiculously low; it was more reasonable to put
it around the half million mark. The immense Dutch end of the island
held something like a million more; but Dutch New Guinea was outside my itinerary.

The tens of thousands we inspected and the thousands to whom
we gave first treatment may be just a splash in a huge puddle of disease. But the very careful instruction in treatment which we offered
to planters, officials and missionaries (in fact to everybody whose
heart was in the work of bringing back a failing population) might
have been more important than anything else we did. I hope so.
Month after month we had been hammering into the white man's
head the grave necessity for pollution-proof sanitary arrangements
under conditions which varied between mushy swamp soil and solid
rock.

CHAPTER VII

WHERE NEW GUINEA WAS NEW

Rounding the northern edge of the great island you come upon the Territory of New Guinea, which was German New Guinea until 1914, when Australia took it over. To simplify the confusion in a few words: the eastern half of the island is Australian-governed, divided into Papua and the Territory. The western half (roughly half) is Dutch New Guinea. That was how the land lay in 1921. Perhaps the horrors of the Second World War will change its geography again.

In May, 1921, when I boarded the *Melusia*, bound for Rabaul, the capital, our decks and cabins were thronged with seventy officials of the civil government, coming in to relieve a military government of evil repute. The newcomers were centered by the Administrator, Brigadier-General Evan Alexander Wisdom, C.B., C.M.G., D.S.O., V.D., whom his King later adorned with an added set of initials and a knighthood. Despite this alphabet train, General Wisdom had a character that went well with his name. He was an Australian Scot, veteran of Gallipoli and the French campaign. I felt that he was a man who could listen to reason and exercise his own. He needed all he had, for he was setting out to face a tangle which would have confused King Solomon.

The physicians he had brought with him for public health work were competently educated men, but inexperienced in tropical diseases. Colonel Honman, the new Chief Medical Officer, was another Aussie–Scot I didn't forget in a day. A hard-crusted, soft-hearted old regular, all he knew about tropical medicine was what he had learned as personal physician to Prime Minister Billy Hughes. He wasn't afraid of liquor or anything else. For seven months I was to be very close to Honman, and to love him for his contradictory qualities.

Aboard ship I had no sooner met him than he suggested that I give them a talk on malaria. I felt that here on the *Melusia* it might be of service to the incoming officials. That night they gathered on the main deck and I told them of my experiences with the disease. How the *Anopheles punctulatus*, whose female is more deadly than the male, travels in the Pacific with mankind in his restless journeying from village to village, from island to island. How I had run my fingers under the lower ribs of thousands of natives and felt the sagging spleen which tells the tale. I went into a subject which the medical men present knew as well as I did — through book knowledge: blackwater fever. This quickly fatal disease gets its name from the dark coloration of bloody urine, caused by the oxidization of hemoglobin, and the bladder condition is called hemoglobinuria.

I had found very few cases of genuine blackwater fever, I told them. Even when it occurs the patient is often dead before diagnosis. The condition, when it comes, is frequently caused by a blind misuse of quinine. Malarial people sometimes neglect the remedy for a couple of months, then swallow a handful. And here I tried to drive home my favorite point. I even had the temerity to quote a German; the world-renowned Dr. Robert Koch had come to New Guinea in 1910 and proved, for the first time in medical history, that epidemic malaria can be reduced by *quinine alone*. Here I took my chance to say that in fever-bitten countries quinine in regular moderate doses is an absolute necessity. Liquor is no substitute. If you abuse your constitution with a daily dozen bottles of beer or a habitual quart of whisky, don't cry "blackwater fever." A white man in the tropics can remain as healthy as in the temperate zones, provided he exercises and takes care of himself.

Wasn't it Kate Douglas Wiggin who said, "It is hard to be agreeable and instructive at the same time"? However, most of the medical men seemed to like the talk. I heard one District Officer for the Admiralty saying, "This quinine business is all bloody nonsense." Perhaps I had gone afoul of his prejudice. You can't talk quinine without arousing some bitter criticisms.

In contrast to Papua's bleak capital I found Rabaul a picture of tropical delight: regular streets were bordered with poinciana, royal palms, coconut palms; betel-nut palms raised graceful, slender stems and flaunted their feathery tops just above clusters of fruit that were like hothouse grapes; Indian laurels loomed graciously over thriving fig trees. The Germans had drained all this land, relieved it of mosquitoes, planted the groves; they had set Government House on a fine eminence overlooking a stretch of water that might have been a Scottish lake.

Rabaul was an extremely shaky Garden of Eden, geologically and politically. Jolly earthquakes came and went with seismic whimsicality, and were so frequent that every hotel, house and office had its heavy furniture lashed to the walls. Otherwise, one might have waked up any morning and found a large German wardrobe in one's lap. Right inside Rabaul's port, Vulcan Island was a particularly bad actor. The Reverend George Brown, the fighting missionary, records its beginning back in 1878 when it blew the twenty-mile channel full of pumice; thousands of boiled fish were washed ashore, and great sea turtles with their tortoise-shell cooked to a pulp. The next big show was in 1937, when Vulcan covered the town with ashy vomit; after that there was talk of moving the capital, but the colonial becomes a fatalist. He has to be.

One morning in 1921 I saw some lumber that had been piled on Vulcan go scattering into the sea like a box of matches, and I saw the huge sheet-iron D.H. & P.G. store curl like a withered leaf. After that Eloisa and I agreed that at the next tremor we'd pick up little Harriette and make for the hills. . . . And let's not forget two very wicked "Shaker ladies," two tall peaks about three miles from town on the mainland, and officially named Mother and Daughter. On the night of Vulcan's birth there was a volcanic growl at the mouth of the Bay, and in the morning Vulcan loomed from the sea, shoved 600 feet from the water and venomous as a newborn cobra. Vulcan is now popularly known as "The Bastard," and so he will be called until he takes a notion to sink again.

Where Papua with her probable 500,000 natives had five official medical men, New Guinea Territory, equally populous, had eight or ten government doctors to serve it. The hospital at Rabaul I found especially well equipped, thanks to a retired German medical staff. The Australians had adopted a German expedient. Well-trained orderlies, under the supervision of medical officers, were sent out to run the lesser hospitals. These orderlies were called "*lik-lik* doctors" or "small doctors" — *lik-lik* means "little." They had a high sense of duty and were remarkably competent. When I was there the natives were being trained simply in bandaging, treating sores and administering physic; then they were given a uniform cap and *lavalava* and sent back to their villages to apply their useful knowledge. They had the title of "Tultul" and their salary was a pound or so a year.

The Medical Tultul was a modest beginning in an important system that was destined to go on. I had studied the mind of the higher type Melanesian and had begun to see that he was far from a fool. I had watched the work of my head boys in the field — men like Ahuia, for instance. What except race prejudice stood in the way of their being educated in medicine and equipped to practise among their own people, whose language and customs no white physician would ever understand?

Even in those days I heard reports of the more progressive Fiji Islands where for a long time they had been giving a sketchy medical training to Melanesians. Most of the South Pacific received the idea with a cynical smile. In Papua I had broached the plan of sending out picked natives, under the direction of laymen, to administer yaws and hookworm treatments over a country so vast that the few white doctors were ridiculously inadequate to cover it. This plan was later adopted. In the Territory of New Guinea I had still better luck; crusty old Colonel Honman had sufficient faith in me to permit the experiment at once. The black boys I chose and instructed in the administration of oil of chenopodium proved remarkably useful, considering the inadequacy of their training.

Conditions we had to meet were similar to those in Papua, only the people were far nearer to the Stone Age than were most of the Papuan natives. Cannibalism was still practised within forty miles of Rabaul. We had to move cautiously out in the bush, but we never carried firearms — with the exception of Chris Kendrick, who faced one or two situations where a pistol proved a very useful tool.

New Guinea Territory, in fact, was at that time harder to deal with than it was before the abrupt political change of 1914. The coastal native, more sophisticated than his brother of the jungle, was dumbly wondering what had become of the Germans, who had ruled them well, all things considered. Natives had been servants of the padroons, and had learned to like them. And what was this new set of white men with a new set of laws which they seemed unable to enforce?

The military administration, which came in with the first World War and lasted for seven years, was a great political blunder, as the best minds of Australia knew from the first; but what could be done about it until Billy Hughes's home Government decided on something less fantastic? The whole business had the nasty look of any sudden political overturn.

Long before 1885, when the Kaiser's Government officially occupied German New Guinea, his thrifty subjects had been working the plantations. This was no pumped-up Sudetenland, for the Germans were honestly in control. They were good planters who studied the soil under tropical conditions on this favored side of the big island. Their colonial treasury showed a surplus; they had increased their acres and become rich padroons; they lived luxuriously. Their Governor's Palace at Rabaul (which the new military administration seized) was a fine example of tropical architecture. Out of a fever-ridden swamp they had made a Rabaul that was malaria-free.

In our time Germany has committed so many crimes against civilization that a crime against Germany may be worth putting on record. Its criminality reacted on all concerned, and especially on hordes of young war veterans whom the Australian Government "rewarded" with free grants of land.

I was settled in Rabaul and enjoying the generous privileges which Colonel Honman gave me in the fine German-made hospital when I learned some details of that military occupation, which a hard working civil administration was by now trying to live down. Everybody was talking about a scandal which compared with our own postbellum days in the South. Field-tried old soldiers were referring with scorn to the "Coconut Anzacs" whom Australia, for lack of better men, had sent to take possession in 1914. The Coconut Anzacs seemed to have been mostly men who hadn't gone to the real war, for one reason or another — raw amateurs without the slightest sense of discipline. Military power inspired many to wanton acts of cruelty and the stupidest sort of blunders.

My daring young man Byron Beach was eyewitness to one outrage. He presented himself as a medical officer to a punitive expedition, and was taken along. A company of Coconut Anzacs had been sent out to chasten a native village, accused of cannibalism. Led by a hard-drinking

officer, himself frightened of the poor, scared cannibals, the troops surrounded a certain inland village to teach the black beggars a lesson.
Maybe they were pretty drunk when they proceeded to shoot up
everything they saw. Men were shot as they ran, women and children
were gunned out of trees. Beach saw the leader of the party put a
pistol to the head of a girl who lay flat on the ground.

And next day the commanding officer found that he had made a
little mistake. He had attacked the wrong village.

Another expedition went to see about a German anthropologist who
lived alone in the bush. He had been there for years and had a way of
locking his books and papers in the little house and going away on
tours of research. When war was declared he was so far away from his
home base that he didn't hear the news. In his absence the frenzied
patriots broke down his door, found great stacks of carefully written
papers and made a bonfire of them. They didn't understand German,
and the writing looked like spy stuff. On his return the scientist found
his lifework reduced to ashes. They say he went crazy.

Maybe the new civil government was too bitter, looking over the
mischief the military administration had wrought. There had been a
great deal of aimless sabotage. For instance, they had demolished the
apparatus in the great radio station. The excuse was that it might be
sending messages to Berlin. It hadn't occurred to the conquerors that
they might save these costly things for their own use.

Now what to do with the German planters? Prime Minister Hughes's
Territorial Government was taking care of that. When I established
myself at Rabaul in 1921 the farce was in full swing, and through no
fault of Governor Wisdom's, who had to make the best of a policy
already framed. The policy was starkly this: Encourage the thrifty
Germans to improve their land with the promise that they might retain
it. In 1921 something called an Expropriation Board arrived, called in
the anxious Germans, and gave them vouchers enabling them to sell
their property back to the Territory, at their own valuation. But when
the Germans turned in these vouchers the Territory's Treasury Department paid for them in orders on the German Government — to be
applied on Australia's reparations claim!

Bankrupt Germans were selling their household goods for anything
they could get. During my stay in New Guinea it was a commonplace
to see vessels departing for Australia, laden with pictures, rugs, silver-

ware. Returning ships were bringing back the same old load: hard
liquor and fresh contingents of war veterans to stray into the plantations, sicken and go home.

Liquor and malaria, malaria and liquor — a vicious circle to worry
the public health physician. These brave soldiers, who never wanted to
hear the word "war" again, were taking Billy Hughes's advice: "Just
go to New Guinea and pick out a fine plantation." They didn't know
how to eat, drink or live in the tropics. There were many stories,
funny and sad. One returned soldier was blithely dumped on the beach
and sent to the wilds with nothing more substantial than a case of
tinned beef, a case of mixed pickles and six cases of beer. Babes in the
wood, what did they know about malaria? Men who should have
known said to them, "Shaky in the morning? Then scoff off a tot of
whisky or a bottle of beer, and you'll feel fit as a fiddle." Green as
grass, the poor fellows thought that coconuts grew underground like
potatoes or on vines like grapes. They starved, they drank, they let
the natives take advantage of their ignorance. They swallowed the
popular "fever cure" and finally tottered back to the returning ship —
if they could.

I looked over the annual import of alcoholic beverages — beer
102,204 gallons, spirits 7,534 gallons, wines 1,500 gallons, stout 1,056
gallons. This was to serve a European population totaling 1,265. The
natives didn't drink, and you must discount the women, children and
missionaries.

I was hardly established in Rabaul when Colonel Honman began
urging me to take full charge of the hospital. That was a flattering
offer, which I at first declined. Between my medical units and myself,
we had to make some sense out of the half million neglected natives
we had come there to study. But I shall never forget the grand old
Colonel's morning calls at my house. A soldier to the bone, he never
complained, but I could see that he was suffering from "New Guinea
fever" — in short, he needed a pick-me-up. It was a habit of my neighbors to borrow a bottle of whisky in the morning, return it at noon,
and borrow it again at night. But Colonel Honman always drank his
tonic on the spot. Without a word I would administer the usual
dose, a drinking glass filled one third with gin and the other two thirds
with French and Italian vermouth. Straight as a ramrod he'd toss it off,

smack satisfied lips over his double row of false teeth, and bellow, "We breed men in Australia!"

He had a leather stomach, a golden heart and a head that nothing seemed to affect. Already we were sympathizing with Governor Wisdom's job, for he was breaking up a racket which was as crude as any invented by Brooklyn union leaders. It was the bird of paradise racket — which may sound fantastic, but it was there, and had been ever since the military administration did its worst for New Guinea. In German days it had been customary for newcomers to shoot and sell enough birds to earn the price of a plantation. But the new Territorial Government passed a law to protect the birds. Like all prohibitions this invited bootleggers who, like all bootleggers, were followed by highjackers. It was so easy to make a rich kill and pass it across the Dutch border, where there were no game-protection laws! — and very convenient for a Chinese trader to wait on the Dutch side and pay cash for the bag. Or you could smuggle the feathered pelts into the hands of a ship's steward. Stewards were getting rich; one of them was able to run thoroughbreds on the track.

District Officers were up to their necks in poaching. One of them came back from the Dutch border with £10,000 in his pocket. He started for Sydney, fell ill on the boat and had to be taken off at Cairns. A sympathetic friend offered to take the easy money to the invalid's family. The "friend" was a highjacker, of course, and had arranged a clever get-away. The poacher died in the hospital.

District Officers had been up to many things never dreamed of in the philosophy of Tammany Hall. One of them revived "black-birding," the old-time slavery. He got a little island offshore, made raids on natives, stored his prisoners there and proceeded to sell them in job lots. When this human meat ran short through brisk sales the official used his police authority and arrested a lot more. Several succeeding District Officers went in for this thriving trade. The military administration tried to break it up. There were some records, for the Keop (District Officer) always made the deals look very legal. But when the Military Governor demanded these records, a handy filing clerk confessed that they had been mislaid.

These abuses were on the wane when Wisdom stepped in, but, even so, he had inherited a pretty kettle of fish. Colonel Honman's principal worry was a lack of doctors who knew anything about tropical medicine. If I didn't take over the hospital, he said, he'd have to draft my services. Well, he did finally.

My right and left hands, Bill Tully and Chris Kendrick, were still with me. Without those two I could never have got through Melanesia. As laboratory assistant Bill used his fine eyes at the microscope, to supplement my dull ones. I had Kenny Fooks too, always good for a barefoot excursion into the swamps, gifted with a constitution that kept him plump through months of hardship. And there was young Byron Beach, an erratic fund of energy. I had picked up two new inspectors, very competent men, whom I had sent out with the other field units. I took out a unit of my own. Between us, we swept north and east over the big hook formed by New Britain and New Ireland; we traveled west under the Equator to Manus and the Admiralty Group; west again to the string of flyspecks, Marou and Ninigo, Matty and Ana.

Chris Kendrick, through fat and lean — usually lean — remained his quiet, reliable self. After his long absences in the bogs and streams and jungles, he'd show up smiling and slap down his neatly written reports, pregnant with a Britisher's genius for understatement. "Had to climb face of cliff. Waited between jumps till surf stopped pouring over it, then jumped again. Tricky business." "Horse broke leg in volcanic rock. Had to shoot him. Too bad, fine animal." "Had to use a lawyer-vine stick on black assistant. First time I ever struck a native. The *lik-lik* doctor here brought me a boy he said had beri-beri. It proved to be a champion hookworm case. In 5 days counted 1,237 worms. Dosed him again in a week. Chenopodium very slow. Got only 25 first dose. Second yielded 1,122. Score going up. Left assistant in charge of patient, instructions to watch stools. When I got back I was annoyed to find that the idiot had thrown the whole mess away. Jungle house-keeping. I might have recovered 4,000 worms." This item gave me a bitter laugh. Things like that have happened to us so often, with ill-trained assistants.

When Chris was with me in New Britain I saw him severely bitten — by a parrot, pet of the Samoan wife of a German planter. Chris was busy making friends when the bird nipped him square across the nose. I treated it, and Chris's diary tersely records: "You never know what to expect down here."

He jotted down one item which a garrulous explorer might have turned into a chapter, and a thrilling one: —

Alone with native crew, big, sulky devils. Couldn't understand trouble. Maybe short on food. They turned on me, with spears and paddles. Covered them with my service pistol, but was a bit nervy for fear 2 or 3 would get me from behind. Finally the D.O. showed up with police. It was rather tricky.

One day en route Kenny Fooks lost his temper and told a coastwise skipper what he thought of him. The skipper retaliated by dumping Kenny off on a sort of desert island. Nothing to do for weeks but count the sparse hookworms and write a weather report. Most of that diary read: "June 14, weather fine." "June 21, weather still fine." "July 1, weather cloudy." "July 9, raining like hell and glad of it." My other inspectors were more active, and I had to scold Byron Beach occasionally for his daredevil tendencies. But he was learning fast and his young vitality made him a splendid worker. My new acquisitions were W. J. McErlane and R. V. Sunners. Fooks and Beach were later sent to the mainland, and McErlane covered the field in Bougainville, an island far to the east and formerly part of the Solomons. These men were not heard from for half a year.

I had been studying pidgin English for nearly a year, but had not reached the point where I could use it in my lectures, as I knew I must. Until I had mastered the idiom I had to depend on a faithful interpreter. Therefore I chose a very cross-eyed native named Jerope; I got him because nobody else in Rabaul seemed to want him. Jerope was so cross-eyed that when he poured my coffee I had to follow the spout with my cup, otherwise he would have poured it in my lap. He was a bush fellow with none of Ahuia's sophistication, and was obsessed by every witch and devil that flies over the Pacific. Before I could take him into the field he got himself arrested for stealing a red lantern off a sewer-digging in Rabaul. When the judge asked him what he wanted with a red lantern he blandly explained. He thought the white men had put them on the streets so that natives could use them to scare off devils. For everybody knows that devils won't attack a man with a lantern.

Jerope languished awhile in jail and improved his education. Because the boy was brighter than the average the Keop who ruled the jail put him in charge of the bulla-ma-cows (cattle herd) and Jerope was faithful to his trust. The day I called and accused him of milking the cows, his eyes crossed in great sadness when he replied, "No, master, him no woman cow, him man cow."

Jerope was not a mission boy; he despised their kind for a lot of sissies. Once when we were inspecting Ninigo away up in the northeast we had with us a well-known English anthropologist, nephew of a great one. Like the Catholic missionaries he had a soft voice and a full beard. He was far too dainty. The Australians called him "Birdie" because he wore a feather in his Alpine hat. Birdie shrank from cold baths, so every morning he minced back and forth across the deck, carrying a little bowl of hot water for his tub. Once when the bowl-bearing Birdie minced by, Jerope turned and spat into the sea. "Him mission!" he growled.

From a medical point of view the Ninigo group was interesting. I made a count of palpable spleens and found an index of 54 per cent; considerable malaria for so remote a spot. In fact this was about the same proportion that I found among the assorted natives brought to the hospital in Rabaul. Hookworm, on the other hand, was only 8.4 per cent as against 74.2 for the whole Territory. Why? Because the group was made up of narrow atolls, where the beaches were the latrines and the tide carried the infecting material away. Malaria and elephantiasis are both mosquito diseases (if you can call elephantiasis a disease — it is merely a symptom of filarial infection). On one of the islands here I saw a woman's breasts so enlarged that when she sat they touched the ground.

Ninigo might serve as a type example of a region with no protection against the insect carriers that are today scattering plague among all the sons of Adam. Rapid transit, open ports, borders wide open . . . It's the same old story, to us of the Health Service.

Do you remember the alarm of ten years ago — how our most modern instrument of speed, the airplane, had carried the deadly *Anopheles gambiae* from Natal in Africa across to Brazil? Brazil was too busy with a revolution to fool with mosquitoes until three or four years later when death-without-bullets felled the population in wet areas. Fortunately the infection reached a comparatively dry belt, so that the mosquitoes were slowed up. Then Brazil joined with the Rocke-

feller Foundation in a gigantic campaign. In 1939 a million dollars was
spent down there, and this year they expect to double that sum in an
attempt to check the scourge before it spreads, heaven knows how
far. . . .

Dr. Marshall Barber, the great authority on malaria, says: "There is
no doubt that this invasion of *gambiae* threatens the Americas with a
catastrophe in comparison with which ordinary pestilence, conflagra-
tion or even war are but small and temporary calamities." I have had
no experience with the *gambiae* in my corner of the tropics: but I am
using him as a bogie to make a point. How tropical are "tropical diseases"? Germs and worms love to visit around. The northern-born
influenza has swept away thousands in the South Pacific; neglected,
its germ may bide its time for a plunge back into the North. Amoebic
dysentery is a "tropical disease" — yes, and a few years ago it appeared
in Chicago. The distinctly tropical filariasis (often manifested in elephantiasis) has been identified in several cases in an incomplete survey
of the Carolinas. Dr. Boyd, investigating in Florida, asserted that our
temperate-climate mosquito can carry a tropical strain of malaria. I
saw how inguinal (venereal) granuloma spread from island to island in
the Pacific; recently I was not surprised to hear of cases in the United
States. Leprosy, which curses the Polynesian, was brought to him by
the oriental; the Polynesian may pass it around — there is plenty of it
in New York today. The white man gave tuberculosis to the black
Solomon Islander, who awaits an opportunity to return the generous
gift.

A few millions of Rockefeller dollars, a few hundreds of Rockefeller
scientists, have gone forth into the seed-beds of disease, to work and
study, and cure, if possible. I say this for the benefit of smug stay-at-
homes who ask us, "Why do you waste your time and money on these
niggers, who live in another world from ours?" Yes, but do they? Our
little planet is moving faster every day. If sanitarians go on bungling
their way through bogs and forests and mountains, maybe it is to save
you from a peck of trouble some fine morning, Mr. Homebody. Or at
least we can wave the danger flag.

In the Kaiser's day, I was told, the German planters sent to Ninigo
to replenish their harems. Certainly the people were terribly thinned
out. I found an island where they were reduced to thirteen, one girl

and twelve men; and all eaten with venereal granuloma. The Hermit Islands had lost their hermit; a friendly planter had taken off the last inhabitant, a healthy young fellow who became a personal servant, too gentle to meet the invasion.

The Admiralty Group is north of the mainland, under the Equator. Manus, a fairly large island, is the center of a wealth of little dots. Some villages here were built over water in the Venetian style of Gaile. Paradoxically, the women were chaste, domestically speaking, yet in Manus I found the only public prostitution I ever saw in the South Pacific. It was an ancient custom here. Discouraged by the Germans, it had come back under the military administration. The incoming civil administration crushed it for a while; but when I was there the custom was flourishing again.

Manus had a certain Gaile-like charm, especially noticeable in the houses. Your canoe entered in the front through a covered opening, so low and narrow that once in you had to crawl on hands and knees. The object of this was simple and practical; if you were an enemy you could be conveniently clubbed as you poked your head into the living room. The houses set aside for young girls were quaint, too. With almost Spanish sternness the maidens were watched over by local duennas, and were carefully caged to the age of puberty. After sunset they were permitted to take the air, still under guard. At first I thought that this was the Manus method of preserving chastity; then I found that it was a mere matter of complexion. Indoor living bleached the skin, and in Manus a pale young bride was quoted at rather a high figure.

A weakness for canoes increased my fondness for this pretty Admiralty Group. I snatched every minute to drop my trouble in the serenity of bright lagoons; great Manus outriggers were wide enough to hold comfortable deckhouses below their coco sails.

Contrast this lagoon-bound holiday with my return trip on the cutter *Siar*, a capable craft with a capable captain; Skipper Bell was the best of the Australian type, raw-boned, handsome, brave. We had reached the New Hanover Group when a hurricane came down on us with a sudden ferocity that seemed to bring sea and sky together. That we stayed afloat those three mad days is one of God's mercies. Our engine was drowned out, we lost all sense of direction, all sense of everything except what was needed to hang on and pray — or swear. When a calm came, almost as violently sudden as the storm. we found that we had drifted over reefs and banks and heaven knows what — we had been blown clean around the large island of New Hanover and were lying in an inlet between it and New Ireland, which we had passed three days before. There wasn't a dry thing on the boat; our cookstove had been doused with the first wave that swept over us.

I have been caught in more tropical storms than I can remember, but this was the worst. With quaking Jerope and such of my gear as I had recovered I went ashore and flagged a schooner bound for Rabaul. Bell and his staunch little ship deserved a better fate than that which later overtook them. The battered *Siar* was towed to Sydney, where she fell a-prey to a favorite island trick: the calkers stopped the leaks with concrete, to save the expense of honest calking. On the return voyage she struck another storm and went down like a flatiron — with poor Bell at the wheel. He was a fine, clean young man who adored his pretty new bride. Well, he was one of the many.

My American medicine frequently competed with native witch-craft, which though it was never an open challenge, was something I felt all around me. Here and there I would catch whispers of this and that laborer who had sickened and died in the field; some *puri-puri* doctor had "pointed a bone" at him. Belief in magic, black and white, had penetrated into some odd places.

There's an elegant little chain of islands off New Britain which old-timers called "Queen Emma's Kingdom." Emma was a self-made queen, the half-caste Polynesian daughter of an American consul. She bought a domain for a few guineas and made a prince consort out of the German nobleman she married. Her descendants were educated in European schools, married Europeans of good family, and came home to enjoy their share in the inherited kingdom. I talked with one of these descendants, a lady who knew Wagnerian opera and Ibsen plays. When it came to medicine her faith was all bound up in the old family witch doctor. Earnestly she told me about some herbs which worked the medically impossible. She was offended at my incredulous smile when I transposed from what Lincoln said of General Grant: "I'd like to know the bottle he gets it from."

No wonder, then, that cross-eyed Jerope was anxious to carry a lantern after dark.

One evening we paused for rest on the tangled brow of a high mountain in New Britain. Incidentally, that had been a most interesting day; I had found rather puzzling evidence of modern sanitation. The tribe here was fierce, savage, cannibalistic — and surprisingly free of intestinal parasites. At some risk I searched behind the village houses and found latrines as scientifically constructed as if endorsed by the International Health Board! The pits were dug twenty-five to thirty feet into the soil, and over them was a support of timber. The deposit fell so far underground that hookworm larvae had no opportunity to invade the surface. The common housefly, bearer of dysentery and typhoid, dared not penetrate that dark well. Rude screens separated the men's latrine from the women's. My compliments to the wise old witch doctor who invented that.

Byron Beach had been to this mountain before me, with a punitive expedition, armed to chasten man-eating. They had climbed 7,000 feet and had forced themselves among tribes that had never before looked on a white face. Beach reported that every village he entered had been equipped with these deep cesspits. They were not mere archaic ornaments, either; the people were using them.

I tried to find out who had taught them, but all I got was "It is the fashion." I had to remember what the immortal Captain Cook said of the New Zealand Maoris when he first saw them — that this primitive people were obeying sanitary laws when the housewives of Paris and Madrid were emptying chamber pots into the streets. It set me thinking. Was not the islander, before the whites came to unsettle his traditions, reasonably self-preserving in his daily habits? My visits to lost Rennell Island, some years later, confirmed the theory.

But that evening, lolling on the mountain brow, I talked with Jerope about dream magic and heard the beginning of a story which, when it was finished, touched me deeply. I looked up and saw that his crossed eyes were not funny any more.

I had asked him if evil spirits could "walk along dreams" and curse you while you were awake. Oh, yes, master, they could do that. But devil-devils can do your dreams great favors, he said. He gazed crookedly at the sunset and told me, quietly as you tell of a proposed subway trip, how tonight in his dream he would visit his mother in the little local heaven. He explained the witch charm which would bring this about. From a great magician, who had been to the Evil One's home on the wild Sepik River, Jerope had bought the skin of a great bat, the enchanted flying fox that could carry you into the land of the dead. "Tonight," he said, "I shall burn the bat's hairs and paint the ashes on my eyes. Then I shall go."

Next morning I asked him if he had gone to his mother. Yes, he had gone; and he told me how, earnestly: —

"Master, me fastem head belong bat close under head belong me, then rub eye belong me along ashes and make fass (shut) eye belong me, and then me tink, and tink, and tink, then me like sleep . . ."

Jerope's head had begun to whirl then — "Me all a same pidgeon." The flying fox became a swift-winging god. "He catch me allesame pickaninny. Me hang on fass too much, then he go up and up and he go quick-feller too much. Him quick allesame nothing.

"Bym-by me come along place where Mamma belong me stop; this one place belong people who die finish." Heaven was filled with Jerope's dead kinsmen. "Master, this place he good feller too much. All man he got good feller garden, good feller house, plenty dog, plenty pig. Mamma belong me he come, he kiss me." (Throughout he referred to Mamma as "he," which is correct pidgin.) "Now me go inside along house belong him. Mamma he got good feller house too much, and yam he big one allesame tree. Suppose altogether people along Heaven he like kaikai fish, he tink, dass all, and good feller fish he must come along saucepan. Man dis place, Mamma dis place he no can work. Suppose Mamma like 'em something; he tink, dass all, and altogether something he tink, he must come. . . . Dis heaven belong Mamma him good feller too much!"

I made no attempt to deny anything, his whole tone was so convincing. He hadn't been dreaming; he had been there and seen a worn old woman having the fine rewards that come by wishing.

CHAPTER VIII

I SAY IT IN PIDGIN

At last the time came when my vanity was tickled to the verge of hysteria; I had actually learned pidgin English. To the native English is pidgin, and if you do not speak it with classic exactitude he simply fails to understand you. Once I had thought that I could pick it up in a week or two, it sounded so like laundry Chinese. Studying it, I learned how iron-bound its rules of idiom and grammar actually are. Twice, before I had mastered the lingo, I had tried it on native audiences and had been, as the actors say, laughed off the stage. But I was tired of having my lectures hashed by casual interpreters; I knew that I must talk straight to the people in the trade language which was common over the larger part of Melanesia. It took a year of hard grinding to learn it. Superior natives, kindly missionaries and District Officers were my tutors.

I must be fair to the reader and show him a few of the simpler twists in the language, and interpret a few peculiarities. Otherwise, the forthcoming sample of what became my standard. pidgin hookworm lecture might be difficult to understand.

The verb "go," for instance. The future is "by-and-by me go," and the past is "me go finish." "Finish" is trickily used to express finality. When a boy is "dead finish" he is dead. When you bury a body you "plant 'im finish." (When a houseboy says he is "killed" it merely means that his mistress has taken a stick to him.)

"Him" is masculine, feminine or neuter, generally pronounced "im," but sometimes "um." "Im" may be joined to a verb, as in "lookim," or separated as in "look im," ("look at him").

"Fellow" or "feller" is another tricky one. "Feller" precedes almost every noun — "One feller house," and so on. "Me go three feller Sunday" means "I was gone three weeks."

A man is usually a "boy," a woman a "mary." But often, linguistically, a man's a "man," for a' that. The personal pronoun is always masculine: "Dis feller mary he go." Repetition gives a verb an increasing value. When you say, "He go, go, go, *go*, GO," that's a long, tired journey. Then for effect you add, "long way too much." "Too much" means "very." Example: "Him good feller too much" — quite a compliment.

"Senake" is "snake" or "worm," and in hookworm lectures you refer to hatched larvae as "pickaninny senake." "Gelass" is "glass," and refers to a microscope, telescope or anything else with a lens in it.

The frequent use of "belong" (or "belonga") is confusing, and "along" is worse. Loosely speaking, "belong" is possessive. "Knifie belong me" is "my knife" and about the only way to translate "Dis fellow knifie belong dis fellow mary belong house belong Keop" would be "The knife of the native woman who lives in the Captain's house" — a pretty clumsy way of making your point. "Along" generally expresses movement or approach: "Ship stop along place." On some remote islands, God is expressed by "Big Feller Walk along Top."

"Blut" is blood (German), and is combined with "sabe" (Spanish) in "You altogether fellow, you sabe string belong blut?" when you want to know if everybody understands the nature of the blood stream. "Altogether fellow" expresses "everybody."

"Kaikai" is "eat." Your heart is a "pump," your lungs "wind," and when you show a hookworm picture in your lecture the "illustration" is a "ficshure."

Their use of "behind" doesn't express much until you are informed that it may mean either "afterward" or "pretty soon." "Behind me show you dis feller" equals "After I have shown you this."

To the uninitiated, pure pidgin does not make the slightest sense. German priests have learned it — and naïvely used its Chaucerian obscenities — without knowing a word of English.

In giving you just a flash of my first public success with the language, I assure you that I have anglicized it down to a point where the pidgin-wise native would have a hard time making head or tail out of it. But head or tail would be lost to the reader if I gave the unedited version.

When I returned to the native hospital at Rabaul and told Colonel Honman that I was prepared to lecture in pidgin, he gnashed pleasantly and said, "Try it on them." Honman was behind me in everything now.

A packed audience was gathered that night to hear my attempt at a new and dreadful language. I mopped cold sweat from my bald spot. Jerope had hung the hookworm chart to a post; it was like nailing your flag to the mast — fight or sink, no turning back. Assistants had passed around our two property bottles, pickled hookworms and ascarides. The natives always admired the bottled ascarides most; they were larger and looked more dangerous. The pause settled my stomach My natural brazenness returned and I bawled for order.

"You altogether boy, you listen good. Me come talk along one big feller sick . . ."

I felt the listening silence. They were taking in every word.

"Altogether boy he got um plenty senake he stop along inside bell' belong boy, he kaikai bell', blut he come, he kaikai blut. Blut belong boy him kaikai belong senake.

"Place belonga me him stop long way too much. You ketchum one feller steamer, you go one feller Sunday, now you come up along Sydney. Now you ketchum one feller steamer, big more (larger), now you go, go, go three feller Sunday, now you come up along place belong me. . . ."

In the native mind I had visualized the distance I had traveled from New York to New Guinea. And now for a word picture of John D. Rockefeller, Senior: —

"Master belonga me him make im altogether kerosene, him make im altogether benzine. Now he old feller. He got im plenty too much belong money. Money belong him allesame dirt. Now he old feller, close up him he die finish. He look about. Him he tink, 'Me like make im one feller something, he good feller belong altogether boy he buy im kerosene belonga me.' Now Gubment (Government) he talk along master belonga me. Master belonga me him he talk, 'You, you go killim altogether senake belong bell' belong boy belong island.' "

(I passed around the bottle of pickled hookworms.)

"Now, you boy, lookim good along dis feller bottle. Dis small feller senake he bad feller too much. . . . He got im tooth belongim. He kaikai bell' belong altogether boy. Blut he come he kaikai blut . . ."

(Turning chart to enlargement of male and female hookworms.)

"You look along dis feller ficshure. Two feller senake. You look;

one feller he man-senake, one feller him he mary-senake. Dis feller mary, him he bad feller too much. Him he stop along inside bell'; him he kaikai blut; him he makim too much small feller egg. Boy he makim something along ground. Egg he come out. Dis egg he small feller too much. . . ."

Open eyes and open mouths confronted me. And now to describe a microscope in pidgin English: —

"He no allesame glass belong Keop (Captain) belong steamer — he nother kind. Glass belong Keop, he make one feller something he stop too far, more big; glass belonga me, he make one feller something too small, more big. Behind (pretty soon) you sabe lookim along dis feller glass . . ."

(Attentive eyes followed the microscope, and I told of the dropping of the egg, the birth of the larva and its destiny . . .)

"Now boy he make im something along ground, egg he come out. Rain he come down. Egg, him he stop. Now sun he cookim. Now small feller pickaninny (larva), close up he broke-im dis feller egg. Him, he walkabout along ground, quick feller too much. You no sabe lookim — he small feller too much. Eye belonga you no good. Now boy he come. Him he putim foot belongim along ground. Now pickaninny senake him come inside foot belong boy, quick feller too much. Boy he scratchim, but he no can catchim dis feller senake. Now he go along string belong blut. Now he go, he go, he go, he go go go go, now he come up along pump belong blut; now he come to wind; him he come up along troat; boy he kaikai him. . . ."

(Pointing to internal organs outlined on the chart.)

"Now he come along bell' belong you, now he big feller little bit; now he gettim tooth belong im; now he sabe kaikai bell' belong boy; he sabe kaikai blut. Suppose you gottim plenty good kaikai — dis feller kaikai no belong you; him belong senake. You eatim, senake he catchim first time . . .

"Senake him kaikai blut belong boy, now boy he no strong; he weak feller too much; him he no like walkabout; him he no like work; him he like sleep all time. Bell' belong him no good, skin belong him no good, leg belong him allesame stick, him rotten altogether because senake he kaikai bell' belongim. . . . Blut belongim water; quick time boy he die finish; now he go along ground.

"Now master belonga me he gottim one good feller medicine. You drinkim one time, behind (afterward) you takim one salts medicine; senake he die finish, he come outside. Now, kaikai belong boy, he no belong senake. Now quick time skin belong boy good, now he sabe walkabout, him he strong feller too much. . . ."

When at last I had finished I heard the frightened sigh that fluttered through my audience. A heavy load seemed to fall from my shoulders. I had said it in pidgin, I had made them understand!

This was the hookworm lecture which, with some improvements, I gave hundreds of times throughout Melanesia, wherever pidgin was spoken; in New Guinea, in the Solomon Islands, in the New Hebrides. Yes, and I took it to New York in 1922, and demonstrated it to the Rockefeller Foundation. When I was asked to address a body of extremely dignified scientific men, Dr. George Vincent encouraged me to repeat my hookworm lecture, for its fame seemed to have arrived before I did. "Give it to them straight," Dr. Heiser suggested when I took the platform. If my performance added nothing to science, it was at least a comedy success. It panicked 'em, as the actors say. When I came to the part that described Mr. Rockefeller as "Master belonga me him make im altogether kerosene . . . Now he old feller. . . . Money belong him allesame dirt," solemn scientists who hadn't smiled for years had to be held up to keep them from falling into the aisles.

CHAPTER IX

"ME CUTTIM WIND, ME CUTTIM GUT!"

The conquest of pidgin cheered me up mightily; and I needed cheering. Toward the close of the New Guinea campaign (October, 1921) I began to realize more and more, through daily practice, that oil of chenopodium was inadequate for the mighty job cut out for it. To do it justice, it did remove worms, quantities of them. The standard method of administering chenopodium was to starve the patient the night before and give him a purge in preparation for next morning's treatment, which was 15 minims, given at two-hour intervals, at 6 A.M., 8 A.M. and 10 A.M. This was followed by another purge at noon, and he was not permitted to eat until the purge had taken effect.

In North Queensland I had found that even these heroic measures had not reduced the rate of infection, because the people were not taking the drug. Then I decreed that no treatment would count unless inspectors stood by and saw the medicine swallowed. In the early morning hours one could get track of a treatment unit by the sight and sound of front doors bursting open and children running wildly down the street. So I decided to modify the dose by one half, followed by a purge. Re-examination showed somewhat better results.

Old-timers who ran the standard chenopodium campaigns were unsung heroes, and the grinding disappointments drove many good men out of public health work. Examination, treatment, re-examination and retreatment — repeated half a dozen times in any given area — made up a method so extremely slow that by the time work in one region was completed the unremoved female worms had again laid eggs inside our patients; eggs which fell with the excreta to infect the soil once more and permit another horde of larvae to crawl back to the human intestine.

When Colonel Honman at last drafted my services and put me in charge of the native hospital at Rabaul, I was given an ideal chance to experiment and observe. Groups of native patients were chosen and locked behind barbed wire; each was given his dose and a gasoline can for his stools. The latter were washed every twenty-four hours for three days, and the worms counted. After an interval each man would be given a very large dose to remove the remaining worms, so that a percentage of effectiveness of the first dose could be estimated. We tried various combinations of chenopodium: thymol, betanaphthol, even betel-nut (which has a certain degree of vermifuge action). We studied the relation of purge and drug, to find out on what ratio they could be given. At best chenopodium was nauseous and produced many severe symptoms like tingling toes, temporary deafness, vomiting; and there was always the danger of profound poisoning inherent in the powerful drug, — untrained dispensers might grow careless and omit the purge, — and that might prove fatal.

To sum up chenopodium, it was about as popular as the Hammer and Sickle at a Republican rally.

Taking charge of the native hospital, although it was added to my duties in the field, was the job I liked best of all I had — new things turning up every day, and plenty to swing to.

I swung to Colonel Honman with ever increasing faith, for he was my mainstay when it came to an argument with Governor Wisdom. The Governor's troubles were piling up on him, and I never blamed him for his stubborn spells. If Wisdom's moods interfered with urgent medical work, it was the Colonel's delight to set his artificial teeth firmly and jump into the scrimmage. He wasn't afraid to go to the mat with the Governor, and at the finish he usually came out winner. I cannot forget his loyalty to me any more than I can forget a set of eccentricities peculiarly his own.

Here is one of my favorite pictures of the Colonel in action. I was in charge of quarantine while he was away, and always on the *qui vive* for any alarm that might come in. Early one morning a disturbing cable came: bubonic plague had broken out in Brisbane, and we must keep a strict lookout for ships from that port. The Colonel was away, making a trip around the group, so when the regular boat from Brisbane pulled in I went aboard and talked it over with a worried skipper. How was he to unload her? Certainly it would be inconvenient if he had to dump his cargo on lighters and move it piecemeal to the dock. I saw his point, and was wondering if I should take chances and let her come in before dark, when I saw the Medical Chief's ship poking around the heads. I went over to it and found the Colonel in his pajamas. I asked him what we were supposed to do about the caller from Brisbane. He hadn't put in his false teeth yet, and his mouth was sunken like a dead crater. "Keep her out in the thtream," he lisped. So I carried the orders back to the Australian skipper, and went home to breakfast. But I said to my wife, "Eloisa, I'll bet that ship will be alongside the wharf before noon." It was; and I knew why. Down in the Australian's hold there was a new Ford sedan for the Colonel, and he wasn't going to risk having it unloaded on a lighter, away out in the stream.

Colonel Honman had his faults, but I grew to love and admire them, with the firm belief that "even his failings leaned to virtue's side."

We had more and more cases of yaws sent in and were administering intravenous arsenicals. The natives called these injections "needla," and it became a popular craze with them — a craze which spread over the South Pacific. It was better than magic; a native would gladly have anything poked under his skin through a needle, no matter what. In Rabaul the native orderlies were always there on injection days; their tongues hung out with eagerness to get a shot of any salvarsan solution that happened to be left over. I have heard them arguing, "Why waste that bully stuff on a lot of ignorant bush fellows who are no good to anyone?" White men were queer in their preferences.

The primitive Melanesians have a holy horror of mutilation — except when they mutilate their noses for decorative purposes, or their fore-skins from custom. The man who has lost an arm or leg is damned eternally, for he must go to the local heaven armless or legless and be the laughingstock of the gods. This belief is a nuisance to the surgeon down there. A native with a gangrenous limb will fight against the knife, tooth and claw. Slow and painful death by blood poisoning is far preferable. Die with both your legs on and you can walk into Paradise, a true man. . . .

When a white man has anything artificial, like a glass eye, a realistic wooden leg, or a set of false teeth, the back-country fellow looks upon him as a miracle worker. One of the oldest stories along this line originated in Papua — how the plantation manager took out his glass eye and put it on a stump to glare at his lazy field hands while he was absent; it kept the crew busy until a native genius thought of just the right thing — he put a hat over the magic eye, and they all went back to sleep.

Toward the end of my term in New Guinea a situation arose in a native ward which compelled me to take advantage of this popular dread of mutilation. Influenza had flared up on the plantations. The plague that laid our soldiers low in American training camps had visited the South Pacific also, in 1918–1919, and played havoc with these non-resistant people. Since then, it had broken out sporadically; but health officers had learned more about it and were holding it down better than before.

I had returned from the field and found the native hospital filled with flu cases; many were dying in the collapse from pneumonia. The sudden deaths among seemingly mild cases puzzled me, until I probed into the cause. Our native attendants hated to lose sleep; as soon as they were snoring, the sick men, hot with fever, would sneak out of a side door and go down to lie in the sea and cool off under the stars. Then they would sneak back to bed and die of shock.

I put a stop to all that. Native attendants had told them how I slit open dead men's bellies. (I had performed thirty-three postmortems to determine the average native content of whipworms.) My ogreish fame had spread among a simple folk who would far rather lose a life than a leg. To them I was master of life and death — *and* the post-mortem table.

Therefore I profited by my foul reputation and marched through the ward brandishing a large amputation knife, and as I passed along rows of quaking cots I shouted: "Suppose you no stop along bed, you sons of bitches, suppose you no takim medicine good feller, now you die finish, me cuttim bell' belong altogether, me cuttim heart, me cuttim wind, me cuttim gut belong you feller. But suppose you good feller altogether, now you die finish, me no cuttim you."

Dark faces turned green. If they died in a state of disobedience their bodies would go to butchery on the postmortem table; what chance would their gutted souls have in a heaven where true men walk high, wide and handsome? . . . After my threat they turned into completely docile patients, and we had hardly a case of pneumonia when they were dying of it elsewhere, all over Rabaul.

Twenty men in this ward had been rounded up and jailed for cannibalism. I went to Colonel Honman and described an experiment I wished to make. We all knew of Dr. Heiser's brilliant success in the treatment of leprosy. Chaulmoogra oil was no new thing; lepers had been given it *by mouth* for a couple of thousand years. When Heiser experimented with it in the Philippines he didn't change the remedy — *he changed the method*. He tried chaulmoogra oil in intramuscular injections, with tremendously improved results.

I didn't expect to obtain any such startling effects. What I wanted to know mainly was whether chenopodium acted directly on hookworms in the bowel, or whether it was absorbed into the blood stream first and was then ingested by bloodsucking.

The twenty cannibals were on the road to recovery from influenza, and for experimentation Colonel Honman selected six who were heavily infected with hookworm. They had already been condemned to hang as an example to their outlaw village, so it didn't matter whether the poor devils died in bed or at a rope's end. My plan was to try intramuscular and intravenous injections of chenopodium.

The result proved harmless to the patients and surprising to the rest of us. In our tests on three of the patients chenopodium was mixed with camphorated oil and resorcin, following Heiser's formula for preparing chaulmoogra oil. These three men were given intramuscular injections in this form, followed by purgatives, and their stools were examined for a period of six days. From Case Number 1 we got only four hookworms in five days; from Case Number 2 two hookworms and one Ascaris. But Case Number 3 offered the main interest. To him we gave an intravenous injection of chenopodium undiluted. After six days we had recovered twenty-two whipworms and only three hookworms, although this patient, like the other two, was heavily infected with hookworm. In Case 3, then, injections of unmixed chenopodium had a far greater effect on whipworms than on hookworms.

In the three who were given intravenous injections results were:

Case 1: — Hookworms: None. Trichuris: 11.
Case 2: — Hookworms: None. Trichuris: 19. Ascaris: 2.
Case 3: — Hookworms: None. Trichuris: 30. Ascaris: 2.

Our experiences with all six cases showed that injections of chenopodium have little effect intramuscularly on hookworm, and no effect on that parasite when given intravenously. But in both ways it had a marked effect on trichuris.

Why was this? Obviously the answer must be in the habits of the two parasites. The hookworm is a superficial feeder, sucking blood from the surface of the gut. The whipworm has a very long head which he buries half an inch into the intestinal wall; possibly he fed only on lymph, which may have taken up a heavier charge of the chenopodium. Ordinarily the whipworm is very resistant to chenopodium, as to all vermifuges. Yet here he showed a high mortality to the drug when it was administered through a new route. Whereas the hookworm, which is affected by chenopodium given in the usual way, showed a high resistance to it in the new method.

I had no time to continue experiments, which were interesting because they were the first attempt to give anthelmintics by intramuscular or intravenous injections, a new route for treating intestinal parasites. Superficially at least, I had settled an argument which had arisen among investigators with more claims to learning than my own. I had established that the action of chenopodium is by direct contact with the hookworm in the gut, not by absorption in the blood stream and subsequent absorption by the parasite. The experimental cases showed that fact clearly, and still more clearly revealed that chenopodium in intramuscular and intravenous injections has a decided effect on whipworm. For the latter there is no other satisfactory treatment. I made these tests without the sanction of the Rockefeller Foundation, whose letterhead should bear the motto, "We Do Not Experiment with Human Beings." When 61 Broadway learned of what I had been doing there might have been trouble for me, but Dr. Maurice C. Hall, chief of the Bureau of Animal Industry at Washington, became my advocate. In a later chapter I shall have much more to say about this Dr. Hall: we are indebted to him for one of the world's great medical discoveries.

And by the way, my experimental cannibals never went to the gallows. After leaving New Guinea I learned that another flu epidemic had struck the hospital. I was rather glad that the six of them died in bed and could go to the Happy Land with all their vertebrae in good order.

I hated to leave the native hospital, which had taught me so many valuable things with which to carry on. I had been working in team with the *lik-lik* doctors and was more than pleased with the technical progress they were making.

Nobody could have blamed Governor Wisdom if he had gone stark staring mad under the pressure of territorial politics. He kept his reason, did his work well, and was retired with a title. The white population was more of a problem than the black; this new government was still in the grab-bag period, every hand feeling out for a prize — anything from an island to a fruit cake.

At one of the Governor's receptions, the fine house on the hill was all in party trim. At an end of the great hall there was a long table, heavy with cakes, sandwiches and bon-bons. After a pleasant hour, Eloisa and I were about to say good-by, but were waiting for our car to drive up in the rain. A minor official's wife sidled over to the big table and said to Eloisa, "Look at those beautiful cakes. I'm going to give a party myself tomorrow." Fitting action to words, she slipped an eighteen-inch fruitcake under her raincoat. We were at the door, telling General and Mrs. Wisdom what a nice party it had been, when the lady with the raincoat joined us. "Oh, Governor, such a lovely time . . ." Her hand went out and the fruitcake slipped. *Splunk!* it messed all over the polished floor at the Governor's feet. Still holding his hand, she trilled, "I wonder where *that* came from!" And fluttered away to her car.

Our little house at Rabaul was a meeting and eating place for my inspectors, drifting in from the field. For a week or two before we left, the lot of them were at my table. In the kitchen their boys gathered around Jerope, matching their tall stories against his. We were a busy, uproarious family, getting ready to push on or say good-by. We had added up our mileage for that New Guinea campaign: 9,958 for all of us, traveling on everything that would walk, pull or float. My score was 3,523, not counting steamer trips to and from Australia — and Beach came next with 1,893.

When young Byron Beach joined our farewell house party he looked like a schoolboy fresh from tennis and a shower. He didn't show a scratch, although by all the laws of chance he should have been dead. For our young adventurer had gone alone 165 miles up the Sepik River, a region so wild and dangerous that only armed expeditions dared it in 1921, and they came back with shuddering horror stories. Beach had tackled it in a frail canoe, paddled by jittering natives — he wasn't literally alone, but he was the solitary white man.

Beach had no business risking his fool neck without a white companion. If he had waited for me I would have joined him.

Almost his first act when he came to our house was to hand Eloisa £400 for safekeeping overnight. He grinned nonchalantly next morning when he took the money back, and doubled it in a tortoise-shell investment. The boy had heroic qualities, but he never forgot that he was a trader.

I wish I had the space to show you the diary he kept on that fantastic trip. I had sent him up to inspect Father Kirschbaum's mission, not far from the wide brown mouth of that mysterious river whose upper waters lie in the howling darkness of the unexplored. With the good Father praying for his soul Beach set out on July 17, carrying plenty of tins for hookworm specimens and blandly intending to offer his wares to a jungle full of naked killers. The lad had the cheek of the devil, and that probably saw him through.

Some of the villages were unexpectedly friendly. In one of them the men were fiercely armed and hideously painted, awaiting another attack from an enemy who had burned half their houses and carried away thirty-seven villagers just before lunchtime. Beach distributed tins among these people, and told them, through a scared interpreter, how to use them.

When the Sepik folk were good to Beach they let him sleep in a Tambarand House, which is a tribal chamber of horrors, decorated with the skulls of relatives and valorous foemen. Artists decorated the family skulls to a semblance of life, and the good tribesmen took them to bed with them.

The natives were disappointed when they found that Beach's specimen tins did not contain red paint for sale. Some of them punched holes through the tins and hung them around their necks. He had to scold them for this.

There were days of paddling into queerer and queerer regions. Time and again Beach saw headless corpses floating down stream. Probably they were the bodies of relatives; enemy meat would have been otherwise disposed of. In another village, bristling with spears, Beach made so bold as to prick a boy's finger for a blood test. At sight of blood the warriors began to howl like wolves, but Beach was there with his everready salesmanship. He smiled winsomely as he presented the tribe with a collection of mirrors and fishhooks. As he wrote in his diary, "I'll say I was thankful. Things were almost jolly when I left."

At Timbunke, twenty-five miles farther up, it wasn't so jolly. On the shore was a reception committee of 200 painted devils, brandishing spears and yelling at the top of their lungs. "I tried not to be in a hurry getting back in the canoe," he wrote, "but the boys paddled for their lives, with all that bellowing mob scampering along the shore. Perhaps they were just wishing me a safe journey. No white man has ever slept there."

All along it was playing poker with death. A fire on the shore might mean that friendly people were guiding your canoe to a safe landing. Or it might mean that the oven was heating up for a neighborhood roasting. Beach visited dozens of these places, and in most instances carried away the specimen tins, properly filled. Some of the villagers were timid, in deadly fear of their neighbors; others were so dangerous that Beach never let them get behind his back. In one of the tamest villages he was knocked down — by an earthquake. At the tip end of his journey 165 miles up the Sepik, he scored his triumph. He cajoled a warrior into submitting to the whole treatment, and recovered 105 worms.

On his swing back, he revisited some of the spots which had seemed especially hostile. At Moim, for instance, he had used his diplomacy, plus a liberal gift of gimcracks, and distributed 95 tins. When he returned a few days later he got them all back in good order. On August 11, after having his canoe swamped in a gale, he reached the mouth of the Sepik and paid off his canoe boys. They charged him thirty shillings apiece, and Beach rounded off his diary by saying that it was no trouble at all to handle the Sepik natives, if you used a little common sense.

Well, the young cub got back to me, smiling and cheerful. It was a mad trip, but I rather envied him the adventure. I think its outstanding feature was Beach's nonchalance in returning to the savage villages and collecting the tins he had left behind.

Now about that roll of £400 which he left in Eloisa's keeping, just overnight. I learned about that later. In approximately three weeks of voyaging to hell and back, he had found time to shoot down a collection of birds of paradise which he sold to a handy trader somewhere on the way home. I sometimes wonder if poaching didn't motivate that fearless voyage.

Byron Beach left me as picturesquely as he had come into my life.

One fine afternoon, off the Solomon Islands, he sailed into the sunset in a trim little schooner that he had borrowed for the joy ride. He had also borrowed a trim little native girl. Neither Byron, boat nor beauty ever came back to that port, or any other that I know of. But I am inclined to believe that wherever he landed he landed on his feet.

CHAPTER X

KING SOLOMON'S GOLD

New Guinea was my jumping off place for the Solomon Islands, and "jumping off" well describes my first trip around that great island chain. I had only a few weeks to work in, and to draw conclusions which were to lead up to years of campaigning along 700 miles of that wild archipelago. If you will recall George Fulton, the man in evening dress whom I met in a smelly trader's store, you will remember his half-promise to send me down to lost Rennell Island on the Lever Brothers' yacht. Well, he had kept his promise — with reservations — and I was at last on the Levers' *Koonakarra*, heading southeast. I had planned to go on the Government's *Bellama*, but she was wrecked in a hurricane. To be transferred to George Fulton's boat seemed like a stroke of luck. Now I could see Rennell Island. . . .

It was nine years before I saw Rennell, for the very good reason that George Fulton didn't want me to see it. He had changed his mind since I talked with him. Rennell might turn out to be a phosphate island, one of those volcanic freaks which quantities of bird guano and submersion in sea water have loaded with valuable crystalline fertilizer. Fulton didn't want Rockefeller people snooping around his potential bonanza. A few years later he found that Rennell's wealth was just another myth of King Solomon's gold.

Alvaro Mendaña, who found these islands in 1568, returned to Spain and told King Philip that he had discovered the place where King Solomon got his gold. Philip rewarded the naughty liar by sending him on a second expedition; but when he returned to the isles of specious wealth he found that they had disappeared. Just another case of bad Renaissance navigation, but Mendaña died hunting for the vanished Solomons. They were lost for 200 years. Monsieur de Bougainville found them again in 1768.

As far as Rennell Island was concerned, for a long while I felt that I had been cheated of my gold. It was not idle curiosity which drew me toward that mysterious spot. If the people had been, as George Fulton said, "practically untouched for ages," I might find there a clue to the origin of the Polynesian race. Many of the ancient invasions have been traced through the evidence of the hookworm. The public health physician, you see, must be a bit of an anthropologist, a bit of a politician and a bit of a historian. . . .

But I had to wait until 1930 to see Rennell Island.

The *Koonakarra* of 1921 was so busy trading, recruiting and supervising plantations that I had to pick up what information I could get between stops. I had an opportunity to draw one large conclusion: that natives from the big islands to the north, near the infesting trade routes, were much the more heavily diseased. Disease diminished steadily as we moved down toward the less frequented parts. My superficial look at a population which, for lack of an accurate census, was estimated at 100,000, verified my theory: *Epidemics are the fruits of island hospitality*.

In those days little could be done to improve conditions. That group of a half-dozen enormous islands, and the many little outlying ones, was served by one lone Medical Officer, and some missionary doctors who strove with a bravery against conditions that should have broken their valiant spirits.

Among the unsung heroes — but no missionary — was my friend J. C. Barley, Oxford M.A., who had voluntarily given his life to a God-forsaken post at Kirakira. In his jungle house he was like something out of Kipling, dressing for the evening, having his spot of gin and bitters before dinner, his sound cigar afterward. He might have gone anywhere in the colonial service, for as a young Oxonian he had outranked hundreds in competitive examinations. But he was too clean a sportsman to play politics. His passion for ethnology and his affectionate responsibility for the natives kept him where he was. He had become the people's advocate, and knew more about the Solomons than any official report could ever tell. His trips for inspection and research were his only relief from solitude.

I only speak of Barley because he was so useful to my future work and because of pleasant memories of his charming mind; in fact I should not write at all of this brief survey, except that I wish to point out a few spots where in later years I returned and marked the changes wrought by contact with the outer world.

Bill Tully and I worked mostly at night, lecturing by lantern light. The ship would be off in the early morning. At Star Harbour on San Cristoval, the largest island on the unfrequented southeast, the naked people carried candlenut torches as they wound down the mountain trail. It was like something out of "A Midsummer-Night's Dream," that twisting stream of light. Few traders and no missionaries had come to them, and they showed a low rate of infection. A friendly, backward Negroid people, they were endangered by their own hospitality. Charley One Arm, the policeman, our fierce black guide, couldn't understand us when we refused the temporary gift of two island daughters. I went away dreading what might happen when more trading ships came in.

Santa Ana lay so near that one of their canoes, bastard ebony with mother-of-pearl insets, could take you there in an hour or two. Yet the Santa Ana folk were light-skinned and their features almost Caucasian. They wore bones in their noses and shark's teeth around their necks. There was more trading, hence more hookworm. I gave treatments to Trader Kuper's two little half-caste sons. It was a good investment, and later I shall tell you why.

Graciosa Bay was so wild that Mr. Mathews, Lever Brothers' representative who had lived there fifteen years with an armed guard, warned us not to come ashore. With knives and fishhooks we lured a few of the untamed to come aboard the launch and be examined. In fifteen years the population had dropped from 3,000 to 500. Somehow, in spite of their savagery, they had allowed vicious malaria and tuberculosis to get in.

Near-by Reef Island showed a different, lighter breed. Somewhat missionized, largely pagan, it had a murderous reputation. It was in its harbor, Mohawk Bay, that an incident occurred which I remembered for twelve years. After a lantern-light lecture I was resting in the whaleboat. In the dim moonlight a naked man came floundering toward me. I reached for a hatchet, and a mild voice told me that it was only Sam, the Christian teacher. I had made a mistake, Sam told me, and gone to a heathen village. His was the Christian village I should have given my magic tins to. And wouldn't I come? It was too late for that, so I let him stand waist-high in the water while I taught him the outline of my pidgin English lecture. I gave him tins and told him to bring them back to me in the morning. He brought them to me at dawn, and I admired

his Christian fortitude. Poor devil — like the others, he thought our tins
were magic boxes that would cure the people. I waited twelve years
to hear the sequel to that story. . . .

At Mohawk Bay I found that a young native was selling the services
of his fiancée to our sailors. Brides were expensive there, and he had
formed a syndicate to buy her, then rent her out until she had earned
the price. It was "the fashion." Not as a moralist, but as a doctor I
asked the question: Who would educate people like these, upon fast-
opening trade routes? Who would teach them self-protection? The
missionaries? Perhaps. But the doctor must follow, or there would be
nobody left to educate.

"Recruiting," that legalized form of contract labor, might act as an
educator. The High Commission Government was already requiring
that plantation hands should be well-cared-for medically and sufficiently fed.

In a lonely bay I saw recruiters at work. One man with a rifle lay
flat in the bow of a cutter, covering every movement of another man
who approached the shore in a whaleboat. The whaleboat backed
water all the way, and the man sent to parley stood up, carefully facing the naked savages who waited on the beach. All during the long
powwow the hidden rifle was carefully aimed. These labor conferences were no job for a coward. So many lone recruiters had been
killed on duty that the Government had made it a law that they must
hunt in pairs.

Considering the vast work which we must soon undertake in the
Solomon Islands, I was encouraged when I found that the intelligent
native looked upon indentured labor service as a blessing, just as it
had been in Papua. An island boy said to me, "I wish the *Hawk* would
come soon." The *Hawk* was a recruiting ship. I asked him why he
wanted it to come soon, and he said, "There are so many sore-legs
in the village." This boy knew what was good for his people, and
I hoped that there would be many more like him.

I never think of Sikiana without a little sadness. Three small
atolls all but link. The Sikiana Group was the last land to be discovered in 1791 and since then very few vessels had touched there.
The inhabitants were pure Polynesian people; and because our crew
was composed of Sikiana men our landing was a joyous homecom-

ing. Every man-jack in the village was lightly lit on homemade toddy; the Ellice Islanders, their blood-cousins, had taught them how to cut the central spathe of the coconut, catch the drip, and trust in fermentation. Unfermented, it makes a fine baby food. In toddy form, it is intoxicating.

There was some heathen religious festival going on, hence the bibulous hilarity. The women, who never drank, couldn't speak pidgin. Much gesturing, and the aid of our Sikiana sailors, who were sharing the toddy, sent swimmers and canoemen to the neighboring atolls to spread the news. And the people danced. Not lewdly, but with the natural grace of unspoiled bodies. They were completely pagan. No missionary had ever settled here. Traders hadn't debauched them; the soil was too poor to produce anything worth trading for.

The girls were lovely with their long, fine, glossy hair; they hadn't learned to bob it as they were doing on the missionized islands. They wore modest *lavalavas* from waist to ankles, and a kerchief which they knotted around the neck and drew under one arm. Some of the men wore their hair long, too, in ancient Polynesian fashion. I made friends with a splendid young fellow named Lautaua, who talked fair pidgin and told me how "in the time of his grandfather" (that might mean a thousand years ago; they had a habit of reckoning time by grandfathers) the Tongafiti had come to Sikiana and killed everybody except the women, and how succeeding migrations from Ongtong Java and the Ellices had drifted there in lost canoes.

I only mention their drinking because it was something of a freak in that corner of the Pacific. The Sikiana folk only made toddy on festival occasions, and never took it beyond the point of exhilaration. Later on, taking the advice of Mr. Barley, who was always their generous friend, they stopped making and drinking toddy. In Sikiana they were gay enough without false stimulation — a friendly, virtuous, lovable people; perhaps their custom of keeping women away from liquor helped maintain their racial self-respect. By and large, I have found the tribes on comparatively sterile islands superior in health and character to their neighbors who had little to do but lie in the shade and catch bananas. It's the same the wide world over; those of Adam's sons who work for a living are better fitted to cope with the cruelties of life.

Young children held our hands and drew our arms around them.

The moon swung high over the lagoon and our returned sailors, quite sober now, daintily walked with their girls, up and down the beach. As we sat on the sand, waiting for the lecture audience to come on, young girls put garlands around our necks, chains which would bind our memories to Sikiana; these were ropes of hair, a strand from the head of every girl.

I had given lectures under odd conditions, but never before like this. White moonlight, pretty, laughing faces, simple people who took it all as the greatest joke in the world, but were so kind-hearted that they followed our instructions faithfully, as one might indulge a feeble-minded person of whom one is fond. Everybody smiled, even the dignified patriarch whom we called Old Number One; he was an unsalaried official representative of the Government. Between Old Number One and Lautaua, everything was arranged for us. Next day when we departed all was in order.

A simple people, allowed to grow up in their own way. Were they the uncivilized ones, or were we? They were not entirely free from tuberculosis; but they seemed to have set up an immunity. Here was a Government without the need of officialdom; no discord, no poverty, no distress, no taxes, no clothing to speak of; and no vices more obnoxious than a little toddy-drinking on national holidays.

I left happy Sikiana with a certain fear for its future. I saw it again in 1933. . . .

I returned by way of Sydney to pick up my family. In a week or so I would be pointing toward Suva, which was the cultural center of the South Pacific — if you disregard the scientifically advanced universities in Australia and New Zealand. Suva was to be headquarters for the rest of my professional career.

Thus far I had worked toward proving my favorite point: Depopulation follows the visitor. I believed what I still believe — that the item which looms over everything else in the question of failing native races *is the introduction of diseases to which they have no immunity*. I had seen its effects so often, right under my eyes.

Moving toward Sydney, I took stock of my South Sea experience, which had covered less than four years. I was beginning to see that one bad old theory was losing ground — the belief that the native, especially the Melanesian, is an economic unit to be exploited till he dies. Governments once blind and cruel were beginning to see light. The British High Commission, controlling five island groups, was struggling toward better things. So was progressive New Zealand with her mandates and possessions over wide stretches of Polynesia.

I considered the stumbling blocks in the way of curing sick Oceania. The Rockefeller Foundation, a vast scientific machine tuned up to deal out mercy in a practical, businesslike way, must have a cooperation which the Pacific administrations of that day were not offering. There must be teamwork, or nothing could be accomplished. Medical authority must come from a central brain. As things stood, the health physicians were political appointees, either lazy and incompetent time-servers or good men baffled by overwork and the whims of local government. When one good health officer retired a successor would come in to undo whatever he had begun. It was medical chaos, and I felt that the Foundation's liberal share in cleaning up the Pacific must be backed up by some unified control. Else the work would be as futile as sweeping fog off a back porch. Suva, capital of Fiji, was headquarters for the British High Commission, and the Governor of Fiji was its head. Suva would be the ideal center for such medical authority.

I considered the problem of leprosy. All along the way I had encountered this imported disease, but there was no census to tell whether or not it was increasing. The cure and prevention of leprosy is methodical treatment with the one known remedy, and segregation of the infected. In all the South Pacific except Fiji there was nothing like a modern leper colony. The island governments should combine to support one.

The shortage of doctors had been very discouraging. Few competent white men cared to endure tropical hardships for starvation pay. From sheer boredom and despair many of them became quacks and drunkards — even if they hadn't started out that way. The answer to that was educated native medical men. . . . I have talked about that a great deal, because that idea never left me. And now I was going to Fiji, where there had already been a crude attempt to teach medicine to Fijians.

As our ship neared Suva, a larger worry was in the back of my mind. Through years of study, from North Queensland to Papua, from Papua to New Guinea, from New Guinea to the Solomon Islands, I had found that oil of chenopodium was not working well enough or fast enough to relieve the million patients who reached out for a cure. In Rabaul's hospital I had given injections of it, hoping to make the drug more effective through a new channel. The experiment had removed whipworms, but almost no hookworms.

I had to look these facts in the face. Chenopodium, on which we had relied as a cure for one of the world's most prevalent blights, was not coming up to our expectations. There seemed no answer to that, until help came from an unexpected quarter.

CHAPTER XI

"SO YOU'VE COME TO FIJI!"

I have such a collection of hurricanes that in self-searching moments I call myself "The Storm King's Target." The wind that blew us around an island, that time we were trying to make Rabaul, is an example. Another was one hot day in Fiji, years later, when our half-caste skipper demonstrated his share of brains: He saw the storm coming and poked our cockleshell into a sheltering cove. For three days we "holed up" with District Officer Bob and his wife Elaine, and watched a Fiji village take wings; the big palm-thatched meeting-house looked like a flying haystack. On the way home I searched for landmarks. Two rivers on Viti Levu had plunged together; an East Indian village had been swept away, everybody drowned. A Fijian town had vanished under a sliding mountain.

Once in North Queensland I saw a galvanized iron roof wrap itself around a telephone pole as you wrap paper around a pencil. I've been lucky; never has a ship gone down under me — quite. Several ships, though, have been wrecked before I had time to get aboard.

Two refuges for the soul in a hurricane are the Power of Prayer and the Power of Swear. Take your choice. Once the big wind roared over a mission station, and the missioner, who didn't care to go himself, sent loyal converts down to bring in his launch, and they saved the boat from the gale's fury. Neighbors made scandal of the wanton risk, but the missionary smiled, "Oh, no. It was no risk. I saw the Spirit hovering over them when they went down to the water."

Another hurricane met our ship coming toward Fiji from Sydney, and I fell back on the Power of Swear. With every comber that plowed through the dining saloon of the old 1,100-ton *Suva* I dug up long-forgotten oaths. My wife and child got through; Eloisa comes of a pithy stock, otherwise she could never have followed me in my curious career. This trip was a soul-shaker. The Fijians have a *meke* song in which they address the powers of the hurricane, "blown from the black mouths of the Ladies of the West." For three horrible days the Ladies of the West gave it to us, straight. The captain tied our propeller-shaft in a bowknot, heading straight into the volley, trying to drag us out of an invisible grip.

I had my hands full, seeing that my eight-year-old Harriette wasn't drowned in our stateroom. An Australian lady furnished a touch "of romance." A hard one would shiver our timbers, she would cling to me, her children would cling to her. "Oh, Doctor, I'm so glad" — she would shriek above the tempest — "that you're here on the ship. I feel so much safer." I imagined myself swimming with Eloisa and Harriette in one hand and the Australian lady (with family) in the other.

When we limped into Suva harbor the sea had turned to glass. Hurricanes have an annoying way of doing things like that.

There on our starboard hand lay the jumbled little waterfront; and on our portside a craggy peak they call The Devil's Thumb; perpetual landslides had marked its face with a perfect **Y**, as though Yale sophomores had been working overnight.

Suva, capital of Fiji, has advanced a great deal in the last eighteen years. Nowadays occasional passenger liners dock there and allow tourists to straighten out their sea legs. The men can buy their favorite brand at Piccadilly tobacconists or London bars. The debutantes can play tennis, while their mothers visit little jewel shops and squander a few shillings on a small handful of silver-gilt pearls that are lovely and have no respectable commercial rating, or take in the museum and shudder at the collection of savage iron-wood clubs which ex-cannibals traded for hymnals, — or buy a four-shilling guidebook at the Carnegie Library, — or inspect the Government Building, that cost about $1,500,000 and looks a size too large for Pittsburgh; that structure was built after the gold rush of '32 when the colony went madder than Californians and started things on a grand scale — for a while. Suva today is like any small colonial capital. Whiskered Sikh policemen in staring red tunics guide the traffic; along the orderly streets walk orderly Fijians, short white *sulus* and bare legs under English coats, their immense, smoothly cut headdresses of kinky hair giving them the appearance of English guardsmen in regimental bearskin busbies. Dignified, broad-shouldered, small-waisted, they seem to be heading for some savage war-dance. Actually they are going to church, or to the native motion picture palace.

Suva in 1922 had one dirt road that ran to Nausori, fifteen miles away. The taxi fare was about $7.50. Your director, to save Rockefeller funds, usually went there on the little *Andi Roronga*, which took from 9 A.M. to 1 P.M. with a stop along the mangrove-tangled Rewa. She started back at two. When you went by taxi you had to cross the river on a funny pontoon with a submerged cable.

I was no longer under the loose-handed control of Australia. Now it was the British High Commission that owned Fiji's 250-odd islands, had a grip on the Solomons, a tiny toehold on the independent Kingdom of Tonga, controlled the Gilbert and Ellice Group and ran some curiously distant isles, like Rotumah and Pitcairn and Christmas Island. The Governor of Fiji was (and is) the temporal head of the High Commission. However, the real government comes from London. Colonials as a rule don't understand Englishmen. Americans, after what happened about 1776, can sympathize. The Yankee slides comfortably into the ways of the Canadian, the Australian, the New Zealander or South African. The born Englishman with his hauteur and peculiarity is another fish to fry. He has ruled his far-flung dominions uncannily well, but his colonials tender him more respect than love.

Yet down there I have worked with Englishmen for whom I felt the deepest loyalty and friendship. Chris Kendrick is one of them. Barley is another, and there are many more. Pretty soon I am going to tell you of another, who was my associate for eight years in Fiji.

Colonials in Suva used to grumble, "Back in London they don't know we're alive." But the politicians knew. Fiji became a dumping place for younger sons and Ministry favorites. Young chaps, green as grass and fresh as paint, were called "cadets," and there was always a new cadet to fill the desk left vacant by retirement or promotion. Against the cadet system the experienced colonial, who knew the land and the people, hadn't the ghost of a show.

Where the English are respected and not liked, the Americans are liked but not respected. Colonials regard us as too evangelical, too insistent on modern shower baths in every room and on having everybody's trousers creased in the same way. They speak of us as rotten colonizers; and these arguments are in the face of our record in Cuba, for instance, where we cleaned up yellow fever and gave the island real sanitation. . . . I remember what an educated Cuban once said to me, "Of course we don't like you, Doctor. You found us dirty and contented; now we are clean and unhappy."

Naturally the British Empire must exact tribute from her dominions or she could not survive. All over Britain's Pacific empire "Buy English" was behind the sale of all the machinery, all the material used in public improvements. Yet it was astonishing how popular American products remained, in spite of the high preferential tariff against them. American cars, burdened with a 45 per cent duty, were eagerly sought in New Zealand, Australia, Fiji. Loyal colonials had their tongues hanging out in their desire to buy British automobiles, yet pig-headed English manufacturers were sending low-powered, poorly sprung cars, built for smooth, hill-less roads. Our own Henry Ford would have adapted his article to geographical requirements. Not so the British maker with his cry, "Buy English!"

Sunkist oranges were everywhere, an example of American trade-genius under difficulties. New Zealand, with her own tropical possessions and access to Australia's and Jamaica's supplies, displayed Sunkist oranges in every remote village. It's still an unfathomable mystery to me, how these California go-getters can drag oranges eight or nine thousand miles, and profit under adverse conditions. Maybe it is because their fruit is obtainable all year round, or because its uniform size makes it attractive.

As my work went on in Fiji I had to put up a fight for one important drug, the arsenical derivative neosalvarsan, often conveniently called "salvarsan," although it is Ehrlich's improvement on his own salvarsan discovery. It is indispensable in the treatment of yaws. On one of my brief trips to the United States I argued the high cost of neosalvarsan with wholesale drug manufacturers who came to a meeting of the American Medical Association. Could the price be cut down if we ordered it in large quantities? I promised that if they would give us a good price we could use $7500 worth a year. When our purchasing agent struck a bargain I don't think the wholesalers regretted it. We used the order soon after the first shipment, and cabled for more. When we ceased to buy in driblet lots, the cost of neosalvarsan was cut four times, and each price was lower than that set by the Crown Agent in London — he being the gentleman whom the Mother Country appoints to collect a large part of the tax on colonies and dominions. Through the deal our purchasing agent made with American wholesalers natives of the South Pacific were saved more than the Foundation's expenditure on building programs, health campaigns and my salary.

This sudden attack on the high price of drugs caused a mild sensation in London, which had governed the purchase of arsenicals up to that time. The Crown Agent responsible for disbursements compared our economical prices with those the colony had been paying. The reaction was true to form. Representatives of the Home Government wanted to know, unofficially, if we were in cahoots with some big Yankee chemical firm. At first an attempt was made to discredit my drug; then the price of salvarsan came tobogganing all through the British Empire.

My reception in official Suva, though polite, was never emotional. There had been a short Rockefeller campaign there in 1917–1918, which had left the Administration markedly unenthusiastic. The Governor, Sir Cecil Hunter Rodwell, was a fine fellow, and I owe much to him and to Sir Maynard Hedstrom, a wealthy merchant who could see much further ahead of his nose than most I met; Hedstrom was with me in all my endeavors.

The Suva Hospital was not stately — a creaky old shack tinkered up somehow. The new War Memorial was finished a few months later when the Medical Department took it over; in spite of its newness it was a makeshift, and so small that it was overcrowded until the building program of 1934. The native nurses, for example, were jammed into an ancient wooden structure, where they had to carry their own firewood and do their own cooking in most primitive style; and these were the girls we must depend upon to raise Fijian standards of living.

There were between twenty-two and twenty-four medical officers whose average brains and conscientiousness were of a high order. I called them "the Old Guard" and was sorry that so many of them were retired soon afterwards; younger ones who replaced many of them had neither the social, educational nor ethical ideals of their predecessors. And it seemed to me that cadets who came out for the civil administration were also a step-down in quality.

There were forty Native Medical Practitioners — natives given a three-year course in simple medicine and surgery. They had no classroom, no charts, only one small book of simple medicine and hygiene, and that was written in Fijian. Teaching paraphernalia was practically nil. These boys attended out-patients, acted as male nurses, attended the doctors on their rounds. Their lectures were given at the hospital by the Chief Medical Officer and the Resident Medical Officer. When these officers spoke Fijian and were interested, the results were good; when they were not interested the formal education was very sketchy.

I studied this system, developed for over thirty years, and wondered if it wasn't an answer to my prayer for something constructive. Some of these boys, though taught so little surgical practice, developed great ability; it was almost as though their cannibal ancestry had given them a particular flair for human anatomy. One Native Medical Practitioner (N.M.P.) was Sowani, who was lent to the Gilbert Island Colony and made a famous reputation as a surgeon; I shall tell of him in the proper place.

There was a system of native obstetrical nursing as well as a training school for European nurses. The native nurses had lectures from a Fijian with the same educational background as their own. One lecture a week for six months each of two years, then the girls were sent with N.M.P.'s to assist Fijian mothers in confinement. Bed-pan carrying for European probationers, mopping, and doorknob cleaning made up their only other training. They spoke no English.

The Chief Medical Officer sat pining at his desk when I made my first call. He was about to retire, and that splendid Englishman, Dr. Aubrey Montague, with twenty years of local experience, was about to take his place.

The soon-retiring C.M.O. rose from his work, offered me his hand and said mournfully, "So you've come to Fiji!"

Yes, we'd come to Fiji. The Chief Medical Officer retained the hairline balance of politeness. The Foundation was a nice philanthropic institution, and it was sweet of us to be interested and all that; but there was no enthusiasm for chenopodium. I heartily agreed with him. We compared notes — without profit. You can't invent a cure-all overnight. There was nothing to take the place of what we had, and nothing to do but go on.

It was a boon to me and to Fiji when Dr. Aubrey Montague took over the desk of the Chief Medical Officer. He was the best of the Anglo-Saxon breed, one of the most helpful influences that ever touched my life. Clear-headed, clear-eyed, he was spiritually incapable of lying even to himself. I never knew him to do an underhand thing or go back on his word — quite a record for an official in the tropics. He was one of the three ablest men I have known in the Pacific and he didn't take third place. A naturally shy man walls himself in. I put a high value on the intimacy we formed when the wall was broken and I could look in on his well-controlled intellect.

His clean life and ideals were free from intolerance; he judged men leniently. I have often seen them fail him, and be forgiven tomorrow after he had weighed them in his kindly practical mind. His administration opened an era of large expansion, especially along lines of preventive medicine. A routine politician would have thrown money around. Montague was economical, almost parsimonious. It was a wondrous thing in those days to see government funds protected by a gentleman's deep responsibility to King and Country.

Governors continually came to him with questions outside his department; advice from his clear mind was never less than valuable. So it was a great shock to me when Montague, after thirty years of service to the Empire, was allowed to retire and to die without the honors he richly deserved. He had done his job unobtrusively and lacked the self-seeking qualities that bid for titles. The only monument he left behind him was an unfillable gap.

Through those first few months we agreed on three ambitious plans. Montague wanted an improved native medical school for his Fijians, a real one instead of a makeshift. His wish was mine, and uppermost in my thoughts; but I wanted this educational project to reach out over all the South Pacific. It was a big idea which might have seemed audacious, but we discussed its possibilities from every angle. He saw clearly the advantage of sending competently educated islanders back to their homes to work among their own people.

We went into the subject of asylum for lepers at Mokogai,* a

* Pronounced "Mokongai," and would be so spelled, except for the typographical feat described on pages 129–130. In most Fijian words I have used the correct Fijian spelling instead of the fantastic anglicized form.

near-by island where the old establishment had been moldering for years. I pointed out that all the poor, small Pacific groups might combine their resources co-operatively and make Mokogai the center, a modernized and enlarged plant where patients could be cared for at minimum cost and with maximum results. Here would be teamwork, the thing most needed over those wide blue waters.

And we agreed on another design for teamwork. High Commission control should be centralized more, particularly in health matters. Quick communications, radio especially, were bringing the islands together. We saw a far vision of a unified medical service; one that would make sense out of the bedlam that existed from New Guinea to the Society Islands. Montague and I were for this plan, and before our preliminary talks were over we had decided that he, Montague, was to secure the backing of the Fiji Government and that I was to bring in the financial and moral support of governments controlling the many Pacific groups around us.

These were long, long thoughts. But before his retirement Montague saw two of his dreams, and mine, come true. The third was partially realized and may be worked out fully in the end. I hope so, for the sake of a million patients. . . . I know that no man was ever more generously helped than I was, with the friendship of Montague on the Government side and with Sir Maynard Hedstrom backing me in the Legislative Council. Hedstrom, by the way, always stood ready to act as interpreter for my Yankee lingo and Yankee methods when I had to argue before cautious governors.

The practicability of a modernized native medical school came home to me. I had had a white man's peep into the Melanesian mind; anthropologists rank him as the mental equal of the Caucasian; the Polynesian stands a grade higher intellectually, with the Japanese; while the Chinese heads the list. Environment, geography and tradition have held so many races back that it is impossible to compare them with our own ingenious and self-destructive civilization.

I had gone over all this when Malakai, N.M.P., was sent to me, and my mind was made up.

Malakai had been made Native Practitioner by the hit-or-miss of the old school. More than half self-educated, his inquisitive mind would never let a subject go until he had mastered it. He was a cannibal's grandson, I have no doubt; so many of the best ones were. His favorite dish was scientific books, which he devoured.

He came to me, a slim young man of twenty with the fine bronze skin of the Melano-Polynesian mixture. Something of a dude, he wore a silk *lavalava* down to his good Fijian knees. His English was imperfect then. In 1924 when I went out on my series of group surveys, I showed him around as a model for the proposed Native Medical Practitioner. He became the best microscopist among the thirty-odd I have trained; his accurate eyes became mine in a work for which poor sight unfitted me. Moreover, he was father, mother, son and valet to me. It was unseemly to set him to small drudgery. Malakai settled that question; when we were in the field he invariably laid out my clean clothes, and did laundry work among savages who were too ignorant for such things. At night he gave me my quinine, and he was always the first up in the morning. The old-time missionary who spoke of the Fijian as "inclined to indolence" should have met Malakai. Once when we were out in the jungle my model N.M.P. fired the native cook and took over the job. Could he cook? Of course!

I'm showing you Malakai, but not as a great exception among Fijians. There are thousands of him on his home islands, only awaiting their chance; they're the handiest people I've ever seen, adaptable, clever, willing, loyal, dependable in emergency. Never once has a trusted Fijian let me down, or failed to put up with hardship and smile in adversity. Treat them with the consideration they deserve, trust them as they should be trusted . . . Well, I've seen many of their fine young men come on, and I'm watching many on their way up. . . .

On my return visit to Sikiana I was troubled by the number of enlarged spleens I found among the people. Malakai was the first to suggest a wide infection of malaria, but I pooh-poohed. Where were the anopheline mosquitoes? Malakai disappeared and came back smiling. "Doctor, I've let them bite me. They stand on their heads to feed, and they have spotted wings." He showed me several captured anopheles and saved me from being ridiculous in my report.

I shall never forget his appearance when he came back from a later mission to the New Hebrides. He had served for a year and a half as the only purely Condominium medical officer. Suddenly there came a cable: "HAVE QUITTED CONDOMINIUM, MALAKAI." It was a matter of color. A newly-appointed official had been born on an island where nobody was exactly lily-white; so he was extremely race-sensitive, and insisted on putting the boy from Fiji in his place. We welcomed Malakai back to Suva because we had let him go at a sacrifice in order to demonstrate the efficiency of native doctors.

The picture of his getting off the boat was something to remember. He had discarded the proud *lavalava* for a pair of trousers. He merely said he liked them, and nobody could pry the real reason out of him. About a year later he showed up with a new silk *lavalava*, and was ready to tell about the trousers. Down in the New Hebrides he had experimented once too often with mosquitoes; an attack of malaria had made his legs so thin that he was ashamed of them. The Fijian dandy's pride is in his swelling calves and slim ankles.

In 1926 when I was going from the New Hebrides to Sydney on the *Makambo*, Captain Tom Brown moved Malakai from second class to the captain's table, a gesture of respect. On my return to the Cook Islands in 1932, the natives asked only two questions: Where was Malakai and what had I done with my big camera? I had been the fifth wheel in the wagon. For three years Malakai ran our yaws unit in Fiji. A European doctor couldn't have done the work as well with four times the money. Malakai's unit was a model.

A European Medical Officer on the Ellice group went alcoholic, so I sent Malakai down for six months. After we had to call him home the local District Officer almost challenged me to a duel; he was going half-crazy, he said, because deputations from surrounding islands were pouring in, clamoring for Malakai's services.

My young doctor's addiction to silk neckties, silk shirts, silk *lavalavas*, fine coats, wrist watches, mandolins and guitars, once ran him afoul of a Fijian custom called *kere kere*. The clans are communistic, and if you happen to be a clansman anything you have is theirs by divine right. That's why he returned from his home town looking like a cat that had been dipped into the sea. His family had trimmed him down to a ragged shirt and a cotton *lavalava*. The highest-born Fijian may get this rummage sale welcome if he ventures into the land of his birth. It quells ambition.

That, of course, belonged to the private life of Malakai. So did his marriage to a handsome wife, who used to accompany him on his trips. When he started sailing alone I was afraid of trouble; Malakai, temperamentally, would have made an ideal guardian for a very old

Turk with a very large harem — no outside assistant would have been necessary. Then there was the matter of his savings. Like all Pacific Islanders he had no idea of a money economy. Why save for a rainy day? The sun will come out; it always does.

Love came to Malakai's life and money flew out of the window. I had badgered him into putting £119 in a savings account; but Malakai got hold of the book. He was having wife-trouble. The first Mrs. Malakai was barren, and the Fijian who hasn't fathered a child is jeered at as something less than a proper man; sterility is grounds for divorce. Malakai had gone courting a native nurse, and the romance had dug deep into his £119. He blew his whole remaining balance on a party to proclaim an approaching heir — on the sinister side. His fiancée was far from sterile — but how to give an honest name to the unborn Malakai, Junior?

Well, I talked to Magistrate Burrowes, who obligingly called two divorce hearings — and dismissed them both because neither Malakai nor his friends, for inscrutable Fijian reasons, would testify to the fact. At a third hearing Burrowes was in a sour temper. Bari and Rafaeli, Malakai's friends, remained mum, but Malakai loosened up a little. Annoyed, the magistrate penalized him three pounds a month out of his N.M.P. salary of nine pounds — probably the first alimony ever paid by a Fijian. On the first of every month the retired Mrs. Malakai showed up to collect. She bled her ex-husband white as a Swede; then came to me for six months' payment in advance to take her on a holiday trip. I argued that three months' cash in hand is worth a lifetime of installments in the bush. She fancied the idea, and finally for fifteen pounds spot-on-the-counter surrendered Malakai for life. Now she could buy presents, buy clothes, go home, save her face. And, quite naturally, pick out a husband. Honor was satisfied. Another instance of native money psychology.

In 1936 Malakai went to the Gilbert and Ellice Islands as Senior Medical Practitioner. When he left there, it required two Europeans to fill his post. He came back to Fiji in 1939, a few days before I retired.

In his ability and in his foibles Malakai was all Fijian. He settled my determination on higher education for such men. Dr. Montague was in the mood for it. If we could have taken that bull by the horns in 1922–1923 our enthusiasm might have swept in the political

consent and money backing of at least eight great island groups. All
we needed was the partnership of the Rockefeller Foundation. That,
I guessed, was merely a matter of asking.

My guess was wrong. I wrote a detailed letter to Dr. Victor Heiser
and outlined our plan. Just a little school with forty undergraduates,
to start with. It could be an adjunct to the new hospital in Suva, but
need not be an expensive set of buildings. Dr. Montague's plans were
modest in price and extremely practical. Governor Sir Eyre Hutson
was enthusiastic. Administrators on distant island groups were beg-
ging for it. Now was the time.

Ardently I wrote:

> The Foundation gives cheerfully to help medical schools for
> Chinese, Spanish, English and what you please, to people who
> are better able to help themselves than these poor blacks out
> here who are as eager for a chance of this sort as ever a white
> man was. The Board could give this school and fund half of
> a teacher's salary; the other half might be made up by the differ-
> ent groups . . . the money would produce results at a far
> higher rate than in England or Canada. . . .

The reply came from 61 Broadway. Dr. Heiser with his usual
sagacity had found the plan reasonable and practical. But the Foundation is so vast that it must be zoned into many divisions, such as a
Division of Medical Sciences, a Division of Social Sciences, a Division
of the Humanities, and so on. And the Division of Medical Sciences
was dead against us; it was out for ambitious projects, and thought
mine very third-rate indeed. Rockefeller millions were going into
the great establishment in Peking. No use throwing good money after
bad, on little squirt schools in the Pacific. After years of my dinging
away at the subject, Heiser himself grew cold and asked me to forget it. Peking and many others were the big health investments. . . .

Well, where is Peking today, after the Japanese have finished? And
Fiji? I'm saving that information for dessert.

It is one of the ironies of our times, and a quaint one, that the
Rockefeller Foundation mailed the Japanese a large check for their
Public Health School on the same day the Mikado's army bombed
to powder a beautiful library which the Foundation had given to
Chungking.

CHAPTER XII

A DOCTOR EX OFFICIO

I was a dog without a collar, medically speaking. Official Fiji had heard about the avaricious Yankee, planting himself on foreign soil to amass a dishonest fortune. In 1922 a law was passed, for my personal benefit, to the effect that no American could practise medicine in Fiji without a "special permit." The special permit was far less potent than a chauffeur's license, and my official status, if any, was somewhat lower than that of the N.M.P. (Native Medical Practitioner). Until 1937 I was not legally qualified to treat anything but hookworm. In the meantime I had treated and been responsible for the care of hundreds of thousands of cases of hookworm, yaws, malaria, tuberculosis, ringworm and so on. Come to think of it, I hadn't been a lawfully qualified physician in Papua and New Guinea. When Dr. McGusty came to power in Suva, he huffed and he puffed and he said, "All nonsense!" — and proceeded to get me a respectable license. In 1937 the Empire discovered that I was in Fiji, and I joined the British Medical Association.

Not that it mattered. Montague and I were together, never slipping a cog. He wasn't the sort who fishes for praise, and he never failed to give me credit, if credit were due.

Fiji was a case of racial decline, with a trend upward. Briefly, the population fell from its 200,000 in the hearty cannibal days of 1870 to 105,000 in the Christian year 1891. The census of 1905 showed an appalling drop to 87,000; epidemics of endemic dysentery and whooping cough had decimated them every year; then measles swooped down on these non-immunes. A pause in the death rate, and in 1911 a slight increase in population which was to continue until 1917 when there were 91,000 living Fijians. They might have risen in eight years to the 1891 level but for the withering blast of influenza in 1918–1919. Once again they recovered from a low of around 82,000 until the New Year of 1937 showed a population of 98,291.

Discounting the World War's gift of flu, which baffled all medicine, Fiji shows how the gradual fall in the death rate can almost
be measured in terms of medical effort. I wish we could be smug and
say that the trick is turned, both in Fiji and Western Polynesia. But
there's the other puzzling factor: the East Indian.

Today in Suva the tourist admires the picturesqueness of these
Asiatics, brightening the streets with turbans and silken *saris*. In the
early '80's they were first brought in as laborers, and succeeding
shiploads increased them to 50,000. With natural progeny they grew
to some 85,000, by the 1936 census. Fiji colonials began by believing
that such immigrants were needed for industrial development; but
in 1916 the indenturing of Indians ceased. Since then more of them
have left than have entered. Those who leave are usually old; the
re-entering ones are usually young adults.

During forty-five years the Indian birth rate far surpassed the
Fijian. The steadier Fijian rate shows a rise. In the early '90's there
was an excess of 7,000 native males over females, but the margin
steadily narrowed until 1936 when the excess was reduced to 2,087.
This indicates a healthy tendency. But wait. The Colony's annual
medical and health reports, 1921–1936, show that the Indian woman out-
breeds the Fijian woman by 25 per cent; soon the Indian population
must overtake the native Fijian. There is a greater loss by death among
Fijians than among Indians. The Fijians lose more people from tuberculosis than the Indians do *from all causes;* the Fijians lose more children under five than the Indians do *from all causes;* the Fijians lose
more from causes other than tuberculosis and death under five than
the Indians do *from all causes.*

Add this up. Fijian mortality is three times that of the Indian, and
the fertility of the Indian woman is 25 per cent higher than that of
the Fijian woman.

The Indians in Fiji are survivals of thousands of ancestral generations of exposure to disease. Fiji with her better food, wages, hous-
ing and free medical attention was an unmixed blessing to these newcomers. Far from the teeming Punjab they dropped the shackles of
caste, and brought with them a devouring hunger for land and freedom. The larger the family the larger the workable holdings; and
there is no stigma on illegitimacy.

In 1922 the East Indians were spreading. Today they are spreading even faster until Fiji is threatened with becoming an annex to India. The Asiatic population is running about neck-and-neck with the native. Something should be done about it, of course, but what? Is it survival of the fittest? Not entirely. It is partly the artificial stimulation given to the oriental through medical science and a vastly improved environment. Some evils have come with the banishment of their old caste system. There is no longer the invisible barrier between Hindu, Brahman, Chamar, Pariah — and Moslem. The Indian found a new freedom in the tropic isles, and the immigrants were mostly very low-caste. Their ideals were vague, their women scarce, the recruiting system led to degeneracy, the marriage tie weakened, little girls were offered for barter. Cult priests from India would froth up fanaticism and loud-mouthed little Gandhis kept the pot boiling. India's Nationalist Movement made a pretty mess of attempted social equality. The Indians had been allotted three seats on the Legislative Council on an equality with elected Fijian chiefs. The Asiatic members put up a howl for a common franchise, and when this was defeated in council, they promptly resigned. Then came the school question. It was fantastically impossible for the Government to build the hundred schools which the Indians demanded, while they declined to contribute their share to Government-fostered mission and private schools. So about a sixth of their children went without education.

I am taking no sides. I only report that the Indians are becoming conquerors by infiltration of an archipelago where the native deserves his own land and customs. In Fiji the Asiatic is developing a kindly fraternalism which Mother India never quite crushed out of him. Very often when one of them has been stranded in India, after a holiday, his friends in Fiji — Hindu, Pariah and Moslem — will chip in on a purse to fetch him back. At one time in our Suva household we had three Indian servants of three discordant faiths: a Hindu cook, a Moslem gardener, a Christian chambermaid. Back in the old home-town they might have cut each other's throats every morning before breakfast. But here it was the song of songs, close harmony. I wish Eloisa had them now. . . .

No, I am not against the experiment to bring back the East Indian. Only I wish they hadn't tried it on Fiji, whose native people I have learned to love deeply.

Now how about the Fijian?

When you number his islands at 250 you include large Viti Levu, which bulks about 4,000 square miles, and its slenderer, somewhat smaller sister Vanua Levu to the northeast; then there is a scattering of fair-sized fellows scaling down to mere pin-points on the map. If some super-Hitler should decide to combine them there would be enough to fill New Jersey, almost. They are heavenly things, the tiny islands, with rounded bases of iron-brown rock and palms dipping toward the sea; so many fern baskets set around surprising blue inlets — blue and silver in the morning. Then you coast around toward larger footholds, elegant cliffs with threads of waterfall and great white shells on the shore, like bleaching skulls. In summer, which is December, the thermometer seldom rises above ninety-two degrees, and July Fourth is in the very ecstasy of spring. I have no real estate to sell in Fiji. So I speak only out of a homesick heart when I say that it is the best winter climate in the world, and the best climate, any time, for me.

Early discoverers called it "Feejee," although the official name is Fiji — and that, too, is wrong. The correct name for it is Viti. Captain Cook made the mistake when he touched at the Tongan Islands, near neighbors, and heard the Polynesians say "Viti" in their own way. This group was honestly named "the Cannibal Islands." The transit of fierce tribes from man-eating to prayer-meeting is miraculous. In 1927 when Martin Egan, as a traveler, saw a long file of sedate natives going to church, he remarked, "From Cannibalism to Calvinism!" And this describes it, although the predominant Church happens to be Wesleyan. It is almost impossible to believe that these quiet, law-abiding people have emerged so soon and gone so far.

The Fijians not only were cannibals, but were inordinately cruel. When a chief's dwelling was being built captives were made to stand in the postholes "to hold up the house," and were buried alive. A chief's canoe was launched over living bodies, human rollers. When there was a shortage of enemy meat, hunters would stalk women and children of their own tribe; women and children were regarded as delicacies fit for visiting chiefs. When there were plenty of captives the resident chief would order out his livestock in the morning, to choose his meat. If one of them sneezed, which was considered an evidence of cowardice, the chief would cry "*Mbula!*" which meant, disdainfully, "I give you life." No proper man ever ate coward-meat. Then the sneezer would reply, "*Moli*," which meant, in effect, "Your words are like the sweet juice of the orange to me." The word "*Mbula*" is often heard today, a pleasant greeting: "How's your health?" "*Mbula vinaka*" is like a casual "My health is good."

I am not so sure that their cannibalism was not caused originally by a protein shortage. There were no four-footed animals, with the possible exception of the rat. The Fijian fainted at sight of the first horse, as the Aztec did before Cortes' ponies. Old tales tell of a maniacal blood-lust: How the father of King Thakombau cut out a disobedient brother's tongue, roasted and ate it. How Thakombau (Evil of Mbau) performed the same feat on the severed arm of a living captive. . . . Widowhood was handled with frightful practicality: during a husband's funeral the widow would lay her head in the lap of a seated woman, who would put one hand over the widow's mouth, the other at the back of her neck; and a relative, sometimes a son, would string a vine around her neck and finish the job.

If some man of the tribe would come forward and claim her, the widow was spared. The very word for widow, *dawai*, is still an abusive term. Little girls who were betrothed to little boys had the vine-noose always waiting. If the boy happened to die it was etiquette to strangle the girl and toss her in his grave. Sometimes she was given a chance to return to her parents and try another marriage. Frequently the parents were so devil-ridden that they sent her back to the executioner. Yet the Fijians were, and are, a child-loving people. I cannot believe that the custom-bound parents who led their daughter back to death were not torn with genuine grief; the nice name for daughter is "rafter of the house." The widow who was nursing a child or was pregnant was sent home to her father's house and lived out her natural life.

The ceremonial over a dead chief would go on for a long time, at intervals. In a hundred days came the final feast. Some of the warriors would show up with a finger or two missing. They had cut them off as an expression of grief.

The first and last King of the Cannibal Islands was named Thakombau, and since most history books spell him "Cakobau" I must dwell on a trick of Fijian spelling that has driven native schoolboys to despair. Johann Sebastian Bach, descendant of the great composer and for years Fiji's public printer, told me how this mad spelling came about so that the island of Mbengga, for instance, is printed "Beqa." In the early days the man who did the missionaries' printing ran short of type. In Fijian every g and d has an n sound in front of it, so to save n's, none were used, the n sound being understood in front of each g and d. Every Fijian b has an m sound in front of it so that letter was understood there and dropped. The plentiful th sound ran the printer out of that character, so he substituted c for th as there is no other use for c in Fijian. The common ngg was replaced by a handy q. A full account of this typographical theory would require pages, but I hope I have outlined the principle, which shows some remarkable results.

This King called Thakombau (and spelled Cakobau) offers an example of the native money sense, that perfect vacuum. His warriors had been merrily destroying American trading establishments, and missions, occasionally pausing to eat the inhabitants. In 1858 President Buchanan sent the *Vandalia* to press a claim for a $45,000 indemnity. The warships looked mighty strong, and Thakombau wasn't getting on very well with his revolutions; the one way out seemed to be to sell his mess of empire for the debt. He offered the bargain to the United States and to England, but found no takers.

In 1874 home politics changed the British mind. According to current myth Thakombau was beleaguered on Mbau's Gibraltar-rock when a British man o' war lay handily offshore. A well-armed landing party scattered the besiegers, brought the King back to his tapa-lined house, and saw him make a cross on a paper which mentioned the payment of debt and the delivery of the Fijis, body, soul and breeches. The story is close enough to the truth. A little later Britain accepted the Fijis. King Thakombau finished with a pretty gesture when he handed over his war club as a present to Queen Victoria. Probably she never used it, but her heart was gratified when she learned that the deposed monarch had exchanged cannibalism for Christianity. He burned most of the heathen temples in his fading realm, but saved his own on Mbau — for sentiment's sake.

The chastened Thakombau took to travel, and did his bit toward importing foreign disease. In 1876 he came back from Australia with a dose of measles, which he spread far and wide.

CHAPTER XIII

HOW THE ANSWER CAME

In Fiji we started out directly for cure and prevention, an active campaign. Chris Kendrick was still with me, my gem of the first water; Malakai was a newly discovered diamond.

On my first tour I saw filthy sanitary arrangements, or none at all. By education we tried to induce the natives and oriental transplant to use ordinary cesspit latrines; our efforts met with more success after the discovery of a new internal remedy had rewarded us with public approval and made the Fijians health-conscious. From then on the pathway was cleared for all our efforts. Dr. Heiser, when he visited us in 1928, introduced the bored-hole latrine, which was the Foundation's enthusiasm at that time. It was a twenty-five-foot hole dug with an eighteen-inch auger, which was a practical benefit to the East Indian in Fiji; but, for the native, the deep pit, covered with a polished concrete slab — which we were by then making and distributing by thousands — was by far the better sanitation.

Dr. Heiser came out again in 1934. In his *An American Doctor's Odyssey* he was kind enough to report those two visits at some length. On his latter trip we made the surveys together and looked over results of our bored-hole work. I have a pleasant memory of our expeditions; how he belied his sixty-third birthday when his long legs walked me lame in Fiji, Tonga and Samoa. We argued like a pair of plumbers on a holiday; subject, Bored Latrine versus Cesspit. I contended that the deep auger-hole was all right for the delicately built Indian, but, even then, in rocky or sandy soil it was no good at all. And for Fijians it wouldn't work. Why? In a land where the natives use palm leaves, breadfruit leaves, stones, coconut husks and hanks of wild grass for toilet purposes, a narrow tube in the ground gets stopped up in less time than it takes to bore it. Then the chap takes to the bush, as of old. It has nothing to do with science, it's just practical mechanics, plus tradition. Our debate had this effect at least; we later modified the bored-hole latrine with a much larger hole, but retained the concrete slab, which was admired by barefoot natives for its reliable cleanliness.

But in 1922, as a newcomer in Fiji and with only such authority as I could get by talking myself into it, this broken jigsaw puzzle looked to me like something no mere human hands could put together. I was a health officer on a rather large scale with nothing so much as a dog license to show for it. It was pretty discouraging, at first. I was like a fireman with a leaky hose, trying to stop a blaze at one end of a building while an incendiary poured gasoline on the other. The government health authorities had a right to mourn over the Foundation's recent attempt to kill the all-pervading parasite. Everywhere I went I saw how little the good work had accomplished. Chris Kendrick would come back from treatments in outlying districts and smile ruefully. "They're quite a mess out there." Like all of us, he was losing faith in chenopodium; and Chris Kendrick's faith would stand a good deal of punishment.

Nevertheless, I was working vigorously to educate the natives in the nature of various parasites and the virtue of treatment. And I was pumping up British enthusiasm with every publicity device I could lay my hands on. As I tooted the Horn of Health they began to look upon me as Barnum's little brother with a rich strain of Rockefeller in me somewhere.

One of my less dignified efforts along the line of health-advertising was a window display I devised for Pop Swann's drugstore, prominent on Suva's main street. Pop was a stanch friend of medical progress. So it didn't take long to convince him that an attractive display of intestinal parasites would help both his business and mine. Most of his customers were Fijians and East Indians, so nothing could be more logical. "Anything in the world to push things along, my boy," said enthusiastic Pop. Between us we set up a charming arrangement in the two windows on either side of his street door, where all who passed could wonder and admire: worms of every variety in the big gallon bottles they call "Winchesters." Tapeworms of infinite length slithered around in alcohol; families of *Necator americanus* swam cozily beside a jugful of oriental Ankylostoma; there was a large bottle devoted to the fat roundworms, nearly a foot long, and to the screw-headed whipworms, and to other, less notorious wrigglers. Pop Swann rubbed his hands as we stood outside gloating over our work in the two windows that fledged his main door. "Doc," chuckled Pop, "that ought to draw customers, if anything will!"

Then a very busy week, uphill and down dale, organizing the campaign and pushing it along. One day, going by Pop Swann's, my way was blockaded by a semicircle of Indians and Fijians, standing at a respectful distance from the great exhibition. Out of the door burst Pop, hair on end. "Doc," he shouted, "for the love of God take those things out of my windows. The natives are so scared they won't pass in between those worms. You're ruining my trade!"

So I dewormed the window and time marched on. But it wasn't marching well for me, or in the right direction.

One late afternoon in February, 1922, I keeled back in my office chair and appreciated the soreness a middle-aged prize fighter must feel after he has taken the count in round one. With a sanitary squad of nine native and Indian assistants and the invaluable Chris Kendrick I had again made a round and seen the dank hopelessness of two races weakened by their own customs and by the unfriendly acts of nature. It was just as Paley had shown: rainfall flooded their shallow wells and mixed with the foulness of their latrines so that both wells and latrines had the same bacterial flora. In some districts hookworm infection ran as high as 98 per cent. This condition was not limited to primitive natives by any means; the Hindu and Moslem of ancient culture were quite as ignorant of sanitation, and more worm-laden than their dark brown brothers.

This filthy stable must be cleaned, but the baffling thing was to find the cure. Our International Health Board was sharing expenses with the Government for a three-year campaign. The question of throwing good money after bad had come up again. Officially, I should have been pro-chenopodium. Actually that drug was the first word in my Hymn of Hate. And the discouraging thing was this: despite the crucial need of hygienic improvements, an effective cure must take first place as an educational demonstration. If you destroy all the hookworms inside the human body, no more of their eggs will fall to the ground to hatch the larvae that make the worms that suck the blood. . . . The whole Jack-built song of consequences with a tropical setting. Sounds very simple, doesn't it? So does astronomy.

I sat at my desk, facing facts and not liking a single one of them. Evening was coming on and I should have been home for dinner. I was too sick of myself and my work to move a muscle. Three more years of this, and where would it get us? Nowhere.

Maybe it was my guardian angel who stole up and laid a still hand over mine. Without knowing what I did or why I did it, I moved my hand across the desk and woke, blinking. I had picked up the Journal of the *American Medical Association*, a November 1921 issue, and an invisible finger seemed to point the page for me. And there was the title: "The Use of Carbon Tetrachloride in the Removal of Hookworm . . . by Maurice C. Hall." Hall was the man who approved my experiment down in Rabaul when I gave those injections to six cannibal prisoners. I respected him, as most of the profession did. As Senior Zoologist of the United States Bureau of Animal Industry, his researches had gone far in his own field. He didn't talk unless he knew what he was talking about.

Here was Hall's report in the modest gray of scientific language, revealing years of most careful observation. His tests had led him to a novel drug — carbon tetrachloride. Queer, humble thing to have fished out of the pharmacopoeia! Hitherto it had been useful only in dry-cleaning fluids and fire extinguishers. He had observed that patients under chloroform anesthesia frequently emit a number of intestinal parasites. Chloroform, then, would be a successful vermifuge were it not for its poisonous qualities. Hall made hundreds of tests down the list of Hydrocarbons until he came to chloroform's close relation. Chloroform's chemical initials are $CHCl_3$. Tetrachloride's laboratory name is CCl_4.

Tetrachloride touched the spot Hall had been looking for. He tried it first on dogs, then on swine, horses, monkeys. He carefully gauged the dosage to 3 cc. for every 10 pounds of animal weight; later he found that 0.3 cc. to every kilogram of body-weight expelled the worms in surprising quantities. After treatment he had performed postmortems on many animals and had examined internal organs which showed no pathological changes that could be traced to CCl_4. In animal experimentation it had been an unqualified success.

In animals, yes. But what of man?

The answer came like a clap of thunder out of Hall's quietest paragraph. *He had tried the stuff on himself.* Audaciously he had taken a 3 cc. dose, gone to bed and wakened in the morning with no pathological symptoms. The dangerous drops he had swigged the night before had had none of the nauseous effects of chenopodium. His animal experiments had shown him that it worked as fast, as safely and more thoroughly. And here was another point in its favor: tetrachloride tried on animals seemed to have no ill effects on pregnancy. Chenopodium had always been a dangerous thing to give a woman with child. It was, at times, among the unsafe abortifacients — often effective if used up to the poison point.

The message of tetrachloride came to me like an answer to prayer. But would the dog-cure turn out to be a man-killer? Probably not. *Hall had tried it on himself.*

With a hop, skip and jump I went to the laboratory used by the Medical Officer of Health. Naturally old Carment, who presided over the collection, wouldn't have the drug. Why should he? Yes, but there it was! A big, brown bottle with the label CCl_4. It had never been opened, of course, and how it got there nobody knows. Strange, useless things drift onto laboratory shelves.

When I went up to Dr. Montague's office I had the brown bottle under one arm and the *Medical Journal* under the other. "Read that and look at this," I said. He read the article painstakingly, then turned the bottle in his hand. "Lambert, try anything," he sighed. That was about the way we all felt those days.

We had been trained in the empirical school. Try anything, if evidence is in its favor. Even the jungle medicine man, for all his black magic, has herbs and simples which the respectable practitioner might include in his remedies. A thousand years before Harvey demonstrated the blood's circulation Asiatic wizards were giving chaulmoogra oil for leprosy — true, they gave it wrong, but they gave it. The Incas of Peru taught us the value of quinine for malaria; they chewed the bark. Before the Crusades, corner barbers were giving mercury to syphilitic noblemen. Up to fifty years ago the medical profession depended pretty much on the household remedies your grandmother used to choke down you; as long as they worked they saved many a fine prescription in abbreviated Latin.

The old empiricals had moved along that line. But men of the new thought, like Pasteur, like Ehrlich, had set out deliberately to fit a drug to a condition. And that was how Hall had worked.

So we were trying to cure hookworm disease with a cleaning fluid. A veterinary had recommended it. True, he was about the greatest vet in the world. I have to laugh now, remembering how we, as green young undergraduates at Syracuse Medical, used to snoot veterinaries and dentists as "hoss doctors" and "tooth yankers." We didn't take the trouble to remember that modern anesthesia originated in a dentist's brain. And since we lacked the gift of prophecy, how were we to know what a horse doctor would someday do with something out of a fire extinguisher?

My mind was made up, but my heart wasn't doing any too well when I went to the native ward and picked out four hookwormy East Indians. I wasn't sure how these fellows would behave, for Mr. Gandhi's Civil Disobedience had become their evening prayer. However, they felt pretty sick and were ready, like Montague, to say, "Try anything." I started them off with a stiff dose of salts.

At seven next morning my faltering hand administered to each of them 3 cc. out of the brown bottle. The minute they swallowed it I felt like a Borgia. It was too late to do anything about it, unless I gave them a quick emetic. If tetrachloride went back on me I'd be responsible for the death of a man, maybe four. Doctors have to become hardened to death, otherwise they couldn't remain in practice. But experimental killing is a different thing. If any of these Hindus died I'd have the weight on my soul. Not only that, I'd lose my job. . . . Already I saw my resignation from the International Health Board being requested by cable.

I steadied myself with an argument: If the Fiji campaign failed along the old line that wouldn't be any feather in my cap either. Well, I was deciding something on a very long chance. . . . My stomach went back on me, foolishly reflecting the pain of my victims. Solid food didn't appeal, so I breakfasted on a pint of coffee, embittered with a new torment. Why hadn't I taken tetrachloride myself, before I tried it on those Indians? *

Dr. Hall had taken a dose of it.

* Some months later I did penance for that moment's slip in courage. A learned man who had studied tropical medicine in London announced that the human

I had dosed my four Indians at seven, and time was wearing on. Tetrachloride, which is a purgative, should have acted quicker. The men were dumb and drowsy. Would this be coma? I felt their lean wrists, listened to their lean chests; pulse and respiration normal. How soon would they take a turn for the worse?

Dr. Hall had taken a dose of it.

Yes, but Hall had been in the prime of health, able to throw off toxic poisoning. These poor fellows were like dry leaves. The very thing that made treatment necessary had weakened them to the exhaustion point. . . . Then I thought: Even if I had drugged myself with the stuff it wouldn't have proved much; what I was trying to find out was its actual effect on hookworm. . . .

I had wandered back to my office, hoping that solitude and a cigarette might tell me what to do next. . . . The door burst open and Chris Kendrick tumbled in on me. His look was grave as he said, "That tetrachloride — "

"Are they dead?" I asked stiffly.

"Dead!" Chris waved his hands. "They're all jumping out of bed, and simply spouting hookworms!"

That was how the news came to me. I had been watching them for hours while local medical officers passed their beds and made long faces which said to my fevered imagination, "See what Lambert's done now!" Then the minute I turned my back CCl_4 had begun to work. For three days while my Indians were, as Chris exaggerated it, "fairly spouting worms," the result was a constant wonder. Cordiality

---

hookworm could infect the pig and be carried by him. This was a serious claim, likely to upset all calculations; especially since he declared that he had proved his theory on a South Pacific island. I wanted to find out for myself, so I went to a friend whose wife had a pet pig that she had raised on a concrete floor to avoid that curse of Fiji's swine growers, intestinal parasites. I examined the pig, found it negative, then hog-tied it and laid it, several times, on a bed heavily infested with human hookworm larvae. It got a severe "ground itch," first symptom of infection. In due time I did a postmortem on the animal and found many abscesses in the liver and kidneys, but no worms in the intestines — fair evidence that human hookworms do not infect pigs.

Then I did the experiment in reverse: got a pig that was extremely heavy with pig hookworm and tied a poultice of the hatching material on my arm. Result: "ground itch," but no infection. Showing, at least, that pig hookworm couldn't thrive in a tough bird like me. I cut open this tender young pig, and a good look at its wormy insides sickened me. As a martyr to science I only suffered through my pocket. The lady had been saving the animal for Christmas dinner, and she charged me five pounds for it.

glowed in an atmosphere which had been none too warm. Doctors gathered around our hookworm count like baseball fans around the box score. The native orderlies were as excited as the rest. First day, second day, third . . . I had gambled with four lives, and won. I call that Tetrachloride Experiment Number 2, since Hall swallowed the first dose; and Experiment Number 2 was a surprising success. Between them my patients had expelled 244 worms after a single dose. The following week we gave them a test treatment with chenopodium — and only got four Necators. The man I mark down as Case 1 expelled none at all. The other three needed no follow-up treatment. In three days Case 1 had shed ninety-five hookworms, and all were discharged as cured. One dose of CCl_4, mind you, had proven 99 per cent perfect.

Mine was the embarrassment of riches. I had worked for the Foundation too long to believe that they would approve of wholesale treatments with so new and untried a drug. If I went on with tetrachloride, as I felt I must do, the only way was to go ahead and say nothing about it.

Dr. Montague's enthusiasm was as great as mine, but I moved cautiously at first. The next set of East Indians I tried it on was less satisfactory than the original four. It wasn't the fault of tetrachloride, but of Gandhi; his sick disciples were so independent that they threw their specimens out of the window before we could make an accurate worm-count. We recovered enough, however, to keep Kendrick and his force of Fijian helpers pretty busy going over the thin washings spread out on tightly stretched gauze.

I look over some of the reports of those experimental days and read: —

> . . . Almost total lack of symptoms in the group that received the purge after the drug. Not one of them was incapacitated for his regular duties . . . with no after-purge there were some who had minor symptoms. Many were sleepy for several hours . . .
> . . . Young Indian working in our office given 3 cc. at 7:45 A.M. . . . by 10:15 gave 85 hookworms. Total for three days 101. Test treatment showed he was cured. This illustrates the rapid expulsion of worms by this drug, which we have observed generally.

The time came when I felt that the whole thing was too important to keep to myself, so I wrote a careful letter to the Foundation. The answer from 61 Broadway with its code-name "Rockfound" was cabled back so fast that it burned a streak across the Pacific: "FORBID USE. WE DO NOT EXPERIMENT WITH HUMAN LIFE."

I took the limp message to Dr. Montague and said, "Well, the jig's up. I'm forbidden to play with fire extinguishers."

Montague thought a long time. Tetrachloride was God's gift to Fiji, he said, and he didn't intend to give it up. He was recommending it for all the institutions under his authority.

Then I found an out. I asked, "Do you authorize me, as your subordinate, to continue its use? Would you O.K. a letter to that effect?" He said he would, and he did. After that I heard no more objections from the Foundation, whose administrators were only too glad, of course, to have the drug tried out on a large scale, as long as the Government of Fiji took the responsibility.

Up to the time when I grew bolder and dosed a whole large Indian school, the new treatment had been tried very quietly. Then it got too public to be kept away from the press. It was at the Dilkusha Mission that we gave this first "mass treatment" — the only practical way of administering a cure to the many. Before that it had been a matter of tedious house-to-house canvas. At Dilkusha we lined up 400 children, and I was about as jittery as I had been when I tackled the four adults at the War Memorial. But I went away smiling, a little cocky about myself. One dose of tetrachloride had removed 99 per cent of the infestation. Meanwhile in Suva Jail Dr. Kalamkar, East Indian physician, had run up a score of 94.5.

All this was news, and Suva had an editor with a keenly developed news-sense. His name was Victor Abel, and among other bold enterprises he ran a paper called the *Pacific Age*. A daring young chap of a good Anglo-Jewish family, he had raised mules in South Africa, made a failure of it, then come to Fiji to raise hogs, and made a failure of that too. His influential father-in-law was Sir Henry Marks, who worried a great deal about the *Pacific Age*.

Sir Henry had set his cap for a place on the Executive Council, and you never could tell what the incorrigible Victor would say next to stir up the Government. The town was always agog, waiting for some new outbreak in his personal correspondence column. It was a completely open forum, that column; under all sorts of fancy *noms de plume* citizens let each other have it, straight in the nose. Then, just to keep the pot boiling, they would change their *noms de plume* overnight and start thundering on the left. When Victor decided to write anything up he trimmed it artistically. For example, there was his famous account of the government yacht left in Suva harbor with her seacocks open. She gently sank, while the officers and crew were ashore seeing a football game.

In the midst of our growing campaign Victor came to me and said he was pretty sure he had hookworm. He had; and tetrachloride did its work very nicely. "Listen, Doctor," he said, "what about this magic stuff? Where did it come from? What's the story? Are you going to bury big news like that in Suva? Tell me about it, let me put it on the wire and I'll have the whole world sitting up."

By that time Fiji was certainly sitting up. Natives were clamoring for treatment. Not until the gold rush of '32 was anything more generally talked about. I wanted Victor to have the story; I said to Victor, "You can run the story provided you keep me out of it — and don't mention the Foundation, either. Just say that Maurice C. Hall's treatment is being given. If that's understood, here are the facts."

Victor kept his word in an appropriately sensational style, proclaiming that Maurice C. Hall was curing hookworm with a thing called tetrachloride. The news thrilled the medical world, scientific men were mulling over the possibilities of a new and novel drug. How would it come out in Fiji? That was the question.

When the tidings came to Washington, friendly biologists crowded Dr. Maurice C. Hall's office to congratulate him, and his reply was characteristic. "You say I've been curing hookworm in Fiji? Hell, I've never been near the place."

In a month I had treated more cases than my predecessor had in fourteen months, and with no increased expense. Tetrachloride worked with such accuracy that there was no need of repeated doses, as with chenopodium. By the end of 1922 the Rockefeller Foundation, which had untangled the Hall-Lambert collaboration and duly forgiven my disobedience, reported 52,000 treatments by tetrachloride.

Of these 50,000 had been given in Fiji, under my supervision.

The history of public health cannot be written by the sure-cure patent-medicine man. We had our bumps, at first, but they were amazingly few. In every district where the Willis salt flotation method showed a hookworm frequency of over 60 per cent we rounded the people up and gave the treatment *en masse*. In regions like the dirty Rewa and Navua districts infection was particularly heavy. In one place we dosed 1,243, and came back in a month to find 1,111 villagers showing negative — about the average sample of our work as it increased to large proportions.

Primitive folk made a carnival of our coming; drums sounded and they all reached out for the wizard drops. They called it "toddy" and said it was fine because it made them drunk. Possibly it did, a little. After a child's-size dose small boys would run around like wild dogs, tear up the flower beds in mission compounds, throw mud and have a perfectly bully time. Full-grown "marys" would caper and dance like Aunt Dinah at an old-fashioned revival; but when their big buck husbands smacked them they would come back to normal with surprising alacrity. Most of the demonstrations were merely put on; our patients usually went wild before the drug could have had time to take effect. However, tetrachloride has a mildly intoxicating reaction, especially if it is not administered with some technical care. But these demonstrations were mostly psychological — the native craving for a big joy party. The British have been more than wise in keeping alcohol away from these people.

After the first two years of wholesale treatments we had to report seven deaths. Postmortems under the observation of able physicians revealed the causes. These seven were all East Indians. One of them, it turned out, hadn't taken tetrachloride at all; it had been chenopodium. One lad who died had a congenital malformation of the intestine, a deformity which would have prevented his living to maturity. Another was a woman who was addicted to the use of alcohol. The remainder were children heavily infected with *Ascaris lumbricoides* (roundworm).

When the deaths came, after forty thousand treatments, I took it pretty hard. I had gambled for success with everything I had, my job, and my professional good name. I felt as though I hadn't a friend in the world. Then who came unexpectedly to my support? Dr. Basil Wilson, whom I had always thought of as a queer sort of Englishman with an aversion to me, if any feeling at all. Stanchly Dr. Wilson did the friendly thing; he postmortemed the bodies and developed theories as to the cause of death so sound that they stand on record today. Among his medical colleagues he became my champion. Worry was aging me years in a day until Wilson's support renewed my youth with courage. Funny Englishman; I could have kissed his long, homely face.

Since that first setback tetrachloride has not caused one death among the thousands of Melanesians, Polynesians, East Indians and Europeans whom we treated.

The fatalities were limited to victims of alcoholism and roundworm. That was interesting; more especially in Ascaris cases. Alcohol was contra-indicated; a few drinks before or after treatment brought complications. Lingering headaches which came to many of the nondrinkers were easy to relieve with an after-dose of salts. But what about the roundworm? Why did his presence in the intestine turn tetrachloride into an active poison? I don't think that question has been settled yet. One theory says that CCl_4, while it does not kill the Ascaris, irritates him to a point where he secretes lethal toxic juices. According to Dr. Lamson and his collaborators, poisoning with tetrachloride occurs in dogs when there is a lowered blood calcium. This chemical poverty may have something to do with it; I make the conjecture, without being able to substantiate it, that there is a relation between a large number of ascarides and a lowered blood calcium.

In the course of the next ten years 286,486 Pacific Islanders were treated, under my personal observation, with carbon tetrachloride and the later drug, tetrachlorethylene.

For the gifted Dr. Hall had come across with an improvement on his discovery, and he asked me to give it its first tryout when I campaigned in the wild New Hebrides in 1925. I used it extensively down there, and optimism sounded in my conservatively worded report. Its work was faster, its toxic effect less than that of his original find. There is no 100 per cent in medicine, but Hall's new polysyllabic drug was hitting an average that was uncanny.

What a wizard he was, this pre-eminent zoologist, who was Washington's Number One horse doctor! Every pet dog wags his tail (or should) in gratitude for his two deworming remedies. The dog's pal, the human, is Hall's debtor — all but the fur dealers. The price of silver fox has taken a terrific slump. Do you know why? Dr. Hall sent his tetrachlorides to the fox farms where so many hookwormy bitches and pups used to die that pelts had become a luxury for the wives of steel barons. When Hall's treatments came to Foxville the breed picked up rapidly and its fur went to the lower department stores; so now every stenographer can have her silver fox — and on her own salary, too. Ask your furrier.

Dr. Hall is dead now. I know it's trite to say that such men don't really die. He has put his own spark into millions of men, women and children who would be in their graves today were it not for what he freely gave. He was an untold benefit to the human race. Most of the human race, of course, have never heard of him.

Then let's sum up the work of tetrachloride over seventeen years since the enterprising Victor Abel first put it on the wire. Dr. Heiser, authority on public health, used to call hookworm the world's most prevalent disease; in all Earth's population one out of three had it, he said. Then the figures on tetrachloride (and tetrachlorethylene) treatments went up and up; 654,896 in 1924; 3,000,000 in 1936. In 1937 I attended a League of Nations conference in Java. A group of us were discussing hookworm treatments. I was pretty cocky about the 500,000 done in the Pacific; so I asked Dr. Chellapa of Ceylon how many they were doing there. Last year had been a pretty bad one, he said — they had only given 1,400,000 treatments on account of the malaria epidemic. They usually got 2,000,000 he explained. I just said, "Very fine, indeed," in a manner I hope wasn't patronizing. I never mentioned our figures. However, in Ceylon they are using the same old Fiji formula and dosage.

One statement may be simpler than these figures. Every year the Rockefeller Foundation used to publish a bulletin of the number of hookworm treatments. In 1938 hookworm was not even mentioned in the Foundation's report, except for data on some still undefined parasite recently found in Egypt. The report had no general heading for ankylostomiasis. The worm which had been the source and inspiration of their world campaigns had dropped out of their ken.

My application of Hall's discovery immediately heightened my prestige all over the Pacific. I don't claim credit. I happened to be the man who stood at the crossroads when a wonderful sort of salvation came my way. I would have been a fool if I hadn't seized it and carried it on. And what a lucky afternoon that was, early in 1922, when I read a little article and found a brown bottle labeled CCl_4. It gave me the courage I needed to strengthen me for a message of my own, which I knew I must work out and make clear in the hard days that were to follow.

PART TWO

PART TWO

CHAPTER I

DEATH AND THE DEVIL

The relation between modern medicine and primitive witchcraft became so important to me during my years of health campaigning in the South Pacific that I think I should say something here to indicate the islander's daily reliance on sorcery's touch with the powers of darkness. During all my work among the remoter tribes I was not received and respected as a university M.D., but as a novel sort of witch doctor who had come among them with a stronger magic than the old. Otherwise I could have made no headway at all. My assistants and I were professional sorcerers, backed by Government; we were that, or we were nothing.

It was some time before I got a glimmer of this native point of view, then I began to take advantage of it. I had to. I had to let them believe that I was a mystic with a ritual that would take away the diseases with which sorcery had cursed them. When I gave tuberculin injections to the wild men of Malaita they believed that I was doing something to remove a wicked spell. In thousands and thousands of cases which I have treated, either for cure or diagnosis, they have gone away with the same simple faith. Good magic has been working against bad. At first I worried about fooling all the people all the time. Then I followed the only expedient that is practical in jungle medicine.

When we regard the native tribe as a unit we must not push the witch doctor aside as a buffoon and a faker. Let's give the devil-man his due and mark the fallacy of the smug European who sits among dark races with the idea of "giving them good laws" and "teaching them morality." This white man forgets that from the dawn of time the medicine man has held a position that is both useful and important to the tribe. Communities with no prison system must be controlled by a hand which, to them, reaches into the Invisible. In the old days sorcery was the prerogative of the chief, and sorcery was a hereditary and honored profession. And even today the wizard, either a chief or a commoner, is there to fend the people from epidemics, to cure their ills, to curse the enemy and to shield his flock from the invasion of evil spells — "and to sustain all those subtle influences that go to form the social cement that marks the difference between a community and a horde of men," as Pitt-Rivers expressed it.

The sorcerer occupies, in his way, the same position as the Christian priests who bless the armies and the harvests and metes out spiritual justice to the sheep and the goats. When he tells the natives of ancient Christian miracles, why should they value his words beyond those of their own miracle workers?

I have remarked on the crude killings of the *puri-puri* men, and their more subtle methods of removing unwanted tribesmen by what seemed to be the power of suggestion; the Pacific native is almost universally a believer in ghosts and devils. Am I going too far when I say that man's first religion was a form of spiritualism? Life departs, but the soul lingers, and the simple believer listens to hear the testimony of the grave.

I had been working in Melanesia for years before I began to appreciate how much they are governed by the powers of darkness, by the casting of spells to kill or cure. In the days when cannibalism and war were unchecked, tribal and personal grudges were settled in a more horrid way. In these milder times it is enchantment upon which the clansman depends for vengeance.

I wrote to Dr. Walter Bradford Cannon of Harvard's Physiology Department, in reply to a query of his: —

"Your letter brings up a very interesting question which is much in dispute. Dr. A. Montague, Chief Medical Officer of Fiji and a resident in the group for thirty years, did not believe in 'voodoo death,' that is, death caused by fear. Personally, I believe he was wrong, as I know of several instances.

"Dr. Phillip S. Clarke, of North Queensland, formerly practised just north of Cairns where he had a kanaka come to his hospital and announce that he was going to die; that he had had a spell put on him, and there was nothing that could be done about it. Dr. Clarke had been acquainted with this man for some time. He gave him a most thorough examination including examination of stool and urine, and found everything normal. The man kept on eating and smoking, but lay in bed and gradually seemed to grow weaker. Clarke was friendly with a better-educated kanaka, a foreman, whom he brought to the hospital ward; this man leaned over the patient, then turned to Clarke and said, "Yes, Doctor, close up [soon] he die." The bewitched man died at eleven next morning, lying in bed with a cigarette in his mouth. Clarke did a postmortem on him and found nothing that could in any way account for the death.

"I stayed ten days at a Seventh Day Adventist mission station, Mona Mona, a few miles above Cairns. On the outskirts was a group of non-converts, among them Nebo, a famous witch doctor. The missionary's right hand man was Rob, a convert. I had been there before and knew Rob. Now the missionary told me that Rob was ill in bed and wanted me to see him. I found that he had no temperature, no pain, no symptoms or signs; but he was evidently quite ill. He had told the missionary that Nebo had 'pointed a bone' at him, therefore he was going to die 'close up.' We got Nebo in, put the fear of God in him and — more important — told him that his supply of food would be shut off if anything happened to Rob; so Nebo leaned down and assured Rob that it was all a mistake, a joke, and that he had never pointed a bone at him. The relief was almost instantaneous; that afternoon Rob was back at work.

"The witch doctor can 'point a bone' from a great distance and the bone is supposed to pierce his victim's body. However, it is necessary for the victim to know that he has been worked upon. Volumes have been written upon this subject, and I can recall endless illustrations of this magic, many of which have come under my personal observation.

"Among native medical students in the senior year I devote one period to the subject of magic, partly because of personal interest in the reactions I get, partly for the emphasis I try to lay on the foolishness of sorcery. There are records of Native Practitioners themselves having died of *draunikau,* and the medical class is always composed about half of Fijians and the rest Polynesians with an occasional Micronesian. The Polynesians of the present generation do not know this magic; but to the Fijians, even to the educated ones, *draunikau* is a dreadful word. When it is mentioned the student's face becomes a mask; I catch the look of worry and fear.

"The practice is still in evidence back in the hills and remote places where in Christian Fiji, with 93 per cent literacy, there are still famous witch doctors. *The only Fijian I have ever known to be unafraid of draunikau * is a man named Malakai, who has been working for me now for thirteen years.* He has actually defied one of the most powerful witch doctors in Fiji to do him any harm. Incidentally, the native theory is that magic cannot affect the white man."

Ndrau-ni-kau is the Fijian word meaning "magic-of-leaves." You might call it the foundation of the old-time religion. No Melanesian believes that he can grow ill or die from natural causes like dysentery or influenza — look for the enemy who has hired a sorcerer to lay you low. Even the diagnosis of the District Medical Officer will not change the native mind. The curse is on him, therefore the cursed will die unless some more potent witch doctor is called in to magic away the spell. The Melanesian's ghost-religion is dreadful. When a man dies and is planted underground his soul loses its kindly nature; your sweet and gentle mother or father or grandfather turns into a *tevoro*, a fiend plotting mischief to his own. And the *tevoro* becomes a principal actor in the long ritual which brings a plague on your house.

The professional making of a *draunikau* is as complicated a process as that used by the demonologists of medieval Europe. As in the cruder magic of the *puri-puri* men, the practitioner obtains a bit of clothing or hair or feces from his victim's person. These things, mixed with leaves, are shut up in a bamboo joint — or more modernly, in a bottle. The mage who follows this craft is merely employed by the hater to work evil on the hated.

Although the approved methods might be roughly classified as the Seven Ways of Cursing, one general practice is for the performer to take his bottle of *draunikau* to some chosen graveyard where the *tevoro* lies underground. The curse called *tava vatu* is said to be the most difficult to beat. Among the graves grows a special plant called *uthi* whose leaves the magician roasts on hot stones, and calls out that this is the *draunikau* by which So-and-so must die; out of the smoking leaves the voice of the victim cries aloud. Then the *draunikau* is buried and the victim will die in about four days, unless the curse is prayed off by a rival expert, who sprinkles his own special brew on the hot stones and repeats, "This is the *sorosorovi* by which the man shall live."

* The word is pronounced *ndraunikau*, the Fijian *n* being sounded before the d, as usual. For convenience I spell it *draunikau*.

The *sorosorovi*, wrapped in leaves, is taken to the sick man's house and displayed so prominently that the *tevoro* will mistake it for the *draunikau* and float into it. So now he's caught, and the benevolent witch doctor throws the package into water. The devil is foiled, and becomes so angry that he will enter the body of the witch doctor who first summoned him, and this man will die in four days.

Kena balavu is a slower torment; every time you heat the *draunikau* the object of hatred becomes ill; when it cools he becomes better. The patient's sickness is determined by the mixture put in the bottle. If it is a hair from his head, then he will have head-sickness, if parings from his toenails, then foot-sickness, and so on. A rival doctor may lift the spell by finding the bamboo where the hell's broth is buried; he will heat the bamboo and rinse it in salt water, then dose and massage the sufferer with magic leaves. The sorcerer who comes to cure is called the "antagonist." Before the antagonist digs up the *draunikau* he must pour kava for four nights over the spot where it is buried. But if the patient dies, then the witch doctor who cursed him must save his own life by stealing to the victim's body and jabbing it with some sharp instrument, or, after the man is buried, he must pierce the grave with a spear. Otherwise the magician will die in four nights. And if friends wrap a breadfruit in mummy-apple leaves and put it under the corpse's arm, the evil wizard will die of heart disease.

Kena leka is another hot-stone *draunikau*, very swift because the death ritual has been said by moonlight. The *tevoro* floats from the grave to some large tree by a lake or river. *Sova yanggona* is among the most popular of the curses. On the grave of one of the victim's ancestors a libation of kava is poured, with supplications for death. *Tei nia*, the coconut curse, is said to have no antagonism. The operator waters sacred ground with kava, then plants a coconut. When it sprouts he transplants it — and his man is dead.

Ndrimi is a Solomon Island importation. Dip your finger in the magic-of-leaves and touch the hated one. The more potent *ndrimi* doctors can bring sickness by pointing a finger. This power gives Solomon Islanders a prestige in Fiji. If a black boy from Bougainville wants a pretty local girl he merely says *ndrimi* — and gets her.

The classic forms have often inter-pollenized, and Christianity and water-front trading have added comedy. There are a number of specialists who mix whisky and the Bible with their efforts to kill or cure.

Hard liquor is forbidden the natives, so a full bottle adds charm to necromancy. One of our native medical practitioners witnessed the work of an up-to-date witch doctor, called in to antagonize a *drauni-kau*. He prescribed a tablespoonful of whisky and a verse from the New Testament, then began taking his own medicine, in liquid form. As our N.M.P. reported it, "He seemed quite drunk."

This modern technique, plus the dreadful *sova yanggona*, had to do with a recent *cause célèbre*, which I am leading up to. Here the magicians used the lantern-and-mirror technique. They went by night to an ancestral cemetery where one man held a lantern, another a mirror and the third poured kava with the death-prayer. Pleased with his drink, the *tevoro* awoke. . . . Look in the mirror and see his cruel face! See, he is shaking the grave-dust from his body! Now ask him to follow you!

What I have heard has come to me after much curious prying. I had been down there nearly twenty years before I could dig any of it out. It is not general knowledge among the whites. The missionaries should have known, but too many of them never turn to see what's going on behind their backs. Superior natives, especially Fijians, have furnished the most valuable data. Benuve Vakatawa, N.M.P., whose work had been among his people, became quite an authority. Once I asked him how the native reconciled the two religions, the old gods and the new God. Did they not call upon Jehovah and Jesus to protect them from the evil old Fijian divinities? He shook his head. I asked, "What is the true religion in Fiji, Christianity or Magic?" He said unhesitatingly, "Magic." Christianity was just a cloak, held up before European eyes to hide the worship of devils and satanic miracles. The people did not want Europeans to interfere with ancient demonology, he said, but Christianity had its place — it was "society," as the European knows it in his dances, theaters and ouija-board parties. It had an amusement value.

I have told how native medical students reacted to my lectures on magic. Vakatawa, however, thought that the old-time religion was losing ground; that the N.M.P.'s as well as the native pastors were drifting away from it. The pastors, for instance, had learned to keep a little iodine and a few simple home remedies around the house and were going to the N.M.P. for medical treatment. But many of these native Christian teachers still saw the witch doctor first, and only got around to the scientifically trained practitioners when the old way didn't seem to work. However, the Native Medical Practitioner with his better education and better methods is getting about, and modern medicine is slowly commencing to take its place in Fijian lives.

What Pitt-Rivers said in defense of the witch doctors is certainly true of the influence they still exert. The old tribal habit of killing strangers because they had "salt water in their eyes" probably dates back to sorcerers who noticed that epidemics followed visitors. Let's say this for the primitive medicine man. He had his own kit of remedies, many of them effective — probably herbs, massage and hydrotherapeutic treatments. He knew about fractures and their care; even today you rarely find there a deformity following a fracture, yet in native life there are many cracked and broken bones.

The witch doctor still bolsters the old moral code. Vakatawa has seen a witch woman tell a sick girl that the gods had cursed her for loose living. The girl was weak with dysentery and confessed that she had cohabited with more than twenty youngsters. The witch said, "Tell everything or you will die." But the poor child died with the last sin unconfessed. Here was a recorded failure in magic in a district where Vakatawa had his hands full; the inhabitants were going to the witch doctor and the medical doctor at the same time. If the patient recovered the magician was praised; if he died the physician was blamed.

Who is the god of gods to whom the Fijian secretly prays for harm to his enemies? Maybe he is Dengei, most powerful of their evil pantheon — yet who is to say, when there are so many? Several of them appear as great sharks, making mischief, bearing ill tidings. There are the two siren goddesses, Yalewamatagi, who lure handsome young men to sin with them, then leave them dead in the bush. Daucina, an oversexed man-god, is the dread of young girls who wander by night. Death often follows his brutal ravishing.

During the gold rush on Viti Levu in 1932 many natives were afraid to go into the mines. Wasn't it known to all magicians that Tui Mateinagata, the Snake-bodied One who hides in gold, was lurking in a cave at Tavua, and that his seven heads of gold and silver would destroy all trespassers? And the witch doctors whispered that the veins would soon play out, for Tui Mateinagata knows how to hide his treasure. There's the old crab-goddess, too, whose bite is poison; but it is to Dengei, lord of origins and of evil, that the magicians fondly turn. He too is a great serpent, and frequents the caves of Nakauvandra in the north. His magic made and populated Fiji. The god admired two eggs in the nest of the kitu bird, and decided to hatch them himself; the issue was a boy and a girl, whom he separated for five years by the trunk of a giant tree. One day they peeped around the tree and said, "Great Dengei has hatched us that we may people the land." Dengei, complimented, produced growing things for food, flowers for adornment, fire for cooking. The first humans would have been immortal, but they disobeyed their god and were punished with sickness and death.

Another story of origins is not so flattering to the Fijian who, according to the tale, was born before all others. But he acted wickedly and his skin darkened, so he received little clothing. The people of Tonga, — Polynesians, by the way, — were not so naughty with Dengei, who rationed out clothes to them which kept their skins much lighter. The white man was the great beneficiary. He was born last, behaved like a perfect gentleman, and Dengei rewarded him with so much to wear that his complexion became the beau ideal.

The Polynesians of Tonga say that the gods held a meeting and decided to create humanity. They baked three figures of clay. The first to come out didn't seem to have baked long enough; he was disagreeably white and looked half-raw. The second was a Tongan, a beautiful olive-brown, and the gods admired him so much that they forgot the third figure until a voice from the oven cried, "I am burning!" Sure enough, the poor fellow was roasted nearly black; so they sent him west and he became a Fijian.

The absent treatment of sorcerers has no effect on the white man, so natives say; but old Thakombau, inwardly infuriated by a snub, might or might not have been the instrument that changed England's royal succession.

In the early '80's, *H.M.S. Bacchante* brought two royal midshipmen to Fiji. They were the Duke of Clarence, heir to the throne, and his younger brother Prince George, who later became King George V.

Ex-King Thakombau was the nearest thing to a monarch that Fiji could produce, and now he was a Christian. He entertained the visitors at a great kava ceremony where the long line of *meke* singers sat cross-legged and clapped hands to the chanted welcome, "*Mbula, mbula mai!*" Dancers had impersonated the animals, birds and fishes, comedians had impersonated dogs quarreling over a bone, long lines of men had coiled across the green in the contortions of the snake-god Dengei, or undulated in the beautiful surf dance. There was the presentation of the *tambua*. To the Fijian this sacred whale's tooth is the prize of prizes; it is gold, it is magic. If a tribesman offers a *tambua* to you, you may refuse the gift; if you take it you must grant any boon the giver asks — even the murder of your best friend, the yielding up of your favorite wife. There's a long tale of crime and punishment connected with the giving of the *tambua*.

This was royal ceremony. Maybe in the back of Thakombau's sly head there was a picture of another *meke* over which he had presided often in his days of power. The Dance of the Cannibals . . . Massed warriors were roaring out the notes to the boom of heavy drums. . . . Human meat was about to be cooked. . . . High voices in a savage tenor would cry out, "*Puaka balavu!*". . . The bodies were ready for the oven. . . .Then, "*Sa rawa tu!*" — "It is prepared."

The English royal visitors had settled under the flower-pavilion and the makers of *yanggona* were at work. They were making kava by the old method — chew the root and spit the juice into a great bowl. The drink was ready. The honorable cupbearer knelt and received a portion in a polished coconut shell, rose and bore the cup to the more important guest. Offering it, he knelt before Britain's heir apparent. But Clarence, who had seen native saliva go into the bowl, was not amused, so the story goes. He pushed the cup aside and made a wry face. Grim silence followed. The cupbearer rose and knelt before young George, whose tact was equal to the occasion. He took the shell and tossed his portion off with gusto; then reached down and spun the cup across the mat — the highest compliment. Loud clapping of hands with cries of "*Mbula vinaka!*"

The time came for King Thakombau to make his speech. With florid generosity he dwelt upon the greatness of England and the benefits Victoria had conferred upon his people. Then abruptly he turned to the Duke of Clarence and said. "You have been afraid to drink the *yanggona* of Fiji. A true man knows no fear. Because you are not brave you will never become King of Veretania." Then pointing to George, "You are a brave young man, you are not afraid of our customs. You will be the King, and a great one."

The Duke of Clarence died without succeeding to the throne. George became King of England. Yet they say that the native *draunikau* has no effect on a white man, and that puts a big hole in the story. From time immemorial, on the other hand, the chief has had the right to bewitch. Thakombau, on or off the throne, was a king; and there is some reason to believe that he used his ancient right.

A recent case of witchcraft struck in high places and involved two of Thakombau's grandsons, Ratu Pope (pronounced *Pope-ee*) and Ratu Sukuna.

Ratu Sukuna graduated from Oxford with a degree in law. Caucasian in feature, handsome by any standard, Sukuna offered himself to the Empire in 1914; because his Empire refused the service of natives, he enlisted in the Foreign Legion, gained his sergeancy and a decoration, and came home with a well-earned wound-stripe. He was one of the few properly educated Fijians. True, Ratu Devi, his brother, later studied medicine in New Zealand. Devi's annoyance was his great personal charm with women in the wards, who wouldn't let him alone. In Fiji he is now an unusually successful District Medical Officer.

Ratu Sukuna holds important government positions in Fiji, where he is in the anomalous position of one who tries to carry two races on his shoulders. In England and France he adapted himself to foreign languages and customs. In his heart, under the borrowed gloss of alien culture, he is still sufficiently Melanesian to avoid the ancestral graveyard after dusk; the educated half of him scoffs at the idea of ghosts, yet he admits freely that when he passes the family plot in the dark of the moon he feels an unpleasant something clawing at his shoulders.

His cousin, Ratu Pope, was a famous character in Fiji, and was always intimate with Sukuna, whom he admired prodigiously. By nature a sportsman, in youth he was a great cricketer. He was schooled at the Methodist College in Sydney, but had the accent of the English country gentleman. His athletic figure was impressive in the short, white *sulu*, above sturdy bare legs and feet; from the hips up he dressed in the British tradition, sports coat for the morning, dinner jacket or tails for ceremonial occasions — much as the well-born Highlander wears his kilt with all the conventional fixings.

He had the charm and wit which we associate with exiled kings. When the Duke of Windsor visited Fiji as Prince of Wales he was delighted with Pope. Pope was, by courtesy, banished for many years to Mbau, the enchanting island his wise ancestors had chosen for their capital; soft winds cool it, blow away mosquitoes; above the royal *bure* looms a great rock, the little Gibraltar where Grandfather Thakombau was supposed to have been hemmed in before he gave his domain to England. Governor Sir Eyre Hutson decided to exile Pope because he had rather innocently defaulted. As chief of his province he had been Assistant District Commissioner, hence a tax collector. It was his free-hearted Melanesian generosity that put him on a bad spot: When you have money, spend it on your people and your friends. Generosity is godlike, stinginess is for the worms. Let me tell it in Pope's own way: —

"I had no trouble at all collecting the silly taxes. Tax gathering is a royal prerogative. So the Government sent me up a little iron safe, to put the money in, you understand. Well, months went by and one day a chap from the Government came in a launch — rather a blighter, I thought. We had a spot of whisky and a cigar and he said, 'Ratu, the tide's turning and I must be pushing on. I've called, you know, to take back that tax money.' I said, 'I'm rather afraid, old boy, that I can't lay my hands on it now.' He seemed a bit miffed and said, 'But didn't we send you an iron safe to put it in?' 'Oh, yes,' I said, 'it's over there in the corner. If you look at it you'll see that the door's wide open.'"

Royal prerogative had scattered the money in several ways — but always for the good of the people of Mbau. Ratu Pope had set up shower baths in all the village houses, and built a reservoir to supply fresh water. The reservoir remained dry while an offended Government interned Pope on his ancestral isle — until he paid the bill. "It's only a few hundred pounds," he complained, laughing at himself, "and as all I have is invested in rather poor coconuts, I'll be Methuselah, I fancy, before I'm free again." However, a relenting Government allowed him to come to Suva to see the cricket matches — he'd have died without that. Also they let him meet the tourist boats, the best possible advertisement for the Fiji Islands.

When the late Martin Egan and his traveling partner Wallace Irwin

were his guests at Mbau, in 1927, they brought back stories that
illustrated Pope's quick come-back. One night they were sitting by
lantern light under the breadfruit trees, smoking the long Coronas
Pope adored. He said, "It's a bit tiresome, being cooped up here. One
longs for travel. I am very fond of the *National Geographic Magazine*." He called for copies, turned to a back page. "I think I prefer
your clever advertisements. Look at this, for instance" — showing the
New York Life Insurance Company's stock advertisement, the one
with the modest skyscraper. "My word, it seems to go up twenty-five
or thirty stories!" Martin Egan told him that Al Smith and his pals
were building a skyscraper that would be about a hundred stories high.
Pope objected, "But doesn't one get blood pressure, going so high in
a lift?" Egan said that everybody in New York had high blood pressure so what was the difference?

Ratu Pope looked at him gravely. "That fellow Frederick O'Brien
who wrote the White Shadows twaddle visited me last year. When
he left I wondered if all Americans were such damned liars."

He showed his guests Thakombau's cannibal temple, the one he
preserved for sentiment's sake. The shaggy thing, on a base of high
stone terraces, is immensely out of scale with the low village houses.
Pope took an honest pride in the deeds of his grandfather, much as
Grant's descendants might in the surrender at Appomattox. He pointed
out a hole in the ground, right in front of the temple, and said, "The
stone of sacrifice used to stand here. It was built rather like a very wide
gravestone, with a depression in the top for the — er — victim's head.
I gave it to our local church to use as a baptismal font. Would you
like to hear the ceremony of a cannibal execution? Grandfather sat on
the second tier and the people formed a semicircle below. Around the
stone the priests drew lots as to whether the poor fellow was to be
buried or — er — eaten. The latter usually won, I'm afraid. It was purely
economic, you see. Well, four powerful executioners came along
carrying the victim lashed to a plank. They held him in the correct
position, and when Grandfather gave the word they would bash the
fellow's head smartly against the stone. They were so very skillful that
I doubt if the poor chap even felt it."

That was Ratu Pope, playboy king who spoke up-to-date King's
English, liked American magazines, excelled at cricket, brought European ideas to a cannibal capital, and then . . .

Late in 1936 he was taken to the hospital in Suva, far gone with diabetes and cirrhosis of the liver. He should have had faith in the British doctors; he knew them all, and respected their work. As he weakened he called for his wife, Andi Torika, and whispered, "I have been bewitched. They have put a *draunikau* on me." His wife nodded. But who was working the black magic? Pope whispered, "My cousin Sukuna."

The accusation, by way of native grapevine telegraph, soon reached the ears of Ratu Sukuna, who was horrified. Why in the world would he want to put a *draunikau* on good old Pope? What silly nonsense! They had been pals ever since they were knee-high. Sukuna went straight to Ratu Pope's bedside. A gifted speaker with a feeling for the niceties of language, he sat beside the dying man and strove with him, gently. At last Pope nodded and asked forgiveness. No, Sukuna could not have brought about the evil spell. But somebody had paid a witch doctor for this *draunikau*. Yes, agreed Sukuna, and went sadly away from the man who had been cursed — by somebody.

A short time afterward Sukuna was in his schooner, sailing from Viti Levu to Lakeba. Suddenly he called out, "Turn back!" For in the water, skimming along his course, he had seen the family totem shark. That could mean only one thing — death of a near relative. When he returned to Suva, his cousin Ratu Pope was dead.

There followed a battle of magic and countermagic, ghost against ghost, throughout Thakombau's old empire. The persons concerned in it were too noble to be ignored. All this, mind you, happened only about three years ago. It began with Ratu Pope's dying whisper into the ear of his faithful wife, Andi Torika. She belonged to the same *matangali* as Ratu Wailala, powerful sub-chief in Taveuni. To Wailala the widow sent a present of ten *tambuas*, a dangerous gift, for under the eyes of the gods the recipient must grant a favor. Ratu Lala, Lord of Taveuni, was on Andi's bad books; he stood in royal succession; if he lived his son might sit on Pope's shadow-throne.

This was politics, in a conflict between two branches of an old ruling family. Seventy-five years ago it would have meant war. Today it was *draunikau*. Ratu Wailala took Andi's *tambuas*, which had come with a request to put a *draunikau* on Ratu Lala, accused of Pope's death by magic. Wailala was also jealous of Lala's title, and went about the curse in classic style. He presented a *tambua* to another chief, with the request that a *draunikau* be arranged for Lala. This chief took the *tambua* to Mosese, a very able witch doctor.

That was in mid-April, 1938. In the dark of night Mosese and Kalepi, his assistant, with a local chief, stole over to the grave of Ratu Lala's grandfather and carried with them the proper leaves and kava root for the *Sova Yanggona* (the Pouring Kava) ritual. They crouched at the foot of the mound where the dead man's legs would be pointing. Mosese, seated between his two associates, lifted the bowl to his lap, then six times raised it to his head. Kava was made according to ceremony. Now it was ready. The performers clapped three times; Kalepi filled a drinking bowl and presented it to the dead chief with the request that Ratu Lala's life be taken away. Six times the libation was poured on the head of the grave to fill the mouth of a thirsty *tevoro*.

The tattler was a woman who had started out before the break of day to fish for prawns. She lost her way, shuddered by the cemetery, then paused in a paralysis of fear. There were voices by the grave of Nagolea, there was the scent of *uthi*, the graveyard flower. She peered, she saw three crouching figures making *draunikau*. For days she was too frightened to tell.

Then, on April 15, 1938, Ratu Lala went to Suva and grew dizzy as he walked. He knew why, and sent for the powerful sorcerer Ngio from Ngau, whom he employed to combat the evil magic. Ngio told him that his sickness started from Taveuni, and there the *draunikau* would be found. That night Ratu Lala had a dreadful dream. A chief who had been dead twelve years came in and poked him with his walking stick, saying, "Who is this man sleeping in my house?" Lala returned to his home in Taveuni, and when another sick spell came on he heard gossip about the three men who had made *draunikau*. He sent for the sorcerers, ignored their pleas of innocence and had them beaten with ropes. They went to the hospital, still denying their share in black magic. Wailala also feigned innocence, but a constable included him with the others.

Ratu Lala's witch doctor, the gifted sorcerer from Ngau, assembled his colleagues, hoping that their combined magic would offset the dreadful *Sova Yanggona*. One night Lala dreamed that he saw the gods in a meeting; a short man knelt at Lala's doorway, holding up a *tambua* with the request for death. A voice wailed, "Ratu Wailala's *tambua* cannot be returned with mercy on Lala's life!"

It was on September 17, to be exact, when I was with Dr. Strode, inspecting the hospital at Suva. We found Ratu Lala in bed with an abscess of the neck, and his morale completely shattered. He had told the world that he expected to die of a *draunikau*.

On Wednesday, September 21, Dr. Strode and I went to a luncheon at Government House. And what did we see? Sitting calmly beside Mr. Monckton, Secretary of Native Affairs, was Ratu Lala. Only four days had passed since he had about given up the ghost, and now he was in high spirits, telling the Governor fine stories and eating with gusto. His explanation was straightforward. Oh, that witch doctor, Ngio from Ngau, had an antagonism that was too strong for black magic to withstand. He had worked from the Bible, and that was big medicine; he would open the Good Book at random and interpret past, present and future; but invariably he would return to the Gospel according to Saint Matthew, and from that he could foil any ghost or devil that ever flew over Fiji.

Ngio the gospel-wizard came to Suva later and boasted of his holy magic to all and sundry.

Exhibitions of fire walking, given by a priestly cult from the island of Mbengga, are too well known now to permit much discussion. Before these shows became popular features for tourist ships and visiting royalty I saw them dozens of times on their native ground. There have been any number of scientific treatises written to account for the phenomenon of bare Fijian feet which remain unscorched after contact with burning stones. As a physician I have studied the condition of the fire walkers before and after the ordeal, and I have always gone away with the feeling that I have seen a miracle. The old Mbengga myth which says that Ra Duna the Eel taught the hero Koma how to do the trick seems about as good an explanation as any I have heard.

Among the dark islanders magic things are usually grim, although there is a faded myth about the *neli* people, a race of elves with long golden hair. They dance by moonlight, and if one of the golden hairs touches a peeping mortal he forgets how to find his way home. They say that native boys and girls who stayed out late usually blamed it on the *neli*. But belief in the little folk is passing.

The giving of curses is a serious everyday affair. In groups less ad-

vanced than Fiji the witch doctor commits simple murder. I have
mentioned the Poisoner's College at Mou. And there is the celebrated
case of Captain Bell, Government tax collector, who went out in the
Solomons on his unpopular errand and was speared by savages, sent
to carry out a practical *draunikau*.

Inspector Bill Tully was down in the primitive New Hebrides. One
morning his breakfast had been laid on a veranda; below many natives
were gathered for a lecture. Tully sat down to breakfast when a witch
doctor, in full paint, stepped up and flourished a bamboo wand, telling
the world he held the magic that would kill. "Go ahead," challenged
Tully, so the magician tapped his wand on a plate. A little powder
sifted out. Scornfully the young inspector blew it away and ordered
his boy to bring bacon and eggs.

Bill finished his breakfast in full view of a very watchful audience.
So far so good. But he had scarcely bolted the last scrap when he felt
a griping in his stomach; cold sweat broke out, and he knew that he
had turned pale green. He must have been a sickening sight, for the
gawping natives screamed and scampered to the woods. It took Bill
some minutes to recover equilibrium. Then he remembered. He had
taken a rather large dose of calomel, and the darned stuff had begun
to operate shortly after the wizard tapped his plate.

Polynesian magic is not so black, perhaps, as that you'll find all over
Melanesia; but it is always there, hiding behind Christianity or even
higher education. In the Cook Islands a father cursed his pretty
daughter. He had elephantiasis, and she had jeered him for his "big-
leg." "Very well," he said, "and may your especially beautiful legs,
which have caused too much trouble already, swell up and become
big as mine." Accordingly her legs swelled, and she was disfigured.
True, she had been sleeping in her father's house for years, and the
filarial mosquito is no respecter of persons.

The Maoris of New Zealand are superior Polynesians. When I was
making a survey there Dr. Ellison, himself half Maori, told me of a
case that had come under his direct observation. The Polynesians, he
reminded me, are practically all spiritualists, and the average Maori
has forgotten more about spiritualism than the European medium will
ever know. Among the Tohunga cult there is power to bring death
by a secret wish; in the Melanesian *draunikau* the victim is not affected

until he knows that the curse is on him. But the Tohungas never telegraph their punches.

Dr. Ellison told me that a Mr. Haberley, half-Maori and an acquaintance of mine, was interested in the Wellington Museum and in search of fine Maori carvings. The quest took him to the region where Rua the Prophet held forth. Haberley found many neglected and rotting relics, but Rua defied him to lay hands on them. However, the collector took them to the museum. It wasn't long before a serious illness overtook Haberley, who fell back on the customs of his mother's people. He was of the Taranaki Maoris, so it was all in good form when he called in another Tohunga necromancer from Taranaki. Out of Mr. Haberley's suavely educated lips came the command, "Save me if you can, and if you can't, finish off Rua." Very promptly the Tohunga put the bee on Rua the Prophet, who died during my survey of New Zealand. Haberley also died.

CHAPTER II

GILBERT AND SULLIVAN, 1924

My share in the application of carbon tetrachloride had been a decided step forward for me, and I had spent two very busy years in Fiji, campaigning both for cure and prevention. But what most engaged my heart and mind was the plan for an improved medical school for natives. Through thick and thin I preached my crusade and hung to the idea like a terrier. In this plan I saw the only salvation for the island peoples.

In February, 1924, when I set out for a brief survey of the Gilbert and Ellice Islands, the idea was still foremost in my thoughts. That was the first time I took Malakai along, just to show them.

The G and E Group, as it is conveniently called, is satirized by young cadets over the Fiji Club bar as "Gilbert and Sullivan." It has a certain comic appeal. Dr. Walter E. Traprock, America's glamour boy among nature fakers, chose these dots on the sea for his *Cruise of the Kawa,* where the national bird of the Filbert Islands was supposed to lay square eggs and cackle "Ouch!" Robert Louis Stevenson was far more serious, describing scenes of blood and beauty along the threading atolls.

Samoans, who once stigmatized as ghosts and slaves all folk who lived beyond them, called their islands "The World's Navel." In this they were somewhat off their bearings, for their Samoa is a bit too far southeast to center the earth. The Gilbert and Ellice group is strung in faint tattoo marks along the very middle of Earth's belly. In all it covers 1,000 miles of sea, with islands so sparsely scattered that the easternmost is some 600 miles from the westernmost. A white man's government has combined these two archipelagoes, but as a matter of geography they lie about 100 miles apart. The Gilbertese are a Micronesian stock, the Ellice folk are typically Polynesian and have a physique, a language and a social organization entirely different from the Gilbertese.

The Gilberts, which have been the meeting place of the races, have become the meeting place of the anthropologists. Originally, these men agree, the inhabitants were a black, smallish, flat-nosed mouse-eared people, called "the Spider Folk" because their divinities appeared in the form of spiders — also of turtles. The Spider Folk were supposed to be dreadful magicians, therefore they were avoided. Then came the invaders, great of stature, red of skin (that is, light brown), who fought them like devils, but still feared the Spider Magic. Songs survive, telling of the conquerors' prowess as sailors; in them they are extolled as Children of the Sea, Fierce Fish of the West.

The mystery of Polynesian or other Pacific migrations is a puzzle that may never be solved. The Gilberts formed a bottle neck through which many waves of migration must have come from the ancestral home, Hawaiki — from which are derived the modern names Hawaii and Savaii. Some pressure, some social convulsion on the continent must have driven them off of the southeast tip of Asia and sent them out in migratory waves — no turning back, a fierce starving horde in a quest for land and a home in the Pacific. Another stream undoubtedly crossed the Behring Sea and traveled southward along the coast; Mexican legends told of their coming from the north. Probably they passed as far as to South America. Our red Indian race must be the mixture resulting from these invasions. They must have reached the continent across the Pacific, or some must have returned from the west coast of the Americas, to have brought the sweet potato to the Pacific. In this time we can appreciate the thrill of horror that went over the peaceful Pacific islands, waking to see strange fleets of enormous canoes pouring forth their hordes of death-driven warriors.

In the sterile Gilberts the invaders found little that they wanted — except women. They lingered for a generation or so, then conquered the Ellices, captured Rotumah, fought their way into Savaii and Upolu in Samoa.

Tradition and genealogy tell the story plainly. About twenty-four to twenty-eight generations ago a return invasion rolled back from Samoa, moving northward. It overwhelmed the Ellices, but was repulsed by the Gilbertese; except that small Nui in the Ellices still retains much of the Gilbertese language and customs.

In total area the Gilberts won't measure much more than 170 square miles. They hardly seem worth fighting over, these bare coral rocks with an occasional drift of soil where coco palms can just hang on. The people must subsist largely on fish and coconut products; in addition, they have the stringy, unsatisfactory fruit of the pandanus and *babai*. The latter is a bastard taro, eaten in other groups only when famine drives the people to it. Yet it takes a mighty struggle for the Gilbertese to raise even these poor things. Over 28,000 population, crowded together on a little land, are never more than a jump away from starvation. Rainfall is sparse, and on the islands nearest the Equator droughts may last for two or three years; at times even the coconut palms have died, and the people have been reduced to sucking the few drops of moisture from fish-eyes. Even after large churches have been built, with a competent watershed from the roofs, many have died of thirst, because they were afraid to drink the water from holy places.

Yet what did I find in the Gilberts? Very healthy specimens, strapping copper-colored fellows with hair from straight to curly; big-shouldered, but not particularly tall. They had the look of men who grow what they eat, and work for it. Their average health was in contrast to that of the naturally handsome, pale-skinned Polynesians in the Ellices to the southeast. To these food came more easily from a richer soil. And must I say it again? There were fewer missions in the Gilberts, whereas the Ellice Islanders were all nominally Christian — as witness once more the greasy Mother Hubbards, layer on layer, pressing oil and germs into their beautiful bodies. Dirt and laziness seemed to have followed the Cross into charming lagoons which once inspired Stevenson's prose poems.

We were traveling on the High Commission yacht *Pioneer,* where Printer Johann Sebastian Bach's son Bill shared the cabin de luxe with me; we had a bathroom of our own, but when the portholes leaked in one direction the toilet leaked in another. I envied Malakai, who bunked on deck. It was one of the morning's ceremonies for Malakai to come down and see to it that young Bach got his bath. Bill was of the age when all boys are anti-soap, and it was worth getting up to see a cannibal's scientific grandson enforcing hygiene on a great composer's descendant; Bill's treble, "Ow, ow!" against Malakai's grim bass, "You aren't finished till you wash the other ear!"

That got us to Rotumah, an island which for some mystic reason is considered a part of Fiji, but lies nearer the Ellice group. Because public health is concerned with sociology, politics, geography, history and anthropology as well as worms and germs, let me use Rotumah as an example of what lavish Nature can do to a people.

The Rotumans were among the world's laziest, their island among the world's richest. Crops grew while you slept; therefore the natives slept or went to a party. This was coconut wealth, prodigal and wasted. Up in the volcanic mountains it took a little work to get at the palms, so they were never gotten at. Nuts ripened, dropped, rotted or fed the island's expensive pigs. Ask an owner about his wealth in coconuts and he'd guess he had plenty.

They were a delightfully mixed race. Their ancestors had been generous to ships that stopped there to "refresh" their crews. In the unwritten history of Oceania the Tongafiti conquerors used Rotumah as one of the steppingstones that let them spread the Polynesian race over the South Pacific. As I found Rotumah, there was little evidence of that fierce and noble background.

To get things done they hired Fijian labor at eight or ten shillings a day. If a Rotuman ran into debt he merely sent his hirelings out to gather a few more nuts — or that was what they were doing when I got there. Some 900 acres of land produced 2,000 tons of copra annually. Mild efficiency could have boosted the output to 6,000 tons. But why be efficient?

Did you want to buy a pig? Well, he would cost you about fourteen pounds. What a price for a pig! Yes, sir, but remember that he's been fed on very expensive copra, and has already eaten twice his value. But why not fatten him on something else? That would be a lot of trouble, sir, and our pigs are used to copra. There's plenty of copra. And maybe, sir, we couldn't afford to sell you a pig anyhow. We're giving another feast tomorrow, and what's a feast without a pig?

In the Rotuman's Melano-Poly-Malay-European veins there was a dash of Negro, and right royal. In the blackbirding days an Afro-American, probably a slave himself, was cast ashore and proceeded to make himself king. He seemed a kindly monarch, and didn't have the tragic finish of the other Emperor Jones. He taught the people how to work, — they say, — but he's been a long time dead.

When I got there they were all Christians; maybe that was because it was so easy to find a church. The Catholic church had a £600 belfry and a splendid mosaic altar. Things like that were prosperity's blow-off, and when the Rotumans didn't know what else to do with their surplus they built another fine concrete monument. There were monuments everywhere, mortuary, honorary, sumptuary. It was like our wealth-parade in the Coolidge Administration. Rotuman pig-feasts were costly milestones in every life. It cost £100 worth of celebration for a baby to be born, £200 for a man to die, £800 for him to be properly married.

And on the doctor's side of this generous picture I found Rotumah heavily laden with hookworm, yaws, tuberculosis and leprosy. Over 90 per cent of the inhabitants were covered with scabies. A sticky, hot, fly-and-mosquito-ridden island, with hardly a breeze to break the dead monotony of climate. . . . A stone wall, built along the shore road, kept in the pigs and kept out whatever breeze might blow. That didn't matter much in Rotumah, where the people seemed too lazy to draw a deep breath.

Most of the elderly men, by the way, had elephantiasis.

Because elephantiasis was something I had to meet as I went along, it may be apropos to explain what I have mentioned before: that it is not a disease, but the manifestation of a disease. The disease is filariasis, caused by the filarial worm, a long, threadlike creature that lives in the lymphatic glands. The eggs pass into the lymphatic and blood streams and hatch into microfilariae. The low power of a microscope will show them in a drop of blood, but their sex cannot be distinguished. They take on sexual form in the body of the mosquito which has drawn up infected blood, and the mosquito injects them into the veins of the next victim.

Now definitely male and female, they make their way into the lymph glands, grow and breed by millions. The female lays her fertile eggs, which complete the cycle by becoming microfilariae. Because there is much destruction of microfilariae in the mosquito's body, and because there is much wastage of the parasites in the reinfection of a human, the disease is rather slow to develop. Mosquitoes may bite millions of times before enough male and female worms accumulate to cause symptoms. It usually takes years of residence in a mosquito-infected native community before these ideal conditions meet.

With the proper number of parasites comes filarial fever, which is accompanied by inflammation and abscesses in the lymphatic and subcutaneous tissues. The inflammation subsides, but some of the swelling remains in dependent members of the body, arms, legs, breasts, vulva and scrotum. These swellings may be caused by dead filaria worms, which block the glands whose function it is to drain a dependent area; thus the dead worms might impede the return flow of lymph and cause an overgrowth of skin and subcutaneous tissue, slowly piling up to a huge size. The skin grows rough like an elephant's hide, and the monstrous limbs add to the elephantine look.

Filarial fever seems to have little effect on longevity, but causes a lassitude which results in a great labor loss. And when it becomes elephantoid it impedes any form of activity.

An interesting phenomenon is connected with these minute organisms. The activity of the microfilariae which the mosquito puts into the blood stream is similar, in one way, to the habits of the mosquito that has carried them. That is to say, if the mosquito is a night-biter, the microfilariae are active during the night only. During the day they seem to rest quiescent, deep in the recesses of the body. But if they have been introduced by a day-biting mosquito their behavior is just the reverse — they are day-active. In the Pacific the disease is transmitted by the *Culex fatigans* and by members of the *Aedes* family. The Pacific branch of the *Aedes* clan is a daytime feeder while the *Culex fatigans* is a night worker. So afflicted island people suffer from an infection that does twenty-four–hour duty.

In the Ellice group so many elderly husbands were disabled by elephantiasis of the scrotum that they often asked for surgical operations in order to restore domestic harmony; for it was "the fashion" for old men to marry young wives. At Funafuti Dr. Mac Finney told me that one swollen applicant, who had come quite a distance, gave his age as ninety. (They date their ages from the coming of the missionary.) The patient looked a trifle passé, but Mac Finney did a clean job, and hoped he would recover.

On a return voyage Mac Finney saw the old boy coming back on the boat to Funafuti. The ancient confessed that he was on his way to jail. Why? Well, when he got off the boat for home, he felt so vigorous that he had attacked the first woman he saw.

The twin groups, Gilberts and Ellices, were a special problem in the spread of this disease. The dark-skinned Gilbertese, living a hundred miles northwest of the light-skinned Ellice Islanders, seem to have been free of filariasis until modern civilization arrived, although the Ellices had been infected for a long time. The writer found this disease moving slowly northward in the Gilbert group. Primitive savagery and that thin strip of water had long kept the Gilberts in a state of quarantine. Then barriers were down, and filariasis reached the Gilberts. The British administration made several attempts to re-establish quarantine, but conditions made it difficult, and they probably knew that it was a bit too late; the mischief had already been done. Only recently has the machinery of infection been understood. In several groups British medical authorities have made valiant efforts to check the blight. Their problem has been made more difficult by the fact that the principal carrier is the "wild mosquito," a creature that lives and breeds in the bush. The domestic mosquito is easier to run down.

In those ten weeks of inspection we covered 6,500 miles, crossed the Equator six times and touched the globe's four hemispheres. In both groups the islands are so low-lying that a few miles away they are invisible; first you see a plumage of palms, then the border of white sand; then the glory of lagoons, some of them looking no bigger than your hand, others stretching a quarter of a mile, brushing their faint pastel colors against the feathering reef that divides them from the Pacific's royal blue. I love lagoons.

Other white men have loved them too. At Funafuti, for example, one of the boys who helped us ashore had a tinge of red in his hair and said his name was O'Brien. The headman of the town and the native magistrate were also O'Briens. O'Briens flocked from every corner until I hoped to hear a trace of the brogue. But the original O'Brien, who must have been a broth of a boy, had long since passed away and left good deeds behind him. In the wicked blackbirding days he had promptly deserted his ship and taken up with an island girl. He saved the people with the advice that they had better stick by him, as his vessel had come to take them into slavery. Blessings on his red head. To keep his Irish memory green, fifty-four O'Briens flourished in Funafuti, out of 250 inhabitants.

Except for Funafuti all the Ellice Islands had closed lagoons, and to come ashore one must run the surf in native canoes, which usually meant a ducking, and always a wet bottom. I have never seen so many churches to the square mile, for the Ellices are highly Christianized, as witness the layer upon layer of dragging Mother Hubbards that cover the women. On small Vaitupu I counted three expensive concrete churches, and found that the London Missionary Society's Samoan teacher hadn't liked the acoustics of the first two, so he had had a third built to suit his voice. In one year, the Ellice Islands had sent $6,000 to *foreign* missions! And $60,000 had been devoted to the piety of 3,000 inhabitants. Churches were objects of superstitious awe. It would be sacrilege, they said, to drink rain water from church roofs, and something awful would happen if they did; their livers might swell up and burst, for instance.

Up in the Gilberts, on the other hand, they were only a few years removed from the absolute savagery of an era when one island waged fierce war against another. As it was, about half of them were nominally Christianized. The Sunday parade to church was a sight worth while. The native ladies wore short fiber skirts and nothing else, except dinky little English hats perked on top of their bushy heads. For hadn't St. Paul said distinctly that no bareheaded woman should enter the House of God?

At Tabatauea on the Gilberts I made a postmortem examination of a dead king. Since the king had been dead a thousand years, I was not surprised that the results were spectacular.

I was led to a palm-thatched shrine where the bones of Korave, heroic ancestor of the island's chiefs, were held in veneration; legend tells of his gigantic size and heroic strength when he led the people of Beru to the invasion. Before I could be admitted District Commissioner Anderson had to get the consent of Korave's entire family connection. We came in a canoe, waded through mud, and as very wet spectators got at last to the assembly hall, the *muniapa*.

The whole village had turned out. The Gilbertese converse in shouts, and the palaver around us sounded like a football game until Mr. Anderson silenced them to explain how important this occasion was. I sat there, looking as majestic as a large fat man can after a dousing in sea water and a sweaty walk. Then the big question. The exalted visitor wished to see great Korave's bones. Immediately the people of Tabatauea went into noisy conference. Abruptly the huddle parted. A headman came forward and said yes, we could see the bones.

Hung to the ridgepole was a large basket decorated with white shells. Two men carefully washed their hands and lowered the great chief's remains. After one glance at the bones, which they had spread on a mat, I had a keen desire to examine them for myself. But could I? There was a terrible hubbub, every branch of the Korave family yelling at each other. Then the headman said "all right" with variations.

There was a remarkably fine skull, indicating that somebody had had a generous brain pan with plenty of room above the eyebrows. At first I found two thigh bones and two tibias, just as any hero should have. When I got around to the two fibulas, the small leg-bones, I found them smaller than their mates, and was tactless enough to ask if their ancestor didn't walk with a limp. Indignant denials. I was more impressed still when I picked up another fibula and tibia — golly, the man must have been three-legged! Also three radii and extra pelvic bones turned up. It looked as if the late king had three of everything to the common man's two. There was a collection of small ribs that might have fitted a great many people, but if they had been assembled on Korave's skeleton they would have presented a new problem in anatomy.

I disturbed Tabatauea's faith as gently as I could by asking if they were *sure* these bones all came from the same man. They were very positively certain. Hadn't the relics been carefully passed down through the generations? And this simple faith may cast light on some of the holy relics worshiped in our Christian churches.

Anderson's flowery introduction had won much respect for my opinion, it appeared, for they asked what I could tell them about their mighty ancestor. Already they had allowed me to sit, just for a moment, on the enchanted stone where Korave used to sit; it was supposed to have a magic quality of coolness. Sure enough, it was quite cool. So I must tell them of their ancestor. The safe bet was to fall back on generalities. I told them that he was a very big man indeed, much bigger than one of his very large descendants whom I saw in the audience. Quite truthfully I praised the size of great Korave's head; no commonplace man could have worn a skull like that. But my praise of the bones *in toto* made the hit of the day. Not only was Korave remarkable in other things, I said, but he had more bones than any man I had ever seen. After Anderson translated this he told me that they were very grateful for the information, which would be treasured among their legends of the hero.

On Kuria it was my professional duty to confer with one of Robert Louis Stevenson's least appreciated characters, District Commissioner Murdock, who had emerged from the days of piracy. Stevenson had actively disliked Murdock; somewhere in his tales of Apamama and King Timbinoka, the novelist had referred to Murdock as "a rat-faced Scotchman with a secretive disposition," and "Timbinoka's cook." The feud stemmed on Murdock's refusal to tell of a thousand and one nights he had been concerned in. He had plentiful reason to keep his mouth shut, for at the time the other Scot was snooping for adventure stories Murdock was a sort of business manager to the savage king who conquered Kuria and terrorized all surrounding islands. Murdock had also acted as contact man between the terrible Timbinoka and the terrible Bully Hayes, pirate and blackbirder extraordinary.

All the pirate I saw in Murdock was his flaring white mustache; the mouth below it stayed pretty tight, and he only grunted, until I won him over with a fancy new spinner for his fishing. Then he opened up and talked about himself.

As a consumptive lad of nineteen he had come there on a sailing ship and won Timbinoka's heart by cooking him a good meal of vittles, and was hired on the spot. From frying fish he had graduated into diplomacy, mostly with Bully Hayes and his slaving deals with Timbinoka. Hayes, who probably hailed from San Francisco, would clean out whole islands and carry away the inhabitants to die in the fields and mines of Australia, Fiji, South America. As a side line, he would swoop down on the pearl fisheries, gathering the pearls and the girls. Out at sea he would repaint his ship with a new set of colors, to fool pursuing naval vessels. He often baited his trap with pretty girls; the ladies of Aitutaki were especially tempting, so he would take on a load of them and keep them in full view as he loitered by various islands. Then the native men, poor fools, would swim out to be captured and chained.

On one occasion, at least, Murdock went as the King's agent to an island where Bully Hayes had carried a shipload of Timbinoka's warriors to punish some of His Majesty's disobedient subjects. When Bully took captives he had the privilege of buying them from Timbinoka. The monarch prospered on this industry, and was a tyrant of the old school. Once he sent Murdock with 300 slaves for coffee plantations in Mexico and Guatemala.

The King's harem was extensive, and uninvited males were promptly slain. A splendid rifle shot, Timbinoka kept in practice by pinking disobedient wives, usually on the run. He owned every blade of grass, chased competitors out of his trading stores, forbade missionaries. He could be hospitable, but when he said, "Get out!" his guest said good-by. He bought liquor, boats and gadgets wholesale. His grand passion was sewing machines; he had a royal collection in various stages of decay; and a trader with music boxes to sell received a royal welcome. European clothes charmed him, and he couldn't wait for the latest styles to come by boat. So he sent two natives to Auckland to learn tailoring. Alas for Timbinoka's vanity! He got so very fat so very soon that the broadest coats and trousers split on him. He spent his declining years in an ornamental Mother Hubbard. Murdock showed me a photograph of him wearing one; so fat he couldn't walk, he was being carried by eight men.

Once he sent Murdock to investigate a wreck on Apamama. The crew was found in a sorry plight; natives had given them food and shelter — but they had run out of liquor. So Murdock got a large demijohn and filled it with rum from one of the King's hogsheads. He reported this to Timbinoka, who asked, "Where you catch im dis feller rum?" Murdock identified the hogshead and his King said, "Hum hum, hum. One time one feller man belong Sydney he like im one feller head belong kanaka. So he pickle him along dis feller rum."

In short, Timbinoka had severed some enemy heads which a trader bought, pickled and sent to a scientist in Australia. After this transaction the enterprising trader sold the rum back to Timbinoka. The monarch found out about it, so he didn't use the liquor. But the shipwrecked sailors got their share of it and His Majesty was vastly amused when he told them what they had been drinking and saw them get sick. He commissioned Murdock to buy their ship for five pounds. Timbinoka assembled the whole kingdom with everything that would float. By main strength and awkwardness they raised the ship, which was repaired and became the Royal Navy. With a regal gesture Timbinoka sent the crew back to Australia, at his expense.

Before his death the King got his useful cook a job as District Officer, a post he served well the rest of his life. Once, he told me, he found an extremely leprous village, so he burned it down and moved the inhabitants to new quarters. From these particular people, he said, he never heard of leprosy again. It sounds a bit fishy, for to this day no experimenter has found out how the leprosy germ is imparted.

One of Timbinoka's royal descendants was at Kuria when we were there. A big man, he had once been handsome, but he was going to fat and his baldness rivaled mine. His morals were everybody's business, even among the Gilbertese, who are remarkably sophisticated for so primitive a folk. Maybe their vices had drifted in from Tahiti, or from an especially low crop of beachcombers. Possibly the discouragement of the harem system had demoralized them. At any rate, the Royal Descendant was no match for a nice girl.

He served as background for a story that came to me as island tales do. Years later I found a Frenchman, Mr. X, looking for a job, and wondered why a man of his education and intelligence should be out of work. He seemed so pitifully anxious that I pulled wires and got him a job managing a trading station. He didn't keep it very long. And this is why: —

He had been a priest, serving faithfully on these islands. Marie was an extremely attractive half-caste girl in his school. With his Bishop's consent he encouraged her wish to become a nun; she preferred this choice to marrying the Royal Descendant, her family's selection. If Father X was in love with her, it was a passion he religiously denied, although he went on with her education while she was a novice. The European nuns in the convent made her life especially hard; they disliked the idea of a half-caste in the intimacy of full sisterhood. She worked for years as a drudge, scrubbing floors. Meanwhile her family were constantly nagging her to leave the convent and marry the aristocrat.

One night she went to Father X, who had been her only earthly friend. Her tears and his efforts to console her were too much for both of them. The Devil he had downed so long came forth. A few weeks later Father X went to his Bishop, a wise and worldly churchman. "Don't take it so seriously," said the Bishop, "those things will happen. Let me transfer you to Australia until it blows over." "No," insisted Father X, "she's going to have my baby, and my child must be legitimate." The Bishop shrugged it off; he shrugged off Father X's priestly frock, too.

Father X, now a layman, went out into the world. The first thing he did was to marry Marie, and when the baby was born he did his level best to raise and educate the child. That might have been easy in a land where clever white men are scarce, but Mr. X came up against a stone wall. He was an unfrocked priest, he had married a half-caste under queer conditions. He wandered from pillar to post, getting small jobs, losing them, feeding his family as best he could.

Then things brightened for him. With his wife and child he wandered to Australia. A clever agriculturist, he invented a cure for some prevalent tree blight, and cashed in. He was now laying aside enough money to support his family; then he would go back to France to re-enter his order.

An ambassador without portfolio, a doctor without a license, I went over the leper situation on the Gilberts and Ellices. The twin groups had their small share of the disease, but when I spoke to certain authorities and asked for co-operation in the model colony we were planning for Mokogai, the response was not too encouraging. Years later a sort of compromise affair was started on Tarawa on the Gilberts, but it proved such a dismal failure that we finally got our way and had the patients transferred to Mokogai.

On this first G and E survey I had gone on preaching my crusade for modernized native practitioners. Government schools in the two groups were effective, although European training can be overdone; the scope of the native mind is circumscribed by the shadow of the coconut tree. Gilbertese intelligence was high. When I looked over such schools as the one at Bairiki and saw bright faces knit in an earnest desire to learn, and when I observed their steady progress, I knew that here were potential N.M.P.'s. They were the sort who could learn medicine, and could return to their home islands to practise and to teach. Malakai was with me everywhere, an object lesson to them.

At Funafuti one of our old school N.M.P.'s, a giant from Tonga named Josaia, came aboard ship. I had known him as a pharmacist's assistant in Auckland before he took up medicine, and we were renewing our friendship when Josaia paused and scowled at a well muscled

native who had shuffled around me. Josaia said, "You have just in-
sulted the Doctor. You have walked across his shadow." Whereupon
Josaia picked the man up, tossed him over his head and through an
open door. Josaia was something of a storm king, and he was tempo-
rarily out of a job. He was an excellent surgeon. If he operated too
often for tubercular glands in the neck, it was because of his lack
of proper training. In those days many practitioners confused yaws
with tuberculosis and acted accordingly. Josaia had been on the G and
E group for a half-dozen years, working his head off for six pounds a
month.

In the highly missionized Ellices there was much religious confusion, although I cannot vouch for the current story about the London
Missionary Society lady. She kept her girls carefully guarded on a
small island with a lagoon. When several showed signs of approaching maternity she asked who was to blame. "The Holy Ghost," they
replied. Immaculate conception was all right, they thought, and didn't
mention boys who crossed the lagoon in the dark of night.

On the less missionized Gilberts, religious affairs once took a more
violent turn. An island had been having the usual squabble between
Catholics and the London Missionary Society — the latter prevailed,
controlled by native teachers. A native preacher fanned up a religious
mania which swept the people. Self-appointed "Apostles and Angels
of God" took over the works, led by a local "Virgin Mary." The Angels rounded up all the Romanists they could find and killed several.
They had locked up the native Catholic magistrate, were marching on
him with a cross, and would have used it had it not been for the courage
of one villager who went by canoe for the District Officer and white
missionaries. The rescue, a few Europeans facing a mass of howling
savages, required tactful argument. Subsequent investigation, which
resulted in the island's paying a fine, revealed scandal among the Angels. John the Baptist had been intimate with the Virgin Mary.

Where the religious problem puzzled the righteous, the medical
questions confounded the doctor. Ocean Island, one of the world's
great phosphate bonanzas, was headquarters for the Gilbert and Ellice
groups. A British syndicate mined the product. Arthur Grimble, Cambridge M.A., was acting District Commissioner and an ethnologist who
had made useful discoveries.

From the doctor's point of view too many Chinese had been imported to Ocean Island, although the Government's very good hospital was doing more than its share. The trouble was that Gilbertese and Ellice Islanders worked beside the orientals; they caught the imported diseases and carried them home. All through the twin groups I saw evidence of infections which the strangers were bringing to a lovely people. Pathologically, the march of disease was beginning to show. Yaws, which seemed to have been brought by civilization, was making heavy inroads. Tuberculosis was working its way into handsome youths, who lacked the European's immunity. Filariasis was a vexing puzzle, because it seemed impossible to control the mosquitoes that carried it. Intestinal parasites were fortunately few; the people lived near the beaches, and tidewater is Nature's handy sewage system.

In my notebook I jotted down "interesting items": —

Gilbertese stick-throwers . . . One man with wreaths of flowers over head and shoulders, the other with pointed, fire-hardened stick about a yard long. Stick-thrower stood away from wreath-bearer only five yards, poised the stick, and *after it had left his hand* named the wreath that would be cut off. He never missed. If a man is accidentally killed by this, there is no legal penalty. . . .

Concrete-topped graves to keep the *tevoro* from getting out. Graves decorated with dear possessions of deceased, derby hats, bottles, bicycles, spectacles, pipes. Saw one piano. . . .

Wreckage that had floated to Tarawa from San Francisco . . . common occurrence because of ocean currents. . . .

Spiritualistic séance . . . two old men and a hag sit in a one-room native house . . . smoking short pipes, they go into a trance . . . you ask them to make prophecies, simple ones like what's tomorrow's weather or when will the boat get in . . . there's a short silence, then you hear the queerest, eeriest whistling along the ridgepole . . . pipes never leave their mouths. You run out to see if there is somebody on the roof . . . bright moonlight, no accessory visible . . . their prophecies are all wrong. They say it will rain tomorrow, but it's clear, and the boat they name for Tuesday is a week late. . . . Probably ventriloquism. . . .

All over the Pacific you hear brave stories of divers who cut the throats of man-eating sharks. When I ask about it they usually say "They do it in the Gilberts." Made a standing offer of £5 for anybody who could do the trick. No takers. In Santa Ana, Solomons, I once saw boys thump sharks on the nose and take fish away from them. Here, when a canoe upsets, the natives climb into the wet sail, to avoid sharks. . . .

But wonderful canoeing. Government is reviving the old custom of giant building. Saw one 109 feet long, sheer as a knife blade and with an outrigger float big as a young canoe. Could carry 150 natives; same people that once steered vast distances by the stars and with charts made of twigs and string. Gilbertese boys now prefer bicycles, but they're making canoes on a grand scale. . . .

District Officer of Tabatauea has one with accommodations like a yacht. I went out in a 30-footer, very fast. When they tack they disengage the mast in the stern and step it into a socket in the bow. Outrigger lifted clean out of the water, three men on it to keep it steady. . . . I got on to add my heavy weight. As we neared the ship, showing off, the outrigger's framework stood almost upright, like a fence. We scooted around again and one of the native "captains" ran around on the uplifted outrigger. Seeing is believing. The swiftest of these canoes can make 18 knots. At the regatta in Sydney Harbor they rule them out — too fast, they always win. . . .

I also made notes on the white inhabitants, and with a touch of sadness. Many of them had been so long away from the outer world and were so hungry for the sight of new faces that they joined the *Pioneer* at the slightest excuse until the boat looked like a picnic excursion. The resident physician was with us. A young cadet named Jones kept sending messengers, saying that he must be seen at once, as he'd had a serious accident. In mercy's name we went to his island, 200 miles off our course — and found that he had nothing worse than a splinter in his leg and a slightly wrenched back. What he really wanted was an invitation for himself and his wife to join the joy ride, and I certainly sympathized with them. But the ship was already crowded to the gunwales.

The island group's treasurer made the trip to check each island's finances. He was a pleasant man, with a decided character of his own. Somehow I wasn't surprised when he mildly informed me that he was a grandson of the frightful Bully Hayes. I had my phonograph along and delighted him by turning on the latest ditties from New York. Yes, he had a Victrola, he said, but the tunes it played were so mildewed that even his children were tired of them. When he got off the boat I gave him a record of "Mr. Gallagher and Mr. Shean," and he was ever so grateful. . . . About the time our ship was turning back toward Fiji I heard of his death. For some morbid tropical reason he had taken his own life.

His story had a ghostly finish. When I reached my office in Suva I found a letter from him, dated a few weeks back, thanking me for the record. It had given the children so much fun.

I was forced to conclude that white colonists of the Gilbert group needed a doctor more than the natives did. Monotony of life there must eventually depress the health of every European. The food was a trial to the civilized stomach; nothing but coconuts, fish and that stringy, tasteless root, the *babai;* and for variety whatever tinned goods the trader happened to have. If the Devil gave me a bad choice, I should rather live on the Ellices than the Gilberts — and rather on Rotumah than on the Ellices. Those are the three spots on the Pacific that I'm least fond of.

CHAPTER III

A LITTLE KINGDOM AND A GREAT QUEEN

The Chief Medical Officer of the Tongan Islands was away on leave. Dr. Minty, his competent assistant and the only other medical officer on Tongatabu, called me in to assist in an emergency operation on Her Majesty, Salote Tubou, monarch of the last surviving native kingdom on the South Pacific. This was at Nukualofa, the capital.

Dr. Minty had no anesthetist, and asked me to help him out; it was a job I didn't relish, for the responsibility would be pretty heavy, and surgical operations in the hot tropics are always something of a gamble. The Queen lay on a bed in one of the royal chambers. Her beautiful eyes turned toward me, her friendly lips said that she was glad that I had come. Her consort, Prince Tungi, bent his huge Tongan frame over her, consoling her and buoying her courage. It was my first personal medical service to reigning royalty, an adventure among giants, for the Queen of Tonga was two-and-a-half inches over six feet and weighed over 300 pounds. She came of a family of giants; her father had been even larger, and her great-grandfather George Tubou the First had been over six feet five inches and built in proportion. She wasn't fat, either. The breadth of her shoulders showed tremendous physical strength. She was a woman of heroic size, a proper mother of Polynesian kings.

Everything was ready. I said, "Your Majesty, breathe regularly, and deeply. If you find the anesthetic is coming too fast, raise your hand and I'll give you a breath of air; but not too often." I started the stuff going and she raised her hand. I gave her air and started again. Again she raised her hand and kept on raising it until I said as deferentially as I could, "Remember, Your Majesty, there is no royal way of taking an anesthetic." After that she was still as a mouse, an ideal patient. Her marvelous chest expansion, breathing in the vapor, was like the opening and shutting of a great accordion; her chest seemed to lift a foot.

Getting her in her bed was no job for a weakling. Prince Tungi was for carrying her in his arms; he was quite capable of it, but I wanted to keep an eye on her breathing and said, "Don't be a hog. Tungi, move down and give me a share." My arms hardly reached under her shoulders and I was relieved when the move was completed safely. She was one of the handsomest, biggest women I have ever seen.

Minty's rapid, efficient job should have been nobody's business; but an operation on royalty is always of great national moment, and the kingdom was agog. Especially in the European section; for Tonga was prosperous enough to employ a great many foreigners to fill government posts. Next morning Bob Denny, the picturesque Scottish postmaster, gave me the first inquisition. "Doctor, didn't the Queen have an operation? What was it for?" I said, "I only gave her the anesthetic." He couldn't understand my obtuseness and shouted, "BUT WHAT WAS THE MATTER WITH HER?" I said, "That's the Queen's and Dr. Minty's business." I knew that if he asked Minty he would be rounded up with a short turn.

In the South Pacific, where everybody's business is your own, Aesculapian secrecy was never quite understood. When Postmaster Denny found that I wouldn't talk about the royal operation he generously forgave me by offering me some pamphlets addressed to a lady who was away. "They might be interesting," he said, "but you'd better get them back in a week. She's due about then, and she's cranky about her mail."

For my share in the much-discussed operation I was rewarded in royal Tongan fashion. The house we lived in was loaded down with gifts of appreciation: rolls of fine tapa, huge chunks of roast pork and quantities of selected Tongan fruit.

These gifts had become familiar to me; in May of the previous year I had accepted an invitation to make a hookworm survey of the Kingdom of Tonga. I spent three months there the first year of the survey. My family and Malakai accompanied me. We showed the Foundation film "Unhooking the Hookworm" with great effectiveness in the local movie theater to large crowds which assembled, docile to the Queen's command. In the remoter areas we fell back on the hookworm charts. The response in specimens was splendid. This was what the Tongans liked — they were already interested in health, and here was something new for nothing. Our examinations yielded little note-worthy in the way of hookworm disease. The infection rate was low and the number of worms per head was low. I judged this was because the Tongans still obeyed the old Polynesian tabus about the disposal of excrement; we also found that most houses in community groups had latrines of a sort, though these were inadequate. But their water supplies were awful. There are almost no running streams and the drinking water was largely obtained from shallow wells, which were subject to great contamination because pigs, fowls, horses and humans shared them.

The pig question came up right away. The Chief Medical Officer wanted me to say that pigs carry hookworm to human beings, and that theory ran afoul of my conviction to the contrary. The C.M.O. and I ceased to be friends after I refused to agree with him. He was a Scot. Scots have about the best medical minds. When they find that a the-ory is right nothing can budge them. You seldom run across one who will devote all his native stubbornness to a shaky hypothesis.

Well, I'm a bit stubborn myself, and on the question of pigs I had my reasons. One of the weaknesses in native diet is the shortage of meat, fresh or otherwise. Europeans coming into native life immedi-ately want to put pigs in corrals. I knew an Irish doctor who didn't rest satisfied until he had enforced such a regulation. He hailed from a land where, according to legend, "they keep the pig in the parlor"; but to the native such intimacy isn't good form. My observation has been that when pigs are enclosed in the corral, the meat supply soon runs out. Why? Because one man objects to feeding the other man's pig; keep them in a common enclosure and they are gradually killed off, with no replacements. When pigs are allowed to run loose in the vil-lages they pick up their own food, or most of it. This is the native way. Much as I have looked into the subject, I know no Pacific island disease that is carried by pigs. Had I agreed with statements to the contrary, to satisfy the esthetics of a few foreigners, I could not have been honest with my own convictions.

Tongans are notably robust and resistant to disease, as we shall see, and I attribute it in no small measure to a generous supply of pork, added to their other foods.

Tongan good feeding and abundant hospitality almost made a wreck of a visiting Fijian football team. I saw the first match of that series,

much to my sorrow, for I am Fijian to the bone. When the boys came
to Tonga they were regarded as much the superior team, and when
I talked with Native Practitioner Savanada, one of the players, all was
confidence. But on the field of glory Fiji was dull and heavy as lead.
Then the saddened Savanada told me why. On the thirty-six–hour
steamer trip to Tonga the Fijians had had little to eat. The minute
they stepped ashore they were confronted with a feast. Poor, starved
Fijians! There were more roast pigs than they had ever seen at one
time, heaped up with trimmings of yams and succulent breadfruit,
and chickens and fish to fill in the crevices.

When they went on the field they were a little like Mark Twain's
Jumping Frog of Calaveras County, artfully weighted down. The
crafty Tongans, by the way, played on empty stomachs. All over the
South Pacific, a sharp trick like this is known as "Tongafiti."

Tonga won the second game, too, with me yelling my head off for
the glory of Fiji. This time Savanada explained it away with a dignity
worthy of his chiefly rank: "Queen Salote was present, and it wouldn't
have been courteous for us, as her guests, to win." But Fiji won the
last game hands down, and every time the Tongan team came to Fiji
the kingdom's athletic pride was lowered a hitch.

Speaking of "Tongafiti," as far as I can find out the word is a com-
pound of *Tonga* and *Viti* (Fiji), and it is probable that the Pacific's
ancient conquerors took Fijian warriors along with them in the days
when they were the Huns and Vandals of their time.

Sikiana had been cleaned out by "Tongafiti" people; there was evidence that they had fought their way via the fringing Polynesian islands
to the west, conquering as they went; at the tip of the Solomons the
people of little Rennell Island had beaten these warriors by luring them
up on the sharp coral, which mangled their bare feet. One end of
Rotumah is still settled by a chief who is descended from Tongan invaders, so is one end of Mangaia on the Cooks. For two or three centuries the Tongans made slaves of the Samoans; at last Malietoa drove
them off, and they promised never to return except in peace. Then
Tonga forgot the arts of war, but in the seventeenth century it became
fashionable for their chiefs to go over to Fiji and join forces with
one or the other of their warring provinces. These trips were a sort
of Grand Tour, a part of their education. They were always welcome

because they were unafraid of charging a fortified position, something that the Fijian always dreaded. Chief Ma'afu, descending on Fiji, would have unseated Thakombau had the British not intervened.

Contact with Melanesia has given the Tongan a slightly browner coloring than the golden skin of the pure Polynesian; those portions of dark Fiji where Tongan warriors and mission teachers were most frequent can still be picked by lighter skins and other Tongan stigmata. Tongans have a stoutness, a fiber, that excels that of all other Polynesians. In many ways they are the superior natives of the Pacific.

Captain Cook discovered them in 1770, although seventeenth-century navigators had sighted them. Because of their kindly reception Cook called them "the Friendly Islands"; he didn't know that he would have been butchered and his boats seized if the chiefs had not disagreed among themselves. A few years later the *Port au Prince* was less lucky. A young boy appropriately named Mariner was the only one saved; Finau Ulukalala, the leading chief, happened to take a fancy to him. Mariner lived there for four years, and after his escape a Dr. Martin took down his enthralling story, which reads like a dime novel.

The missionary followed the white trader, and Tonga was a cockpit for religious factions. The last chapter of that bitter feud was written as late as 1924. It was Methodist against Catholic at first; finally Methodist against Methodist — actually Wesleyan against Wesleyan. Taufahau, a giant chief of the Kanakupolu family and destined to be king, first saw the writing on the wall and joined the Wesleyans; by that time the Tongans had lost their old religion, the worship of Polynesian deities. Taufahau may have yielded to a greater magic than he knew. He may have become a true Christian, although this seems difficult to believe. Certainly he seized the opportunity to weld the group into a political unit. A great warrior, a great strategist, a great man, he was enthroned in 1826 and lived until 1894. Under his kingship all Tonga became Christian, mostly Wesleyan.

In his later years, around the seventies and eighties, scandals arose in the Church. Much money was exacted in religious offerings, and after the missioners had feathered their own nests, the balance was sent out of the country. Tonga, mind you, was just emerging from the Stone Age — yet she was supporting foreign missions! Finally Taufahau, now King George the First, decided to head his own state Church, the Free Church of Tonga. There were cruel persecutions of Wesleyans who wouldn't recant; many were killed, thousands driven out of Tonga. George the First had a renegade Wesleyan missionary named Baker as his guide, and the guide became Prime Minister. Although Prime Minister Baker served the kingdom with some permanently wholesome laws, his rule degenerated in the course of years. As much appears to have been wasted through him as through the former rule of the missions, and things came to such a pass that the British High Commission had to intervene and institute a protectorate over Tonga. The Free Church pursued its erratic way through the reign of George the Second of Tonga, who died in 1918, and into the reign of Queen Salote. In 1924 she joined the Wesleyan Church, and the Free Church ceased to be Tonga's official faith. The Free Church left a bad financial record, and had little regard for honest business practices. For many years Tongan religion had been largely a matter of politics. Whenever a monarch switched his religion there had been a corresponding switch in the opposition to the Crown.

The Tubous are the sole survivors of numerous native dynasties which the first white men found in the Pacific. The Tongan kingdom has outlived the greedy gobblings of Western powers, and the people have kept their identity through every political crisis.

The Tubous have a past longer than that of any other ruling dynasty today. Their kings first came from Eastern Samoa, probably from Ta'u, which seems to have been the cradle of great Polynesian kings. The Tui Tonga was the spiritual and temporal head of the state, and Aho'itu was the first of the Tui Tonga. A later Tui Tonga wearied of the double burden and turned temporal affairs over to his brother Tui Haatakalaua, and Haatakalaua finally passed his power over to another brother, Tui Kanakupolu. When King George the First took the throne, he abolished the title of Tui Tonga. Joeli, last claimant to that ancient title, died after my first visit to the kingdom.

This seems a pretty sketchy way to pass over a thousand years of history. When I first saw Tonga its two great historical strains were joined in marriage. The Haatakalaua and the Kanakupolu families united in Tungi and Salote. The royal wedding was in 1918. With three sons the dynastic succession seemed safe.

In 1924 the reigning couple were more highly educated than most of their subjects. Salote had studied in Auckland and Tungi had gone to an excellent school in Sydney. Ata, one of the great nobles, had also been to Sydney for his education. Otherwise only a few half-caste children had enjoyed foreign advantages. Generally speaking, the people knew only a few words of English.

The Tongans were great nationalists with a mortal dread of being taken over by one of the Powers. They were even afraid of England, although they seemed quite safe in that direction. The British protectorate over the kingdom was (and is) a very light one. Great Britain was selecting Chief Justices and Auditors for them, and quite naturally the Tongans paid the salaries. The British Consul and Agent acted as adviser to the Queen, and it was his duty to approve any financial expenditures. With these restrictions, Tonga is today a free constitutional monarchy, with a parliament and the Queen's privy council.

The point of friction has always been the British Consul's right to veto expenditures. If he was well trained in the British civil service the plan worked out well. But the job occupies not more than an hour of the Consul's day, and too many of them have used the leisure to indulge in petty statesmanship and tyrannies far beyond their official authority.

The financial veto is a powerful weapon, but the check in expenditure has been Tonga's salvation. It is hard for Western civilization to understand the Polynesian's utter lack of money sense — or the Melanesian's, for that matter. From early childhood the European has learned the art of getting and spending. Not so the Pacific Islander. Although in many ways they may excel us intellectually, it is next to impossible to make them understand that coined metal isn't something you pick off trees and throw around for the moment's enjoyment. It's all great fun, while the party lasts. Only by hard knocks will the native learn money economy. Oftentimes his education comes in jail, where he can study at leisure the disadvantages of Western methods over his old-time communal system.

Wild extravagances of Church and State forced Great Britain to set up a protectorate to prevent Tonga from falling into other hands. The British Consul, with keys to the treasury, had to span the great void which is the Tongan money sense. Today I know of no other nation so financially sound as Tonga — no debt, internal or external, and a surplus of £150,000, about twenty-five dollars per head. For the United States this would be a capital of well over three billions, with no debts at all. Not so bad for Tonga, a land that saw iron for the first time about 250 years ago. And the kingdom's wealth is well distributed, too. Every Tongan male at the age of eighteen receives from his government eight-and-a-half acres of fertile land and a town lot to build his home on.

The white man goes through these islands and sees many things that may be comic from his biased viewpoint. But shouldn't we turn the laugh on ourselves in the light of New Deals and Planned Economies? While Western civilization is eating its accumulated fat and beginning to gnaw its own vitals, I wonder if some Tongan Brain Trust might not lead us out of our wilderness of bureaucratic taxes, and teach us what the Abundant Life really means.

In 1924 Queen Salote was in her young twenties, but her mind was matured by experience in government, and she was quick to see the help our Foundation could give her little realm of 25,000 souls. We were working like devils to give Tonga an adequate water supply, and I wore my diplomacy threadbare trying to convince the Scottish C.M.O. of the obvious need. Although I am a chronic admirer of the Scots — and haven't I seen them survive and carry on in posts that would have demolished a less sturdy breed? — this Medical Officer remained a prickly thistle that drove me to distraction. I'm a peaceable man, as the Irish say. Certainly I've managed somehow to get along with a great variety of human types.

But not with this one. The few faint hairs that remained on my head bristled at the sight of him. He bothered those hairs worse than the Tongan flies that swarmed around breakfast at Bill Smith's boarding house; there I learned to cover my bald spot with a knotted handkerchief. No handkerchief could shield me from the Scot's irritating perversity. I had to confer with him, of course, or I couldn't have worked at all. He was a very competent surgeon, particularly skillful in eye surgery — a rare accomplishment in the South Pacific. As a health officer he had done some splendid work, especially with yaws. But I had got off on the wrong foot when I disagreed with him about pig hookworm. His great fault — if it be a fault — was his firm conviction that he was a final authority on everything.

One of his assistants, a brilliant young fellow who suffered as long as he could endure it, then accepted a high post in Australia, gave me all the help he dared, and that was useful. But the Scot had an anti-Lambert complex. We were trying to install model latrines all over the Tongan Islands, and we had to choose a type that met with his approval. Nothing I offered was satisfactory, and it was impossible to find out what he wanted. If I hadn't finally resorted to a "Tongafiti" trick I feel sure that nothing would have been accomplished. At last, in complete despair, I went to him with one of the plans he had rejected and said suavely, "Well, Doctor, I've finally come around to your original idea, and I'll go with you on this plan." Without a murmur he accepted it. I had discovered a system.

Probably Tonga was fortunate in having so good a man at the helm. For the kingdom had been hospitable to some quacks, both clerical and medical.

A prominent trader was saying good-by to friends at the boat and remarking, "Glad you're going while you have so good an impression of the women," when a well-dressed stranger with a lady on his arm strolled up and said, "No man is good enough for a good woman." This knightly champion's name doesn't matter, except that it went on the Tongan medical register with the string of initials "M.D., Phy. D.O., M.S.R.U.I., S.A. and Harvard University D.O." The S.A. might have meant something, but his fantastic list of degrees remained as much a mystery as why the Tongan Government appointed him to a high medical post. Later on he admitted to me that he learned all his medicine as a hospital wardsman.

He was the only physician available when Queen Salote gave birth to the Crown Prince. His elegant bedside manner combined with his official prestige had elevated him beyond criticism. The accouchement took place, according to tradition, in the royal suite; following old custom, the great nobles waited in an antechamber to hear the birth proclaimed. Now and then the much-titled physician would pop in to take a look at his patient, then pop out to smoke a cigarette and shoot his cuffs. Finally a capable half-caste nurse, who had been constantly in attendance, poked her head out and announced that the baby was coming. The titled one hurried to the bedside a minute late; the child was already born. He stepped over to the nurse and whispered confidentially, "And what shall I do next?" It was his first obstetrical case.

Well, the nurse must have taken care of it, for when I was in Tonga the Crown Prince was a charming little boy. The obstetrical curiosity was not dismissed; he served the kingdom for quite a while. When Fatafehi, father of the late king, finally succumbed to his family's hereditary disease (old age) our hero was on something of a spot. He was told of one royal funeral where the body lay so long awaiting the family's arrival that the pallbearers had had an unpleasant task in bearing away the casket. It was decided to embalm the remains of Fatafehi — which stumped the poor fellow again. Finally he compromised by filling the lead coffin with formaldehyde solution. On the way to the grave the pallbearers wondered why it was too heavy to manage. They had to bore holes in the side and let out the solution before they could lower the coffin into the grave.

At last the good doctor was faced by a flu epidemic. He couldn't handle it, so he went to Fiji for "medical supplies," and never came back. I didn't know much about him when he came around to me in Suva and impressed me with his charming manner. I wanted a competent doctor to take my place while I was home on leave, and his fine talk almost decided me to take him on. "All I want," he said, "is a chance to treat the natives. Just for my board and keep. I love the natives." When I asked the Tongan Consul about him the answer didn't quite satisfy me, so I changed my mind.

He went the way of all flash: a very minor sanitary inspector in Fiji; then a job as little doctor on a little ship; then a move back to Tonga to settle down to beachcombing with a native wife. He could at least lay some claim to having brought a royal heir into the world. Even though he hadn't known what to do next.

If the Saga of Tropical Medicine has a comic section, some of the Tongan M.D.'s legitimately graduated from the pick of the universities deserve a place in it. One very able physician was a practical-joke addict. In his office was a skeleton, jointed and movable, with which he scared natives by jerking the strings. At night he would rub phosphorus on his bony playmate and take him driving in his buggy; the ghastly hell-light threw the town in a panic. When old Bridges was Collector of Customs the fun-loving doctor brought in a "drug order" which included a great many household furnishings. To dodge duty, he gave the furniture large Latin names: like *Carpetorum brusselorum* and *Hattus rackus*. This got by the native inspector, to whom Latin was all Greek, but Collector Bridges stopped the racket.

They told me of another doctor who was anxious to become C.M.O. Over in Haapai he quarreled with Chief Israeli, who was a great swell in Tonga and closely related to the King. Some minor skin disease took Israeli to this doctor, who found his revenge in saying, "Man, you've got leprosy!" He kept poor Israeli interned for six months outside the village and started a dicker with the Tongan Government. He craved promotion to Chief Medical Officer, he said, and if they handed him that, Israeli would be pronounced cured. The doctor got what he wanted, and proclaimed that his treatment had saved the patient from a leper's tragic end.

When I began hookworm treatments the royal family were the first to take the medicine, as a good example to Tonga. For me that was a delicate assignment. The household numbered forty in all, for Tongan hospitality kept the palace bulging with relatives and near-relatives. Keeping up the establishment must have been quite a drain, although Salote had a competent income and Prince Tungi was well-salaried as Premier; both had landed estates. But they were rich relations to two large families, and feudal tradition imposed on their generosity.

Feudal tradition encountered modern medicine when it came to dosing the Queen. The tetrachloride had to be mixed in a special mug; for custom demanded that no common mortal should eat or drink from any dish or cup that royalty had used. However, the Queen and Consort took their medicine gracefully, and allowed themselves to be photographed taking it. An anxious populace waited outside the palace, and there was a murmur of relief when it was announced that our medicine had taken its normal course.

As a special favor I was given "back-door privileges" at the palace, and it was an honor I valued highly. Here on quiet mornings I would find Salote sitting in loose, easy clothes, a relief from the British-made silks and satins of her state appearances. Our talks got me very close to her quick mind and her eager desire to learn what was best for her people. Taufaahau, the heir apparent, and his two brothers would be playing around the place. Sometimes I would see them riding the giant turtle which has never left the palace grounds since Captain Cook brought him from the Galapagos in 1773, a gift for the King of Tonga. I always had chocolate bars or some other sweet for the children to nibble when they decided to sit on my knee. That was sixteen years ago. The turtle is still alive and the Crown Prince has graduated with honors from Sydney University. He is going to Oxford to study law and anthropology. Salote and Tungi have a right to be proud of this tall, splendid young man. Lord, how time has slipped along. . . .

Many and many times I talked my plans over with Salote, and especially my fixed idea that there must be a modernized Central Medical School in Fiji. She was a constructive listener. She looked upon the people as her children, and was grieved by the tricks that had been played upon them by alien races. Once I asked her if politics and religion weren't the same thing in Tonga, and she said: "Doctor, I think you're about right."

A true Christian, she had an intense admiration for Queen Victoria. Once a year, robed for the occasion, she would open Parliament, and be seated in the red chair of state, with her adored Tungi at her side. She insisted on ceremonial black for the parliamentarians assembled, and before the great day there was a tremendous scrambling for European clothes. Once a small boy scampered into a trader's store and demanded a pair of silk stockings. He was a Queen's page and had to put on full regalia.

Ancient suits were hired or borrowed for the occasion; dress suits, dinner jackets, antique cutaways and obsolete Prince Alberts, anything so long as it was black. Once I contributed my winter-weight dress clothes to an appealing noble and watched him join the long, sweaty line of lawgivers that filed in to the boiling ceremony. And the minute it was over ministers of state sneaked away crosslots, suffocating coats over their arms, tight shoes in their hands. They were stealing home to their comfortable and sensible *lavalavas*.

Major-General Sir George Richardson, Governor of Western Samoa, told me of his presentation at court when the Queen was very new to the throne. Richardson, a crusty Britisher who had gone through the mill at the Court of St. James's, may have exaggerated the incident. In the presence of young Salote, he said, he had approached the throne, made the proper bow and backed the prescribed distance. Out of the silence the Queen clapped her hands: "Johnnie, bring the gentleman a whisky-soda!" She hadn't yet learned all the European formalities, but hospitality told her what a Britisher seldom refuses.

Salote, with the pride of an ancient dynasty behind her and the problems of a modern world facing her realm, was the connecting link between the old and the new.

Strangers, dropping off at Nukualofa, have looked over the ancient stone relics there, have wondered at their monumental size and have heard, perhaps, smatterings of their legend. They have seen the great Haamonga (Burden on the Shoulders), a trilithon with side pieces fifteen feet high; one piece is twelve feet wide by four feet eight inches thick, the other is nine feet seven inches wide by three feet eight inches thick. These are above-the-ground measurements, as they are set very deep. They stand ten feet apart and are grooved at the top to support a crosspiece that is fifteen feet long, five feet wide and twenty-one inches thick. These stupid, literal measurements describe a colossus, and nobody knows where the stones came from. Tradition says that they were brought from Wallis Island in ancient Tongan canoes.

The great squared arch is the gateway to the old sacred *marai* (family ceremonial ground) where the Tui Tonga worshipped until the rise of temporal power moved them to another *marai*, a few miles away. On the old *marai* where the Burden on the Shoulders stands there is another relic important to the lost religious history of Polynesia. This is called the Leaning Stone, and is a slablike pillar nine feet high, five wide, two thick.

The Tongans, you must remember, were fast losing their old religion when the white man came. They knew that the trilithon and the leaning pillar were of sacred memory, but what they signified was not clear. It was not until I visited the Cook Islands, where I saw similar relics and heard the young chiefs recite their poetic myths, that I realized what Tonga's stone relics signified in the old paganism.

Almost everywhere in Polynesia the symbols were the same. The arch represented Hina, goddess of fertility, and the leaning pillar was Tangaloa her husband, god of life's origin. After I found similar pillars and arches on the Cook Islands I concluded that Tonga's ancient worship must have been phallicism. I submitted my theory to Prince Tungi and he consulted with keepers of the old tradition; they all agreed that this was probably the explanation. Tungi told me that there were caves on Tongatabu which were called Hina because of their archlike shape, and that on Vavau there was a very realistic cleft stone, also called Hina.

When I describe the Cook Islands I shall elaborate a little more on the Hina (or Ina) and Tangaloa myth, for the Cook Islander still remembers.

Tonga's third wonder is the Royal Tombs, the Langi. There are five Langi, generally pyramidal in shape, and covered with from three to five layers of stone. They measure about two hundred feet on a side; their outer stones, some of them twenty feet long, are nicely squared and fitted. Each was built for a Tui Tonga.

During one of our back-porch conferences Queen Salote told me that she had recently allowed one of her relatives to be buried there, because he was of the Tui Tonga line. The Queen was also of the same ancient family, so she was the only witness, except the Haatufunga, honorable buriers of the royal dead. The chamber into which the body was to be lowered was deep down in the center of the Langi. It was covered with an immense slab that had lain there four hundred years, and was raised with great difficulty. They found a vault, about twelve feet long by four wide and three deep, walled with artfully fitted stonework.

I beg Her Majesty's pardon if I misquote her, but this is what I remember her saying: "I saw the body go down into the dark vault. When it was first opened we found the skeletons of three men. One lay face down, and must have belonged to a very powerful man. The other two were more slender, and their bones showed that they died in a sitting position."

The seated skeletons were probably those of the Haatafunga, whose duty it was to prepare the bodies and wrap them in fine mats. In the old days they were permitted to remove the costly cerements and take them away as perquisites of office — if they could work fast enough. They were given just the time it took to poise the slab over the tomb, and lower it. The pair squatted on either side of the noble skeleton had been a minute too slow, and had been sealed in.

Later Tonga grew more humane, and the funeral workers were not permitted to touch the mats; they were given safe exit before the lid fell. Certain valuable things, equivalent to the funerary spoils, were set aside as their reward. The Queen told me that Joeli, lineal descendant of the Tui Tonga, had opened a tomb a short time before and found a beautifully carved ivory pillow. She had wanted to present it to the scientific world, but Joeli had re-interred it.

The Tongan people, always having lived under communism qualified by an aristocracy, still offered an example of socialized medicine in daily practice. Sickness was treated free. If it was often not treated at all, that fact was partly due to the wide scatteration of little islands, and partly to the incapacity of an understaffed medical department. Voyaging around the small, forgotten islands I groaned over dirt and flies and the ignorance of simple hygiene which spread yaws, dysentery and typhoid. General weakening from these diseases had made the people easy prey to the influenza epidemic of 1918, which swept away eight per cent of the population. What they needed most was proper soil sanitation, proper water supplies, *and education in these necessities*. So many deaths were unattended by a physician that it was difficult to estimate the mortality figures covering typhoid, for instance.

The question of infant mortality — deaths of children under five — was to grow less crucial year by year. I have learned that by stimulating one branch of public health the physician is apt to stimulate many others. Our hookworm campaigns in Fiji, for example, worked toward the reduction of infant mortality; from 200 per 1,000 it fell below 100, and in one banner year was as low as 89.

The Tongans were a pithy breed with a will to live and an eagerness to learn — if you got around their ancient prejudices and the new peculiarities imparted by various mission sects. Proselytizing Mormons and Seventh Day Adventists had confused the issue. The Adventists had been popular when natives found that this faith gave them two workless days a week. They were less ardent believers, however, when their preachers forbade smoking and the eating of pig. The Mormons were anti-tobacco, too. Visitors at the mission stations of either sect had to keep cigarettes and tobacco locked away from light-fingered converts.

I sometimes wondered if civilization had done these people any good at all, except to shake off the abuses of the nobles. The ancient communism with nobody rich, nobody poor in a self-contained island group that fought away intruders — would that be the simple answer today? Over a hundred years ago Mariner thought so, when he asked good Dr. Martin to write into his book: "Captain Cook brought the intermittent fever, the crooked backs and the scrofula." (Probably tuberculosis.)

And Vancouver brought the bloody flux, which in a few months killed a great number of them. . . . To any man of humanity, nothing can be more distressing than to cast his eye on the island of Otaheite, a spot blessed by nature with everything that can make life pleasing . . . but now become a scene of general mortality, and a prey to disease, which to all human appearance, will in a few years render it a desolate wilderness.

But when you run a thumb over Mariner's *Tonga Islands* you are forced to believe that the old cures were sometimes super-Spartan, although the savage doctors recognized tetanus long before the discovery of bacteria. Says Mariner: —

> In all cases of considerable wounds produced by pointed instruments the patient is not allowed to wash himself until he is tolerably well recovered, nor to shave, cut his hair, nor his nails; for all these things are supposed to produce *gita* (tetanus).

Mariner reported that convalescents "happening to wash themselves too soon, spasms supervened, and death was the consequence." Observers told him that "wounds in the extremities . . . are liable to produce tetanus. . . . They never allow females to be near men thus wounded, lest the mere stimulus of venereal desire should induce this dangerous complaint. . . ." One man was "eight months without being washed, shaved or having his hair or nails cut. . . ."

Now for the old treatment of tetanus, an art they learned from Fiji, where warlike habits made *gita* very common.

> . . . consists in the operation of *tocolo'si*, or passing a reed first wetted with saliva into the urethra, so as to occasion a considerable irritation and loss of blood; and if the general spasm is violent, they make a seton of this passage, by passing down a double thread, looped over the end of the reed, and when it is felt in the perineum they cut down upon it, seize hold of the thread . . . the thread is occasionally drawn backwards and forwards, which excites great pain, and an abundant discharge of blood . . .

Several times Mariner saw this cruel operation; the jaws, he said, were violently closed for a few seconds, but lockjaw never developed. The recoveries, he thought, were about forty per cent. They also let blood in this way for ridiculous reasons, like wounds in the abdomen; but they had a theory (rather in line with some of our advanced scientists) that passing a reed into the urethra had a rejuvenating effect on the debilitated. The King of Tonga, in Mariner's time, had this operation performed "and two or three days later he felt himself quite light, and full of spirits."

The operation called *boca* was castration in cases of enlarged testicles (probably elephantiasis). Tourniquets were skillfully made of native cloth and the instruments were razor-edges of split bamboo. Dr. Martin wrote: —

A profuse hemorrhage is mostly the consequence of this operation; it was performed seven times within the sphere of Mr. Mariner's knowledge . . . to three of which he was witness. Not one of the seven died. . . .

Sounds gory enough, doesn't it? But those native sorcerers, working with tapa and banana-leaf bandages, cutting with split bamboo, displayed an art and a knowledge of surgery which had been cultivated through generations of experience. This wasn't just voodoo. It was applied surgery, practised by men who needed only the touch of modern science to equip them for the great work.

In contradiction to what I have said about native deficiency in money sense, I found the Tongan developing into a keen trader in a small way. The *Tongafiti* game wasn't lacking in his deals, and many European traders were going bankrupt because the native was too sharp for them. The old Tongan was a babe unborn when it came to expenditures, and there are stories of primitive natives playing pitch-game with shipwrecked trade dollars. Not so today.

Salote and Tungi were studying finance methodically, patiently, to learn modern economics. Up and down the beaches their subjects were sometimes sharpening their wits in a very practical way.

Trader Algy Slocombe told me of the only times he ever got around a native in a deal. Living next door, a Tongan family let a couple of their trees hang over his fence and interfere with his tennis. He approached the native wife, who talked to her husband, and there was a long Tongan dicker. The husband admitted that he was grateful for the water he got from the Slocombe well; so that was something to bargain with. Algy said to the native's wife, "If you'll cut down those trees I'll let you have all the coconuts that drop into your yard from the palms on my side." The Tongans say, "*Fa moli moli,*" when they mean "Many thanks," and there was a far-off look in the woman's eyes when she said it. For years she had been gathering those same nuts, and no questions asked. But a trade was a trade.

A native from Vavau came to Algy's office proposing to deposit some tobacco against a loan of one pound. He said he was mayor of his town, had a good plantation, dealt with Lever Brothers. Algy wanted a day before closing this big transaction; just for curiosity he wired Vavau and found that this man had never had credit there. The customer returned — without the tobacco, of course — and said he must have the money at once, as the boat was leaving for Vavau. Algy merely smiled, *"Fa moli moli,"* and his applicant departed without the slightest sign of ill-feeling. His five-dollar build-up had been as elaborate as that of the New York confidence man. But that was all right. He'd find a touch somewhere before the boat left.

Neither in Fiji nor Tonga did the natives have family names; though some of the better-educated were beginning to affect the European way. I ran across a Tongan named Joni Motocawiah. If you say it fast it sounds like "Johnnie Motor Car Wire" — just what it means. The day Joni was born his mother saw her first automobile, and a roll of barbed wire was washed up on their beach. There was also a baby named Atalosa, which sounded sweet. Before the baby came her mother had sniffed something they told her was attar of roses; "Atalosa" was the way she said it.

Remodeling the English language wasn't confined to Tongans. Eloisa and I were quartered for a while at Bill Smith's boarding house, where food was delicious and flies abundant. Bill Smith was the reigning Mr. Malaprop. Once when he cornered me in a learned medical discussion he referred to "A man's tentacles and pinnace." He knew more about the cookbook than the dictionary, and told me how to bake ham under a layer of mud so that it "brought out the intersticine juices."

A Tongan's own language served him well if he didn't happen to like you. Needy aristocrats, beginning to learn the value of money and liquor, had perfected a little trick of giving a high title to visiting Europeans and making them "members of the family." If the European was romantic snob enough for the game, he freely lent money and whisky to the noble donor of titles. When money and whisky played out the titles vanished also, and the once-honored one was unceremoniously removed from the family. This old army game was a bit of *Tongafiti* that was practised in Samoa as well as Tonga. The generous Polynesian was beginning to learn that you don't give something for nothing in this wicked world. Chief Ulukalala, a pretender to the

throne, had titles to give that sounded extremely noble. He gave one
to an official, and another to a resident doctor's wife. Between the two
honored ones there was contention as to which should rank the other
at native ceremonies. Her title was *To'e Umu,* literally "Scraps from
the Oven." His was *Kuli Haapai,* which in English is "Dog of
Haapai."

The relics of early missionary blue laws made it very easy to go to
jail. It was forbidden to do any sort of work on Sunday, even on your
own premises. When I was there Dr. Ruhen, a medical officer, was
arrested for breaking the Sabbath by picking a bunch of bananas in
his own yard. Despite his protest that he was only gathering food, he
was duly fined. Sunday games were prohibited. Algy Slocombe's tennis
court got him into trouble with the puritans. We had some splendid
Sunday games there, and Algy felt secure because his court was
screened by a hedge. Some holy peeper caught him finally, and all his
players were haled before a native magistrate and fined. Fortunately
that happened after I went home.

All crimes lead to jail, or are supposed to. Going to jail in Tonga
seemed to be quite a merry social affair. Back in the days of old George
Tubou one of the royal relatives was a prisoner. Every afternoon the
King's carriage would wheel up, take the culprit for a drive and for
tea in the Palace, then return him at six o'clock, the closing hour.

A friend told me that when he first saw the Vavau jail there was a
sign over the door "All prisoners not in by six o'clock will be locked
out for the night." When I was there the jailers complained bitterly
because there were no prisoners, and they had to do all the work.
Tongan prisoners were great gadabouts. In one village there had been
several burglaries of provision stores, and the police were baffled for
days. At last they located the loot, hidden under the jail where the
inmates could delve in, when they pleased, for a midnight snack. It
seemed rather remarkable that such good boarding houses were losing
boarders.

That was Tonga as I saw it, going in and out for many years. Like
all Pacific groups, it was a land of marked contrasts. At sunset an old
witch woman would stand on the cliffs "calling the sharks." She would
throw scraps into the water, then raise a high, queer chant and the
beasts would poke their noses through the surf. And in the palace at

Nukualofa an educated, civilized woman sat with her consort, planning to meet the conditions which a new world had imposed on her kingdom. Because their rule was good, and the British Protectorate a wise one, Tonga continued to improve greatly, both in health and in understanding.

I never let Salote and Tungi forget that the native medical talent was right there in the kingdom, waiting to be developed. Every time I visited her islands I told the Queen how the pick of her young men could go to Fiji for a first-class medical education, if we had the money to back such an enterprise. There was always that big If. Salote's common sense and patriotism told her that I was right. Her generous wish was not limited to her own realm; she saw how the native races of Oceania could not be helped until they learned to help themselves. But when I talked this problem over with her I realized that little Tonga was not rich enough to effect a program that would cover the whole wide Pacific.

One day in 1926 I was very discouraged when I came to Queen Salote with my troubles. I told her of a letter I had just received from Heiser; he had decided that I must abandon the School idea altogether. It was no fault of his, he had done what he could. But the case was hopeless.

Queen Salote listened carefully to what I had to say. In her thoughtful hesitation I saw that she was agreeing with Heiser. I had put up a four-year fight for an impractical ideal.

Then suddenly she raised her kind eyes and asked, "Doctor, is it such a tremendous amount that we can't bear our share?"

It wasn't a spendthrift Tongan speaking. It was the voice of a woman who had considered the question carefully, and had come to see the road to a sick kingdom's recovery. She knew that there was a competent treasury balance. She had been with us from the first. Her influence had helped reduce Tongan infant mortality until it had become the lowest in the Pacific; she had encouraged mothers to come to doctors or government dispensers for supplies of baby food; this had given medical officers a chance to check up on the condition of young children. Salote had encouraged war on tuberculosis, and had seen that every house in her realm should have sanitary arrangements, even if they were still crude. The medical men she backed with moral support were cleaning up yaws with arsenicals. No one more than Salote knew the health situation in Tonga.

And couldn't Tonga bear its share in our School, so that the Pacific would at least have competent native medical service? Before she had spoken, my School had been taking its last gasp. Now it was alive again.

I went to Samoa and quoted her offer to the old Governor, Major-General Sir George Richardson. "Well," he grunted, "if Tonga is willing to do that we'll come in too."

The fight wasn't over, even then, but the wall was breached.

When I left Tonga for the last time the Crown Prince Taufaahau was on the ship with us. He had come home to the celebration of his twenty-first birthday and had been given the high title of Tubou Toa. He was a splendid boy, one I would have been proud to have claimed as my son. Two young anthropology professors from the University of Chicago were with us and were charmed with his conversation, always on an intellectual footing with theirs. Gigantic as his ancestors, he kept fit by exercising with fifty-six–pound dumbbells. He laughed, remembering the chocolate bars I used to feed him. I was telling him about a chief of a lost Pacific island who had asked me to come back and be his guest for life; the Crown Prince fell into a long study, the way his mother did when she was deciding something for herself. Then he said, "Doctor, I invite you to make your home with me in Tonga. But of course," he said, "that will be after I have assumed my place in Tongan society."

I know of no happier place for my old age.

CHAPTER IV

THE LAND OF THE TALKING MEN

I only stretch the long-bow lightly when I say that Western Samoa's political troubles began with a small medical problem and ended with a great one. Certainly the finish of the Mau Rebellion was a picture of hatred's reaction upon public health.

The *malanga* of 1924 was in full swing, and I was one of the party. From days of old the *malanga* has been a royal progress, an annual window-dressing on the march, as it was in England when a grateful populace turned out to greet Henry VIII with polished hauberks and freshly dry-cleaned plumes. In Samoa's year of plenty, 1924, the *malanga* was still an impressive show. His Britannic Majesty's proconsul, Governor of New Zealand's ten-year-old Mandate, had full-costumed a military display and was accepting the feasts or listening to the bands and musical orators all around Savaii.

Since Samoa's dawn of time the *Tulafale* (the orator or "talking man") had commanded leadership. No funeral, wedding or political controversy in the *Fono* (meeting place) has been official without a competition of orators, first on one side, then on the other, showering palaver or threats neatly wrapped in compliments. In the years of the Mandate the Talking Men were still importantly featured, and that wolf-gray, bullet-headed old British soldier, Major-General Sir George S. Richardson, had made many stops along his two weeks' march, to examine the well-being of a people he governed all too kindly.

Under this *malanga's* careless pageantry I witnessed a small pregnant incident. It dropped another of the seeds which, in a few years, sprouted into the wicked flower of an insurrection already germinating. In my report to the Foundation I described this official tour as "unique in my experience and remarkable for its results in obtaining the confidence of the native and his co-operation in measures for his own benefit. In the party there was the Governor, the Commissioner for Native Affairs, the Resident Commissioner of Savaii, the Chief Medical

Officer, the Collector of Customs and Taxes, the Governor's A.D.C., Dr. Buxton and myself." Fau'mui'na, high chief, led thirty Boy Scouts called *"Fetu o Samoa,"* the Star of Samoa; there were native police, carriers and attendants. The Fetu went in front, beating a drum, behind them was the flagbearer, next the Governor with his retinue, then the endless queue of followers. It was a parade to touch the imagination of a people susceptible to pomp and ceremony.

In the village reception house there would be the usual kava ceremony, the food presentation, the long hour devoted to exchange of courtesies. Then the *Tulafale*, the professional orators, would unlimber their eloquence for the benefit of the Governor: "We in our ignorance and humility turn to you for the light of your wisdom, as the flower turns to the sun. We are the children, you are the father upon whom we depend for guidance. We know that you love us, and we return your love. . . ." When you hear this doled out day after day you begin to believe the Orator. The simple Samoan child of nature — and watch out or he'll have the shirt off your back. Witness how his shrewd diplomacy all but had the United States, Germany and Britain tearing at each other's throats in 1900. When Germany got her cut in the colony the Samoan's connivance worried her to a point where she only tried to control them with punitive raids. . . .

But in the Governor's *malanga* of 1924 the Orators were laying it on thick. They would look into every gift-basket, call out the donor's name with praise if the taro were big and the fish well-cooked. If the contribution looked stingy they would be very frank about it, amidst popular mirth.

Public health was never relaxed in this bright journey of inspection. The Boy-Scoutish Fetu, wearing nothing but the *lavalava* and a cap with the emblem Star, would give the people exhibition games, object lessons in simple sports that would keep the villagers away from picture shows and dissipations in Apia. The Administration was sensible in showing the all but naked bodies of the young Fetu, to illustrate the health advantages of light clothing in the tropics. The Administration was always rational and kind.

At one of the settlements the orations and ceremonies had been unusually long. As in every place we stopped, the doctors had lined up the population for quick inspection of ulcers, skin lesions, eye conditions, enlarged spleens, or any other sign of disease. Our time was more than up, we had to be pushing on. What happened then was certainly no fault of Dr. Ritchie, a Medical Officer whose patient and enlightened work in restoring a failing race had earned him a crown in Heaven, twice over. It was a fault of tact, reacting on that interesting intangible, the Samoan temperament.

We had been there long enough for the natives to report any sickness in the region. Now we were hurrying to board the launch. What happened then was characteristic of Samoan dilly-dally. Several natives came running up with the cry: "There's a woman who has been having a baby for five days! It's half in, half out!" (They were describing, I suppose, a "hand presentation.") All Savaii had known that we were there, but it had just occurred to them to call a doctor. Dr. Ritchie, on the march, had no instruments with him, and experience told him that the woman was as good as dead. To examine her would mean an out-of-the-way trip, and Governor Richardson was impatient for the pompous *malanga* to move on. So it moved.

Even then I felt the seriousness of that diplomatic blunder. Here was a chance for the Administration, out for show, to make a beautiful gesture. Of course there was no hope for the woman, but it would have made an immense impression of kindness if the party had turned their launch around and wasted a day with the dying mother. It would have had the dramatic effect they wanted.

But the mistake was made among a people who were nursing many grievances, most of them imaginary. When the calamitous Mau Rebellion broke in 1927 that incident was remembered. Years later, after the messy thing had subsided, one of the Mau leaders, Fau'mui'na — since promoted to a good government post — told me that official neglect of the woman did much toward fomenting revolt. That and the shooting of Tamasese, exiled as a nuisance and a royal pretender. . . .

No war-captured country ever had a better government than these islands enjoyed after New Zealand's soldiery took over in 1914 a group which the League of Nations later changed from German Samoa to the mandate of Western Samoa. It was in refreshing contrast to Australia's early rule in New Guinea. Even before the uniformed Anzacs had left Samoa there was a clear-headed scientific attempt to look into social and health conditions. New Zealand, with her high cultural

standards, had long studied the splendid race of Maoris, whom she had
governed well. At home a million-and-a-half New Zealanders lived
alongside 70,000 Maoris whose population had increased and whose
rights had been maintained under a benevolent rule. Yes, Western
Samoa was fortunate in her new government which had never shown
a selfish financial motive behind any of its acts. But the Mau Rebellion
came, and its "cruel oppressions" have been so sensationalized by newspaper propagandists that the average reader asks: How did the administrators come to grow hoofs and horns overnight? Well, they didn't.

In 1923 Dr. T. Russell Ritchie came in as Chief Medical Officer and
his four years there were as remarkable for scientific achievement as
anything accomplished by Gorgas in cleaning up Cuba and Panama.
In civil administration you'll find mistakes everywhere this side of
Heaven. But even the mistakes were motivated by a fiery zeal to show
the world New Zealand's disinterestedness. Education and public
health were the features in a program so thorough that it should not
be forgotten.

It was a demonstration of preventive medicine unexcelled in the
tropics. By 1926 a death rate of over thirty per thousand was reduced
to twenty in four Samoan districts. Yaws was practically eliminated,
infant welfare work had brought down the average mortality under
five years to the lowest in the Pacific — before Tonga worked out
that problem. Soil sanitation had become the rule instead of the exception; in 1921 New Zealand had sent a commission to Australia to
study the Foundation's hookworm campaigns there; Ritchie had
adapted it to Western Samoa with marvelous results. He was bringing
in pure piped water; on islands like Savaii, which is very rainy but so
lava-porous that it has no streams, he had overridden Polynesia's super-
stition and used church roofs as watersheds for storage tanks. New
Zealand's successful medical work was becoming a model for other
island groups. There could not have been a better one. Germany's last
census in 1911 showed a population of 33,476. In 1917, after three
years in possession, New Zealanders counted 37,196. In 1918 pandemic
influenza, a scourge that baffled world medicine, mowed the natives
down. But the Mandate's care brought them back so steadily that in
1933 — despite the hellish work of the Mau Rebellion — our yaws campaign workers counted 48,300. This last estimate, I think, was about
1,500 short of the actual number. Confused conditions, following years

of revolt, made the count extremely difficult. In 1936 the census showed 55,000.

From 1921 to 1931, half of those years consumed by the Mau's hateful destruction, New Zealand had given to Samoa between £12,500 and £14,000 annually for medical purposes alone. None of this was in the form of a loan; it was free as a birthday present. Add to this New Zealand's gifts of public works, — like the native piped water supplies, for instance, — and you have a total of some £250,000 devoted to Western Samoa with no expectation of any return but the moral satisfaction of seeing a race revived.

Then what was the matter with Samoa that she wanted to rebel?

Samoa has been plowed over so often by romance-hawkers, big and little, that it would hardly be worth my time or yours to try to re-visualize the moonlight and song, the deep-grooved valleys, the lacy waterfalls infested by golden girls with tumbled raven hair. On my frequent professional visits I saw their unromantic side, yet always admired a people who refused to be coaxed or slave-driven into the sort of work which, to them, seemed unnecessary. Don't dismiss the Samoan as a happy good-for-nothing. On sterile Savaii I have seen them carrying farm produce on their backs, mile after mile; it was the old way, and they were working their own land. If Samoan racial pride seems to you to be no more than backwoods vanity, remember the Polynesian brain, one of humanity's best. And remember that in both Samoas, Western and American, there are as many people, perhaps, as you'll find in one of New York's longer streets. The old days are done for; the days of brave canoe-voyaging over uncharted blue waters. Among their ancestors were baffled Alexanders, weeping for more worlds to conquer. The worlds they found were so small, so scattered . . .

They have settled down to a small-town complex. For hours on end they sit around the kava circle, talking, talking. We are outnumbered, they say, but we are still Samoans. The New Faith is well enough. We must still observe our ancient ceremonies, our rules of courtesy, our carefully graded social distinctions, and every complication of our political structure. Listen to that old chief over there. He can recite his ancestry for thirty or more generations back. He is an aristocrat, and his memory is long, they say. All our memories are long.

This is not all poppycock. The Samoan is a born gentleman. Although books have been a stranger to him since the dawn of history, he is reading now. He is a nationalist and his reasoning mind has told him that his nationalism will have international support. Inwardly he believes that he is smarter than a European, and he wants a Samoa that is governed by Samoans. He looks across toward the Kingdom of Tonga and asks, "If they govern themselves, why can't we? Tongans don't work for Europeans. They hire them."

All such ideas are splendid, if impractical and slightly ridiculous. They had much to do with the disastrous Mau.

The good Samoan mind is still factional. When the Dutch explorers first saw Apia they found a people who lacked the solidarity that welded Tonga. Each of Samoa's three main islands had its own complicated aristocracy and tribal intrigue. It was Japan without a Mikado. You would have thought that the descendants of voyaging warriors would have developed the leadership that pulls a country together. Perhaps the Samoans were too innately civilized to crave a Hitler and a generation of massacres. It was the European's job to drag them out of the Stone Age into the Bomb Age — all in a century and a half. By 1900 they could use rifles well, as witness the small butchery of Marines that led to the partition of the two Samoas between Germany and the United States.

Cloying praise has shared in spoiling the native Samoan. Robert Louis Stevenson was the worst sinner. It was too easy to sentimentalize their sweet and gentle women, their courteous patriarchal chiefs, the waterfalls that sang like fountains day and night. Before Hollywood went South Sea and flattered them with the camera, Stevenson had told us in charming, balanced sentences how he had lived among Greeks in Eden's Vale. Samoan conceit became elephantoid under this pretty coddling, and the abundant orators around the kava ring told them again that they occupied the Navel of the World. It was never raucous boasting. As I have said, the Samoans are a race of gentlefolk.

The medical problem in Western Samoa was more than a matter of lining them up, treating them, sending them home. In American Samoa, our Navy tried the efficiency method, but it didn't work very well with a people who live on ceremony as much as Japan did under the Shogunate. A sick Samoan, if he has rank, pays for his operation a thousandfold before he is home and recovered.

The Samoan social system could ramify its way across a hundred library shelves. To be brief, its core is the *Matai*, or master. This title goes to the head of the *Ainga*, or family, and is handed down like an heirloom. The title *Tufunga* is high, and carries with it the greatest dignity, and the honors that go with it have always been recognized.

To the practical modern doctor the old ceremonial is what can't be cured and must be endured. Take the ceremonial journey they call the *malanga* — if a Samoan goes visiting relatives and takes the whole village along, it becomes a *malanga*, and the visitors are apt to eat the host's provisions down to the last taro, while he bites his nails in secret and publicly implores his guests to stay longer. But this generosity has a true Christmas spirit — you give something and expect something back. Pretty soon the host will be on a *malanga* of his own — then it will be his turn to do the feasting, and yours to pay for it.

Treating a sick Samoan is an ordeal for the doctor and it is not always so easy on the patient. N.M.P. Ielu Kuresa, an honored graduate of our School, wrote an article for our medical journal, the *Native Medical Practitioner*, in which he described the rigmarole which surrounds a simple surgical operation. This is his account, in brief: —

"To be operated on by a doctor does not mean the doctor's bill only. Custom and etiquette must be complied with. In the first place, the scene will be at the patient's own home. . . . Having come to the conclusion that he must be operated on, he will first inform his immediate family of his intentions. At this stage a daughter or son, perhaps residing some distance away, will have to be sent for in order to participate in a family meeting to decide whether the sick person's wishes should be carried out, or whether a further try of other native medicine or treatment be applied." Every Matai, under these circumstances, must make peace with his kinsmen; otherwise "it means carrying with you bad luck and perhaps better chances of dying. Samoans are very particular about their selection of physicians and will travel miles to get to a good surgeon, leaving another doctor who might be close to their village."

All the related Matais are informed of the coming event. Then the Orators are brought into play. They assemble at the sick man's house, and there is a contest of eloquence, wishing the patient "all good luck and God's never-failing help. . . ." So the Orators must get their pork and the sympathizers must feast — ". . . food in such a quantity as befits the title of the sick person . . . a whole roasted pig, or even two, bread or biscuits and of course taro by the score . . . the first installment on operating expenses." Any other stricken member of the *Ainga,* a wife or child, gets the same ceremony, scaled down to the social importance of the sufferer.

"The first expense, then, can be from £1 to £5, to be conservative." If the Matai happens to be hard up he must borrow pigs from his in-laws. "At times, just to conform with Samoan customs, if no pigs are forthcoming from the son-in-law or the daughter-in-law, or the sister, the *Ainga* must resort to parting with a share of the family lands, or some other form of property."

This blow-off ends the first scene. A boat is probably necessary to carry the patient to the hospital. The crew offers its services free — But wait. The expedition is called *ole si'ingama'i,* "party-carrying-the-sick." The boating expedition swells to a heavy-laden fleet. And don't forget the *Tulafale,* the all-pervading Orators, bringing their wives and children and in-laws.

Etiquette demands that there shall be a stop or two on the way. Etiquette also demands that leading families provide a splendid barbe-cue. Samoan hospitality, carefully gauged by the family code, holds the patient long enough to get well — or else. The visitors know that it is their ancient right to demand food, and that their hosts will be their guests someday and there'll be another big picnic. The visitors make gifts, too; usually fine mats and tapa cloths. These gifts are a part of the prevalent gentleman's code.

The patient gets to the hospital — alive, let's say. "Parties-carrying-the-sick" are not allowed in wards, so they are settled in a base-camp in a near-by village, as guests of the *Ainga* there. The visitors contribute more pigs, and mats which cost from one pound up, according to historic value. These expenses, Ielu writes, "will no doubt appear absurd to the European mind. . . . It may all be in the course of life, according to the Samoan way of living, yet a pig is a pig and a fine mat is a fine mat."

Then comes the operation. The native pastor and an Orator have been at the patient's bedside. The parson and the *Tulafale* have said their prayer, made their speeches. Back in the camp there is wholesale cooking. The occasion demands . . . "something to mark the occur-rence. The presentation will be done publicly and the food announced aloud wherever it is being presented. The announcing is usually done

when the patient has been brought back to the ward after the operation."

The sick man, if he got well, was in for such an entertainment bill
as never faced Lucullus. If he died the funeral would be on the same
lavish scale and his family would have to pay for it.

Ielu tells of operating on I'inga, an aristocrat. Ielu was a brilliant surgeon, and the patient's elephantoid scrotum was such a simple matter
that he let him walk a short distance to the hospital. That should have
cut the cost. He didn't need boats or a base camp or a lusty entourage.
However, this proud I'inga was compelled by custom to make a large
food presentation every day of his illness; daily 100 loaves of bread
with sugar and butter and two whole roast pigs went down to his
account. His title of Matai was a high one, therefore he had to pay in
fine mats for the daily *sua* (pig) presentations. The party cost him
five pounds in bread, and pigs were worth about seven pounds apiece.
The whole job set him back forty-four pounds, thirteen shillings.

Surgical and hospital fees came to four pounds.

One night in 1924 I was dining at Vailima with Governor Richardson, who lived in the romantic house which Robert Louis Stevenson
used to occupy. Above it loomed the steep hill which is topped by
Stevenson's tomb. So many tourist-ladies have climbed the mud-slip-
pery trail to visit this shrine that I blush to mention it.

Governor Sir George had risen to high office by force of sheer
ability. War had advanced him from the rank of drill sergeant to
general command. A born Englishman, he had immediately won New
Zealand's respect for his Mandate administration. You had to admire
him. He had the middle-class Englishman's anti-Yankee prejudices; a
brush with our United States Navy control in American Samoa hadn't
helped. Don't think that he was any martinet when it came to native
administration. Devotedly, honestly he wished to be the father of his
flock. But he seemed rather too self-satisfied. Touchy Samoa politely
resented his attitude, "See what we are doing for you. Come to us if
there's anything you want done." I longed to tell him that he was
doing too much for the Samoan, feeding him with modernism faster
than he could digest it. But you didn't tell things to Governor Richardson. He told you.

At that meeting, as at many others, we had discussed the need of a modern native medical school in Fiji, and as usual Richardson had been favorable to the plan. The expenses of governing a country that had 3,000 chiefs to 40,000 population was the only thing that held him back until Queen Salote's generous offer in 1926, when he pledged Samoa to share in a scheme in which he had always heartily believed. During that long evening's talk in 1924 I didn't mention the woman on Savaii who died in childbirth. But if a competent Native Medical Practitioner had been on the spot that day the story of Richardson's administration might have had a happier ending. I think he had a right to feel proud of the medical situation, for the Mandate was already training native nurses in the model hospitals, was using one of our old-school Native Medical Practitioners, and had socialized medicine to a point where every Samoan paid a head-tax of about five dollars a year for all treatments.

Years of administering that model colony bred a certain smugness in the good Governor Richardson; and smugness is always dangerous in handling native affairs. Early in 1927 he went to the New Hebrides on a Royal Commission with Governor Sir Eyre Hutson of Fiji. Richardson was on the crest of the wave, feeling his oats in every pore. When the party got back to Fiji I wanted to return his Samoan hospitality, but Richardson's mind harbored a single thought: go up to Government House again and tell Sir Eyre how to run Fiji. Hutson was one of the smoothest products of the colonial school, and he had learned enough about the treatment of native races to have made Fiji a model for all students of island administration. However, Richardson got to Government House and told Hutson; and Hutson smiled rosily, suavely agreeing that he ought to study Samoa and get some tips on how to run Fiji.

When Richardson finished telling Hutson and returned to Apia, the Mau Rebellion broke right in his face.

As a doctor I cannot diagnose Samoa's illness without looking further into the causes that led up to it. The status of the half-caste in Polynesia was at the root of the disturbance. While in dark-skinned Melanesia a touch of white is often a stigma, it is a matter of pride to the peach-tan Maoris, Cook Islanders and Samoans. The European may turn his shoulder on the half-caste, but the Polynesian forgets his insular pride in an eager mating with Europeans; every child with a trace of Northern blood is looked upon as something which approaches the racial ideal. The Samoan highly respects the child of a mixed union — provided the native mother has not been deserted by her husband or mate. There is the case of one distinguished British scientist who experimented with going native, chose a Samoan woman, wore a *lavalava* around his belly and a hibiscus flower over his ear. Called back to London to account for himself, he left the girl where he found her — and the baby. It was no disgrace that she had to do washing; needy aristocrats often do that. Nor was she ashamed that she couldn't show a marriage license. She hung her head because Johnson (I'll call him) had deserted her, and before the baby was born. Johnson wandered to Chicago, where he died; but his beach-widow carefully guards her beautiful son for fear that some of his father's relatives may come along and claim him.

I heard two half-caste boys quarreling. One howled, "Jonisoni!" and the other yelled, "Anisoni!" They were not accusing one another of bastardy, but raising the accusation that their mothers had been deserted by Johnson and Anderson.

When Germany ruled Samoa every man whose father was registered as a European could himself register as a European. Some so classified were less than one thirty-second white, and many of them could not speak a word of English. When New Zealand took over she had to accept the Made-in-Germany rule. The mental and moral worth of these mixed bloods depended, of course, on the quality of their parents. The product varies; but the more I travel the more I see the brilliant results when two superior beings of opposing races are bred together. After a while I'm going to tell about a few New Zealanders who are legally classed as Maoris.

The fuse that led up to the Mau explosion carried one very dangerous combustible — half-caste jealousy of European social prestige. The jealousy was mutual, I think, for the European wife grew watchful of the lovely half-caste girl with her soft, long-lashed eyes and velvet skin. This girl was getting an education and her parents were grumbling because she could not step into the social sphere which her mind, her manners and her beauty demanded, in all fairness.

Insurgency centered in O. F. Nelson, a half-caste who possessed genius both for business and for political leadership. The chain of

Nelson trading stores had bulked him about $1,500,000, an unthinkable fortune to be gathered out of Samoa. Like Nelson, the discontented half-castes had educated their daughters in colleges and upper schools, yet had gained no status for them in European society. The full-blooded Samoan looked up to Nelson, one derived from their own race and so powerful that the Government had to come to him for favors. When he rode out in his handsome car he displayed a coat of arms as large and gaudy as the Governor's own, and his A.D.C. was in uniform. The native majority was under his control.

Mau means "Stand Fast," and the stand was against real and fancied wrongs. Trouble brewed when Western Samoan traders howled because American Samoa was outbuying them in the copra market. The quarrel became a crazy patchwork, with Richardson trying to patch the patches. Half-castes were clamoring to be counted as Europeans, even though the change would have endangered their rights. Then Prohibition, that indomitable mischief-maker, raised its old silk hat. Because the Customs House, through an error, got more than its share of liquor on one consignment, the League of Nations, which controlled the Mandate's thirst, ordained that Western Samoa's Europeans should have liquor for medical purposes only. Up to then strong drink had been wisely forbidden the natives. Under Prohibition, indignant Europeans taught Samoans to make a vile intoxicant called "bush beer," and to help themselves to a share of it. All this added native drunkenness to the pattern of revolt.

The Orators were putting their heads together. At every *Fono* the Talking Men intoned "Samoa for the Samoans" and suavely asked the aristocrats, "How can nobles and chiefs serve under this common fellow Richardson?" The mess, which largely interests me from a medical point of view, harked back again to the Governor's *Malanga*, which I described at the opening of this chapter; it included two officials who were later accused of corrupting Samoan youths. A schoolteacher who showed us around Savaii was also involved. Two suicides resulted from the scandal, which set the Talking Men off again, asking why the Europeans sent such people to teach them morals.

On top of these grievances, and dozens of smaller ones, came the Mau. At first it was passive resistance, then in 1928 there was bloodshed. Tamasese, a justly exiled pretender to Samoa's shadow-throne, came back to Apia with a howling demonstration. Richardson, tired and

sick, had resigned in favor of Colonel Allen, a New Zealander with a
cool blue eye and guts to spare. When the mob battered in Officer
Abram's head with a stone Allen's police fired on them, as they were
ordered to do in case of violence.

That was all the blood spilled; but it might have been better for
the Samoans if the rebellion had been stifled by force of arms. It went
on for years, passively. Nelson was banished to New Zealand, where
he managed his revolt by wire. After the quarrel was settled, over
the festering carcass of Samoa, there came Nelson's Napoleonic return.
But there was no Waterloo; only a popular clamor to give him the
place of leader in the native parliament as well as to admit him to the
European Legislative Council. The new Administration refused him
this bi-racial privilege with the remark, "You can't wear trousers and
a *lavalava* at the same time."

As you study small life under the lens and watch the microcosm
work out its cycle, so you can look at Western Samoa and see the
after-effects of war over this wrongheaded world. The doctor rushes
in afterwards and tries to patch up the innocent and the guilty. Samoa,
when the Mau subsided, knew a terrible aftermath. The Samoans hadn't
got back Samoa; all they had received was a resurgence of the native
diseases which a careful Mandate had struggled so valiantly and successfully to cleanse. Devoted men had worked for many years to
accomplish what five years of rebellion had undone.

It was five years after the Mau began before co-operation between
the Government and the Rockefeller Foundation could begin salvage
operations. When I returned to Samoa to have the Foundation's share
in cleaning up the Mau pigsty, I shook my head at the sorry change.
The beautiful Samoan children — and nothing can be more beautiful —
were pitiful little things, their skins a scab, their faces eaten with yaws.
The tea-rose skin had faded to gray; intestinal parasites were sucking
again at their blood and lymph. The Mau had turned against its own
people instead of its enemy. Argument had triumphed over reason,
the Polynesian had junked his high intelligence and become an Intellectual.

Samoa for the Samoans! Ignore every order of the white intruder
with all their nosy medical men, dinging away at keeping clean, keeping the water pure, reporting sickness. Ignore their impudent instruc-

tions about repairing fly-proof latrines. Ignore vital statistics. Tear them up. Ignore everything but Samoa for Samoans.

The latrines rotted or were torn down by the indignant. Water supplies festered. Clean in his habits from days of old, the Samoan jettisoned the ancient tabu and gave over mischievously to soil pollution. Fields and villages stank with a foulness which defied the Administration while it killed the Samoans. It was hard to approach some of the settlements, they were so odorous of decay. Samoa had certainly cut off her nose to spite her face.

It was impossible to collect vital statistics during that spell of madness. The death toll was a matter of eye measurement. We plunged in with rolled-up sleeves to give all possible help. Tragic as it was, the devastation proved to be less than that of the influenza epidemic in 1918. Yaws was the principal problem, almost universal with the young. A giant campaign was organized, our combined workers gave 89,000 injections, including treatments and re-treatments. For experience has taught medicine that this disease is stubborn and may reappear in deep-seated conditions after the superficial symptoms have vanished. However, in our wide mass treatments our main effort was to cure the open sores which spread infection.

In 1933, when New Zealand took its yaws census of Samoa, the figures showed the population on the upgrade again. The forward march will go on, I think, unless some Liberator decides to turn these islands over to Germany or Russia or Italy. Then again there will be hell in warm water.

American Samoa, Uncle Sam's split in the three-cornered deal of 1900, I did not survey until my Pacific adventures were nearing a close, although after 1926 I visited it briefly every year. The reason for my delay is simple; I had to wait for Uncle Sam's invitation. Working so long on the other side of the line and rather feeling the American lack of interest in an American enterprise, I'm afraid that I was rather prejudiced against the administration of our lovely little possession, centered in Pago Pago.

In many ways I was happily disappointed when I came at last to make a short survey — all in spite of the fact that I was annoyed by the unfairness of our home folks in their comparison of the two Samoas. So many sweet lady-tourists from Boston and Keokuk have sailed into Pago Pago's bright waters, which lie smooth as a lake inside the leafy oval of a dead volcano. There's the old Flag again and our gallant sailors in white. Why, this is the naughty land of Miss Sadie Thompson! Why, we've all seen that lovely, wicked play called "Rain" — but the scenery doesn't do Pago Pago anything like justice. . . . It's all so peaceful and orderly, isn't it? Quite different from Western Samoa over there, where they've certainly made a hash of it. See the handsome Commandant, who seems to boss Pago Pago with a velvet glove. Let's call him "Uncle Samoa"!

This is a sort of autopropaganda, born of national pride. Overnight trippers cannot see — how can they? — that Uncle Sam has guinea-pigged a race, or that part of a race which is identical to the people on the western islands. The tourists haven't had time to find out that the New Zealand Administration, working against great odds with a population about four times as large as that which America controls, is a shining example of government for the people who must be governed. And in spite of the Mau Rebellion, New Zealand is building up a better racial spirit. The people in their Samoa are better educated, better prepared to meet civilized conditions. They speak better English and are far, far better mannered.

Uncle Samoa, in fact, is an honest quarterdeck hero. His real interest in his share of the islands is to maintain a naval base; and that, in all common sense, is extremely necessary. He salutes the Regulations and does the best he can. It is certainly no fault of his if some antediluvian chapter in the book limits his service to eighteen months and orders him to sea duty or paper work or rolling hoops. Orders is orders, and tomorrow he'll be saluting the next man that comes along to hang his cap on the official hat-rack. It's the same all down the line. The Governor is just getting the swing of his job, then he's off; the Chief Medical Officer is just beginning to organize his theories of native diseases — then good-by. In the schools there's a continual change of teachers, hence a general sloppiness of instruction. The impermanence affects the enlisted man, often not unpleasantly. He chooses a temporary mate, raises a few children, and when the time comes to sail back to the States he hands his family over to some newly arrived buddy. Pago Pago is full of wistful college widows, scanning the sea with dreamy Samoan eyes and wondering what the next ship will bring.

A great many of our "administered" natives, I found, were enlisted in the Marines with the same pay as American boys. The results were often unfortunate. Certainly it was another move toward taking away the Samoan's national character.

This is all on the black side of the slate, — to mix a metaphor, — the white side showed a great deal to American credit. In 1918 our Navy successfully quarantined influenza when it was almost decimating Western Samoa. But I must remind you that only one ship arrived in our Samoa during that year, whereas the New Zealanders' group had the job of overhauling vessels from all the Seven Seas. However, our work was thorough and promptly quelled the scourge.

It was remarkable to me how well the Navy's medicos carried on, in spite of handicaps. The newcomer would pick up his predecessor's unfinished business, work it out in his own way, and hand the job over to the next one. Of the twelve thousand inhabitants whom he was there to supervise he would find twelve thousand spoiled by coddling on the one hand, unexplained discipline on the other. We had been pursuing the American way, serving them large doses of democracy overnight, forgetting that democracy to the aristocratic Samoan is like raw whisky to a newborn babe. From the chiefs down to the humblest kanakas a "Hello, buddy" attitude was all too general. Nobody could tell the natives anything. False prosperity had come with the Navy's colossal expenditures, and among a people to whom a handful of pennies had once meant fortune this easy money was demoralizing. The native official and the native houseworker clamored for higher pay and shorter hours. The "gimme" habit was an ubiquitous nuisance.

Four Chief Medical Officers, coming and going, had developed some good teamwork. The first of the four had very sensibly framed a policy he could hand on to the next one, and the results were good. The indifference of the people was always a stumbling block. It was up to the Navy to install a decent latrine system, and no native would lend a helping hand. They expected everything to be done for them — and it was.

I admired the field and hospital work of the chief pharmacists' mates and the petty officers under them. Most of them were university graduates, technicians in dentistry, entomology, pathology, bacteriology, X-ray and all the other necessaries. Watching their performance, you had to bulge your chest and say, "That's a Navy job. No American parents could ask a better training for their sons."

One superior of these medical gobs had had rather a crude way of distributing benefits. If natives didn't show up for treatment they were hauled out and given the get-well-damn-you orders. In case an inhabitant refused to be hauled out, lusty police came and hauled him properly. Education by force stopped a general yaws infection, which was good. But it dampened Samoan confidence in America's kindly rule, which was bad.

There was an organized body of trained Samoan nurses; the regulation pay was fifteen dollars a month, increased by a monthly dollar for each year's service. Good pay, but the tendency was to get married and go home. This wasn't at all bad, since it brought new blood into the work, and those who retired formed an alumnae body and became health missionaries in their villages. Their training was excellent and included the all-important items, baby feeding and dietetics.

An acute conjunctivitis generally called "Samoan eye" was prevalent in both groups. One school of thought still maintains that it is a form of trachoma. When you say *"Fa'a Samoa"* down there you are saying "Samoan fashion," and that style of treating the eyes isn't so good. When natives go blind, as so many do, it is usually due to their inherited witch-doctoring. They use a *Fa'a Samoa* treatment, which consists in scrubbing the eyes with coco fiber soaked in salt water. After a good course of this the entire eyeball is destroyed. It was encouraging to see how the chief pharmacists' mates, who ranked as District Officers, were going at the problem. Every newborn baby got its drop of argyrol, and school children had their daily treatment. Adults were harder to handle; they were apt to wander away and try *Fa'a Samoa,* then come back stone-blind.

Fa'a Samoa for deafness was another medical annoyance. It consisted in tucking small shells into the afflicted ear and, in most cases, destroying the drum. Commander Paul Crosby, then Senior Medical Officer, deserves high praise for his supervision of eye and ear cases, and for the improvement all around in native health.

The Mau was shorter in American Samoa than on the other side, but it came to the Naval Administration before it reached New Zealand's mandate. Part of our Mau was a sad story, and promptly hushed-up for the good of the Service. Trouble started among half-castes and traders. Then it was known that some of the Naval staff were in the conspiracy. Zealots even confined Governor Terhune in his house. I knew Terhune back in the days when I practised in Mexico, and remembered him as an upright officer and a square-shooter. But a Board of Inquiry came sailing down to Pago and would have called Terhune to account for something or other, if he had been alive. Over his dead body he was absolved of all blame. The guilty officer was punished; and I hope that tardy justice cleansed the memory of poor Terhune, who had decided to die like an officer and a gentleman.

But it was a curious finish for the ruler of what one colonial news lady headlined "A Kindly Despotism," commenting on the Governor who happened to be in office, "With astonishing disregard of American constitutional principles he combines in his person executive, legislative and judicial authority." The lady otherwise flattered our Naval Administration, and made allowances for the difficulties it had overcome. I make allowances too. It's a bitter thing to be responsible for the work of colonial empire.

Along Miss Sadie Thompson's haunted beach I was reassured by a fringe of modern privies, built firmly. Tourists might have been offended by this, but to me it was far more beautiful than if the beach had been left to pure romance and soil pollution, which have combined to destroy so many tribes.

I was glad to scribble in my notes: —

Medical conditions excellent — have never seen schools so clean as at Ofu and Olosenga under Chief Pharmacist's Mate Campbell. *Ta'u* under Harris far better than the average, but not so good as Campbell's work. Little or no ringworm and no conjunctivitis among 300 school children. Campbell and Harris had reached independent conclusion that eye manifestations in Samoa can be controlled by argyrol, therefore no trachoma. Teachers instill drops daily in children's eyes. Scars on lids and cataracts are due to native treatment. . . .

And to go on:

Mrs. Harris told about The Sanctified in L.M.S. mission here. If you're Sanctified it means you've led a pure life, so you're socially exalted and allowed to wear a hat to church. You're not in the Club unless you keep up your dues, $1.50 every six months. Before communion The Sanctified meet and confess, to find out if they're still fit members. The ones who admit that their morals have slipped during the month are fined twenty-five cents, which entitles them to be re-sanctified and take communion. Mrs. Harris tells of her servant who had been wrestling with her soul. Question: Should she blow $1.50 to get herself sanctified, or save her money and have fun? Finally she decided to have fun.

These two Samoas, because the population was so small, were like handy laboratories for the study of racial breeding, its decline and its rise. They offered such opportunities for new knowledge on the subject of one all-important disease — filariasis and resultant elephantiasis — that I suggested to the International Health Board a special study there, as the debility caused by filarial fever was cutting into labor efficiency all over the Pacific. Commander Phelps, an extraordinarily able physician, found that in Samoa the daytime microfilariae did not differ from the night variety. Dr. Buxton of the London School of Tropical Medicine thought the *Aedes variagatus* the principal offender. No satisfactory cure has been found, but Commander Phelps experimented with intramuscular injections of chenopodium, and with good results. These were much the same as the ones I gave the six cannibals down in New Guinea, with a decided effect on whipworms.

The roundworm question was an important one in Samoa, and always had been. An early observer, nearly a hundred years ago, remarked that the natives were infested with *"lumbrici."* In my time the Governor himself vomited one up, much to the sailor's delight. Strangely enough, hookworm was scarce; moisture, heat and soil pollution invited the pest, which did not seem to respond. In spite of Pago Pago's handsome fringe of waterside latrines, the building of them was a problem among the islands. If they were made of wood, fierce winds blew them down. Concrete was fairly expensive. Lieutenant Commander P. J. Halloran came across with the best idea yet for tropical arrangements, and although the humorists called them "Halloran's Privies," many were set up and proved entirely satisfactory. A unit cost $400 and would accommodate ten, five on a side. Molded in quantity — for they were practically all concrete — they would cost about $250 per unit, built over a concrete trough with an automatic flushing system. I lack space to go into detail, but to tropical administrators of public health this plan ought to be a boon.

The Navy was going at the job in its own way, and in many regards was extremely thorough. In the hospitals it even made blood tests to determine Samoa's racial origin. Hawaiians, as blood-examination has found, are in Group A, the world's largest racial stock, the Caucasian or Caucasoid. But some of the Pacific blacks are also heavy in "A." The aborigines are usually in Group O, as witness the American Indian. But blood donors in the hospital at Pago Pago revealed such a predominance of Group O that, from that angle at least, it would prove that the Polynesians are of a mixed stock.

Mixed in blood or mixed in ideals, I still have faith in the Polynesian's ability to survive against a civilization that has been thrust upon him. To our credit, the native population of American Samoa has about doubled since we took command. In 1900 it was 5,679, and in less than forty years it had risen to 11,638. America's experiment is restoring health to our Polynesians. In doing so, I hope we have not lost them their way of living, which was a very good way indeed.

Although quite unfortified, American Samoa, centering in Pago Pago, is a powerful link in that chain of steel we are drawing across the Pacific. And what if an aggressor should happen to want it? Well, it's one of the great fueling stations, and oil is the food of war nowadays.

CHAPTER V

PIG ARISTOCRACY

The Adventist pastor who had only two converts led me into a dark, gnarled jungle. With every step I was forced to remember that this was not Samoa with its kindly government and courteous natives. We were on one of the blackest spots in the New Hebrides, and right across the stream was wild Malekula where the Big Nambas had added liquor and firearms to the ancient art of man-eating. "This way, please," whispered the Pastor, as if it were a prayer meeting. Ahead of us broke a light from many torches, moving ceremoniously around a great square.

Now and then a rifle cracked. Musicians were whistling on reeded Pan's pipes; *oom, oom* sounded the enormous wooden drums. Over the spectacle towered graven images, demoniacal human shapes and forms of swooping birds. It was a barbaric choral scene, everything centered on the star performers. Then I turned my eyes — and saw it. A painted man stood on a high stone pulpit, gesturing and counting. Below him another painted man wielded a mallet. Victims were being hauled up, screaming, only to be silenced by a crack on the skull. There was a chanted hymn of praise. The donor, who had contributed the sacrifice, held an honored place apart. Crack went the mallet again. Another body was dragged away. . . .

They were killing pigs.

This is a glimpse of the New Hebrides as I saw them in 1925. On other groups we had already launched curative campaigns as wide as our numbers would permit. My plans for an advanced School to train Native Practitioners had not come to anything definite, and there I stood alone on one of Oceania's plague spots. Well, not alone, for I had Malakai with me.

I had come full of curiosity, hoping to check up some of the causes of racial decay in the New Hebrides, that unfortunate double chain of islands where the population had been dwindling for well over a hundred years. Jogging shoulders with suave Samoa on the one hand and tamed Fiji on the other, these thirty wild islands remained the lawless stepchildren of a bad government called the Condominium (aptly nicknamed "Pandemonium"), a sort of Siamese-twin arrangement made between England and France in 1907. There was a Frenchman in one Government House, a Britisher in the other. The only occasions I ever saw the Condominium get together were on the King's Birthday and July Fourteenth.

The heroic pig-killing was a rather open session of one of the native secret societies, which have controlled the New Hebrides from time immemorial. In my study of depopulation I was glad to have seen it. Because it was a cause of racial decline? Quite to the contrary. For uncounted generations it had been the social pulse of tribal life. European meddling was weakening the fabric of these mystic orders and giving the native no substitute. Let me remind you again that races die out for three established reasons: imported disease, the decay of custom, and a lack of will to live. Imported disease is easily the most important of the killers, but the three together produce results dismal to behold.

It was on the tiny island of Atchin, off wild Malekula, that I saw the pig ceremony. My survey was half over, and I had already seen enough demoralization to understand what happens when the ruling white man is too indifferent or poorly equipped to take up his burden. In Vila, the little capital where M. D'Arbousier, a cultured mulatto gentleman, governed for the French, and Mr. Smith-Rewse, a kindly Britisher, did his lonely best to hold up his end, I had seen a comic-opera demonstration of authority. The French half of the twin, it seems, was selling the natives their worst enemies, liquor and firearms. It wasn't lawful, but what of the law? The native liked to drink and shoot, so why not accommodate him? The British pretended to frown on this. How much their frowns meant is herein illustrated: —

We were playing tennis behind the neat British Residency when a police official was suddenly called from the game. He sauntered away and found the trouble, a noisy altercation over a police patrol which, for unexplained reasons, he had set in front of a trading store. Trader Le Meskime was in a dither; the show of arms was scaring away natives who had come to buy toddy. A large number of them, mixed with Tonkinese, were huddled outside, not daring to approach. *Incroyable!* What an outrage to keep an honest Frenchman from his honest profits! So the accommodating British police official moved his guard and the dark customers filed in to spend a week's wages on a Saturday-night jag, as usual.

The sale of booze and bullets to a Stone Age people made the French very popular, you may be sure. French ships with supplies of opium for the Tonkinese, and some for the natives, were popular, too. Ask a discouraged official if there were no laws in the New Hebrides and he'd groan, "Plenty of them." Perhaps he would show you a "Joint Resolution," passed in May, 1922, for the Island of Tanna and beginning, "The Joint Order of January 2nd is repealed." It was a nice piece of paper, which seemed to cover everything in the way of land claims. The only trouble was that the French and British settlers between them had put in more claims for property than there was land in the New Hebrides. In the old days any pioneer who came along would trade a bauble with a native chief for "all the land from here to there and as far back as I can see." The native, who probably had no claim on the land, would cheerfully make his mark on a piece of paper, call in a friend as witness — and another rainbow sale would be more or less on record.

The Joint Court was supposed to settle the quarrels that rose over shaky claims. But since the Court postponed its meetings from year to year, the witness who opposed a claim was usually dead before they met. The judicial body could not function unless all members were present, and some were always on leave. Soreheads proclaimed that the Court preferred it that way — the fewer witnesses the less trouble.

The French had a way of shooting the natives off land on which a "legal" claim had been filed. The dazed aborigines, of course, hadn't the vaguest idea what it was all about. But the canny Frenchmen knew. They always raided native plantations where the trees were bearing and gathered the nuts until their own newly planted acres began to yield.

Black men on Malekula, Santo, and Malo were doing as little as possible to help the unwelcome white man, though their murderers ran to the missions to be handily converted and missionaries often sheltered refugees from the rough work of "recruiting" for contract labor. French planters were tricking men into service, holding them indefinitely in the chains of drink and debt. Only about 13,000 of the possible 50,000 inhabitants were under any semblance of government control. There were eight government agents to enforce what order they could with a handful of sketchy native police. In a perfect climate, blessing a soil that flowed with milk and honey, there were but four British plantations. The French had crowded the others out.

The public health physician must study a population from all angles, and New Hebridean angles were odd. It would require volumes of anthropological data, with charts, to outline the cobweb of family structure on these islands.* In one rough sentence: The northern and more Polynesian half of this double archipelago was matrilinear (inheriting through the mother) while the negroid folk of the south were patrilinear (inheriting from the father's side). Among the bearded natives of Malekula the wives were squaws, while their lords slept with rifles and bottles of toddy. Women were forbidden the men's sacred enclosure. A true man cooked for himself and never let female hands defile his food.

Women had their value, however. On one island off Malekula I watched native boats every morning, being shoved off; the women were rowing across to work the "gardens" (truck farms) on the opposite shore. Their husbands sat at bow and stern, bristling with rifles; they took no chances on their drudges being picked off by rival Nambas, sniping from the bush.

In a roundabout way I have Mr. Smith-Rewse, the British Resident Commissioner, to thank for Pastor Parker's hospitality and for the pains that earnest Adventist took to show me the cannibalistic pig-killing. With the Commissioner's party I had set out from Vila on an inspection tour of Malekula and Santo, for health conditions on these notoriously savage islands demanded my attention.

Except for two excellent physicians in the Presbyterian hospitals, overworked and always embarrassed by a shortage of medicine, I found white men in the New Hebrides grossly ignorant of the causes, cures and prevention of tropical diseases. In Papua plantations were places where sick men came to be cured; in the New Hebrides plantations were seed-beds for infections that the workers carried back to the

* *The History of Melanesian Society*, by W. H. R. Rivers, describes the fantastic genealogical tabus on marriages inside the family line.

villages. Natives had become so enfeebled that the French were importing Tonkinese. These yellow strangers were contributing a new dis-
ease-picture to a land that had not yet set up an immunity to the
scourges brought in by Europeans 100 years ago.

As to hookworm, the *Necator americanus,* I found the prospects
pretty doleful. I was told that if I asked for specimens on Malekula
the Big Nambas would either take a pot shot at me or run howling to
the jungle. Even the missionized ones feared that I was collecting
fragments of excreta for purposes of witch-doctoring. One of them,
whom I tried to convince to the contrary, shook his bushy head
stubbornly. "No, master. Dis would spoil me fellow altogether." However, through the help of a few responsible white residents, I made
enough worm counts to suspect that the general infection in the New
Hebrides would run to something over 94 per cent. That meant that
on our future curative campaign we would have to treat the whole
population.

On the way to Malekula the government yacht *Euphrosyne* touched
at little Atchin. The mission bell was ringing lustily, but when services
were over only four sad natives came out of church. Pastor Parker
took us to his house and fed us on the fat of the land — strictly vegetable
fat. After dinner we smoked pipes and cigarettes around the table,
and neither the Pastor nor his wife said a word. The Commissioner's
sins were to be respected. Anyhow, we'd be off for Malekula in a
day or so.

But on the hour when the *Euphrosyne* was about to depart Smith-
Rewse said to our host, "Parson Parker, I expect you to see that Dr.
Lambert doesn't go into the Big Nambas country." A bush war was
going on over there, and the Commissioner's word was law.

The Big Nambas and the Little Nambas, let me explain, are two .
savage cults among the innumerable divisions and subdivisions in the
New Hebrides. They go naked, except for a wrapping of dried banana
leaves around their genitals. This wrapping, called the *nambas,* is large
with the Big Nambas and small with the Little Nambas. Both cults were
rather untamed in those days. Mr. Smith-Rewse told me about his
last trip to Malekula, and the murderer he brought back. The man
couldn't understand why he was arrested, although he had just buried
his infant daughter alive. All the way back to Vila he pleaded, "Master,
me no like go jail. More better you make me belong police." That

happened in peacetime, the Commissioner said. In wartime Malekula needed a major general more than it needed a doctor.

Later on I saw plenty of Malekula.

So I was left alone with Pastor Parker. I went out on the veranda, lit my pipe and heard his gentle voice saying, "Doctor, I'm afraid you'll have to stop smoking in the house or on the veranda. I must enforce the rules of our faith." A chronic smoker, I struck a compromise. I'd move to the lawn and let the Pastor talk to me from the veranda, if he didn't mind shouting. This was quite satisfactory, except when it rained. I had much idle time on my hands. Atchin was too small to afford many conclusions, except that the people were pretty heavily infected.

Mostly in shouts, Pastor Parker unloaded his peck of troubles. How his predecessor had moved to another station and all his converts had backslid when he stopped paying them a salary. He had worked on the patronage system, and his expensive conversions had drained the mission exchequer. Pastor Parker had never had enough money to make a wide appeal. In several years of purely spiritual effort he had only made two converts, a pair of primitives who were living in sin with heathen wives. The wives always accompanied them to church.

Trouble had been waiting for Pastor Parker when he took charge. The week they moved in, the place was raided by Big Nambas, who had plenty of guns and did plenty of shooting. The barricaded Parkers might have furnished long pig for the pig lovers but for a rescuing party of Presbyterians. To Parker's Adventist mind Presbyterians were limbs of Satan, but they saved him just the same, and advised him to move out. The Pastor informed them that he had come there to preach the True Gospel, and by Jehovah, he'd stay.

He was brave according to his lights. Once, in a desperate appeal for converts, he went alone among the Big Nambas and invited them to shoot him. It was a sort of sanctified attempt at suicide with all the charm of martyrdom. The savages laughed and sent him home. Either they admired his courage or they thought he was "touched."

He told me that he believed there was a great deal of cannibalism on Atchin. Offered a meatless Adventist diet as an alternative to maneating, I could well understand their attitude. Flatulent with three windy meals a day, I gazed morbidly at my host. I asked him if the pig-killing ceremony he had shown me was not a symbol of cannibalism. He thought so, vaguely. Later talks with ethnologists assured me that my guess was right. In the Pre-Pig Era, when man-eating was the rule instead of the exception, human beings were led up to the sacrificial stone, and with every stroke of the mallet were counted off to the credit of the fortunate donor. The pig is a comparative new-comer in the Pacific, but the ritualistic ceremonies are old as Time. It is remarkable how the pig took center-stage in New Hebridean life. He became the unit of wealth, of social position, of tribal power. When I was there, although his cult was vanishing with other folk ways, he was still being bred in strange shapes for sacrifice. Wives were still valued as swineherds, chiefs exalted for the number and odd variety of their hogs. Murders were committed more often over pigs than over women.

It was something out of *Gulliver's Travels*. Up to the time when misapplied Government and applied Christianity had weakened the pulse of the tribe, the secret society ruled these islands with a power that was super-Masonic. There were numerous lodges, each desig-nated by some emblem-leaf and special tabus. A boy coming of age passed the harsh initiation, which included circumcision or, more often, incision. Among the incisionists the medicine men were still operating on the young initiate by standing him in water up to his waist, thrust-ing a blunt stick under the prepuce to stretch the skin and using a feather-edge of split bamboo to cut the foreskin longitudinally from end to end. The wound was packed with herbs, which might have been astringent and antiseptic. The boys, treated *en masse*, were locked away for long days of fasting. I never heard of one who died.

The ceremony I first saw was to celebrate the return of a boy from the sacred island of Aoba, where he had gone through the cruel final tests which would admit him into the lowest rank of the secret order. He might work for years, maybe a lifetime, to accumulate enough pigs to raise him a degree in native Masonry. Now he was distinguished by a woven strip of fiber, worn something like an apron. Initiated boys danced in front of him. Yams were stacked like cordwood around the space where torches flared. Musicians pounded ten-foot wooden drums, shaped like fat cigars. The tops of the drums were painted with identical faces; the face of Tamaz, the Unseen God of All.

The ambitious native bought his way into high position in the order, and to chieftainship, through his contribution of pig monstrosities, especially raised for sacrifice. It was near Bushman's Bay, Malekula, that I first saw one of these freaks, a boar with artificially curled tusks. These tusks had grown toward the upper jaw, then turned in a circle backward as far as the lower jaw, where they were growing upward again to form a spiral. He was fourteen years old; if he lived to be twenty-one, he would be prized beyond money valuation — the pig with the three-curled tusks. The curl is produced by knocking out what correspond to our eye-teeth. With these gone, the teeth below have full play, and begin to twist backward at the end of the climb. Sometimes the curving ivory grows into the lip and tissues of the jaw, sometimes into the jaw itself. The animal must suffer constant pain. By the time he is ready for the altar he is fairly tough food, yet the man who can offer such a sacrifice to the noble dead is well on the way to mastership of his lodge.

The donor of several boars with curled tusks is immediately ex-alted. Such things are important to the great Tamaz; for when a high-grade native dies his soul goes to a high-grade heaven. The commoner, known as "man rubbish," must do with a pretty cheap Hereafter. Spiritual merit is achieved at the great ritual, but there is a minor ceremony known as "killing small," which is more prac-tical. Here the donor merely taps his pigs on the back, to show that they will be sacrificed when the time comes. The idea is to hold a surplus of pork, which might otherwise all be eaten at one grand party.

The Big Pig Ceremony goes on for weeks of splendidly rhythmed dancing, warriors chanting the saga of the tribe, grandees parading in elaborate masks while many curl-tuskers die for glory.

Sometimes a white man with an eye to business has gained chieftain-ship through feats of pig culture. One I knew attained high nobility by offering his collection of freaks. He took his rank seriously and went about in complete undress, save for a *nambas* and a pair of curled tusks around his neck. A friend who had known him in his other life asked him aboard his yacht, and was so shocked by the white chief's fashionable nudity that he wouldn't let him stay to dinner unless he put on a bath towel.

All through the New Hebrides there is a carefully guarded strain of sows which produce a certain number of pseudo-hermaphrodites with every litter; they produce them consistently and have a special name among breeders. I didn't believe this until I saw several alleged bisexuals being tenderly cared for. Undoubtedly they had both male and female characteristics, but in every case one sex or the other predominated. They could not breed, of course; but I was informed that they were amorous. There was a general opinion that only the matrilinear people bred these *ragwe* for high sacrifice and that the patrilinear groups shunned them as devil-devils.

The communistic New Hebridean builds a stockade around his vegetable patch in order to keep out the roving pigs. With no knowledge of crop rotation he moves his garden every year. Neighbors pile in to help him break ground, and he reciprocates. He cleans his patch when the *neurav* blossoms and harvests his yams when the cicada sings. And here's where the pig comes in, literally. Tribal law permits the yam-grower to shoot the low-bred trespassing hog. But if the interloper happens to be a tusked boar, hands off. Shoot him and you're fined in pigs of equivalent value; or else the owner goes gunning for you. Hence many very ugly pig wars.

The pig-poor commoner can't afford polygamy; women are scarce. Multiple marriage is a luxury for the rich, and for surprising reasons. I asked a wealthy chief on Aoba how many wives he had. Oh, about six, he guessed, but one of them might have died "of a pain in the heart." He had about a hundred pigs to take care of and they were increasing so fast he'd need at least two more wives.

Pigs were increasing, humans thinning out. That was true of almost all the islands I visited. In most districts the birth of boys far exceeded the birth of girls — a danger signal that marks the decline of population.

Finally we were working into the forests of Malekula which Mr. Smith-Rewse thought too dangerous for a white doctor to tackle. Shaggy black men, each wearing a chronic scowl and a beard that would rival a Scottish terrier's, lurked and peered or trooped down on us with their handy muskets. To make even an approximately accurate hookworm-survey was like trying to pry buttons from a live rattlesnake. When it came to yaws I found the men more obliging, for here as elsewhere they admired the needle, which New Hebridean pidgin called "stick medicine." It was a trifle disconcerting, however, to "needle" a man who squatted with a loaded rifle across his knees,

ready to repel a surprise attack from Little Nambas or to rebuke a
Foundation doctor whose technique proved unsatisfactory.

A few years earlier the Nambas, Big or Little, had fallen upon white
planters, butchered and eaten them. Then an Anglo-French naval
force landed on a punitive expedition. They made about fifteen miles
inland, burned some houses — and never saw a native. Another night
came on, and the Commander knew that people were hiding in the
bush; there was desultory firing and a few casualties. The landing
party retreated in the early morning, the bush-fellows picking them
off as they ran helter-skelter for their ship and safety. Their retreat
was scattered, with wounded men and abandoned firearms. The forest
cackled its jeering laughter, "Why don't you come and get us?" The
hidden savages had tied guns to the trees so that muzzles covered the
trail. They had fastened long strings to the triggers and sheltered themselves behind rocks where they could pull at a safe distance — an old
Malekula trick. There was plenty of meat for the ovens that night; and
when the bad news straggled back to Vila the bi-national Government decided that there should be no more reprisals. Natives must be
approached with tact. That was about the only policy the Condominium ever decided on, and we followed it, you may believe, in
our subsequent task of cleaning the uncleanable. Working on my findings of 1925, I sent Inspector Tully down there, and later some of our
best N.M.P.'s. What they accomplished in the face of native perversity was quite remarkable, and they had good government backing.
Tully reported that one mission body rather resented his coming into
their areas, because they had been charging a fairly stiff price for yaws
injections, and we were giving them free. The missionary attitude
was understandable, for we were buying the drug much cheaper than
they could; and after we furnished them our source of supply and
gave them the advantage of exchange, the difficulty was ironed out.
When the missionaries charged for treatments the natives were more
than willing to pay. The "needle" was always immensely popular with
them.

Before I left Suva for the 1925 survey Dr. Maurice C. Hall had requested me to try his latest discovery, tetrachlorethylene, on hookworm patients. I was the first to use it. Malakai and I selected a number
of patients at the Residency at Vila, treated them, counted the worms,

then re-treated them to see the percentage of efficiency. Results were splendid, and physical reactions to the drug were few.

Later on a shipping strike in Sydney stranded us at Bushman's Bay, Malekula, and there I was able to make a field test to determine how well tetrachlorethylene would work if given by laymen. On the fine Matevan Plantation I examined 102 laborers and found 97 infected with the Necator. We were working all over the island, so we had to move into the interior, but before I left Matevan I gave Fleming, the planter, a supply of the new drug with instructions as to dosage. Malakai and I got back in two weeks; again I rounded up my 97 patients, and was delighted to find that only 16 of them were even lightly infected with the worm. When I considered that the work had not been done by medical men, the results were very gratifying.

On this Matevan plantation I found that filariasis was so general that one force of 69 field hands had lost a total of 34 days in the past month. No wonder the French were importing Indo-Chinese. But a bad compromise . . . The natives seemed to enjoy it when we took blood smears and let them peer through the lens at swimming microfilariae. "Snakes in the blood!" they shouted admiringly. Back in the bush villages, when we were making hookworm tests, the old snake-in-belly argument always worked. What worked still better was the growing opinion that our medicine was some sort of booze. Results were often disconcerting. With thirty Big Nambas milling around, flourishing guns and shouting praise to Tamaz, it was up to your director to sit very tight and remember what the Government had said: Use tact.

Hookworm lectures in the villages, when we could drum up an audience, never lacked the element of surprise. One day we expected a fair number of natives but nobody showed up. Then a shy pagan sauntered in and explained that they couldn't come today "because an old man had to hang himself." We set out with police and missionaries, but the party was over when we arrived. The old man had had all his pigs slaughtered and given the neighbors a splendid feast. In the flush of revelry he had gone into the house, put a noose around his neck and thrown the end out of a window. His friends had obligingly pulled the string, then gone on with the free feed, vowing that he was a nice, generous fellow, but too old to be much good.

In the back country the old and feeble were often buried alive. A

Catholic priest told me how he had started his congregation. He dug up an antiquated couple who had just been dug in, revived them, baptized them and gained two splendid converts.

On Santo I saw one man who had been arrested for planting his father in a deep hole. This patricide was just as puzzled as the Malekula fellow who had buried his newborn child.

As a divertissement in pandemonium we had on our hands Dr. P. T. Buxton of the London School of Tropical Medicine. A distinguished scholar, Buxton was often a thorn in the side because of his definitely pro-Buxton opinions. I first met him in Samoa where he was patronizing New Zealand's great medical work, then London sent him with us to the New Hebrides. Before our boat touched land he endeared himself to his fellow passengers by remarking, "Aren't colonials quare people!" At a tea party in Vila his hostess asked, "Which of the Colonies do you come from, Doctor?" Buxton's eyebrows went up. "I only come from England!"

Malakai, who had been busy as a bird dog, was guardedly polite to this very learned entomologist, and I wondered what black revenge was simmering in the Melanesian heart. Malakai owed Buxton a grudge; up in Samoa the Londoner had twitted him about having hookworm. To disprove the accusation Malakai had examined his specimen by our regulation field method, and had found his case negative. "Suppose you try my Clayton Lane technique," challenged Buxton — this method was splendid for hospital examinations, but too complicated for field-work. Malakai was game. He tried Buxton's method on himself — and got one solitary, smallish hookworm. So Dr. Buxton had told the world how he had the laugh on a poor N.M.P.

Malakai bided his time. The malaria situation was not acute, because May to November is the "dry season" in the New Hebrides — meaning that it doesn't rain very hard and mosquitoes are comparatively few. We were on Malekula, and Dr. Buxton had returned from a month's tour, combing the islands for anopheles. In all his search he had only found two damaged-looking specimens. Where were the mosquitoes? Malakai looked over the sad little exhibit and never turned a hair.

Then one morning on Bushman's Bay my favorite N.M.P. turned up with a large number of anopheles in his specimen case. Buxton wanted to know where he got them. Oh, explained Malakai, he had

just cut a hole in his mosquito net and used himself for bait. Having
had their fill of blood they had gone to rest inside the net, so in the
morning Malakai had gathered them in. With a pretty gesture he
handed the scientist eighty-seven specimens to carry back to London.
I wonder if this gave our visitor a little more respect for the N.M.P.

This neat rebuke was all too subtle for a land where murder was the
popular way of showing annoyance. If I wished to get rid of anybody in particular I would just lure him to the New Hebrides, push
him off a boat and forget it. Should anybody get around to ques-
tioning me — which they probably wouldn't — I would blame the dis-
appearance to "blackwater fever," always a handy explanation for
missing persons. Or if I were a native I would shoot first, then run to
a mission and get converted. To bask in righteousness was always fairly
safe for the escaped trigger-man. (At one mission service the Nambas
lurked in the woods, well supplied with ammunition for a couple of
sanctified runaways, while the congregation inside was singing with
much fervor: "Anywhere with Jesus I may safely go.")

Another, if less popular, refuge for the guilty was to "recruit" into
contract labor. Women offered themselves to recruiters, too, but for
a different reason; they were usually in flight from "old men" husbands
or embarrassing family troubles. I saw one big black girl approach a
house and ask the planter's wife to take her on indefinitely. She was a
runaway, quaintly wild, naked except for a G-string pad and a small
mat on her head; she used the mat for a pillow. Down her back, suspended from her forehead, she carried a calico bag and there were a
few coppers in a leaf-purse at her throat. The bag contained all her
earthly possessions encased in sections of bamboo (*bahbu*). She showed
us her treasures: a piece of taro and a hatchet. She was all ready to
set up housekeeping.

At the British Residency in Vila there was an excellent servant I
called "Bush-Fellow Santo," just to watch him grin. A few years before
a chief had ordered him to shoot a rival chief, so obedient Santo had
poked a rifle through the bush, a foot from the doomed one's head.
Poor Santo pulled the trigger, and the thing missed fire. The annoyed
chief picked up the fallen gun and Santo made for the shore under a
rain of bullets. Luckily the Government's yacht lay in the stream. He
was pulled aboard, swearing eternal devotion to the white man. And he
kept his word.

The general practitioner, who attends one patient at a time, must know something of the sick man's habits, environment and psychic condition. The health physician in primitive countries has these problems multiplied by thousands. He must regard mass behavior — and examine the files for the rate of tribal advance or decay. He must know something of the history of his multiple patient to form a workable theory concerning the dangers or benefits of foreign contact. He must strive to be a diplomat and make whatever contact he can with the Government in power. . . . Then he must work with the best tools and knowledge that are at hand.

In the mad Condominium, where there was no reliable census, we had to pit fact-finding against an estimated population of around 55,000. The real figure, as we estimated it, was under 45,000, and steadily sinking. Evidences of depopulation showed in the long-deserted villages and in the discontinuance of many tribal ceremonies because there were so few old men left who knew enough of the mysteries to perform the rites. Long since these grand masters had been swept away by epidemics. Old planters would point out spots where they had seen tribes almost blotted out in the course of thirty years.

Yaws was second to hookworm and malaria. On pleasant Tanna, to the extreme south of the group, it was a painful sight to see the poor fellows hobbling to the fields, as though walking on hot coals. They were suffering from "crab yaws," which causes the feet to split oddly. Others, further gone with the disease, were given sitting down jobs, cutting copra near their quarters. Little attention — except in the hospital here — was paid to the condition and its cure, but what information I gave was welcomed. In more settled sections of the island a few injections with arsenicals were being given with the usual striking results. On parts of Tanna I found the natives themselves so eager for a cure that they were paying for the cost of salvarsan, and so earnestly asking for it that the supply was constantly giving out. When our outfit returned on later visits to give mass treatments the people were so grateful for the improvement in their health that they took up a collection and tried to present Tully with thirty pounds.

Everywhere we were busied by a variety of cases. We discovered an odd dozen of lepers and decided that the disease was spreading through the unprotected shores; there was no attempt to segregate the patients, although two at the Presbyterians' Tanna hospital were being successfully treated with chaulmoogra injections. Queer cases swam into our ken. Here was a sick warrior who had tried to dry up his yaws by smoking them over a fire. Here were patients being treated for tuberculosis when they were suffering from tertiary yaws, or treated for malaria when they were sick with filariasis. Here were missionaries complaining of prevalent syphilis — and it was yaws again. Here we became emergency dentists and examined pyorrhea, one result of anemia. Here were Christian teachers who wondered why so many children died, especially girls in a land where more women were needed. We tried to lecture them on the rudiments of infant feeding; the Presbyterians were doing their best to supply milk. On Tanna I found that good Dr. Nicholson had been breeding goats and teaching the babies to suckle the nannies, direct from producer to consumer. It was a sensible idea, since there was no effective way of storing milk out of reach of filth-carrying flies. The nannies had come to regard the youngsters as their own kids. Once, experimentally, I picked up a small baby and growled at it. There was a worried "*Baah!*" and the mothering she-goat came at me, tail up and horns down. No foreigner was allowed to fool with *her* children.

Where there was a scarcity of drugs there was always a plenitude of witch doctors. These wizards lacked the dignity of the ancient tribal seers, who undoubtedly exerted a certain protective influence over the flock. Now they had degenerated to annoying rain-makers, wind-makers, sun-makers, generally called "poisoners." If rain, wind or sun failed to appear on schedule, the Nambas had a jolly habit of shooting these specialists and calling in new ones.

I went with the Commissioner to round up a couple of wizards at Malua Bay, Malekula. They had been making mischief, setting family against family; then shooting had begun. Mr. Smith-Rewse, personally conducting the arrest, said that he would have let it blow over if the Adventists hadn't kicked up such a row. We went up to a plateau where the missioners were starting a village, and there was Pastor Parker, offering his services. Natives hung around in a wide circle, but they had left their rifles in the bush. They were not allowed to carry guns to public meetings.

If they had wished they could have picked us off like tender fowls for Sunday dinner, for nobody knew how many were hiding behind cover. We were entirely unarmed, except for four policemen in

dungaree uniforms — opposed to a whole island of untamed savages
who openly boasted of cannibalism. It was surprising to see their
frightened faces as they came up and shook hands with the missionaries; they were too shy to talk to government officials. Then with the
suddenness of all savage things a thin, tall old man appeared. His beard
and his eyes were somehow alike, wildly roving. He was the first of
the accused wizards. I had expected an arrogant figure, threatening us
with all the powers of sea and air. He slunk up, a picture of abject
fright. The other, who followed soon after, dragged back at every step
like a schoolboy about to be spanked.

They had fallen into a trap. The Resident Commissioner had given
it out that he had come to discuss some abuses on the part of the
"recruiters" who haul in contract labor. The natives huddled around,
hanging on Smith-Rewse's words — then abruptly he turned his questions on the two witch doctors, who seemed to have lost the power
of invisibility. Four policemen seized them, and as they were dragged
to the boat the air was filled with pleas for mercy. I was only sorry
for them.

For three days, going toward the Vila jail, the older one was just
a plaintive, seasick old man. He gave me a nicely curled pig's tusk, a
pledge of friendship, and admitted with the artlessness of a child that he
had planned to kill off the converts in the new Adventist mission. He
grew more and more downcast, and as we neared Vila he asked in
quavering pidgin, "How soon will you eat us?" I didn't know whether
to laugh or to cry. The poor old devil thought that our expedition was
a cannibal raid.

The Vila authorities sentenced him to a jail term long enough to
untwist his imagination. When I saw him in the jail yard he was very
docile. He even allowed me to treat him for hookworm. That was
something of a triumph for modern medicine.

The witch-doctor affair didn't end with the arrest. Nine days later
an Adventist convert named Harry, working in his garden, was shot
from ambush. He had been spokesman for Mr. Smith-Rewse during
the capture of the magicians; also friends of the sorcerers accused him
of having informed on them. After the shooting he lay for a long
time on the beach; riflemen in the bush dared the rescuing Adventists
to come ashore. Then one missionary recognized an acquaintance and
arranged a truce. I don't know whether Harry lived. He had gone to

the village of the magicians to assure the women that the wizards were only under arrest and would come back. The villagers had decided that he was there to seduce their wives — or that was the story they told.

I offer these scenes as samples of a country where a Foundation doctor was trying to make medical sense. Later on, when I made my return visits, we met every possible condition, good and bad — mostly bad — and often went alone among the most backward savages. None of us was murdered, but there was still a chance of a white man's blood being shed, if some fanatic should arise with a crusade against the oppressor. It had happened before.

For instance, there was the prophet Ronivira. Once in the early yam season he awoke to find that his navel was blown out. The uninitiated would have put it down to too much yam, but Ronivira arose and proclaimed that ghosts in his belly had given him power to raise the dead; price one pound to revivify a male relative, ten shillings for a female, five bob for a child. He didn't do any revivifying, but made a huge impression. His platform was the Bible, his program anti-white. He built warehouses to receive goods from a sympathetic United States — for the New Hebridean believes that all Americans are black men.

Finally the Resident Commissioner took him aboard the government yacht. In the midst of cross-questioning a storm broke with a clap of thunder; and thunder was so unusual in those parts that the Commissioner, so I was told, lost his nerve and let Ronivira go. After a time doubting Thomases began asking the prophet why he didn't raise any dead. When his wife died he stood over the corpse and made all the passes in his repertory, but Mrs. Ronivira didn't respond. To bolster his falling stocks he said that white magicians were working against him. Therefore all white men and their sympathizers must die. A high mast was erected on the beach for the hanging of all native skeptics; and when a white rag fluttered from the yard-arm it meant a European must die before sundown.

They murdered one white, at least, ate part of the body and threw the rest to the dogs. Finally the Resident Commissioner arrested Ronivira in earnest; but the yacht taking him to Vila met a storm that all but wrecked it. Although his trial was prolonged by witnesses afraid to testify, the authorities finally hanged the Great Resurrector.

Otherwise the Condominium's frail hold on the native might have collapsed.

Any white man's stories of cannibal revels should be checked with care. The primitive is a shy bird, and he knows that cannibalism has been blacklisted. Therefore he works cautiously. Old-timers in the New Hebrides say casually, "Oh, yes, it is going on." But I have never found one who has actually seen it.

When Bill Tully was running our yaws campaign in a remote part of Malekula, guards appeared around his house one day and forbade his going out. Through the chinks he could see a glow of fire, hear drumming and fierce cries. Bill knew, as if he had seen it, that they were cooking long pig. The patients who came to him next day were especially quiet and subdued.

One afternoon, on Atchin, Malakai came back from an inspection across the island and said that work had been delayed by a ceremony. The messenger of a chief on Malekula had come with a gift for a chief on Atchin. It had come carefully rolled in pandanus leaves. Maybe the chief was less secretive than he would have been before a European, for he allowed Malakai to look on while he opened the package. It contained a human hand.

What Malakai saw was part of an old courtesy-custom. When a chief makes a kill he sends some part of the body, like a hand or foot, to a chief bound to him by kin or friendship. Within a certain period the recipient is supposed to return the gift in kind. There is a delicate code: If the meat of a common native is sent to A, then in due time A sends to B flesh of a similar social status. If the cut is from a chief, then chief-meat is expected in return. In old days when white men were easy game the exchange was often in white-man's flesh. But nowadays bagging Europeans is a dangerous sport, so the meat of a "clothed man" takes the place of this delicacy. A "clothed man" means any native who has been educated to European dress.

This pernicious round-robin, I was told, had got on the nerves of some chiefs, who had learned to prefer peace and pig. But when the pandanus-wrapped package came they knew what was expected of them.

Man-eating is far from an everyday amusement in the New Hebrides, but in 1923 even white men were not entirely safe. Ewan Corlette, a planter on Bushman's Bay, Malekula, sent his native wife to the neighboring island of Santo to visit at the home of his friend, Klapcott, who had a trading store, and a native family. Later the place was found a shambles, a welter of blood. Klapcott had always kept a rifle handy, but evidence proved that, when he turned to take down some goods, one of his native customers had brained him with a hatchet. Evidence also showed how the women and children had run, trying to escape, before the savages finished them.

Traders didn't like to tell cannibal yarns because it "gave the place a black eye." They were something like the San Franciscans who saved face by calling their earthquake a fire. The face-savers along the beach were inclined to scoff at tales of white men having taken photographs of man-eating revels, although some such pictures, I am told, have been shown to the public.

The Negroid folk, if they ever talk about man-eating, will tell you that it has a religious significance. The merrier, slightly Polynesian people to the north and east are more candid. One of their chiefs, who had probably finished a quart of bad French wine, said simply, "Me like im long pig too much." He just liked what he liked. His people had a record for cruelty. In the bad old days their trained garroters went on long hunts, stole upon sleeping islands and strangled the sleepers, quietly, with a looped vine. They were reputed to have kept their prizes in pens to fatten them. Island peoples with a higher mental capacity than their neighbors have often been the bloodiest cannibals and tormentors. Witness Fiji, witness the New Zealand Maoris. Cruelty seems to be the brat of young imagination. The ape-man bashes his enemy with a club; he can think of nothing cleverer. His more gifted neighbor becomes a virtuoso in the art of giving pain. Yet superior peoples like the Samoans and Cook Islanders have not been notorious man-eaters; whereas the flat-headed Goaribaris are still at it. In spite of this paradox, I have found some of my most enlightened native friends among grandsons of cannibals.

Meanwhile anthropologists debate the subject: Do men eat men to satisfy an animal hunger, or has cannibalism a religious significance? Scholars who associate the Christian Church's sacramental bread and wine with the ancient custom of devouring a sacrificial hero will appreciate the remark of one big black convert. It was Communion Sunday, and when the wine cup was passed to him he drained it and shouted lustily, "Fill um up anudder time, Master. Me like im dis fellow Jesus too much!"

Perhaps at times I have given the missionary less than his due. I stand rebuked by a letter I picked out of a recent *Pacific Island Monthly*. It quoted an eminent authority who wrote in the middle of the nineteenth century and reminded his readers that the missions had appreciably reduced "the power of an idolatrous priesthood — a system of profligacy unparalleled . . . infanticide . . . bloody wars where the conquerors spared neither women nor children. . . . In a voyager to forget these things is base ingratitude; for should he chance to be at the point of shipwreck on some unknown coast, he will most devoutly pray that the lesson of the missionary may have reached thus far."

The letter-writer reminds us that the author of these words was no missionary, nor was he rated a good Christian. Many called him an atheist or freethinker. He was Charles Darwin.

I have criticized some missionaries as I have criticized some of my own profession. But I have stumbled so often, late at night, into little lonely mission houses, to be welcomed by their poor best; I have depended so much on the missionary's co-operation in my medical work, and so frequently seen his eagerness to learn the nature and the cure of diseases that were afflicting the tribes, that I do not wish to seem unfair.

I am speaking of the best. And I shall not take back a word I have said in disparagement of the others. Even among the best there was frequent jealousy and backbiting. Opposing missionaries were too often "sheep stealing." Once on Ambrym I heard Smith-Rewse ask a missionary why he hadn't been to Vila lately. "I can't get away," he said. "Every time I leave, those Seventh Day Adventists steal one of my villages."

Missionaries are excellent men, average men, poor men and evil men — about like the rest of us. I do not agree with their claims of making such large numbers of *true* converts; but their claims as educators, humanizers and civilizers are often justly founded. Not so long ago in the Pacific the whole burden of education was left to them. And as humanitarians I praise the Presbyterians in the New Hebrides — without their intervention over the past hundred years the last native there would have died. And I have seen the quiet work of the Melanesian Mission in the Solomons where the workers are High Church, yet drudge and slave with evangelical zeal. The Melanesian Mission, I think, is doing better medical work than any of the other sectarians down there. And, not excepting the devoted Fathers of the Sacred Heart in Papua, I would call the Presbyterians of the New Hebrides the best religious civilizers.

In the Melanesian Mission were educated men and women giving their lives and all for the Cause, which paid them £40 a year. They were often short on equipment, but their hospitals were better than could be expected. Brave people, mostly celibates. I can almost forgive Bishop Baddeley for helping to wreck a great humanitarian plan by writing, in effect, "I will accept no boundaries to the Kingdom of Christ." Baddeley had served as a colonel in the First World War, and he guarded his boundaries with a soldier's sense of duty.

Let me offer the Reverend Frederick J. Paton as the best example of a Presbyterian missionary. A frail-looking man of fifty-eight, crippled by a missing leg and a twisted arm, he took me in his creaky little motorboat over to Onua on Malekula. Before he had unlatched his gate I caught a scent of roses and verbena. The rich soil of the New Hebrides had grown a garden that might have smiled in Kent or Massachusetts. But his fragrant little garden contrasted with the awful untidiness inside his house. Items in the litter were too numerous to mention, except to say that he dined off one end of a long table in his big living room, and the rest of the table was given over to books, binoculars, scraps of food, discarded watches, a typewriter, some clothes — in fact about everything that Mr. Paton had put there and forgotten. He usually did his own cooking, but in our honor he brought in a couple of native teachers who stirred up a frightful mess in a very dirty kitchen. He had a bathtub, which Malakai insisted on giving a triple scrub with disinfectants before he would let me get in. I don't know where Mr. Paton bathed, but he was always neat and clean, if shabby.

When I talked with him I realized why he was the most useful missionary in the New Hebrides. His father before him was the famous missionary-bishop, and his son Frederick's life was devoted to distributing the John D. Paton Fund. Mr. Paton was too busy with good works to bother about his surroundings. His doors were always open to stray natives, who wandered in day and night; they just curled up on the floor and slept. While provisions held out Paton never let them go away hungry. This Australian Scot had inherited some money; however, his pocket never held two pennies to rub together.

I think it was his ambition to die poor; but when money was needed for his work he could be shrewd. He would pack and go to Sydney, where a Mission Board was never quite able to resist his plea.

Medical experience had taught me that a pure spirit often dwells in a broken body. When he was a baby a careless nurse had spoiled one of his arms; he had lost a leg when a motorboat fouled a hidden rock, during an emergency call. His success in handling natives was envied, even by his co-religionists. His converts were nearer Christians than most I saw. . . . I don't know why I speak of him in the past, for as I write he is very much alive, seventy-three and going strong. We have been corresponding for years, and I bless him for the way he took up my cause for the Central Medical School. His daily work had shown him the need of it.

I can't forget the way Mr. Paton had the laugh on me one night when I was lecturing the natives in a church at the quaint village of Pangkumu. With unique co-operation he had assigned the contribution box to receive hookworm specimens. The people were pretty badly infected, so I strained my pidgin English to express the horrible fecundity of the female Necator. See the hundreds of snake-eggs she could lay in twenty-four hours. . . . "Look out!" Paton whispered. Right in front of me a woman with scared eyes was holding a baby. In her fright she let it drop. I had to stop the lecture to look over the casualty, and when I found that no bones were broken Paton laughed softly, "It doesn't pay to be too sensational."

Paton knew his natives, and he knew the Condominium well enough to have an incompetent district agent removed now and then. When my Native Medical Practitioners ran afoul of European prejudice Paton never failed to take their part. A French physician objected to our N.M.P. Peni visiting the villages when a whooping cough epidemic was raging — and whooping cough can be deadly down there. The Frenchman wanted the sick to come to his hospital, to sleep outside in leaky shacks until he was ready to treat them. Paton advised Peni to go straight to the villages and save the patients from the shock of being moved, and he acted on that advice. When Mesalume was there — the poor boy who died on duty — Paton often got out his motorboat at small hours in the morning and hurried him to emergency calls. The Government had no launch to send.

During my first visit to Onua I treated 300 hookworm cases, and nearly half of them were women; a remarkable record in a land where women were especially guarded by the feces tabu. Whenever I found a people susceptible to medical advice I always found a good mission in charge. Paton's was 100 per cent.

The New Hebrides needed dozens of Patons. And Patons don't come in dozen lots.

I had finally the meager satisfaction of knowing that the population was taking a slow turn upward — but too slow to hold its own. The men still outnumbered the women; there were not enough of the latter to carry on the breed. In some regions where public health was beginning to pick up I found that the sex balance was working toward a normal equilibrium. That was a good sign, though all too faint. Its promise was dimmed by graver threats of racial annihilation. You can't draw clean water from a stream that is polluted at the source. The New Hebrides, with no enforced quarantines, no concerted effort to look into the causes of epidemics, no program for restoring the best and healthiest of the native customs, no educational system, and apparently no sincere wish to divorce the savage from liquor and firearms, were well on the road to racial extinction. The slum-scum of the Orient would take over all the jobs of the sick islanders, and succumb to the same diseases. That's a gloomy picture — but an illustration of what may befall any community, tropical or temperate, where public health and education are not enforced by a strong central authority.

When I was working among the plantations around Male I stayed with M. Peletier, who owned a wide domain, 800 acres of it rich with coffee, cacao, cotton and copra. M. Peletier was equally rich in children from wives and concubines. He had come there as a stranded French sailor, and in middle age his ambition was to retire and live in Los Angeles. The sanitary habits of his laborers were fairly well looked out for — which was refreshing, since I had just seen indescribable filth on near-by plantations.

Well, on Saturday night I retired early in one of M. Peletier's clean rooms, and had just fallen asleep when the quiet was shattered by drunken native voices. Next morning the natives who had promised to come for a lecture failed to show up. They were sleeping it off.

In the afternoon I drove with the Peletiers to the home of M. Margot, who had the usual store in the back of his house. We were having a glass of wine on the front porch when a crowd of natives appeared and began to file around toward the store. They were none too steady and it was obvious that they had come for more liquor. The Margots gave me an embarrassed glance. *Comme c'était embêtant!* With a Foundation doctor looking on, knowing that they were selling grog to the heathen! M. Margot rose to the emergency and staged a powerful scene. Blue with indignation, he faced the rioters and asked them what they meant by coming on Sunday, of all days, to buy kerosene and tobacco? Then, turning to me, he explained gently, "They're just children. If they happen to want kerosene and tobacco they pay no attention to my rules. Such children!"

Meanwhile the children were howling some island French word that sounded like "Poison," or maybe "Boisson," but obviously referred to booze. Their college cheer, "Me want Boisson," was pointed-up by one big voice in the bedlam: "Suppose you no pay me my five pounds wages along grog — me want Boisson!" And the Margots were loudly protesting that they had never heard of such a thing. Neighbors ought to be ashamed to give grog to those poor boys.

We left in the midst of the embarrassing scene; left Margot to unbolt a side door and begin serving the customers. I let out a vulgar American horse-laugh. How furious the Margots must have been at Peletier for taking me there on Sunday! Peletier drove moodily away and tried to continue the argument about natives wanting kerosene and tobacco. When I asked him if I looked like a jackass he changed his tune. You had to sell grog, he said, if you wanted to keep anybody on your plantation. Even the British did it on the sly.

M. Margot's side-door trade was mild compared to what I saw on another island. Saturday night again. Nude figures were dancing around a fire. In the center of the group was a fat Frenchman, naked except for a grass skirt. He was leading them all, contorting and howling. The ground was strewn with empty bottles. I asked the man with me if this fellow had "gone native." "Oh, no," he said, "he is the owner of a big plantation. But he prefers to dance with the people. It keeps them contented."

In going among the islands we would come occasionally upon scenes of well-being that raised our hopes for the future. Even now I stroke my waistcoat, remembering the large hospitality of F. J. Fleming's plantation at Bushman's Bay. Here was a New Zealander who had succeeded against all odds. His acres were lush with luxury. Blooded cattle grazed in his fields, his yards were filled with fancy ducks, turkeys, chickens and guineas. One native boy was devoted to a single job — supplying Matevan Plantation with fish. Dinner at Mr. Fleming's table was something I often remembered on hard cross-island hikes. It was here that I made the tetrachlorethylene experiments, for in spite of the plantation's prosperity there was much disease.

Mr. Fleming dwelt in the Land of Canaan and knew all the ropes. He kept his plantation clean with blooded Herefords which multiplied so rapidly that there was a surplus over the needs of his menage and his labor quarters. Once a week he had a young bullock slaughtered, and he knew how to keep the meat tender and wholesome. The only provisions he had to buy were tea, sugar, wine and flour. Matevan baked its bread in its own ovens, and was not bothered by labor shortage, because the good eating was famous among the natives. This project flourished on dangerous Malekula, a smiling picture of what the New Hebrides offered to the right man.

While Mr. Fleming fed on the fat of the land discouraged planters over the hill were starving on tinned beef.

This survey didn't end with very cheerful conclusions. The New Hebrides group offered a picture of a race being murdered by European invasion. Fiji and Samoa had been invaded too, but their conquerors had set about making amends. Outside of sporadic attempts to discourage cannibalism, what had the pale-faced intruders done to improve this race whose labor they so bitterly needed? . . . I had worked my level best and given all the advice I had to give.

We were coming back to the New Hebrides someday, with all the medicine and all the knowledge at our command. I told that to Mr. Paton just before I left, and he was mightily pleased. I couldn't prophesy any results, but now that I look back on our subsequent years of work down there I know that in many regions we turned the tide of health. Yet it has still not turned fast enough to restore a dying population. And if it dies, what then? Well, the Axis Powers can always pour in slaves to upset Oceania's racial and economic balance again. I hate to think of that as a solution. But the Condominium Government as I saw it was inviting its own fall.

I didn't dwell on doleful things when I said good-by to Mr. Paton and told him that we were coming back to cure and not to question. Before we shook hands he smiled and said, "Mr. Rockefeller has given us so much in the work you are doing for my people that I want to give him something in return." He brought a package and when he opened it I saw a roll of tapa cloth, very old and unusual with a faded velvety texture. The markings were so faint and frail that he had to trace them out. He said, "This came from Efate over in the east where there's quite a mixture of Polynesian. The missionaries who first touched there over a hundred years ago found the natives worshiping this cloth. Nobody knows where it came from, but there's a myth that it was brought in a foreign canoe." Mr. Paton rolled up the tapa and handed it to me, with a letter to John D. Rockefeller. "Just to thank him," he said. "I don't think there's another tapa like it in the world."

On my way for a month's leave in the States I went by Sydney, Fiji and Tonga, carrying the old tapa back along the course it must have followed centuries ago. At Tonga I unwrapped it and showed it to Queen Salote. She looked it over carefully, and so did the wise old ones. They all said that it must have come from Futuna, one of the French Polynesian islands just north and west of Tonga; they told me that it was of a type made nowhere else. "It must be very old," Salote said, "because it was not pounded with a stone, as they do it nowadays. It was scraped with a shell, and that gives it the velvet texture. And the stenciling is finer than the modern style." She marked out the graceful feather design, almost indistinguishable. "They never made feather designs in Tonga. Tapa is still scraped in Samoa," she said, "but this one is a double tapa, and they do not make that kind." The old people pointed out the thin reddish color that still tinted the surface and said that it was *lengo*, which is turmeric, a sacred plant-juice worn only by chiefs. Futuna was on the old route where traders brought in turmeric for the body and garments of royal personages. "The feather design is royal too," the old people said. "This tapa was worn by a king. So a king must have visited Efate."

I went on my way, carrying something that amounted to a lost crown jewel, a proof that Tongafiti conquerors had once touched the New Hebrides. When I reached New York I sent that tapa with Mr. Paton's letter to Mr. Rockefeller, who dropped me a note saying that he was putting the relic in a museum. I hope he did. I hope it wasn't tucked in the family attic where a housekeeper would junk it someday among unidentified family scraps. If that should happen, the Rockefeller estate would lose a unique treasure.

CHAPTER VI

NEW ZEALAND'S LITTLE SISTER

Before I take you into the Cook Islands, where our war on disease landed me late in 1925, I must deal briefly with Polynesia's humane and thoughtful big sister, New Zealand. The kinship of her native Maoris with those she was called upon to govern in the Cooks is so close that one can scarcely refrain from naming the two in the same breath. I have made several visits to the Dominion, both to learn and to teach, and have written hundreds of pages of reports, never without admiration for the Government's progress in rehabilitating a magnificent race which, but for a generous conqueror, might have perished from the earth.

I grant you that their program for education and health has been marked by errors of judgment, and that their pioneering was like most Pacific conquests, selfishly concerned with taking away a native people's God-given right to its own land and its own way of life. Perhaps New Zealand's temperate climate worked on the temperate mind of the Anglo-Saxon when he finally set himself to govern the greatest number of Polynesians in any of Oceania's racial zones. This might have brought about the bright change. But I am more inclined to believe that it came largely through the native Maori's natural genius for government.

Consider the lusty fighting Maori of two centuries ago. They numbered perhaps between 200,000 and 300,000 souls. In 1896, when Government conscience awoke, the Maoris had fallen to 40,000. Then came the resurgence, forced through channels of education and public health, so that today the Polynesians on the mainland have passed the 85,000 mark and are steadily increasing. In the year 1937 the Dominion spent well over £1,000,000 on education, building, sanitary improvements and pensions for the Maoris. Public schools were thrown open to their children. Industrial training fostered the Maori's natural ingenuity with tools. Too much, perhaps, was being done for the native;

it is only human for a spoon-fed people to do as little as possible to lift the spoon.

On the Pacific New Zealand is unique: her million-and-a-half Europeans outnumber her natives by tremendous odds. This may sound easy for the Dominion, but Government, every step of the way, has been forced to tackle a variety of problems: ancient and well-earned grudges against the *Pakeha* (white man), a tendency to lean on a dole, carefree indifference to modern hygiene — a hundred and one cross-currents. I have seen the subsidized Maori farmer on the East Coast, dressed in British clothes, looking like any tanned European and proud of modern farm machinery. I have seen the model dwelling houses which the authorities set in the back yards of native schools to inspire the Maori housekeeper. I have seen British ladies striving to teach back native arts which the natives had forgotten. I have seen lazy boys playing pool during work hours and pertly asking, "Why work when the *Pakeha* pays?" And all this time, in the primitive village which he ruled with a rod of fear, Rua the Prophet lay dying of a rival witch's curse; when he died his followers sat for days, expecting him to rise again.

In 1926 New Zealand was governing her own Maoris, their cousins on the Cook Islands and beautiful Niue, and had control of Western Samoa. She was ruling 152,000 Polynesians. It would be better for the Polynesians, I think, if she were to govern them all.

The British New Zealander is not especially race-tolerant, nor has he always been an idealist. The surprising thing is that the Maori's rise from death to life came about largely through the genius of certain Maoris, of one generation at least, who seized the opportunity and so brilliantly improved it that their zeal revived the flagging soul of a conquered people.

Let me name a few of that generation. Some had a light strain of British blood, but their minds and hearts were Maori. There was "Jimmie Taihoa," later knighted as Sir James Carrol, a lawyer whose scarifying logic so outmaneuvered Parliament that the *Pakeha's* unjust land laws were enfeebled by *reductio ad absurdum*. Sir Apirana Ngata, probably the greatest of these Maoris, deliberately set himself to learn European ways that he might protect his race against the *Pakeha*. With a cabinet portfolio he served for years as Minister to the Maoris. When his fire blazed too hot the Prime Minister put him out. But only to invite him back, because as an outsider he was even more destructive. His land laws stand today, a bulwark between the Maoris and the land-grabbers. He is still living and fighting. Highly Europeanized, his great wish is to have his people return to their tribal ways.

Dr. E. P. Ellison, a Maori, was last Director of Maori Hygiene, and served in the Cook Islands with distinction as Chief Medical Officer. Dr. Peter Buck (Te Rangiheroa) began in the same post, developing later into one of the world's great ethnologists. He was visiting professor at Yale for two years, and in Honolulu he became director of the famous Bishop Museum. I have heard that he is returning to New Haven.

These distinguished Maoris graduated from Te Aute College, and the new generation has not produced such leaders. Possibly it is the fault of a changed educational system for natives. Possibly it is because unusual men are born, not made.

Sir Maui Pomare died a few years ago. We were close friends from the day I met him with Lady Pomare, also a Maori aristocrat. He held down three ministerial positions at one time; but for his racial origin he would have been Prime Minister. Graduate of an American medical school, he began his career as Maori Medical Officer. Once young Dr. Pomare handled a three months' typhoid epidemic without a soul to help him. As Director of Maori Hygiene he treated a whole race over scattered areas. His preachment of modern sanitation and racial self-respect were lasting things. Often Pomare's theories ran counter to Ngata's, for his great desire was to close the gap between two races.

Memories of an ancestral thoroughbred always pleased Sir Maui. About the time the Ministry of Health for New Zealand and the Ministry of the Cook Islands were conjoined under his authority, there was an anniversary service in one of Wellington's oldest churches. Eloquently the preacher dwelt on the Christian beatification of a certain old-time savage, Pomare's great-granduncle, who had given the ground the church was built on and money to endow it. The sermon so honeyed the good works of the converted barbarian that the news got around to Pomare, who asked the clergyman to come to his office and hear the real story.

Great-granduncle, a cannibal and head hunter, had led the first Maori War and held the British at bay so long that an embarrassed Crown Governor put a price of five hundred pounds on the rebel's head. The

Maori King called in a few chiefs, who might have been a bit pro-British, and made this counter-proposal: "I am honored by the offer of five hundred pounds on my head. Five hundred pounds is a lot of money, and if any of you want my head, suppose you come and get it." The chiefs made no reply. "Well," said the King, "I think I know the value of heads. Suppose I put my price on the Governor's, an exchange of courtesies. My offer is sixpence."

Sir Maui informed the clergyman that his ancestor had endowed the old church after he had laid aside his well-worn spear and become a Christian. The gift had to do with horse-racing. The British had built their race track in Wellington, and the craze had spread among the more prosperous chiefs. The retired King, old and feeble, had imported a thoroughbred and entered it for the great meeting of the year. The elderly Maori lay on his deathbed too ill to go near the track, so he posted relays of runners all the way from the course to his bedside. When a messenger proclaimed that the horse had won, the old man straightened up, shouted, "A victor to the last!" and fell dead. His success on the track enriched a church endowment, and a winning horse had crowned his string of victories over the white man.

With relish Sir Maui told me how the old gentleman did a stroke of business. He sold the present site of Wellington to the granduncle of Sir Francis Bell. The deed is recorded, and the price was something like this: two kegs niggerhead tobacco; three dozen red flannel nightcaps; a dozen pipes; a dozen umbrellas; two flintlock pistols; assorted muskets with powder; half a gross of jew's harps.

When I asked Pomare if it didn't make him sick to think of his ancestor selling the site of a great modern city for a mess of junk, he said, "It was only a fraction of the land Great-granduncle had. And he got what he wanted. Can't you imagine the old man walking away, wearing his red nightcap, hoisting his umbrella, playing his jew's harp and laughing over the way he stuck the white man in that deal? Everything's relative in this world, and when it came to money-sense — well, he was a Polynesian."

It was at Pomare's request that I visited the Cook Islands toward the end of 1925 and into the early months of 1926. He asked me especially, as a director for the Foundation, to look into the hookworm situation there, but also to include in my survey the general aspect of native diseases. He had not then been long enough in office to organize the public health work as thoroughly as he desired, and there was the usual shortage of competent doctors. Sir Maui had a special affection for the Cook Islanders, as he was closely related to them. He often suggested my looking into the pre-Christian religion on the Cooks and the relics it left behind.

Medically speaking, the Cooks were a great relief after the New Hebrides. Although conditions were far from perfect, I found no serious problems. Public health was above the Pacific average, but there were some indicated dangers, and I was obliged to raise the red flag. Population had begun to fall in the eighties, but had been slowly coming back since 1900, when New Zealand took over. Up to then the group had been utterly neglected, save by the usual despoilers. Twenty-five years is too short a time to work a radical change in any people. The Maoris on these tiny, graceful clumps of land now numbered over 10,000. The group lies some twenty degrees below the Equator, cheek-by-jowl with Tahiti — too close, perhaps, for health.

Rarotonga, so often described by romantic novelists, has suffered some injustice from flights of imagination. It is the main island in the little Cooks and is a collection of small towns, one of which harbors Government Headquarters. To the native mind it had the lure of Paris for the Peorian. Cinemas, public entertainment and private vice drew with the loadstone's charm, and the combination was probably dangerous for the pleasure-loving Maori. Gonorrhea, imported from generous Tahiti, was on the increase. That was true of Rarotonga, but not of the less populated and more primitive islands. The Polynesian is a great gossip, and when an infected townsman came home from his big spree the whole village knew it, and shunned him accordingly.

Dr. Ellison was working like a beaver with an understaffed department, yet what could he do but just shuffle along and make the best of it? I had Malakai along, my Exhibit Number One. At once he became a popular idol, a social and scientific success. When Ellison saw his work and realized what a native physician could accomplish, and I told him that our Central Medical School, once it got going, could turn out hundreds like Malakai, Ellison was all for the School; he'd do anything to put it through.

My hopes were running high then. Dr. Montague had just written a letter, announcing that all the High Commission groups, five of them, and all the groups controlled by New Zealand were ready to sign on the dotted line. And there was Sir Maui Pomare, clear-thinking and powerful in his faith that the native mind was receptive to the highest education.

My hope was to be blasted by an act of Pomare himself. He had suffered a slap in the face, something no well-born Maori will endure. I shall go into that later.

In Rarotonga it was pleasing to see the young people, the boys in white trousers, the girls in simple frocks, throwing their souls into the dances of 1925. European clothes and European ways seemed to be their destiny, and the Government had encouraged innocent dances, away from the temptations of bush-beer and petting parties on the beach. This music and youthful pleasure was in sharp contrast with the plight of the unhappy New Hebridean, robbed of his tribal ceremony and given nothing to take its place.

In less conventional surroundings girls were still dancing the hura, more graceful than the Hawaiian hula, but they were contorting for the leer of visiting sailors. Gonorrhea, already gaining in 1925–1926, was not entirely blameable on that old scapegoat, Tahiti. The Hollywood movie had become the popular notion of European behavior. Imitate clothes, imitate morals. The local girl had acquired a craving for silk stockings and high heels, things that must be paid for with *Pakeha* money, however she got it.

Disease-bearing Tahitian boys were coming over with a bribe which few Rarotongan girls could resist — bottles of French perfume. For this the girls deserted their local sweethearts and husbands, flew to the scented strangers, and were sorry afterward. The bright lights of Rarotonga were luring so many from surrounding islands that overcrowding threatened a higher infection of tuberculosis. Polynesian hospitality invited the germ, for relatives came pouring to be packed like sardines in the coral houses. They ate so much that many hosts went undernourished between parties.

Speaking of forced sophistication, a little native nurse in one of the best hospitals approached me shyly and asked for an examination. I brought in assistants, had her put on the table and ignored her protests over the delicate job at hand. When I had finished I asked her why she had made such a fuss; she ought to be used to doctors. "Oh, but

Doctor," she said, "I thought you were going to examine my chest!" She had expected me to use a stethoscope. It was the same all over the Cooks. Put a stethoscope to a native's chest and he thought it was magic to cure whatever ailed him. What ailed the little nurse happened to be pregnancy.

Here's another example of the naïve sophisticate. I was with a local merchant, admiring the beautiful sunset, when a pretty native girl stopped her bicycle. She was trig and slim in a white duck dress, white shoes and a flaming red scarf around her neck. What she said sounded like something you learn by rote: "I-am-looking-for-the-doctor, to-come-to-my-mother, who-is-very-ill." I asked my friend if her mother was ill and he said, "That's something she learned at school and is trying on us."

She smiled primly and my friend asked her where her lover was. She said, "Luff? That is no good. Some boys talk luff, I say 'Go way, I am too strong. I no go down to the beach.'" Her name, she told us, was Ngapuku, and she was sixteen, fancy free. "I am a Girl Guide," she announced. With every breath she went on talking about "luff," which did not interest her because she was a proper Girl Guide. Where and how she guided the stranger came out in the next sentence. Last week when a New Zealand gunboat came in she met a sailor who talked "luff" and was indignantly repelled. However, since Jack ashore wished to be guided, she took him around to the other sort of girl and charged a fee of twenty-five shillings, five for girl friend and twenty for herself.

The Cook Islands had no half-caste question because there were no half-castes, socially speaking. All were members of the local community, and a light-skinned baby was a welcome arrival. There was no slightest stigma on illegitimacy. Married natives were eager to adopt such children. One British trader I knew had a native wife and four daughters; long before a newcomer was born a delegation came to the house and begged for the privilege of adopting the baby. The prospective mother finally promised it to a childless couple, if it should be a girl. But if it was a boy she would keep it. She had no boys.

I heard of one native who quarreled with his wife and left her. But when he learned that she had been living with a white man he returned and implored to be taken back. He wanted the privilege of fathering her expected child. The Maori here seemed to be moving toward another race, and I hoped that it would be for his betterment. Children with a European strain usually got ahead faster, not because they had more brilliance or character, but because their lighter skin seemed to cast an aura of superiority. Parents favored them, schoolteachers, however fair-minded, unconsciously moved them toward the head of the class. I am not sure that the full-blooded Cook Islanders were not the best type I saw in the Pacific. Although the women were inclined to sloth and fat, the men were thin and well-muscled, hard workers and innately industrious. All day long they labored in their gardens, or carried produce miles to load it on the steamers offshore. At home they did the cooking for their lazy wives, who, like most Polynesian wives, were spoiled by their husbands.

As an inquiring physician I noted the fine condition of the men; handicapped by imported disease, inadequately defended by a medical system not yet well organized, they seemed to be building up their bodies against many of the ills that attacked them. The principal occupational disease among them was hernia, result of lifting heavy loads.

On my second visit there, 1932, I wrote to the Secretary of the Cook Islands, urging him to take advantage of the larger number of Native Medical Practitioners we were then able to offer. I pointed out one paradox: sophisticated Rarotonga showed less confidence in European physicians than I usually found in the primitive outlying islands. Everywhere there was a faith in witch-doctor remedies, which was astonishing considering that these places had been in contact with Europe for over a hundred years. During my first visit I used Malakai more than once to scold and wheedle sick natives away from their ancient superstitions. He could talk to them as man to man, which was more than any European could ever do. I missed him on my second trip.

Some of the impressions I am giving deal with my later stay on these islands, but they are mainly true of the Cooks as I saw them in 1925–1926.

Captain Andy Thompson of the *Tagua*, which took us from atoll to atoll, was a Yankee from Minnesota. As confirmed fishermen, Andy and I were soulmates. In those waters you might land anything from a minnow to a hammerhead shark. What happened one afternoon might serve as a Polynesian parable, and Andy was the philosopher to interpret it. Andy's line grew rather taut, and as he pulled it lazily in he said, "Just a little one!" The fish was halfway in when the line started out to sea. "Guess it's a big one," Andy decided, holding on. Then as suddenly the line slacked; there was some dead weight on it. Andy pulled it in, 300 pounds of kingfish, which might have weighed considerably more if half its tail end hadn't been bitten off while it was being hauled into the boat. Put me down for a liar, but this is what I saw. The big fish had swallowed the hook so deeply that we had to slit its belly. In the postmortem we found a thirty-pound cod attached to the hook, which it had just gobbled when the kingfish grabbed it. Further scientific curiosity caused us to open the cod and find a two-pound mackerel. "Well," drawled Andy, "that's the Pacific all over again! England swallows New Zealand, New Zealand swallows the Cooks. . . ." He was like a Roman augur, interpreting guts at the altar. I studied the kingfish and wondered what sea monster had eaten its tail. And would this be the fate of Pacific empire when its shrinking population had grown too feeble to serve European needs and hordes of orientals swarmed over the plantations to overthrow the economic balance until some monster military machine would swim up and kill a fish it was not quite able to swallow? 1940 was to threaten the world with that very thing.

This fishing interlude came when we were approaching low-lying Mauke, where I was entertained by hospitable traders, many of whom had native wives. The Cook Islands might well be named after the prevalent good cooking; the tenderly roasted sucking pig and Mitiaro eels, found nowhere else, are something to recall with watering mouth.

Our work in the New Hebrides was sometimes delayed by native hostility, but more often it was native hospitality that set us back, in the Cooks. Not all native, either. On the beach at Aitutaki was Whiskey Smith, reputed to be the Pacific's most disagreeable trader. Sourly he defied us to have a drink of his home-brew bush beer, and in vain hopes of establishing cordial relations I tasted it. Whenever I think of it my head begins to ache. In subsequent meetings Smith refused to know me, then one day he barked, "Come in and meet the wife!" He produced a dingy grotesque of womanhood and said with a flourish, "Ah, a perfect type of native beauty!"

As soon as our ship was sighted whole islands would put on gala dress. They were going to have official visitors, a chance to entertain company! Everybody turned out, from the schoolmaster to the village idiot. Houses were decked with flowers, pretty girls wore fashionable dresses that traders had brought from Wellington. Out came the local string orchestra, playing American jazz and British hymn tunes.

Then the anticlimax. What a blight fell over the festival scene when it was known that the foreign doctor had come only to examine them for hookworm! That was a tedious test, likely to spoil any party, for it required forty-eight hours of dull dosing and unpleasant purging; when it was over we should have been about as popular as Mussolini after his castor-oily march on Rome. But the Maori has a reasoning mind. One of my patients, a chief with a wide white smile, said, "Now we'll feel better, so we can go on with the dances in your honor." They would line up the girls and regale us with remarkably loose-muscled huras. Then the orchestra would play prewar tunes from Broadway or Piccadilly. All over the Cooks, wherever I found boys and girls who co-operated in my treatments, I would give them lessons in the fox-trot, the latest wrinkle. I carried this fancy step with me, like a message from another world, and gave dancing lessons on every island I visited. If I wasn't popular as a doctor, I was a toast as a dancing master. And there was always a feast. Stuffed with tender pork, chicken, turkey, fish, tomatoes, taro, native oranges, I politely ate my way through the islands. This was no place for a fat man.

In Rarotonga's hard-working, understaffed hospital they were beginning to work out the New Zealand plan of visiting nurses. There were two European nurses, one who supervised the Rarotonga hospital, another who took care of babies and other things at Aitutaki. One schoolmaster's wife was a Government Nurse.

On that first trip I was covering the ground and studying the needs, and on the later visit we campaigned for a latrine back of every house in the Cooks. It was all prearranged and set to go; and it did go in all the lower group. The Foundation was sharing in the overhead; otherwise a paternal government paid for the whole job, with the exception of the labor which the natives contributed. The buildings were made according to the best economical design, and the islanders rivaled one another in producing decorative effects. They were becoming esthetically health-conscious.

Speaking of esthetics, I must mention a social event among the Europeans, known as "the Privy Tea-party." Its host was Mr. David Brown of the Cook Island Native Store. It was an official opening of the model latrine which had been endorsed by New Zealand and built on the Foundation's plans. The building, garlanded with flowers, was set up on one end of the lawn while at convenient tables tea was served to Rarotonga's élite. The ceremonial unlocking of the door was spectacular. Then the master of ceremonies delivered his speech from the throne. This was horseplay, but splendid propaganda; for the whole official personnel was there and heard a clear outline of the benefits which more little throne rooms would bring to the Cook Islands. There were some jokes at my expense, but I didn't mind in the least. The core of the speaker's argument was something that I had preached a thousand times: "When you build a house, build a sanitary latrine first, then a sanitary kitchen; then parlor and bedroom arrangements to suit yourself."

On Mauke, above-mentioned for its hospitality, I lived with the Resident Commissioner, Mr. Dwyer, who not only showed me that young octopus served with sauce of salted ground coconut can be a dish for the sea gods, but made us the guests of the island. Mana, son of King Tamuero the Second, made a fine point of Polynesian courtesy when he moved in with his wife and took charge of the household, to see that we were comfortable. Like most good husbands, he was confidential only when his wife wasn't listening; if she heard him explaining things to me she would warn him not to talk to strangers. However, he found a chance to tell me about the three kings of Mauke who built the London Missionary Society's famous old church.

Remembering what Sir Maui Pomare had said about the old religion and the new, I was anxious to see that church. Mana took me there and showed me the big structure of coral and lime with two separate paths leading like low causeways up to the door. He pointed and said, "That path is for the men." I looked again. Two fourteen-foot stone phallic pillars were planted on either side of it, and on top of each was a roughly hewn stone hat. The other path was for the women; across it was a heavy stone arch, Ina's phallic sign. Strange wedding of paganism and Christianity.

Inside the church, the altar rail was set with hand-carved panels of hardwood; there were thirteen panels, and each was studded with a silver disk. Looking closer, I saw what they were — old Chilean trade dollars. Figures of the sun and moon were painted on the ceiling, symbols of the procreative divinities, Tangaloa and Ina. I have mentioned the priapic images, male and female, which I saw in Tonga. But here, in the sanctity of a puritanical church . . .

Mana, son of Tamuero, explained. The first missionaries who came to Mauke did much prosperous trading. Their store paid Chilean trade dollars for copra, then got them back when the natives bought axes and calico. The Maoris saw how the good men cherished the silver tokens. So when the natives built the edifice out of respect for the missionaries, they finished the chancel reverently — and into the panels they set the dollars, each one an image of what they considered the white man's God.

The pillars and the arch outside had their own story. The three kings were converted and the people followed *en masse*, as Polynesians will. The leader of the kings studied his Gospel devoutly. But in the back of his head he wondered what Tangaloa and Ina would think of these doings. Well, it was safe to drop an anchor to windward. So he set up the pillars for the men to touch when they went in to church, and the arch for the women. Thus they could worship the new God and still give no offense to the old divinities.

And how about the stone hats on top of the pillars? The business missionaries gave English straw hats to the three kings with the understanding that hats were something like crowns; only kings and Englishmen could wear them. King Tamuero, the most enterprising of the three, decided that he might offend Tangaloa by wearing a royal headdress when the god had none. Therefore he wove two coco-fiber hats in imitation of his own and set them on top of the twin pillars. So the god was again appeased. It took a generation or so for the missionaries to realize what the strange stones outside the church really stood for, then they were so shocked and grieved that they ordered them torn down. A common-sense New Zealand government was in control by that time and protected the Maori's right to do as he pleased with a church he himself had built. Tangaloa's two straw hats had worn out after a while, and admiring natives had replaced them with permanent stone ones. I hope they are still there.

It would require a Homer to recite the endless myths of Tangaloa and Ina. Like the Greek Apollo, Tangaloa could walk the earth as a man or ride the heavens as a god. He had two wives. One controlled

NEW ZEALAND'S LITTLE SISTER   261

the sun, and since Tangaloa was the sun, she darkened the land to wintry gray when she took him on pleasure trips. His more illustrious wife, Ina, had a father named Rangomatane, the Club.

This information, and a great deal more, came from Mana, who was at first extremely reticent. It wasn't cricket for a Christian Maori to talk too much about things which, in his heart, he believed. When I journeyed to Atiu, second largest island in the group and magnificently walled with coral cliffs, Mana referred me to a man named Maka, who would know more. The aristocratic young Maka served as sergeant of police for the District Agent, and was heir to the chieftainship. He was outwardly so missionized that it was hard to make him talk — at first. But Maka was too much of a goodfellow Maori to offend me with secrecy, and he was renowned for knowledge of the old ways. One afternoon he led me down among the coral walls on the beach and showed me two curious niches cut in the formation. Deep inside these recesses were the Tangaloa and the Ina symbols, sculptured with anatomic realism. On this island, and others, I saw women bowing to upright stones, offering up prayers for fertility.

Maka told me more of the myth than I could translate and put down in that short visit. *Tanga-loa* meant Man Everlasting. His first-born son was called The Beginning. Tangaloa gave fishing tackle to this god-boy and bade him cast his line into outer darkness. The lad gave a mighty tug, and when the Cook Islands came to the surface he cried, "Father, I have brought up the land!" In another aspect Tangaloa was called Maui (He Baited the Hook). The first name he gave the Cooks was Nukatea (Fruit of the Land), but he changed it to Tepapa (Firm Rock) for this reason: proud Tangaloa bade the land to come to him, but it defied him saying, "I am the firm rock." Then the angered god seized hold of Ina's father, The Club, and beat the land until it split open and his second son, god of southern winds, came forth. Tangaloa had seven sons with mighty names like The Shelter, The King of Peace and The King of Heaven.

The aristocrats of Mauke and Atiu claimed divine ancestry. Ina loved best her youngest son, Ariki, and for ages the islanders favored him. Maka knew that his heavenly ancestor was Rangomatane, the Club, and spoke of him as you would of a distinguished grandfather. The lordly sergeant of police took me up to the flat ground and showed me an interesting relic of the old cult, ruins of Tangaloa's Worship House, two long stone walls some half-mile apart, one side shorter than the other. And here had been the sacred *marai* called Arangirea, or Heaven, where the people gathered, calling out the names of the heavenly sons, and of Tangaloa, and of Ina. They sacrificed pigs, and cried, "Tangaloa, Everlasting, Everlasting!" When the great priapic sign was raised the women danced the hura, sacred to the god.

One point in his long story confused me, and I wanted to know who was the mother of all Tangaloa's sons. He looked self-conscious, and I knew I was treading on delicate ground. I had touched the family skeleton, for Maka was descended from Rangomatane, the Club, therefore Ina was his ancestress. Once upon a time Tangaloa was so insistent in his husbandly demands that Ina descended from the moon on a banyan tree; look at the full moon and you will see the shadowed banyan. Ina fled in vain, for Tangaloa followed her, and seven sacred sons were the result. Maka told me earnestly that he only revealed the scandal in the interest of truth, and it was nothing to be proud of. By many signs, he said, you knew when Ina was near. White clouds were her tapa, and when they grew red it was her father's signal, "Come to earth." Thunder and lightning meant that she had obeyed and her divine feet had touched the ground. The rain was her tears, the emerging sun meant that she was drying her clothes.

Maka told me how Ina, like the Phœnix, renews her youth — but not by fire, by a dip into the sea. When I asked him who created Tangaloa he puzzled a moment, then said, "He was the son of the Unknown God. And nobody will ever know who created God."

The prevalence of leprosy on the Cook Islands interested me impersonally, as a medical investigator; as a human being it interested me because of an unpleasant incident which threatened to wreck my plans for the Central Medical School.

Twenty years before my first visit there Dr. Maui Pomare made a leprosy survey and took some interesting notes. Penrhyn Island was a notorious type case; five per cent of the inhabitants were afflicted when I saw it in 1926. On Penrhyn the great Maori physician looked into the local history of the disease and found that a Penrhyn Islander who had lived with a leprous woman in Samoa brought it back with him in 1885. Forty-four cases stemmed from this man; over a course of twenty years thirty-one of them had died, for leprosy is a slow killer. One boy came down with itch, was declared "unclean" and shut away with a real leper for many miserable years. When the sick man died his companion buried him. Pomare found that this boy showed no trace of leprosy.

At that time lepers were isolated on the rim of Aitutaki as well as on Penrhyn, where through fear of the disease they received no medical or surgical care, and scarcely any food. Once a month a whale-boat would dump rations on the beach. The only contact the sufferers had with the outside world and their families was a few words shouted to the boys in the boat, lying safely offshore. An inlet on Penrhyn lagoon, connected with the main island at low tide, had become a trash-heap for lepers.

Pomare wrote: —

> The poor unfortunates do not get enough to eat. There will be no need to ask for a volunteer keeper, as we have already an unrecognized Father Damien, in Meka and his young wife, who volunteered to live on the island in order to be near their adopted son. I really do not know what would have happened to these unfortunate British subjects if Meka had not volunteered. He does all the fishing and looks after the sufferers; for this he receives no recognition from the civilized world in either funds or praise. Perhaps when the great Master will call His own He will say unto him, "Good and faithful servant, enter into the rest of the Lord. . . . Greater love hath no man than this, that a man lay down his life for his friends."

World-wide experimentation has shown us very little of the etiology of this disease. The cause of infection remains almost as mysterious as the cause of cancer; but unlike cancer it is definitely contagious. For thousands of years it has been treated with chaulmoogra oil, taken by mouth, which showed better results than any other drug, but was so nauseous that an adequate dose was impossible. In 1900 Dr. Victor Heiser, working at Manila, gave it in injections intramuscularly, and made the first step forward in the long history of the disease. Today modified chaulmoogra oil is the chosen treatment.

Conventionally, we shrink away from leprosy. Biblical stories of the "unclean" and lurid passages from popular novels like *Ben Hur* have played upon the imagination until we have given leprosy leadership among the bogies. Among primitives, where the treatment is not understood and the extremities gradually slough away, growing so anesthetic they do not respond to the touch of a red-hot instrument, the picture is unpleasant. But the disease is so leisurely that it takes years for it to arrive at its final horrifying aspect. To the experienced physician diagnosis in the early stages is a matter of routine, and the modern method is simple. Today, if I were forced to choose, I would rather have leprosy in an early stage than tuberculosis. But the world was slow in taking up preventive work. Isolation and treatment were everything until recently when the American Leper Association began to study the mode of leprosy's transmission. They could only find a few old men who knew anything about the disease, so the Association had to train young investigators to look into the causes.

Its transmission is a knotty problem. We know that infection is general in leprous communities, but how does it infect? Medical martyrs have tried to infect themselves by wearing leper's clothes and sleeping in leper's beds, but these tests have brought no results. Natives have lived with leprous women for twenty years without contracting the disease, but Pomare found forty-two cases that had been conveyed to Penrhyn Island by a man who had lived with a leprous woman. There is a theory that it is acquired in early infancy and does not manifest itself until later life, under circumstances favorable for the disease. But what are favorable circumstances? Nobody seems to have found out.

It takes a keen expert eye to mark out leprosy in its early stages; the experienced sisters on Makogai can spot it at once; slight discolorations, slight skin anaesthesias. In the Pacific where civilized early treatment is given you see no such horrid sights as meet you at every turn in India and China. In 1926 we were rounding up Cook Island lepers and sending them to the Mokogai colony.

Leprosy is not indigenous to the Pacific, and there are evidences of its rather recent importation. It has been there long enough to have a folklore, and natives generally believe that a leper can will his sickness on an enemy. These natives know that the disease is transmissible, but if the patient is your friend you can live and eat with him. If he is your foe, do not touch anything he has touched. In Tahiti they tell of a goatherd who was caught in a sudden rain and borrowed a shirt from his pal, who happened to be a leper. When people asked him if he wasn't afraid of catching it he said, "Why? He's my best friend. Why should he want to pass it on to me?"

Aitutaki offered a plain picture of two diseases which have only recently scourged the Cooks — elephantiasis and leprosy. They seemed to have no native name for the disfiguring offshoot of filariasis; it was too new for them to have given it a name. Aitutaki's burying places showed that they had been a larger race only a few generations back. The bones were longer and sturdier and the skulls showed clean white teeth. Among the living, I found all too many cases of dental decay. Their white-toothed forefathers had not tasted sugar, nor become dependent on the trader's white flour. From what I could find out, the Aitutaki of 150 years ago had known no serious infections except yaws, which they called *tona*, as all Polynesians did.

About seventy-five years ago a man from Tahiti imported leprosy and nobody could make out what it was. Then the belief grew that the curse came to those who defiled the sanctity of those family ceremonial grounds, the *marai*. They tell of a European who burned a trash-pile on an ancient *marai*, and was cursed. Nobody felt sorry for him; they had warned him of what would happen. The *marai* was so sacrosanct that none but members of the family were allowed to weed the plot, and *nobody* could build a fire on it. One on Amuri was so vengeful that its black stones poisoned the nuts falling from surrounding trees. Those who ate these nuts would be afflicted with swollen lips. Ancestral ghosts are jealous guardians.

On Christmas Day, 1925, I gave a party for the natives who had helped me generously with my work. To foster competition and please myself with a pretty show, I offered a prize for the best hura dancer among the girls. One of the prettiest creatures that ever shook a grass skirt was a light-colored native named Ann Masters, winner from the start. After her lovely hura she put on European clothes, and looked as though she had just walked off Park Avenue. In my role as dancing master I taught her the fox-trot. We danced for two hours, I imagine.

Afterwards, one of the residents asked me if I knew about Palmerston Island. Palmerston? Well, yes; it had a bad reputation for leprosy. And my friend asked if I knew that an Englishman named Masters had brought the disease there, and that his descendants were known as "the leprous Masters"? Did I know that Ann was the daughter of a Masters who had moved to Rarotonga? I wasn't much flustered, hearing about Ann. Why worry the doctor who had given reward-of-merit fox-trot parties all over the Cooks?

Two years later I went with Dr. Heiser to inspect the rapidly improving leper colony at Mokogai. The island was divided into a "clean" side and a "dirty" side. On the clean side lived the resident natives and the hospital staff, a respectful distance from where the lepers were kept. I had no sooner crossed the deadline to the "dirty" than I heard a sweet voice in the peculiar jargon of Palmerston calling out, "How do you do, Doctor?" It was Ann Masters, still trig and young to outward appearances. The doctors said she was too far gone to get well, but later I was happy to hear that she was on the road to recovery. I have a photograph of her, one I took at the Christmas party. Today, with my increased experience in spotting the symptoms, I can see many indications of the disease in that pretty face.

On that same visit to Mokogai I had another surprise. Two familiar figures strolled down the beach and waved their hands at me. I recognized the cook and housemaid who had served me so well when I lived on Aitutaki in 1932.

Certainly it is a slow, conservative germ, and I stand as a human example. A dozen years ago I must have been exposed to it a number of times, yet I show no leprous symptoms.

One woman I examined on Atiu haunts my dreams. Because she showed suspicious signs I made a hasty bare-handed examination — conditions were too crude for the physician to protect himself with rubber gloves. My fingers went under her arm to examine the ulnar nerve — and struck a big, mushy ulcer. I couldn't find soap or even fresh water, so I walked for nearly an hour until I could wash my hands.

In 1938 Dr. Ellison conducted New Zealand's last big roundup in the Cooks, combing the islands for lepers. On Penrhyn he was entertained by Phil Winton, a wealthy pearl trader. Winton fed Ellison royally, and at the end of his stay the Doctor went to thank the cook for her distinguished meals. He took one look at her and said, "You'd better pack up and come with me on the boat." Winton had made the mistake of forgetting that leprosy could come in by the back door.

A few months after my return to Fiji I went on leave to the States, to be gone until the beginning of 1927. Meanwhile Sir Maui Pomare, always anxious about the leper situation in the Cooks, had chartered a ship and gone there to take patients off for Mokogai. Leaving Suva for home, I was on the crest of a wave. The Central Medical School was an assured fact — practically. Now I could boast to New York and Utica that four years of propagandizing and wire-pulling had achieved the unachievable. All the groups controlled by the High Commission and by New Zealand would send the money, send their quota of students. Soon we would be breaking ground for the long-deferred project.

It was a case of crowing before you are out of the woods.

When I returned to Suva Dr. Montague's long face proclaimed bad news. What had happened in my absence was worse than I had expected. The Cook Islands had withdrawn from the Medical School scheme, and not through any fault of parliamentary politics. It was Sir Maui Pomare himself who had suddenly quit the game. But when I learned the truth I held no resentment against the great Maori.

It seemed that Pomare had gone in his rescue ship to a spot in the Cook Islands where they dumped lepers and left them to die in their own way. Under his administration the situation had bettered somewhat, but it was still a poor makeshift. Pomare's one desire was to get the poor devils to the modern leper colony.

The boat you charter for the haulage of lepers isn't exactly a luxury liner, and the trip to Mokogai was slow, dirty and dangerous. At last he got them there, some thirty patients, and was taking the greatest care to see that they were properly landed. When that job was over he came down the gangplank, not a very presentable Cabinet Minister; rough travel in a rough boat had soiled his clothes, exposure had darkened his complexion and he hadn't shaved for a week. Down on the wharf he was stopped by a dandified young Medical Officer, obviously fresh from London, who held up an arresting hand and twittered commandingly, "Colored people this way, please!" I don't know how many kinds of hell New Zealand's Minister of Health gave the efficient youth, but plenty I imagine. Pomare inherited temper from a long line of Maori chiefs.

Pomare took the next boat to Suva, went straight to Montague, then to the Governor. To both he said that the High Commission hadn't sense enough to keep these brats away from responsible positions. He had seen what he saw on Mokogai, and he was through. So long as he remained in office, he declared, no health project favored by the High Commission would ever get the shadow of a red cent out of his ministry. And that broad ultimatum withdrew the Cook Islands' co-operation from the Central Medical School. Without the Cooks, we were just where we had been before, helpless to go on.

Children say, "He'll get over being mad." With a strong and stubborn character like Pomare's, this softening of the temperament was not so sure. I tried to steady myself with the knowledge that at least six important Pacific groups were still behind our plan. I remembered Queen Salote's generous question which had given me the first big encouragement: "Are we too small to do our share?" But time was precious now, and whatever we did must be done at once. Pomare controlled a section of Polynesia which we must include, or quit.

It was January, 1927, when Montague retailed the bad news, and I gave myself a few days to worry. Then I went over to his office and asked, "What about it?" He said, "Lambert, you know Pomare, and I don't. You've worked with him, he likes you and he'll probably respect whatever you have to say." I had already thought over what Montague proposed next. "Why don't you take the boat for New Zealand, see Pomare and try to talk him over? It won't be easy, but I can't see any other way."

In about two weeks I was in Wellington, where I went straight to Pomare's office in the Government Building. I hadn't announced my coming, and when I reached his desk I saw his look of friendly surprise. (I made the mental note, "At least he's smiling.") Well, he said, he didn't know I was in New Zealand; and what had brought me there at this time of year? I said "I have come down to get better acquainted with you. The last time I was here it was so cold that I went to Auckland to write my Cook Island Report. Now I just want to visit." Impulse was urging me to bring up the subject which I knew was foremost in both our minds. But it would be fatal to seem too eager. Our conversation drifted into impersonal channels; Dominion politics, welfare work among the children, native health problems — a little of everything except what had brought me there.

I wasn't going to play the first card. Then gracefully, as if there had never been the slightest difference between him and the High Commission, he asked me how the School was progressing. This was my opening. I eased into the subject, as though he had never heard of it before. He listened for an hour, interrupting occasionally to make his own comments. In every detail this great Maori showed the same grasp of essential points that he displayed on a later visit to Fiji when we gave him the honors of a chief and Eloisa cooked her best dinner; Montague was there, a superb physician himself, and was convinced at last that a Maori could excel. He was even more convinced when we took Pomare over to Mokogai and landed him, in state, at the same spot where a whippersnapper had once said, "Colored people this way."

. . . After that hour with Pomare in his Wellington office the difference was surprisingly smoothed out. He was cordial, beaming. Why, of course the Cook Islands would be in on the Medical School. Of course well-trained Native Practitioners would be the only solution. Of course the Cooks were in.

When I left his office, dazed by this splendid turn of luck, I could not restrain a chuckle. Had Pomare ever intended to hold aloof? Hadn't he withdrawn from the High Commission scheme merely as a demonstration, to show the *Pakeha* that he could not insult a Maori without the danger of reprisals? He had shown them that he held the power, and that he could use it. Then with a magnanimous gesture he gave them what they asked for.

Out on a Wellington street I mopped my brow and tried to realize that we had crossed the last bridge. The hard pull of four years was over. I was going to have my School. Now ground-breaking would begin in earnest. Now we could send all over the Pacific, bring in eligible native boys and teach them what modern medicine really means.

CHAPTER VII

HALF A LOAF AND A SLICE OFF

I should be sloppily sentimental and call the scene which is to follow "My Dream Come True." The dream had backed in a little crookedly, knocking over a few ideals and dumping at my feet a short measure of fine gold. But who was I to complain? Something substantial had materialized out of six hard years of constant hammering for results. I think I was excited, for I could scarcely follow the earnest, dedicatory voice that rang through the new lecture hall, fragrant with fresh paint and plaster.

That was the morning of December 29, 1928. I sat on the platform with bigwigs of the Colony: Sir Maynard Hedstrom, U. S. Consul Roberts, the Secretary of Native Affairs, the Colonial Secretary and sundry others. His Excellency Sir Eyre Hutson, Governor General of the High Commission, was making a speech.

"It is fitting that there should be this meeting today to record the opening of the new Medical School in Suva, which has really been in being for some weeks, from November first, but officially as a Central Native Medical School in the Western Pacific will enter on its career, which we hope can be no other than a successful one, from January first, 1929 . . . had its origin some years ago with Dr. Lambert, a member of the Medical Staff of the Rockefeller International Health Foundation . . . whole-heartedly supported by Dr. Montague. . . . And the various Administrations in the Pacific, who have co-operated in the scheme, owe a deep debt of gratitude to Dr. Lambert for his strong faith, for his persistent advocacy of the proposal with the governing body of the Rockefeller Foundation . . . without which we should not be in this building today. . . ."

I looked over the upturned faces, brown and white. I counted the eight native boys of the graduating class, and thanked God that all the undergraduates wouldn't have to sleep in the little firetrap of a dormitory, which would only accommodate twelve. The new dormitory could pack in twenty-eight, and there was room for forty in the dining room. The new main building, over which we were making such a fuss, would be fairly cramped quarters. It needed space for laboratories, pathological, bacteriological, biochemical. And the dissecting room wasn't much bigger than my grandmother's cupboard. . . .

Just the same, my dream had come true, even with a string on it. The modest buildings we had achieved were modern-built and filled with students.

Now the Governor, his kindly, eupeptic face rather flushed with December heat, was addressing the student body: —

". . . You are receiving opportunities with limitations, which are unavoidable, of becoming members of a very honorable profession, not only for your personal benefit but mainly for the good of those men, women and children to whom you will be called on to give medical and surgical aid and treatment to the best of your ability and knowledge . . ."

Then it was over, everybody had shaken hands, and I was being interviewed by the press. I told the reporters what I felt, that his Excellency had been too modest in disclaiming his own important share in bringing the School to life; how the project had been a partnership between Dr. Montague and myself, and how I might have given up early except for his quiet persistence; and how Queen Salote of Tonga and her Prince Consort had offered financial aid in my hour of deepest discouragement; how their loyalty to all the South Pacific had inspired other groups until at last they had touched the purse-strings of the Foundation. . . .

Outside on the half-finished grounds I saw students filing into the classrooms. There was a score of dark-skinned Fijian boys with shocks of kinky black hair, sport shirts and *sulus*. They had the look I have always admired in their race, that of intellectual honesty and will to learn. The Polynesian boys were in *lavalavas*, and like the Melanesians they were bare-legged and unshod; some of them had the pale, even features and straight hair of Caucasians. There were a couple of boys from the Solomon Islands, wooly-haired and almost plum-black. The light-faced, worldly-looking ones were from the Cooks. There were a couple of well-dressed East Indians. The Condominium was sending us New Hebridean students, but they hadn't come yet. The Fijians outnumbered the others, for there were twenty in all, and twelve of them were graduating from the old school, which had only accommodated sixteen students in all. Almost overnight the enrollment had increased to forty, and I was wondering how the boys from far-off groups would get on with the Fijians, when more of the outsiders came in. The fair-skinned boys from the Cooks and Samoa had one great advantage; they knew more English, whereas the Fijians were handicapped there and would have to learn hard lessons in a strange tongue. For the same reason all the Melanesian lads would have a tough time at first. New Zealand had been wise in giving her mother tongue to the Polynesians. . . . But I knew the Fijians, men like Malakai and Charley, who had mastered every hard subject that came their way.

More boys would be eligible for the school. We would have to refuse some for lack of space, and look very carefully into the mental qualifications of every applicant. . . . There would be a tendency on the home islands, I knew, to play favorites for political reasons. Some of the officials would promote candidates because they were "good batmen" — meaning that they had served them well personally.

All that must be straightened out, for we would never have room for slackers. . . . I wondered how soon we could promote a decent school for native nurses; that was a part of my plan for enlargement. Now they were living in a crazy shack where they did their own cooking, and in the hospital they scrubbed and emptied slops for dainty British nurses. Samoa was giving her native girls an adequate training. We could do no better than follow her lead. . . . I wondered if students would ever come from Papua and New Guinea, where N.M.P.'s were dreadfully needed. The Canberra Government was standing pat on White Man's Australia, and the "blackfellow" was not supposed to have a head on his shoulders. Papuan and New Guinea natives, they said, were not adequately prepared for higher education. I knew better, for I had seen those boys, and worked with them. . . . According to Australia's yardstick students from the New Hebrides and the Solomons were also inadequately prepared; but they were entering our first class. Australia forgot that her Territories had been missionized by Fijians, Tongans and Samoans. . . . Dr. Strong, the progressive C.M.O. at Port Moresby, had offered to pay the expenses of Papuan students, if Canberra would consent. . . . But why argue the point? Australia was jealous of little Fiji's rise as a medical center, and had decided not to send a student or to permit an N.M.P. to work in her possessions. . . . I wondered if she would ever change her mind.

Up to the day I retired the Foundation was always a little nervous about what I was going to do next. They were usually asking, by inference, "Where is Lambert going to pop up now?" Dr. Heiser's immediate reaction to whatever I put up to him was a simple, "No," and I had to pound away at him until he gave up. As I have said before, he was very careful with Mr. Rockefeller's silver dimes, and his honest stubbornness deserves great credit. Dr. Sawyer, who bossed me during my early days in the Pacific, was a strong advocate of the Central Medical School, for he knew the needs of the islands. Sawyer is now the Foundation's Director of the International Health Division, and still a little nervous about me. He wants me settled on a Californian farm where I'll be out of mischief. Sawyer is one of the most brilliant research scientists of our time. Considering his environmental background he is extremely broad-minded — he comes of a family of clergymen. I shall never forget the time I led him up to a North Queensland bar where the Australians were sneering "Wowser!" at every prohibitionist. Sawyer ordered ginger ale, drank it and made them like him. With the same puritanical gusto he backed me up in the Medical School. I shall always be grateful to him.

I had estimated that it could be financed by a contribution of £1,500 each from seven island groups. Fiji's sudden decision that she could start a School of her own on a one-horse scale had given more point to my argument when I went back to the States and put it up to the Foundation. I had talked pretty steadily for half a year, informing the unsympathetic ones that Fiji's stingy plan would set the School back about twenty years.

In 1927 I had come back to Suva with the Board's promise in my pocket. They would fund half the expense of the larger plan. This was economical still, and hardly adequate for what we needed; but we had enough now to get things going. I had wrestled with the Foundation's Department of Medical Sciences, to whom I had to appeal for the sort of funds required. To give out money to the very finest medical schools and raise their already high standards was the Department's end and aim. To finance a little idea like ours gave them an almost physical nausea. I didn't get anything out of them, except to make them admit that some lower grade of medical education might be useful, until their high-flown notions had time to turn out crack specialists to serve the teeming millions who lacked anything but witch doctors to care for them.

The Department of Medical Sciences remained adamant. I finally got the money from the International Health Board itself. This was the first time they had given financial support to the building of medical schools. Up to then it had always been in the hands of the Department of Medical Sciences.

The time would come when we would need more buildings and equipment, that was obvious. The time might also come when some jealous local politician would attempt to wreck the School, or drain it white. A little man can do big mischief, as we found later when a domestic colonial secretary worked his political best to destroy our planned Unified Health Commission, for the petty reason that Fiji's Chief Medical Officer would head it with a few pounds larger salary than his own. He was of the old anti-American type, which has done so much to promote ill feeling both between England and her colonies and England and America. His kind, I hope, is passing. This little man was not quite able to interfere with co-operation in the Mokogai Leper Colony, which we started back in 1923 and saw built into one of the finest leprosaria in the world.

But the School was open, and we were down to the realism of immediate figures. We could admit forty, and the cost per student would be ninety pounds. There was a wooden dormitory, a main building seventy-six by thirty feet, and the Principal's house. We were well staffed with the Chief Medical Officer, the pick of the government physicians and local practitioners. We also had the Government's pharmacist, a dentist, the Government's bacteriologist and chemist, and the Rockefeller Foundation's modest representative. We had plenty of textbooks and scientific instruments. In fact we had about everything but room to turn around in.

I wasn't dissatisfied that afternoon in 1928 when I made another inspection of the buildings. Our feet were on the ladder, we were going up. The other things would come, though there was plenty of fighting ahead.

I had to reflect on the slow and painful beginnings of the Native Practitioner system, some forty-two years before. In 1875 the Colony was frightened by the measles epidemic which burned the Fijians down, and with only the puniest attempt at medical aid. Thirteen years later the British residents were appalled by the danger of smallpox, brought in by the East Indian invasion. The Government well knew that the most important medical need was vaccination, but the expense of European vaccinators in this work seemed overwhelming. Health in those days was in the charge of Dr. Corney, Fiji's second great Medical Officer. Sir William Macgregor, later Governor of Papua, was the first, and Dr. Montague was the third of the great ones. In Corney's day the Colony, in desperate need, was sending out natives to administer vaccine to an endangered population.

Corney saw how dextrous these men could be with instruments and how quickly they won the confidence of half-wild villagers. Perhaps the Colony's financial embarrassment was what touched off his imagination. At any event, in the late eighties, after the Government had voted small sums for vaccination purposes, Corney surprised them all by suggesting that the native boys be given some systematic medical education. In January, 1889, eight Fijians passed the examination and were given certificates.

These early students got only the bare bones of a living. They were huddled together in a *bure* in the old Colonial Hospital grounds, and spent a good deal of their time working their gardens for enough vegetables to keep going. They had no lecture room, no models or diagrams; postmortem examinations were not easily obtained and almost the only apparatus for anatomical study was a set of bones. When medical officials had time to teach these boys they casually handed them some practical work in the Hospital. Most of the nursing duties fell on their shoulders, as the Matron was the only trained nurse in Fiji. There was some improvement in 1900, when a lecture room was built. Somewhat later improvements advanced as far as a wooden students' quarters.

In 1898 the students went on strike, which resulted in the improvements of 1900. As a body they called upon the officials and announced that they wanted the whole-time services of a cook, otherwise they were going back home. The authorities concluded that they were probably human beings, so the point was carried. After several years the eight-student school had turned out approximately twenty Native Medical Practitioners. These men were working for something like seven pounds a year, all told, but they were given free gardens to cultivate for themselves. They earned two pounds ten as Provincial Vaccinators, and in 1905 their salaries jumped to between eighteen pounds and fifty pounds. Seven years later their usefulness was recognized by another increase in salary; this time they were divided into first, second and third class. A first-class N.M.P. was getting as much as one hundred pounds a year. When the new School was opened, they were making around one hundred and fifty pounds.

The products of this low-paid, rough-and-ready education won their spurs early. In the devastating influenza epidemic of 1918 three of the old students died at their posts as dispensers in the Colonial Hospital. Eight in all died, out of a total of forty-eight. In no case was there any complaint that an N.M.P. had failed in his duty so long as he was able to lift a hand.

In December, 1928, a new order was coming to pass, I hoped. The door was open, not too wide, but young men were passing through with a keen desire to get the best that modern methods could give. That door would have to swing wider. It mustn't close again. Neither politics nor prejudice nor indifference must slam it shut in the faces of those who had come so earnestly to learn. I was canny enough to suspect that there would be the same percentage of failures you will find in any college anywhere — ten following years of experience taught me that the average was less. They had something more than the desire to get on in the world, which inspires so many European professional students. That December evening I talked with several of the incoming class, the boys who were not too shy to speak out. Why did they want to go into medicine? The answer I got from them was usually the same: "Because I want to do something for my own people."

It was about then that I pulled in my belt and promised myself that so long as I was alive and in Fiji I wouldn't let them down.

PART THREE

PART THREE

CHAPTER I

OLD BRANDY AND NEW EGGS

First let's try to peg the story down to the spring of 1931, when I put a bottle of rare old brandy under my arm and went up a very New Yorkish elevator to see Mr. Raymond Fosdick. The brandy, worth its weight in gold, if you could price it at all, had been given to me in exchange for three dozen fresh eggs.

Mr. Fosdick, as legal advisor to the Rockefellers, was also an important trustee of the Foundation, therefore my business with him was legitimate. So was the brandy, although America was then in the throes of Amendment Eighteen.

As I waited outside his office I almost asked his amiable secretary if I hadn't better smuggle the bottle under her desk and say nothing about it. I was conscious that Mr. Fosdick's brother was the Reverend Harry Emerson Fosdick, pastor of Mr. Rockefeller's great temple of sobriety on Riverside Drive, and the Rockefeller family were honestly in favor of prohibition. And how about the big Rockefeller executive in his office over there? Representative of a great temperance family, brother of a great preacher . . . No, I had better hide that bottle somewhere. . . .

Then his secretary said "Dr. Lambert," meaning me, so I picked up the bottle and went into his office. I had been told that I would meet one of the most charming men on earth, and I wasn't disappointed. But our conversation hadn't gone very far before I noticed his eyes straying toward the wrapped bottle I was holding in my lap; he was wondering, I suppose, if South Sea doctors always carried their own liquor. Maybe I was getting off on the wrong foot, but something had to be done. I pulled off the wrapper and handed him the brandy. I began, "I don't know how you stand on prohibition. This happens to be rare old stuff — but if you have any prejudices — "

"Prejudices!" He stared at the faded label. "It's 1835! Yes, I have prejudices — in its favor." Relieved, I said, "Well, it's for the black sheep of the Fosdick family."

Still nursing the bottle, he laughed, "My brother Harry is so strict I have to balance the ship. Now let me uncover a family skeleton. My great-grandfather was a distiller before he became a preacher. His distillery failed because he endorsed bad notes for friends, so he turned to the Baptist pulpit for consolation. In those days they had high pulpits with a steep stairway in the back. My ancestor used to keep a bottle under those stairs, and before sermons he would brace himself with a couple of good spots; then he would mount the ladder and give his congregation and the distillers hellfire for two solid hours. . . . No, Doctor, I don't mind your telling all about the family. I've often said to Brother Harry that it would be a good thing for him if he imitated the old gentleman. But Harry seldom listens to my wiser suggestions."

The brandy perched on the desk like a silent diplomat, opening the way to confidences. Mr. Fosdick had studied at Colgate when I was at Hamilton, and when I told him that I was on the team that knocked the living perfume out of Colgate our entente was established. He asked about progress over my six million square miles of sea. Maybe he had read my reports, but there were so many reports blowing in from all points that I sought briefly to refresh his memory. With education and tetrachloride, I said, the hookworm disease was getting under control and populations were on the upgrade, where the High Commission and the Foundation had a free hand. Wherever we worked with the New Zealand health authorities we got fine results. We expected the Cook Island natives would show an increase of 20 per cent in the decade between 1926 and 1936. The Mau Rebellion had set back New Zealand's work in Western Samoa, but they were making good headway again, the Foundation doing its share. The awful Condominium was still making a mess of the New Hebrides; and the Australians — well, they weren't playing ball.

The Central Medical School had graduated two classes, but without the thorough curriculum which the new students would have. Soon we would be able to throw more well-educated N.M.P.'s into the work. . . . I am not sure that Mr. Fosdick remembered our little School at all. Fiji is a long way from lower Broadway. When he had commended our modest project, a few years before, he had thought of it as romantic; yet when he fixed his signature to the plan, buried among the vaster projects, it was one of the most fruitful acts of all his useful life. Many Rockefeller millions, for instance, had gone into the great school in Peking, and into field work in China. Five or six years later the Sino-Japanese war blasted away those handsome contributions. The little school at Suva was destined to grow steadily and bear an annual crop of trained native talent.

I told him that our work was now directed toward mass treatments for both cure and prevention. The big, shaggy Solomon Islands were black spots in the Pacific which we were doing our best to penetrate with modern medicine, and with what few responsible white men we could find. They were injecting thousands with neoarsphenamine, for yaws, dosing thousands with tetrachloride and tetrachlorethylene for hookworm. I had made a short survey of the Solomons in 1921 and later on, through Montague, had started things going that way. I had visited there again in 1930 and this trip had taken me at last to the lost Rennell Island. . . . I tried to tell him about Rennell Island, small as a mustard seed in a pond, yet unique in all the world because it was inhabited by a people who were 20,000 years behind our modern times. . . .

I told him of two of our excellent men, working in the more attainable Solomon Islands — if anything down there is "attainable." Gordon White and Dr. Steenson were outstanding. White was an Australian small doctor made over from a pharmacist, and he was doing wonders with the hardest assignment in the world, "blackfellow treatment." Dr. Steenson was a scientist of large caliber, although physically he was about vestpocket size. The Dean of the New Zealand Medical School knew what he was about when he recommended Steenson to me.

These men would send me their journals, written from the field when they worked up and down the double chain of six or seven big, wild islands. There were plantations and missions around the edges, but the interiors were usually inhabited by unregenerate killers. Malaita, for instance, was a little larger than Long Island, and twice as tough. When black Malaitamen worked on the plantations they had to be carefully watched; they had a nasty habit of turning on their straw-boss. No Malaitaman ranked as a true male until he had killed his man. There was the case in 1927 which newspapers played up as

"The Malaita Murders." Captain Bell, a tax collector, with his white assistant and fourteen native police, fell under massed spear-points, and when the guilty ones were tried for murder they made no attempt to deny anything. Hill-grown Malaitamen don't know how to lie. Somebody had "sent" them to do murder — a witch doctor, most likely. Without a sign of fear they walked up to the hangman.

Dr. Steenson had drawn a very accurate map of Malaita, in four colors. The colors, he explained, had been made for him by mission boys, out of plant juices. He and White both carried phonographs, and when patients came in too slowly the white medicine men would turn on stale music-hall pieces. "Show Me the Way to Go Home" was a favorite. Mission boys learned it, formed male quartets and butchered the tune horribly, far into the night. Malaitamen loved the needle — sick or well, they demanded it. But on adjacent islands they would run and hide, scared to death of it. When audiences failed to show up the interpreter would say, "Big kaikai" — whether they were eating men or pigs was never revealed. Earthquakes were a commonplace, leaf houses tumbling, young parrots falling out of the trees, natives scrambling under a barrage of coconuts. Lollipops were always in demand; stalwart warriors would wait for a dole of candy before they would talk business. Sometimes a native, who had never been near a treatment, would curl up and die of a heart attack or gallstone colic or whatever ailed him. Invariably his fellow tribesmen would blame the death on "stick medicine," hypodermics, and it would take a wealth of diplomacy to argue them down. This situation was never less than dangerous. Steenson carried his Bible with him, and on Sunday mornings, when the missions enforced leisure, he would open it at Genesis and pull out a file of papers entitled "Yaws Campaign Notes." He wrote me: "There is one thing in this Bible with which I do not agree. I refer to a sentence in 'The Equipment and Working of a Yaws Unit (Samoan Experience).'" Dr. Steenson was basically religious.

Quaint letters came from native mission teachers, White and Steenson sent them to me as comic bits: *"My deer friend Dr. Steenson,* I am David Ikala write this letter to you, about all your boys, on this night, you put Goaril to look after all your things, now behind you he went down to Raresu, he going on Mother's house and he do a trouble there, he catch hold the girls. . . . And another time he brake the roof of there house. . . ."

This letter was signed "With a great love."

It was a horse of a darker color when surreptitious notes were slipped into Gordon White's hand, saying, "Don't go down to Wanderer Bay," and telling how the natives there were waiting to club the white men. Gordon White wrote casually, "Wherever I go the local lads come along with their various relations, and there is no sign of trouble or discontent."

White had the services of Charlie One Arm, the policeman, who with his single arm could knock out all comers. Charlie's maxim was "Treat 'em rough." Around mission stations he would shock the pious by shouting to women who wouldn't take their medicine, "Listen, you sunnabitch fellow!" But when I read White's reports of threatening letters I saw Montague; we had White, Steenson and Charlie One Arm moved to safer, tamer ground. We couldn't afford to have another Malaita murder. . . .

Gordon White rounded off his report by telling how a flock of naked cannibals, well armed with clubs and spears, swarmed down and surrounded his tent. Had they come to finish him off? No, it turned out, they were bearing gifts. Gordon wrote, "The Malaitaman generally wants as much as he can get for anything he has to dispose of, and giving things away he looks on as sheer madness. But here they were showering me with presents, and with no apparent strings on them — cowrie shells, kai-kai spoons, a bow and a few arrows, a basket of fruit, and a middle aged rooster — I should say about forty-five." Just a little tribute to modern medicine, and no flowery speeches; solemnly the Malaitamen strode back to their jungle. . . .

I did not tell all this to Mr. Fosdick, a busy man on a busy day. But I had time to outline enough of it to hint at the problems we had to face among the howling pagans of the Solomon Islands, where the missionaries, good, bad and confused, were merely nibbling around the edges. Tuberculosis was prevalent in the Solomons, and we expected to tackle it on a grand scale when there were more N.M.P.'s.

Before we shook hands Raymond Fosdick asked: "But what about this wonderful 1835 brandy? Is it so easy down there to get hold of such rare stuff?"

"It is," I said, "if you find the right man. I got four bottles of it in exchange for three dozen strictly fresh eggs."

Then I told him how.

CHAPTER II

ANOTHER ISLAND NIGHT'S ENTERTAINMENT

Late in 1930, shortly before I broached the egg-and-brandy riddle to Mr. Fosdick, the beautiful yacht *Zaca* pulled in at Suva. Templeton Crocker, who had inherited richly from banks and mines in California, was taking friends on a world cruise. He had a thirst for anthropology and scientific exploration, and it was rumored that he might later equip his fine ship for research in far places. I am afraid my sigh was a bit envious as I watched the *Zaca* steam gracefully in. I had scoured the southern seas in so many tubs, junks, bumboats, leaky launches and cockroach-ridden steamers that my bones ached at the very thought of them. Crocker's explorations were *de luxe;* most of mine had been *de louse.*

Templeton Crocker came to my office, a well-favored man in his late forties, pleasant and almost boyishly anxious to learn. He seemed much impressed because I was just back from Rennell Island and its little neighbor, Bellona. Did they come up to my expectations? Yes, I said, when you fly to the moon you may be sure it will come up to your expectations. His curiosity was on edge; had I taken notes, could he see some of them? I handed him a small batch of rough dictation, not enough to tell him all by any means. I could see by his excitement that Rennell Island had the same pull on his imagination that it had had on mine all the eight years that I had awaited an opportunity to see it.

When we dined on the *Zaca* the owner showed me around and explained that she was an enlarged "bluenose." The main dining room was also the lounge, but the Crocker party ate mostly on deck, tropical style. Everything was roomy, the cabins plain but comfortable, equipped with electric lights and fans. Gus Schmidt, who managed the galley, was a real chef, and there were quantities of refrigerators to help him out. The ship carried what they called "frozen foods" — Idaho steaks, Long Island duck, fresh peas and strawberries — about all the luxuries for which we tropicals were hungry. Crocker had a plentiful supply of wines, used with judgment; when there was an occasion for it he could surprise you with a rare vintage.

He was at our house a great deal, always asking about Rennell Island. When he didn't dine with us he dropped in for a rum cocktail. We played bridge, and I was surprised to find that he was making money; a rare feat in Suva, where the game is sharp as a razor blade. When we dined on the *Zaca* my inner mind kept exclaiming, "Think of following a health campaign on a ship like this!"

The night before his boat sailed he came around with my notes; I knew he couldn't have made much out of them, the stuff was so scrambled. At dinner I complimented him on the *Zaca's* cook, and he said the great trouble was getting fresh eggs. On the *Zaca's* long hauls even refrigeration wouldn't keep them fresh. I mentioned doing something about it — then Eloisa gave me the matrimonial look. Wherever Eloisa settled down, she started to raise chickens; she had a way with chickens.

But on Crocker's mind there was something heavier than an egg. It was Rennell Island, I knew before he had said a word. Finally he said, "I wish you would tell me all about that trip." He and I were having coffee on the veranda, and I said, "You remember that girl of the Arabian Nights who had to tell the sultan a story between dark and dawn — or else? Well, we'd better have a fresh pot of coffee, because this story is going to be pretty long."

"I can stand it," he said, and waited for me to begin.

Last May [I said] I was in Tulagi, capital of the Solomon Islands, looking over our health campaign. I don't have to tell you how long I had waited for a chance to see Rennell Island; and mine wasn't all an explorer's curiosity. When George Fulton told me, back in 1920, that the Rennellese were "practically untouched" I had wondered if these seemingly archaic people were infected with one of the known varieties of hookworm. Or if they were infected at all, would it be a variety hitherto undiscovered? If so, I might be able to furnish valuable data on the origin of a race that had been so long lost to the world.

From inquiry and general reading I knew that Rennell Island, and its tiny companion Bellona, had been visited in the past; but those visits were few and far between, even in the Pacific sense of the term.

Some sailors might have penetrated to the interior. Two brave bishops, Selwyn and Patterson, touched there in 1856, and fifty years later C. M. Woodford and A. G. Stephens had made geological surveys around the shore. Dr. Northcote Deck, of the South Sea Evangelists, visited several times with a companion missioner, between 1908 and 1911; Deck made a gory mess of proselytizing. Resident Commissioner Kane, on his official inspection of 1925, might have been the first white man that ever went into the interior. A few years before that, the powerful Lever Brothers had "recruited" some labor from offshore; but the natives were so unresistant to disease that the recruiters had decided to take back the ones who survived. In 1928 Stanley and Hogbin made a geological survey for the High Commission, and reported that they had found absolutely nothing of commercial importance.

The next year the Whitney South Sea Expedition went there collecting birds for New York's Natural History Museum. The young men from this expedition, on its second trip, were the ones who brought me into the story. Rennell lay only 150 miles to the southeast of Tulagi; it was hard to realize that it was so near, or that in 1930 one could turn back the book of mankind's history for thousands of years and read the living page; that the voyager of today might thrill as Captain Cook thrilled when he first saw a Pacific island.

Well, I talked about Rennell to Captain Ashley, Resident Commissioner at Tulagi, and he offered to take me there on his next cruise. He'd have to drop me on the beach and pick me up when his yacht swung around that way again. But Rennell Island wasn't very safe for strangers, he said. A few years ago when Dr. Deck of the South Sea Evangelists had sent three native missionaries there the Rennellese had killed them off; eaten them, probably, for nobody ever found the bodies. No, the safest way to see Rennell would be behind an armed guard.

Time was precious and there was no telling when Captain Ashley's boat would take a notion to come. Then I saw a stout but battered little auxiliary schooner lying offshore. It looked like a turn of Providence, for she was the same *France* that had taken the Whitney Expedition to Rennell three years before. A crowd of young men came ashore, looking more like hoboes than naturalists. Their leader was Hannibal Hamlin, grandson of Lincoln's Vice President, and an old

Yale football player. I pricked up my ears when Hamlin said that they were heading the *France* for Rennell Island again, if they could make it. My ears stood higher still when he said that he was the second white man, perhaps, to have gone inland as far as the Lake.

I wasted no time, you can well believe, in asking them what dicker I could make to go along. Hamlin showed true American generosity. They were indebted to Captain Ashley for a lot of things, and if I was his friend they'd do anything to oblige me; only trouble was the Whitney Expedition backers hadn't come across with their check. They were out of provisions. All right, said I, provisions and trade were on me. Let's take them on and get started. At the Burns-Phillip Store Hamlin took on some very odd supplies, including a great number of adzes, hatchets and trade knives with wooden handles and blades six inches long. When I asked him if we were going to use them on the savages he said, "No, but that's what they'll want." I could understand the jumble of cheap mirrors and scissors. When he called for calico and beads he always asked for red. Why red? "That's the color they'll want," he said, and started dickering for three pasteboard trade boxes with flimsy locks.

Our only stop was at Gaudalcanar where Gordon White was heading one of my Solomon Islands treatment units. He was an especially valuable addition to the party, as he had been to Rennell Island on the Stanley Expedition, two years before. On this trip he was to act as my microscopist.

We were a careless, happy company, getting dirtier every hour. We had with us a youngish German named Walter — I can't remember the rest of it — who was a shell collector and looked the part. Our skipper was an ancient Scot, sour with religion. Gordon White had brought on three Solomon Island attendants, and he lent me a very black one named Ga'a, four feet high, aged fourteen, and proud as Punch to be serving a white gentleman. Service consisted mostly in opening tinned food and throwing the empty tins overboard — or letting them roll. The main cabin was so small that you couldn't stretch without banging your elbows; here we ate amidst fumes from the engine. We only used the engine in dead calm, when it could make four miles an hour. We had a small lavatory and a shower, neither of which worked. I was more than grateful to my companions when they allotted me — out of respect to my superior girth — the largest berth on the ship. It was right off the cabin, and there was no privacy. But privacy was a stranger to the *France*.

There was a place for nothing, and nothing in its place. Walter the German strewed shells, Hamlin and Coultas stuffed birds and scattered feathers so that some of them always managed to get into the stew. Our native deck-hands slept in places where you couldn't help stumbling over them. Gordon White, when he wasn't trying to find where he had stowed his microscopic outfit, turned on the phonograph and shouted.

We were on our way to Rennell Island — maybe. And just another touch to our oddity: We had a stumpy black Hercules who helped the cook by spilling soup, waited on table by dropping dishes, cleaned the cabin by pushing the dirt across into another corner. He was an ebony figure of the Masculine. And his name was Bella.

When the report came that we would reach our destination next day I began looking into the physical condition of all aboard. If the Rennellese were as primitive as I had heard, any introduced germ would catch like wild fire, and we might spread a scourge. Harry, our Solomon Island cook, had developed a nasty eye condition; he was a spectacle in the galley, with that dirty rag over his eye. White and I treated him and he began to improve. Still I was worried, wondering how his infection would react on the people we were about to visit.

I looked them all over. There were no common colds, and that was satisfactory. How about that quick-moving venereal contagion, gonorrhea? To the embarrassment of some, and the merriment of many, I lined them all up, from black crew to white captain, and gave them what the Army calls "short-arm inspection." They were all negative. Satisfactory again. Also there were no visible signs of skin infection. We seemed to be, all told, a very healthy lot.

Then I got my thrill when Hamlin called me on deck, pointed over the bow and said, "There she is!" It lay isolated in the sea. I saw a straight line of cliff, sheer as a prison wall, lifted some 400 feet and running as far as the eye could travel. Scraggly foliage showed faintly at the top. What except an airplane could get anybody up there?

Hamlin, all out of patience, told me that there was only one dent in the cliff, a narrow passage called Kungava Bay, the "White Sands." If the Scotch skipper hadn't been so stubborn we could have sailed straight into it. As it was that day was gone and most of the next before we made our final tack and found the opening in the cliffs which marked Rennell's only landing place, a pin-point approach to an island that was fifty miles long and some fifteen wide. Those guardian cliffs were relics of a strange volcanic action which pushed the Pacific's largest atoll into high prominence. The island was so tightly ringed with a collar of coral-stone that Sinbad himself could not have found the entrance without a chart. Fortunately Hamlin had one which his navigator on the former trip had made for him.

We shot through the reef and found anchorage inside a beautiful, sheltered bay; it was especially serene because the cliffs protected it on two sides; below their impressive height the beach curved like a white necklace. Things began to move. Two rudely built outrigger canoes came paddling up to us, and I got my first glimpse of these strange people. There were two men, a woman and a couple of small boys. They were not like anything I had ever seen before, and I remembered what Fulton had said: "About twenty thousand years behind modern history." At the risk of being trite, let me say that the men, very tall and handsomely muscled, had the figures of Greek gods. Around the loins they were swaddled in folds of clumsy tapa (*kongoa*), made grotesque by a palm-leaf fan stuck in the back. The fans, I learned later, were for protecting the hair when it rained, or for brushing away flies when it shone. Their heads were impressive, dark as to hair and brows, and with strong, well-modeled features. Their hair, almost straight, was coiled in a bun at the back. Their dark, expressive eyes were somewhat slanting, but not Mongoloid fashion, more like the American Indians'. Although they wore small tortoise-shell ornaments stuck through the septum, their noses were slenderly arched. There was nothing negroid about their gracefully cut mouths. What were they like? Somehow you couldn't call them either Polynesian or Caucasian. Yet there was something indefinitely Caucasian in their features.

The woman was shorter, nude save for a long strip of tapa, bound so tightly around her hips that it seemed to hold her legs together. Those legs were her imperfection, for they were short, stocky and knock-kneed. I wondered if this peculiarity, which I saw later in the majority of the women here, had something to do with the tight binding of the thighs. Or was it an occupational distortion, caused by carrying heavy loads? In the Kuni dwarfs of Papua I have remarked on another sort of occupational distortion — they were pigeon-breasted and duck-footed from climbing hills all their lives. This Rennellese wife, like the man, was well tattooed except for her face and back. The designs seemed to be all in the same pattern.

They had hardly gotten aboard before they were all over the ship, prying into everything, handling everything, including ourselves. Delicate, dirty fingers felt of our shirts, felt of the buttons on our shorts, patted us all over to see if these strange beings were real. One of the small boys patted my stomach, not satirically, but in admiring surprise that it could be so big. One of the men went into the galley where he tunked the tin pans and chuckled strange words in a dialect which was not quite Polynesian.

Hamlin and I went down the ladder to look at their canoes, strange hulks gnawed from thick logs — gnawed is the word, for they had been hollowed out in the most primitive possible way.

Hamlin said, "Yes, they char the wood and hack it with shells. But these canoes are better made than the ones I saw before. I gave them some hatchets, and they're working with them. They're crazy to get iron and steel. They'll do anything for it, give you anything they've got, and that isn't much — mostly women."

Back on deck I saw the woman making up to Bella, the cook's powerful helper. There was danger ahead, I feared. Not the danger of being clubbed to death, as they had clubbed the mission teachers; but the trouble that comes to any island visitor when crews go ashore to "refresh."

The people who had come aboard spoke a little queer pidgin English, just a word here and there which they had picked up God knows where. They didn't know much of it, for when we first spoke to them they returned a polite, blank stare. Then the woman saw an empty beer bottle, and said "Me want," in a pretty, husky contralto. But when we tried more pidgin on her she was dumb. "What does she want with an empty beer bottle?" I asked Hamlin, and he explained, "The men break them up to shave with. Until beer bottles came the older men were all bearded. The young bucks pulled 'em out by using clam shells, like tweezers. I guess you could buy the island for a dozen razor blades."

Then a few more canoes straggled out to let men, women and children clamber aboard, to make themselves at home. They had never heard of privacy. Why should they have heard of it? They were the primitives of primitives, therefore naïvely communistic. They poked their fingers into every hole in the main cabin, turned up our mattresses and wondered what they were, tried to find out why locked boxes and cupboards wouldn't open. Occasionally they would slip some small thing like a shoelace or a beer-bottle cap into their tapa sashes. A few of the girls could say, "Me want knifie," putting a caress into their voices as they handled our shirt collars. Late that night unmistakable sounds from the crew's quarters indicated that some local beauties had remained to earn a knife or bottle.

(Here I paused to give Templeton Crocker the last cup of coffee in the pot. Then I went on.)

When we were at meals they'd leave us alone — and that was the only time, why I don't know. Right after dinner or breakfast they'd be back. We tried to play cards, but with beautiful torsos pressing against our shoulders, backs and arms, it was hard to concentrate. . . . Two new arrivals came into the cabin, and Hamlin recognized a friend of his former trip. He got up and rubbed noses solemnly with a bright-eyed, nuggety little fellow, whose look was quick with intelligence. "This is Buia of Kanava," Hamlin said, and then of the taller, younger one, "he's named Buia too. He's Buia the Bastard. Buia of Kanava is heir to one of the Big Masters — that's what they call their chiefs here — and he speaks a little pidgin."

At once I decided that Buia of Kanava should be my very own for the duration of the trip. His pidgin was quite bad, but intelligible. When I asked him how he learned it, he said the Japanese sailors had taught him. He was a progressive spirit, far beyond the island average. One day he had swum out to a Japanese pearler, lying offshore, and offered his services for a trip of a few hundred miles. He was there to learn the white man's ways; Japanese or Swedes were all the same to him.

To bind his service securely I took Buia to my cabin and laid an offering out on my berth; an adze, a hatchet, a trade-knife with a six-inch blade and one of the pasteboard lock-boxes Hamlin had been foresighted enough to buy. He gazed, dumb with fascination; he was like Aladdin at first sight of the jewel-filled cave. "Belong me?" he murmured. Yes, they were all for him, *if* he would be goodfellow boy, show me everything and tell me everything. When I got a key and opened the box Buia was mine for a lifetime, if I wanted him that long. I replaced the treasures in a cupboard, but every afternoon while we were on the island he would appear in my cabin and beseech me to let him look at them again. I would lay them out on the berth and watch him gloat, rubbing his hands. He would be a very rich man.

By piecing Buia's words together I gained some knowledge of a religious and social structure which had only moved forward a third of the distance from the Glacial Period.

Buia told me that Rennell Island was divided into five districts, each ruled by a kingly chief called a Big Master. The two most powerful Big Masters were Tahua, Lord of the White Sands, and Taupangi, Lord of the Lake — the lake was Tenggano, lying in the center of the island. The people did not worship images and they had few devils. They adored an unseen God (Big Master Walk along Sky, according to pidgin). The Big Masters were the most powerful because God lived in their heads. ("God does *what?*" I asked.) God lived in their heads, Buia insisted earnestly; so they were wiser and stronger than other men. Once a year, at the harvest festival up by the Lake, Tahua and Taupangi could wish God to leave their heads, just for the period, and dwell behind the brows of some chosen subordinate. Then the subordinates were very strong and wise, but God always came back to the Big Masters. The harvest festival was being celebrated right now, Buia said, and that was why Big Master Tahua was not on the White Sands.

Then Buia came out with a scandal which somewhat alarmed me for the future of these "untouched" people. It was a real-estate deal with more of Hollywood's flavor than Rennell's. Probably the five big chiefs were descendants of five sons of the early conquerors, and Taupangi, Lord of the Lake, was of the eldest line; at least he was the most powerful. Once he ruled both the Lake and the White Sands; but the beach looked useless to him. Perhaps God told Tahua of Kanava that beach property had a future. At any rate Taupangi was induced to give Tahua temporary use of the White Sands, but when he saw vessels anchoring there, with good trading in iron, Taupangi realized his mistake and ordered Tahua out. This started a war, and the enterprising Tahua must have won it, for when we got there he was well established as Lord of the White Sands.

The yams on the Lake were small and poor, but the beach was a different matter. Iron was gold. Iron would put Rennell on its feet. Rennell had girls, the incoming ships had knives, axes, scrap iron. With a corner on iron Tahua could become master of the Big Masters.

As a public health physician I didn't like the sound of this. Trading love for iron was going to work havoc with these natives, unless this form of commercialism was soon discouraged.

Since the main object of my visit was to look into hookworm infection, if it existed, and to study the nature of the parasite which, if they had it, must have been borne by their ancestors generations before the dawn of our modern history, it was necessary to use Buia as a go-between. If he could get it through his head that we were here to examine feces specimens, he could explain it to his people. But after two patient hours of careful pidgin I saw that I was making no headway. Buia simply didn't understand what I wanted. I had been using the lingo almost daily for thirteen years, and had never before had such trouble in making myself clear. Then it dawned upon me that it wasn't entirely the man's faulty knowledge of pidgin. He had no conception of disease, as we view it. All sickness was punishment from their offended god, penalizing the evildoer. That was the only reaction that I got from him after steady pegging away. Finally we changed the subject.

Gordon White and three boys went ashore and erected a tent and fly where we could go properly to work on our examinations. Walking along the sparkling beach I was surprised to find only one house, such as it was, a leaf-building with a steep-sloping roof, eaves that almost touched the ground and no doors. But where did the people sleep? In caves? On the bare ground, with the rain sifting over them? When I knew them better I found that was what they did.

I got around to the subject of murder, for I never quite forgot Dr. Deck's three murdered evangelists. I asked Buia what he would do if somebody tried to kill him. "Who would want to kill me?" he asked, surprised. Suppose somebody should steal his land? "But who would want to steal my land?" Then I got around to Mr. Deck's slain teachers; Rennell people had certainly killed them — and I had heard that they had eaten them, too. Buia's face clouded. "Those mission boys were very bad fellows. They asked our people to build them a house, and when the work did not suit those mission people they were very cross. They gave no presents although they were rich. So our people killed them." And ate the bodies? "No!" Indignantly. "My people have never eaten men. It is not the fashion." I knew he was telling the truth. Cannibalism might be like many another curse, imported. The Rennellese had never acquired a taste for long pig, or for pig of any kind. Their diet was simple in the extreme: the small variety of fruit and vegetables they could grow, what fish their clumsy wooden hooks could bring in, what birds their arrows reached. They ate just one thing at a meal. If it was fish, it was fish and nothing else. If it was yams, it was yams alone.

There were many things they couldn't understand, but their bright minds were quick to learn. Our ornithologists were out for specimens, and Hamlin had given a few native boys their first lessons with a shotgun, half an hour's target practice on the rare birds flying about. Then he had casually handed guns to the boys and told them to go to it. They came back loaded with feathery game. What was still more wonderful was that nobody had shot himself in the foot.

So I sat down at my typewriter to write a report, something that couldn't be done in sociable Kungava Bay. The boat was swarming. Native heroes and their women had gone into about everything on board, and were helping themselves rather freely. It was neither politic nor polite to offend these charming people by telling them to go home and stay there until they were invited. As a counter-attraction I had set the phonograph up in the bow and ordered little Ga'a to keep the needle going till it wore out. The ghost-music attracted part of the crowd part of the time, but they always came back to me. The phonograph was all right as a miracle, but what really puzzled and charmed them was my portable typewriter.

A baker's dozen of the brown-skinned young things lolled over my shoulders, touching the keys as they flew, drawing their fingers over the ribbon to see the ink come off. What was this strange box that made such straight tattoo marks across a very white sheet? Finally I gave up all pretense of working and called Buia. His eyes, like all the others', were fixed on my portable. He said that they all wanted to know what I was doing. I told him that if he would push the girls back a few inches I would try to show him. This machine, I said, made talk. Those things I was tattooing on the white sheet were words; if Buia were to carry the sheet as far as the albatross flies, a man on the other end would just look at it and the words would talk to him. Buia's bright eyes were standing out of his head as he murmured, "Me no sabe dis fellow talk." "I'll show you," I said, and tick-tacked on a piece of paper, "*Hamlin, please give Buia a tin of cigarettes.*" I told what the paper would say to Hamlin, and sent Buia below.

Presently he staggered back, a tin of Chesterfields shuddering in his hand. Furtively he whispered the miracle to the huddled islanders. And it *was* a miracle in a land where there had never been the slightest trace of a written language, not even picture writing. In their excited faces I saw a hungry eagerness to learn. Experimentally I lined them up, and as each one told me his name or hers I would typewrite it and have the bearer take it down to a man in the engineroom, who would read it out to them. This game lasted until my fingers were tired of hitting the keyboard. Some of them tried to help me; mischievous fingers would poke at random, and the ship would be a gale of rough contralto laughter when a key flew up and struck the paper.

That night I wrestled with Buia again over the subject of hookworm. Carefully I told him of the snake that hung to the human intestine and sent its eggs out with the bowel motion. In my jungle campaigns I had informed the most backward and savage Melanesians that they had "senake in bel'" which their witch doctors could not cure because they only removed the ghost of a snake, but we could fetch the real thing. I had worked in safety among tough cannibals and found that they were afraid to attack a man who could do such magic.

I thought that my detailed explanation had at last got under Buia's skin. He was politely impressed, and I felt sure that he would act as my friend and interpreter tomorrow when I would begin the delicate work of collecting specimens of feces.

Next morning Gordon White and I went to the beach with our microscope and little tin containers; the first thing I did was to give a container to Buia, and ask him if he remembered what I had told him. Now Buia seemed unable to understand. Gordon White came to my rescue and said, "Doctor, I'll go and demonstrate to these bastards, personally." With Buia and a retinue of small boys he retired into the bushes. Silence. Then a perfect bedlam of frightened yells. Small boys came scampering out, hands in air, mouths open, screaming. And Buia followed the panicky retreat. They ran as though a mad dog were after them, nipping.

At last Gordon came out, dejectedly holding a tin. "When I put the specimen in and closed the lid," he said, "they stared as if they were accusing me of an atrocious crime." The natives of the beach kept away from us for a bad half-hour; we were isolated among a lot of savages who had interpreted our well meant attempt as the grossest insult. These men carried spears and clubs; we knew how they dealt with those who offended them. Whether or not they had eaten Deck's missioners was only of academic importance. What happens after you're dead doesn't matter much. The main thing was to keep alive. . . .

Then Buia came sidling back to our tent. His look was portentous. He said, "Master, dis fellow he something altogether tabu. Him he tabu too much. Suppose Big Master Tahua sabe something belong dis fashion, he altogether too bad along you fellow me fellow" — Meaning that if we went on with our search for hookworm eggs Tahua would kill us all, including Buia. We heard the noise of people scrambling down the precipice. Buia told us that they were from Lake Tenggano. And as we valued our lives, he said, we mustn't even hint at what happened in the bushes. Otherwise terrible things would befall us for breaking their tabu.

Well, there we were, on the third day, absolutely bunkered on the main object of our trip. When I went back to the *France*, feeling that my investment had turned out a total loss, I found the people of the Lake swarming over everything, and among them a grandee of the White Sands, an adopted son of Tahua. And there was Tamata, too, adopted son of Taupangi. They seemed to be a reception committee from the Big Masters, inviting us to the harvest festival at the Lake.

Hamlin had warned me of difficulties going overland to the Lake. But our failure of that morning had roused all the mule blood in me. If I went to the Lord of the Lake and prevailed on him to cancel the tabu and let me make the necessary examinations I might accomplish the purpose of my visit. After all, it was only a walk of seven or eight miles, I was in fair condition, and impatient when Hamlin argued that I had better not try it. I didn't know what I was in for. . . .

(Here I paused and looked at the empty coffeepot. "Guess I'd better make some more," I said to Templeton Crocker. When I got back with the coffee I asked, "Are you tired of listening?" "Lord, no!" said Crocker. "And I hope you're not tired of talking." "I'm never tired of talking," I said, and went on.)

I was rather glad to be away from the *France* for a while. The sociability on board was getting on my nerves. I had already learned that their dialect was akin to Polynesian and that the word *tabu* was feared and respected. But it wasn't at all like the German *verboten*. We didn't use *tabu* properly or understand it properly. A thing could be tabu one minute, I discovered, and not tabu the next. When I found standing room only in my cabin, everything in it being pulled up or pulled down by curious island fingers, I would smile mildly and say, "Tabu, tabu!" It wouldn't do to lose patience and push them out. They would be tabu-ed out of the main cabin, but we only had to wait a little before a head, then an arm, then a leg would appear slyly in the companionway. Then they would all ooze in again. We had talked it over among ourselves and had decided that they were Polynesians, kind and courteous to friends; but an uncouth word might rouse their tempers to a fury.

We started on our little stroll to the Lake. At Hamlin's suggestion I put on a pair of heavy army shoes with stout brass screws in soles and heels — seemed rather a silly precaution. Buia was guiding us and we had a few carriers for our light packs. A tin of sardines and two ship's biscuits would be enough for each of us, in case of famine. My pack included a light change of clothes and toilet necessities. Also we had a bundle of tribute-gifts for Tahua and Taupangi. Hamlin had been foresighted enough to include tea, butter, sugar, salt, pepper and a benzine tin to make tea in. Otherwise we expected to live off the country.

Our march began with a climb up 400 feet of cliff, up a sort of ladder trail which generations had scooped out with shells. The coral stone seemed to be so many little daggers, slicing at me until my hands and knees began to bleed. Once on the summit, there were slopes of coral; everything on the island was coral, except thin patches of earth that had caught on the surface. I think that the people got what they ate by moving from patch to patch and picking whatever grew there. We found a grove of pawpaws. The carriers were eating the fruit green, so I tried a paw. They were not bad. Green pawpaws are full of papain, with an action similar to that of pepsin. . . . Walking along, nibbling, I began to feel that the difficulties of the trip had been overrated. Then beyond the grove I looked across the bleakness of the land from which a healthy people had hacked their bare living through ages of struggle. Over the trail in front of us was a mass of briary vines. Must we go through that? Buia led the way.

I wore a helmet and was sorry, for the rest of the way we had to walk at a crouch through a tunnel of close-woven twigs. Vines pulled off my helmet, tripped me up, flung me about. Two good men with machetes could have cleared this trail; but there were no machetes in this land of little iron. There was always coral underfoot, cutting with thousands of minute edges. Beyond the vines trees were growing out of solid coral; the forest was so dense that we were in twilight, all the way to the Lake. Perspiration oozed out of us, rain oozed in, wetting us through. Yet we were so thirsty that we must stop every half-mile or so to swig from our water-bottles. A cigarette would have helped, but they were saturated by misty rain the instant they came out of the box.

The barefoot carriers didn't seem to mind the jagged stuff; they would step daintily around a bristling lump which could have opened an artery. Now I knew why Rennellese legs were always scarred up to the knee. The gods of Rennell Island had thrown up another barrier against strangers. When we approached an especially bad lump Buia would point it out in time for me to balance myself on my cane to avoid a fall that might have scraped me to death.

Maybe you have scared your children to sleep by telling of obstacles, natural and supernatural, which the hero must overcome in his climb to the ogre's castle. On that walk to the Lake fissures would appear in the rock, spanned by rain-slippery, mossy logs. Buia would stand on the slimy thing, agile as a monkey, and pleasantly help us across the void. I wore two pairs of woolen stockings when I started out; now they hung in shreds against my bleeding calves. At the first step on a log I saw that the thick leather of my shoes was torn as if it had been scraped across yards of barbed wire. Now I knew why Hamlin had thought that I couldn't finish this little tour. By the time we reached the muddy shores of the Lake my dreadnaught shoes had about gone back on me, and the brass-studded soles were flopping about like broken wings.

On a knoll some fifty yards from the Lake we came upon another of those queer Rennell houses, practically all roof with eaves a couple of feet from the ground. There were no doors or windows, so you got in by crawling under the eaves. There was nothing inside but a great pile of coconuts. We were told not to touch them because they were extra tabu. Coconuts were very scarce. Hog-dirty, dog-tired, White and Hamlin and I tumbled down and panted, quite willing to die among the coconuts, if only they let us alone.

Somebody was crawling in after us. It was Buia with a couple of handsome natives. Buia said that we had better hurry up, as the Big Masters, Tahua and Taupangi, were waiting to receive us. So we were up again, mucking our way through a mile of lakeside and up to a so-called village. There were shackly palm-leaf canopies on crooked poles — where people slept, perhaps. There were caverns in the coral over yonder, which might serve as apartments. We came to another Rennell house, slightly larger than the one we had been in. In a palace like this there is no question of Majesty having obeisance paid it or of a court officer instructing one how to bow and kneel. You crawl in on all fours, and on all fours you greet the reigning sovereign. Taupangi, Lord of the Lake, sat in state on a pile of native mats, and was properly dressed for the religious ceremonies. Around his waist he wore a wide tapa and a fancifully woven mat. His hair was in a knot at the back of his head and he was smeared all over with sacred yellow turmeric. He was still young, and about the biggest man I saw on Rennell Island, with shoulders like an ox's yoke and a wonderfully proportioned body. All of the Big Masters that I saw were handsome men, none of them running to fat as Polynesians do in middle age.

At the other end of the house sat a younger, still handsomer man, enthroned on mats. He had the perfect classic profile and his tattooed torso was magnificent. This was Tekita, who had acted as the Big Master's substitute during the ceremonies of the week; during the ritual God had passed from Taupangi's head and into Tekita's. He was being king for a day, as it were, for the great spirit (Tainatua) owned every stick and stone on Rennell Island, and the man whose head possessed him spoke with the voice of God. Taupangi, for the nonce, was only human. Soon, when Divinity resumed its seat in his brain, he would again be all powerful over the division of labor, crops and everything else in his little realm.

Tekita, the substitute, had been chewing betel-nuts, and seemed excited, as well he might be considering his lofty rise. Superficially he behaved like quite a conceited young fellow. He spoke pidgin English fairly well — he might have been one of those whom Lever Brothers' yacht had taken away on an unsuccessful attempt at recruiting. With all the gestures of royalty Tekita seated himself next to the Big Master and graciously did some interpreting. As he talked he rolled his eyes and every few moments he would go into a silent semi-trance. He was going on much like any charlatan trying to impress an audience. In a prophetic voice he admitted that he was glad to see Hamlin again. "Hamlin fadder belong me," he said. And promptly wanted to know what present "fadder belong him" had brought. This honorary fatherhood, although it cemented our friendship with Taupangi's people, was becoming a bit of a nuisance.

I found more pidgin than I had expected, at first. It was gradually filtering in. (I can't forget Tekita's lordly farewell, spoken between trances: "Me too sorry belong you fellow you come along here." Meaning, of course, that he was glad; but he had somehow mixed his adjectives.)

I wanted to see Tahua, Lord of the White Sands, but when I asked this favor of Taupangi, the Lord of the Lake, he was jealously evasive. Our tribute of an adze and axe changed his mind (which was Tekita, speaking with the voice of God). Guides led us over to a miserable little hut of sticks and vines. Apparently Taupangi wasn't being too lavish with his rival. But there was enough room inside for the bearded, muscular Tahua to sit in state opposite his divinely inspired substitute. Tahua relaxed to a somewhat cupidinous smile when we presented him with an adze. This meeting wasn't much, but it was what a bond salesman would call a "contact." I knew that I would have to gain Tahua's good will before I could even attempt hookworm examinations on his side of the island.

Tomorrow would end the festival, with the ceremony of putting God back into the heads of the Big Masters. I was too tired to care. I had sloshed through mud until I found fresh water, made a pretense of washing my face and hands and came back dirtier than before. Now I could see why the inland Rennellese went unbathed, except when it happened to rain on them. I crawled into the guest house — not daring to touch the pile of sacred coconuts — and eased my feet with clean socks and tennis shoes. Then I spread out my blanket and got on it.

"Oh, sleep! it is a gentle thing," said the Ancient Mariner. In Taupangi's domain it was a mixed blessing. When I started to drowse, our courteous hosts came in with a rough wooden bowl filled with *pana*, a glorified sweet potato. Although they had peeled the vegetables with their dirty fingers, the smell of food woke me pleasantly. Since leaving the *France* we had had nothing but a few sardines and one sea-biscuit apiece. I had watched the natives cooking; Rennellese fire-sticks were pieces of rotten wood which they rubbed until the spark came. They lined a hole with coral stones, started a fire on them and kept it going until the stones were white hot. Then they wrapped food in leaves, laid it on the stones, covered it with earth and let nature take its course.

Except for a small clamshell, which they used mostly to scrape the meat from coconuts, the wooden bowl was their only eating utensil. At festival dances they used the bowls as drums. These, and big wooden drums, were the only musical instruments they had. I was sorry that we had forgotten to bring them jew's harps, which would have charmed them into ecstasies.

To say that I slept that night would be a gross exaggeration. Every man, woman and child who could crowd in became our bedmate. Communism and comfort seem to be strangers. We lay all coiled together, Gordon White and I sharing the common lot. The rest of our crowd had had sense enough to find some sort of shelter outside. Before we slept — if it could be called sleeping — a burly, blustery fellow named Panio came in and showed all the specious heartiness of the typical politician. Instinctively I felt that we might have trouble with Panio. If I had known, as I learned later, that he belonged on the beach, a henchman of Tahua, and was one of the three that had killed Deck's missionaries, I might have slept even more lightly than I did.

Lying on the floor, cuddled very close to me, was Tamata, son of Taupangi, and on the other side, equally intimate, was Tahua's adopted son. I could see why the house was so popular, for the night was quite cool; outside in the ridiculous leaf-and-stick shelters only a mat protected the sleeper. I had seen women lying in the open, babes in arms, snoring serenely with cold rain sifting all over them.

The house inside reminded me of Mark Twain's description of

Brigham Young's bed; if anybody turned they all had to turn. Far into the night, pidgin English questions were pegged at me from this side and that. They all wanted to learn a little more while they had the opportunity. Indoors or out, it was the crudest existence imaginable, not far removed from the animal. Yet they thrived on it, to all appearances. . . .

Next morning, after we had implored our hosts to break their one-meal-a-day custom and cook us a fish, we went over to the harvest festival, which was drawing to a dramatic close.

(I paused to light a cigarette, and Crocker prompted me with "What happened then?")

Well (I said) the show was held near Taupangi's house. He and his rival, Tahua, with several other Big Masters, were the features. They had laid aside their bunchy loin coverings and wore nothing but strips of tapa between their buttocks and around their waists. From head to foot they were yellow with royal turmeric. Tahua's first gesture, when he saw me, was to point at my bare legs. I didn't understand, until I learned that Resident Commissioner Dick Kane, the first white man known to have penetrated as far as the Lake, had worn woolen stockings. When the natives were curious, he told them that in civilization only big chiefs were allowed to wear stockings. Next time I visited Taupangi I restored my status by covering my calves.

There was a rough dirt court, about fifty yards by ten. They had fenced it with sticks and leaves, higher than a man's head. This was to keep women out. If any female looked in on the ceremony she would surely die, they said. There was some trouble about letting us into the enclosure. We were told that the gods, angered at our presence, might do us harm. Finally, as a measure of protection, Taupangi sat between us and danger. Before he rose to take part in the ceremonies he insisted that another Master, a very old one, should sit in his place, so that at all times we were well insulated against the supernatural.

The precious coconuts which we had been sleeping with were now piled in the center of the court; beside them was a rude platform where sat the two young men who had substituted as godheads for the two Big Masters.

Then the Masters — there were about twenty of the minor ones in all — began filing slowly around the coconut pile, their faces turned heavenward as they chanted. First Taupangi would take up the theme, then the others would join in a sort of obbligato. The walk sped up gradually to a curious leaping, first on one foot then the other; they hopped by rule, two on the right leg, two on the left. The pounding of drums and food-bowls, the howling song and general yelling increased to a hubbub. Abruptly the dancers would sit down, and the racket would cease. Finally Tekita (still monarch pro tem) rose from his platform and distributed coconuts from the pile.

The big moment came. The celebrants began working God out of the two substitutes and back into the heads of Taupangi and Tahua. The faces of both Big Masters were set in earnest religious devotion. The lesser Masters formed a line, four abreast, and hopped some distance toward the house where Tekita had been sitting. Singing at the top of their lungs, their hands outstretched toward Heaven, they hopped back. Their slow retreat and progress brought them nearer the house each time; they came at last within six feet of the eaves. At last with a bloodcurdling howl they rushed up and struck the roof with the flat of their hands. Then, apparently, God flew from his temporary dwelling back into the heads of Tahua and Taupangi.

The minute this transfer was made Taupangi's substitute seemed to come back to normal. He had lost the superiority complex altogether, and was a relaxed, courteous and jolly fellow.

That night our bird hunters brought in some ducks, which we ate half raw, because the natives only knew how to scorch them. Themselves, they never ate ducks; ducks were unclean feeders, the people said. Thinking that we might protect ourselves from the sociability of the house, we set up a tent. In fifteen minutes our tent was jammed with self-invited guests. The frail canvas came down two or three times during the night from the pressure of those inside getting out and those outside getting in. In the weary, dreary morning, plagued with thirst, I tried drinking water from the Lake, where the natives seemed to get theirs. On the coral-jagged march back to the beach, I found to my embarrassment that the Lake was quite unfriendly to a white man's digestion.

When we reached the White Sands some interesting gossip was going the rounds. It was about Tekita, who had been substituting for Taupangi. By all the rules a substitute was supposed to be very tabu during that period, especially for women. But when God got back into Taupangi's head he told on Tekita, who had broken his tabu with a certain village maiden. So God visited his punishment on Taupangi, not Tekita, and told him that he could not go down to the *France* while she was in the bay. Somehow the Almighty must have reversed himself, for Taupangi visited us a few days later.

While I was at the Lake I never for a moment overlooked the problem of hookworm examinations, nor did I fail to put in a great deal of time making a census of the people for apparent diseases. Since Buia had warned me not to mention hookworms to the Big Master, I was still searching for a way to go ahead. Then Buia fixed it. My guess was that he spoke to Mua, son of Taupangi; for both the Lord of the Lake and his son had first class minds. Tahua, Lord of the White Sands, was reputed to have less "power" than Taupangi; that is to say, he was unable to go into a "sweating trance" as the chief of Lake Tenggano could, they said. Mua told me that Taupangi could kill by wishing, through his closer connection with the Grandson God.

At any rate, when we were back on the beach Buia told me that if I could give him and Mua the specimen tins, and would make examinations before the two Big Masters came, maybe it would be all right. I had offered a large fishhook and a small fishhook for every specimen, which may have been why we got a few. We found a light infection, but under such adverse conditions we were unable to determine whether the hookworms were ancient, modern or what. It was interesting to observe the watchful care with which our tin containers were returned. Each man would squat in front of our worktable and never take his eyes off the specimen until we had finished and thrown it into a hole in the sand. They were taking no chances on our being witch doctors, come to make black magic.

If I had been given the ghost of an opportunity I might have reached some conclusion; I might have washed out their specimens according to the regulation field technique and studied the parasites under the microscope. This might have added important clues in the search for Rennell Island's history, for the hookworm contents of a race may tell a great deal about the origins and migrations of a people. Dr. S. T. Darling, eminent in tropical medicine, had developed theories on this parasite, which he collected all over the globe. He demonstrated that the original habitat of the *Ankylostoma duodenale* was north of twenty degrees north latitude, while the *Necator americanus* stemmed from a region south of that line. This is a point which has not been given due weight by anthropologists. All my work over the Pacific added validity to Darling's theory. Certainly I found that both Melanesians and Polynesians living south of twenty degrees north latitude — provided that they had not been contaminated by Asiatics — carried only the *Necator americanus* — an evidence that their origin and migration must have been from south of this latitude.

You can imagine my disappointment in learning so little from the tabu-haunted Rennellese, to whom the intimate details of a worm-count would have been a capital offense. On all the island there was nothing like a latrine; like the followers of Moses, these primitives dug holes in the sand and carefully covered "that which they had done" — this as a precaution against some witch's charm. Sand, however, is far too porous to hold down the enterprising larvae, especially when the hole is only a surface scratch. We devoted much time to examining blood for filariasis, which was conspicuous for its absence. Our spleen examinations revealed no malaria, either on Rennell or its little neighboring sister, Bellona, although both were definitely in the malaria belt. Neither did we find an anopheline mosquito.

The complete absence of dysentery was interesting, because it had once been brought there by an apparently clean ship, and had decimated the population. It had died out, probably because the Rennell flies, although they flew in swarms, did not seem to light on human beings; also there was no water supply to be contaminated — the beach natives drew water from holes at the bottom of the cliffs, the interior natives drank out of the Lake. Food was no carrier, for it was cooked in the skins.

There was little sign of past devastations, although there was evidence that the few visiting ships had brought them influenza and an infection of gonorrhea, from which they had recovered.

Wandering about, I finally came upon a few miserable beings, hidden away from intruders. They were suffering from yaws. The people had not talked about yaws. They seemed to be ashamed of it. It was quite evident that they had kept the disease from spreading by an age-old, self-taught practice of segregation.

The Rennellese wore their one garment until it was threadbare; by day it was trousers, by night pajamas. Since the water in the Lake was hard to get at and the water below the cliffs came in driblets, only expert swimmers knew the pleasures of bathing. They rather disliked the touch of salt water, but this prejudice was not responsible for a certain skin condition.

Scabies was present, but not serious. The prevalent disease on Rennell, I think, was something they called *onga-onga*, a sort of itch. The inhabitants claimed that it had been brought there by Dr. Deck's unpopular missionaries. Apparently it only appeared as a dermatitis, the result of scratching. Constant scratching was a native gesture. When the disease first came, they told me, everyone went mad, ran to the bush, threw away their clothes and dug their nails into every part of their bodies.

Within a month after we left the island all of us came down with it. To me it was a most unpleasant visitor. It began at my thighs and covered me from knees to waist, like a pair of shorts. I could see no discoloration, save where my nails had torn my skin. Hot baths irritated it. Successive days of treating myself with saturated solution of salicylic acid in strong tincture of iodine, then with Deek's ointment, brought relief. My skin peeled completely away from the infected area, and I haven't heard from *onga-onga* since. . . .

Shortly after we had re-established headquarters on the *France* natives from the interior came flocking to trade mats and baskets for beads and knives and fishhooks. Obviously the situation was growing touchy, with jealousy between inland-dweller and beach-dweller. There were one or two wrestling matches, not too good-natured — strange combats, in which two strong men pulled each other's hair until the weaker fell. These were dogfights, and we were the bone of contention.

The situation tightened when Panio, Tahua's strong-arm who had helped do away with Deck's missioners, came aboard and proceeded to make himself obnoxious. Panio was unlike the other islanders. He dramatized himself as a murderer. With much diplomacy we had reached a point where we could keep the people out of our cabins for short intervals — but not Panio. In blustering ward-heeler style he would walk in, throw out his chest and take possession. He was angry with Buia for getting more than his share of good things; also he had a social bee in his bonnet; his daughter wasn't being recognized by the local *haut monde*.

Yes, it was getting ticklish. Like all bullies, Panio was putting up a dangerous front because, probably, his gang was behind him. For all I knew we were a dozen against fifteen hundred. All the rights were on their side; we had come unasked, and they had entertained us with the best they had; on the *France* they were merely returning our visit, and it was impossible for them to understand why we shouldn't give them the run of the ship and whatever they fancied in the way of food. When we asked for privacy they no doubt thought of us as stingy, grasping strangers. Remember, these people were all born communists.

Our nerves were wearing thin. Something must be done about Panio. One night when we cleared the cabin he refused to budge. This time I made my voice firmer than Rennell diplomacy required; he stood his ground, looking not at all pretty. I told Hamlin and White what I was going to do, and when they nodded I used my clearest pidgin on Panio. Would he get out or be thrown out? Rather a ridiculous question, for he was years younger than I, immensely powerful and in the pink. Facing him, I thought, "I'm in for it now. I'll *have* to put him out. . . ."

(Here I paused to drip cold coffee into my cup. Templeton Crocker asked, "And did you?")

What happened next (I said) was a sort of psychic curiosity. Panio stood firm and looked for a long time straight through my glasses into my furious eyes. My glance didn't swerve. Suddenly his nerve seemed to ooze away. He dropped his eyes, shuffled, turned and marched out of the cabin and up the stairs. When I got on deck he was gone.

I don't mind confessing that after the thing was over I had the "wind up," as the British say; so much so that I went to my grip and found my pistol. Next morning the relations between us and our guests seemed a bit strained, and I was dreading the consequences — when back came Panio, carrying a broad grin and a tribute of baked *panas* for me. To this day I don't know how I subdued him, with only a look. Possibly he was afraid that my glasses would slay him with the spell of the evil eye. Possibly I had quelled him the way, I am told, you can quell wild beasts, by a fixed and powerful stare. . . . I should hate to try it on a Bengal tiger.

The native name for Rennell Island is Mungava (Big Rennell) and for Bellona Island it is Mungiki (Little Rennell). The *France* hadn't visited Bellona on its other trip; very few Europeans had ever dared to go ashore there. After Buia told us that one of the kings of Bellona was his cousin and might make things easy for us, Hamlin was particularly anxious to touch there. Then all the population of Rennell Island clamored to be taken along. Mua, son of Taupangi, was the most clamorous of all. I promised to take these two young men, provided and agreed that they would smooth the way for me to get plenty of hookworm specimens. If we hadn't taken Mua, his father would have been furious because his son had been left behind and Tahua's representative had gone with us.

After talking things over with their two Big Masters, Buia and Mua made a quaint suggestion. The people of Bellona might be "cross too much." As we were approaching the shore Mua and Buia had decided that it would be a good idea to dress up in European clothes, put shotguns over their shoulders and look like hunting naturalists. This disguise would impress the natives, for some undisclosed reason, and after that everything would be smooth going.

We reached the little bay in the little island, which was a stone-walled Rennell in miniature — about four miles long and three wide. It had much more soil on it and looked much more fertile. When we found anchorage we shouted and fired guns to attract attention, but nothing stirred. Jagged masses of coral endangered our anchorage; on a windy day we would have been beaten to pieces. As it was, our keel got a terrific bump on a hidden snag, the anchor chain parted and we were set adrift. The four-mile engine got us around at last; we worked all night and finally dropped an improvised anchor. Our survival was a compliment to the stout teakwood hull of the *France*.

In the early morning canoes appeared, coming out to us. Buia and Mua hastily arrayed themselves in white men's raincoats and hats, and when the natives drew alongside our amateur detectives began shouting at them in the vilest and most profane pidgin English — evidently their conception of trading skippers approaching an island. Buia and Mua looked their parts so little that you wouldn't have thought they could fool a baby. But the Bellona folk stared anxiously up at them, and when our impersonators began to address them in their native language the listeners were bewildered. Who were these foreigners who spoke so fluently in the speech of Bellona?

Suddenly Buia and Mua threw off their disguise. A sigh of wonder went over the reception committee, then a shout of welcome swelled to an ovation. It was a breath-taking occasion: native boys had actually come as guides to a European vessel! The people of Mungiki, very like their relatives of Mungava, swarmed aboard and rubbed noses with their heroes. Every visitor bristled with bows and arrows, spears and clubs; they looked fiercer and wilder than the Rennell folk. Surrounding us, more curious than hostile, their every gesture seemed a threat. The few who could speak pidgin went anxiously among us, asking, "Captain, Captain?" They wanted to know which of our party was top dog.

Finally Buia led us ashore, and we were surprised at the neat little houses among the heavy palms. Everything we saw was clean and well kept, including the villagers. For some lost reason they seemed to have learned the art of taking care of themselves. When we returned to the boat Buia's cousin, one of the three kings, sent word that he was ready to receive us. We returned the compliment by asking him aboard, only to be told that it was tabu for a king to come on a stranger's ship. There had been war between the three kings; and how in the world there was room for three wars between three kings is another South Sea mystery.

As the soil looked richer, so the people looked healthier than those of Rennell, where epidemics had killed many elderly folk. On Bellona there were many of the old and wizened. They were fine-looking, very light in color, their features well cut. When I sent again to the three kings, telling Buia to say that they wouldn't get an ax or an adze or any other dainty unless they came, their Triple Majesties showed up. They were polite enough, and after I bribed them with an ax apiece I told Buia to tell them the object of my visit: hookworms. Whereupon they informed me that they did not want doctors, they did not want missions, they did not want government, and they would give me no census. Quite courteously, they preferred our room to our company.

Even an overnight inspection showed the good results of quarantine against foreign-borne disease and custom. Although pathologically I was unable to look into the case, they seemed to have nothing to fear, except petty wars. Their teeth were poor in comparison to the handsome mouths of the Rennellese. This was due, perhaps, to a different method of betel-nut chewing.

Then we sailed back to the White Sands, where by the demonstration they made we might have been to Peru and back. Big Master Taupangi grabbed my shoulders and tenderly rubbed noses with me. Marking my surprise, he shook with laughter and extended me an invitation to attach myself to his court and stay there the rest of my life. For one with God in his head, he was feeling very jovial and stood back to back with me to prove that he was an inch taller. When I went over his chest, thighs and belly with a tape-line he was proud as a peacock to know that he was larger all around than the largest European on the vessel. Each day before we left he came back, as God's vicar in Tenggano, and presented me with a basket of yams and a basket of *pana* in trade for a tin of bully beef, a tin of salmon and a few ship's biscuits. This human reservoir of divinity was extremely fond of tinned fish. So were they all. Every few minutes a Rennellese brave would show up and say, "Master, belly belonga me he hongry too much." Our Solomon Island crew looked down on these people. Once Hamlin said to me, "Doctor, these Rennellese live almost like dogs." Whereupon little Ga'a chipped in, "Master, dis fellow he no dog. Dog he know somet'ing."

Our departure was the end of a field day. Tahua, always a businessman, had been selling us the finer mats and baskets which the Lake people had made. Mats were coming in faster than we could handle them, but we still gave in exchange the best we had to these kindly, likable islanders. Everybody wanted a lock-box, because I had promised one to Buia. I had only one left, and that I gave to Tahua, out of respect for his superior station. Tekita and Mua were clamoring for ones just like it. Then down came my old college chum, Taupangi. If Tahua had a lock-box, where was his? Imagine my embarrassment. Finally I found an old wooden box in the engineroom, got Bella to hinge a cover on it and to nail on the brass locks of my own tucker-box. The Lake people cheered *en masse* at the presentation, but Buia and Tahua looked very glum. The small pressed-paper boxes I had given them were nothing compared to the grand prize which the Lord of the Lake carried away.

The people saw that we were actually going, and the prices of mats and baskets fell to almost nothing. Rennell's little stock exchange was having a slump. Before we started for Tulagi I doled out fishhooks to the two rival kings. I served out the hooks with Spartan justice, first two to Tahua, then two to Taupangi. I started in with a box of large-sized ones, and when that was finished Tahua hastily picked up the box of smaller ones and thrust it in my hand. He was afraid I might forget about it, or change my mind. Appreciative laughter from the crowd, who probably realized that Tahua was a chronic go-getter.

Lock-boxes, however, were the treasures of treasures. It wasn't until we were out at sea that I realized why. To them these things, with lids that you could fasten with your own key, represented privacy. Here was something where you could store away small objects that were your very own. From birth to death in Rennell's primitive society there was no such thing as a door to close or a curtain to draw when you wished to be alone and mind your own business. Instinctively the untaught savage longed for a sanctuary, away from prying eyes. I had to have lived on communistic Rennell Island to understand and value civilization's greatest boon — privacy.

When we got back to the comparative civilization of Tulagi we found that Resident Commissioner Ashley had worried because we were overdue and had started out on an expedition to find us. He had taken thirty armed policemen aboard the *Renadi,* for the luck of former visitors to Rennell Island had given the place such an evil reputation that the Protectorate had ordered that nobody should approach it without an armed guard. Captain Ashley had put a machine gun on the *Renadi,* and Dr. Steenson had gone along with a hospital unit.

I wish Ashley had seen me rubbing noses with the chiefs when we bade farewell to Rennell. . . .

(Templeton Crocker looked around the porch and said, "Good heavens, it's daylight!" Sure enough, it was. "I'd better be getting back to the *Zaca,*" he said. "We sail at noon. But tell me one thing, Doctor. Will these queer Rennellese go on, pretty healthy and contented, just as they've always been? Or what?")

"Something will have to be done about them," I said, "and the thing to do is to let them alone. What worried me most was the business enterprise that the Lord of the White Sands was showing. Anything for iron. Trade the women's services for a knife or a busted chisel. Rennell is leaping from the Shell Age into the Iron Age. They've never touched the Stone Age, because they hardly know what stone is. Before somebody brought in the white man's ax they did surprisingly well with a clamshell on the end of a stick. They don't seem to like missionaries, but they're mad to learn European ways because that knowledge will bring more trade. Their 'virtue' as we call it? Well, virtue is about the same the world over. In some countries women are tabu. They don't happen to be in Rennell, where the women are the only thing that appeals to the white man as trade. From a doctor's angle, virtue's great virtue is this: It's prophylactic.

"Imported disease; that's what threatens Rennell, sure as God made little apples. Now they're healthier than the average in San Francisco, say. From what I could find out, their only ills have come from the few visits white men or Japanese have made there — except hookworm. I wish I knew more about that parasite on Rennell.

"They're so susceptible to imported germs that I'll tell you what happened. Before the *France* came to the White Sands, remember, I examined everybody on board for the slightest trace of anything 'catching.' Except for the sore-eyed cook, whom we tried to keep out of the way, we were all apparently clean as a whistle. Yet we hadn't been on the island ten days before an epidemic of head colds swept the people. They didn't know what was the matter with them; they didn't even know how to blow their noses."

"Where did they pick up those colds?" Crocker asked.

"They caught them from us. Our noses and throats were full of latent germs to which we had an immunity, whereas the Rennellese had none. They wore few clothes, they slept out in the rain, they were exposed to winds and drafts, yet the common cold was an absolute stranger to them. They had had an influenza epidemic, once; the white man brought it. They had had gonorrhea, once; the white man brought that too. Once they caught dysentery, from a ship that was supposedly clean of it. Bring in more ships and Rennell will go down and out, as so many other islands have. And I don't want Rennell to go down and out."

"Because they're a unique people?" Crocker asked.

"Because they're the only living relic, that I know, of a prehistoric race, changed so little that they will make an invaluable study for scientific research. But not for casual sailors and traders. There's nothing on Rennell Island worth trading for. . . . What I should like to see done is this: Have the Government put 'No ADMITTANCE' on both Rennell and Bellona — except for an honest scientific expedition, coming there for no other reason than legitimate research. For those islands are nothing more or less than studies in the history of mankind."

So Templeton Crocker went back to his ship.

And all this led up to my brandy-and-eggs conversation with Raymond Fosdick. In fact, it also led up to one of my most interesting adventures.

For when morning broke, after my Arabian night with Crocker, Eloisa reminded me again that he was in need of fresh eggs and that we had plenty in the hen-house. "I've gathered three dozen," she said, "and you might put them on the *Zaca* when you go down to the office."

I took the eggs over to the *Zaca*, which was busily preening herself for a long haul. I left them with my compliments and best wishes. The *Zaca* sailed at noon.

A few days later a messenger came over from the Fiji Club with something wrapped in the *Times and Herald*. Unwrapping, I found four bottles of 1835 brandy. There was no address on the package, and I thought there was some mistake. I asked Amos, secretary of the Club, and he said: "Well, if you don't want the stuff, I do. But Mr. Crocker seemed to say that it was for you."

I wrote my thanks to Templeton Crocker, and this opened up a lively correspondence. He was about the way I had been when I first heard about Rennell Island. He couldn't drop the subject, and as months went by his keenness seemed to grow. Early in 1933, he wrote that he had made some changes in the *Zaca* so that it would be more handy for collecting scientific specimens. He finished by asking me to go along and show him the strange country I had told him about. Of course I wanted to see Rennell Island again, but I secured an invitation from the High Commission first, then wrote Mr. Crocker, "I'll go willingly, if you'll spot me around where I can inspect our work in the Solomons and make a tuberculin survey." I also suggested that he bring an anthropologist along. He found the man and added a plant collector and an entomologist to the *Zaca* party.

That was the way Eloisa's eggs came to roost, if I may scramble a metaphor. In a roundabout way they gave me a chance to revisit a spot which interested me more, perhaps, than anything I had seen in the Pacific.

CHAPTER III

THROUGH THE SOLOMONS TO RENNELL

Let me begin with a scrap from my diary of May 4, 1933. We had been on the water three days, moving toward Vanikoro.

> . . . We are a little crowded, but not too much. *Zaca* is beautiful; 118 feet long, 23 feet beam, 125 tons, 22 tons lead on keel, draws just under 15 feet of water. I have had my share of fortune in vessels on survey trips and plenty of hard times . . . now I blink, looking around me, and wonder if I'm awake. I should like to keep the daily menus, they are so varied and excellent. First night we had grilled steak, perfect; next night Long Island duckling, and I gorged — Christmas dinner every night. Always fresh vegetables, just like home (U. S., not Fiji). All Frosted Foods . . .
>
> Roomy cabin, electric fan over bunk, reading light over bed. Two bunks, one of which I use for scientific gear, a chiffonier and two drawers, under the bunk, which Malakai and I share, as well as a roomy clothes closet with hangers etc. I share Mr. Crocker's elaborate bathroom with Maury. We eat on deck at two bridge tables under an awning, as the mainsail is not raised.
>
> . . . Was somewhat worried, coming on this trip, for fear we might have to conform to millionaire standards of dress. This would have been cruelty to me and would have hindered, as it always does, the success of the work. On some small boats I have been on trips with Resident Commissioners who felt that they must uphold good old British prestige by putting on black coats and choker collars every night; I remember one who ran out of boiled shirts and had to eat in his stateroom to conceal his shame. But Crocker out-Herods Herod. *Lavalavas* are the order of the day, and in the evening a singlet if it is too cool. Day and evening, Crocker wears a *lavalava* or a very short pair of shorts — nothing else but a bandanna handkerchief around his neck . . .

We did not lack scientific equipment or scientific brains. Mr. Crocker and his secretary Maurice (Maury) Willowes collected specimens of anthropological and marine-life interest. Norton Stuart was a botanist, and Toschio Aseida a Japanese photographer of submarine and surface phenomena. Gordon Macgregor was an anthropologist from the Bishop Museum, and our ship's surgeon, Dr. John B. Hynes, did blood groupings on the various islands we visited. This may sound like a hero list out of the "Iliad," and I may add Homerically, "with me always were Gordon White and my long-tried henchman, Malakai Veisamasama." Malakai found the stateroom so comfortable that it rather surprised him. Between island visits he sprawled on his bunk, always reading. It was usually *The Martyrdom of Man*, which I gave him once for a birthday present. He carried it with him as you'd carry a Bible.

The *Zaca's* white crew had been mostly enlisted in California. The stewards were soft-footed and dextrous. When we sat under the awning of long, starlit evenings I had the impression of being on a crack ocean liner. We had everything but an orchestra, but there was a phonograph wired throughout the *Zaca*, and a very powerful Morse station of R.C.A. . . . No, this wasn't real. I wasn't the Lambert who had slapped mosquitoes in a Papuan whaleboat and been stranded on a New Hebrides island, waiting for anything with steam-power or gas-power or paddle-power to take him off.

I wanted to see the Solomon Islands again, for my inspection in 1921 had been a hurry-up affair, at the whim of Lever Brothers' busy island inspector. My visit to Tulagi in 1930 had been mostly directed toward Rennell Island. In 1921 ill luck had kept me from seeing Malaita, the most savage spot in the savage Solomons. On the Crocker trip Gordon White and I were equipped to make tuberculin tests, for little was known of its prevalence in the group. Above all things, I was anxious to compare my new notes with my old ones. What had happened to the health of the islands I had seen twelve years ago? And what had happened to Rennell Island in three years?

In the *Zaca's* comfortable lounge my only worry was that I might get too fat to waddle ashore, what with Mexican beer and a snack at 11 A.M., cocktails and a snack before dinner, highballs and a snack in the evening. Being by nature a sensualist, I had to pray to my Puritan forefathers to save me from myself until our ship touched the White Sands.

Visiting Tucopia, a dot on the southeast tip of the Solomons, I met a problem almost unique in the Pacific — overpopulation. This island, too small to warrant a stop-over, was another Rennell in miniature, with the same lake in the center. And the people who came paddling out in canoes were strikingly like Rennellese, perhaps more like the tribes of Bellona — more Melanesian than either. They had the same style of tapa breechclout, the same palm-fan sticking in the back, the same way of knotting their hair. The Fijians have another island, Thikombia (Tucopia in Fijian), which lies just north of Vanua Levu. It is undoubtedly one of the old steppingstones to this second Tucopia and Rennell. The Tucopians whom we found here spoke a language with so much Fijian in it that Malakai could speak a few words with them; he said that they looked like the light-skinned tribe on Thikombia, who were supposed to have come from Futuna.

A native missionary informed us that "people were growing like weeds." District Officer Garvey had been there shortly before and wondered what to do with a race that was increasing faster than their food grew. For this fertility the missions were responsible, indirectly; when they came they said that every man should have a wife. Formerly only one son in the family was allowed to marry, the restriction being aimed at keeping the population within the bounds of subsistence. After their Christian teachers changed the rules Tukopia's birth crop became embarrassing. . . . Well, that was something I couldn't settle for them, except to suggest more recruiting for work on faraway plantations. That wouldn't have been so practical, either, for the Tucopian had the same savage home-love as his Rennellese cousin. I went away chuckling. Here was a native race whom missionizing had increased. The men who came to our ship had a well-fed look. They seemed to be on the upgrade, though overcrowding might endanger their future.

We sailed toward Vanikoro, and saw Tinakula flaming across the sea, a volcano that seemed to be in constant eruption. Black smoke obscured it, then winds would clear it so that we could look to its sharp summit; at night it was a pillar of fire. Vanikoro, which lay beyond, had a total population of ninety-five. It was a noteworthy illustration of the decay of native races. When the early voyager La Pérouse was wrecked there, the island teemed with people.

We saw the Duffs, where the dark people looked Melanesian and spoke Polynesian; Macgregor told me that they chewed their words so that he couldn't understand them. They scorned our tobacco because it was a grade too good; it seemed that the Burns Philp store had sold Crocker some of the better sort of rope-tobacco made by East Indians in Fiji. The minute the natives smelled it they turned in disgust. They wanted the rank trade tobacco made in America, and you couldn't fool them with a substitute. A disappointment to our anthropologists, when they tried to collect museum specimens on the Duffs, and got nothing . . .

We swung around to the little land I learned to love on my visit there twelve years before. Sikiana with its three charming atolls, three links in a chain. I remembered its unspoiled, laughing Polynesians, its modest, pretty girls who had draped us with wreaths of flowers. I remembered its jolly, handsome men, who had been inoffensively drunk with toddy the day we got there. I remembered the bearded patriarch we had called Old Number One; I had thought of him as one who ruled only by example in a pagan democracy which had no laws, no worries, no debts, no crimes, no serious diseases. I was full of forebodings as our ship neared a palm-fringed lagoon. What had happened to little Sikiana since last I saw it?

Two canoes came out across the reef, and I recognized an old friend, Lautaua, who had done me many favors on my last visit. We were glad to see each other, and his pidgin was garrulous, describing his trips over many waters during that dozen years. Most of the Sikiana men who had been our sailors on the Lever Brothers' cruise had died or strayed away.

And did I know what had happened? Well, the Melanesian Mission had come to their little Polynesia. Over the ten miles of soft lagoon Lautaua told the story. How they had sent in preachers and teachers to improve them. As Missioner-in-Chief a very black boy had come from Guadalcanar. His name was Daniel Sande. At first the people would not join the Church, and many were still holding out; but the Polynesian will yield to persuasion, if only for a show of politeness. Lautaua had offended Black Daniel by moving to another island; then he got so homesick that he came back, a shorn lamb, and found four black Melanesian teachers ruling the roost for Lautaua's proud, light-skinned neighbors and relatives. I asked Lautaua his confidential view on the new religion. He bowed his handsome head. "Master, some fellow he talk man die he come back; me tink man he die he go along ground finish. He no come back. Me no go along school [catechism]. Me no go along water behind [baptism]. Me tink Story [Birth of Christ and miracles] he altogether gammon. Mission he spoil him altogether people."

Sikiana, where once they had danced by the light of the moon, had a look of dull propriety. Good heavens, there was a church! A conch shell sounded — and the Sikiana girls were filing in, dressed in white pinafores. Beside them marched sad-looking Sikiana men. It was edifying, it was shocking. Salvation had entered Paradise. Government had entered, too, for here was the official shack where we were to bunk and try to eat the awful messes a native cook had thrown together. Malakai took one sniff at the mound of indigestibles, then he did what Malakai would. He shouldered out the cook and took over the saucepans. For the rest of our stay there we ate wholesomely and well.

There was an undercurrent of discontent in Sikiana because a hurried Government Secretary had swooped down on them when Old Number One died and had asked in haste, "Who's chief now?" An enterprising impostor named Tuana had presented himself and made a glib selling talk which got him appointed in twenty minutes, more or less. The Honorable Secretary went back to his boat, too full of business to wait and find out that he had broken Sikiana's traditional line of chiefly succession. Such a miscarriage of justice is not characteristically British; but there are always puffy officials, meaning well and doing badly.

I learned about Black Daniel, who seemed to be a hard-bitten slaver in the name of the Lord. This was his day's routine: Sound the conch at 6 A.M. for church; sound it a little later for the children's school; sound it again at ten for the bigger boys and girls; school for grown-ups at 4 P.M., where the study was catechism; church again at 6 P.M., with much singing and a long, strong sermon. This was the week-day program. Sunday, of course, furnished a constant grist for the mill that never ceased turning. When religious duties didn't interfere the inhabitants could work; but they weren't working very hard. Sikiana was getting lazy.

When I had audience with Black Daniel I found him a big, smiling fellow with a boil on his nose. Several Sikiana girls were fanning away the flies; these light-skinned damsels had the look of trained nurses who didn't much care for their assignment. Daniel had something of a Father Divine technique, a way of bursting into ecstatic patter, then coming down to practical affairs. Quite an able man, I thought. He had a record of births and deaths by age and sex, which he had kept since he came there three years ago. Also he had kept a census, very useful to me when I started to work.

Arcady had vanished under the heel of religio-totalitarianism. I wondered if the dark-browed missioners were "taking advantage" of the pretty girls around them. But I found that this was not so. The girls were looking out for that. They were too Polynesian not to shrink in disdain from black-skinned lovers. Not that their hearts were as pure as the Bishop of Melanesia might have wished. They cast yearning eyes toward our good-looking sailors; those were white men, and quite a different matter. I heard one sailor speak softly to a pretty girl named Ana, who looked nervously toward the mission. "Master," she said, "me fright too much come along you. Big Master Stop along Top he look along night too."

Our sailor learned, however, that these affairs could be arranged through special dispensation from Black Daniel. If he liked you, and the girl was a heathen, the church would bless the temporary mating. Daniel liked the sailor, so that was a granted privilege. However, the romance fell unripened. When the couple decided that their love was sanctified they were discouraged by a crowd which followed them constantly. It was all very funny, and tragic. I wondered how long these people would remain purely Polynesian. Their Melanesian teachers had the Supernatural on their side, and the time would come, I thought, when the breed would become very mixed.

Poor Old Number One, how his bearded ghost must have worried! A year before our visit a fanatical trader named Buchanan had run amuck and burned down all the heathen temples. Not only that, but a crew of Japanese pearl fishers had insisted on coming ashore. When the people told them that they were not welcome, they turned a machine gun on a village and forced a landing. Machine-gunning islands seemed to be a Japanese habit. They stayed long enough to fish all the shell out of the lagoon and quartered themselves in Lautaua's house. When they left they became generous, gave Lautaua 1,500 cigarettes, a toothbrush and an old pair of swimming goggles. He was clever enough to imitate the glasses with wood and scraps of windowpanes.

Pukena, the cook whom Malakai had discharged forthwith, but who remained as humble helper, told about Tuana, the misappointed chief. Tuana was a grafter, and like many grafters, lazy. The Administration had entrusted him with medicine for the people. When the sick applied for help, Tuana would reply that his stock had all run out. In short, he was keeping the good stuff for himself and his henchmen. Lautaua, being obviously the superior man on Sikiana, should have been entrusted with these things.

We were there four days, all of us very busy except Crocker, who had a badly infected foot.

I had been carrying on wholesale injections of tuberculin, and had found that the prevalence of tuberculosis was alarmingly high. On my first visit I had had only time to make sketchy tests, but certainly the disease had gained great headway. Gordon White and I went over the whole population. Lautaua, the religious rebel, blamed the missionaries for the disease. Yet the population had made a satisfactory increase in the past twenty years; and that was hard to understand. There was plenty of malaria, and we were finding acute, unguarded pulmonary tuberculosis. Possibly the change in custom, brought in by the missions, possibly added infections which may have resulted from contact with them, or with the Japanese, might have resulted in the many acute chests we saw. Or possibly it was due to the small amount of additional clothing which had come in with the new way of living.

There had been almost no traders, and few foreign vessels came that way. But the very isolation of these atolls, plus Black Daniel's scientific inadequacy, added to the weight of native ills. Among the plentiful mosquitoes we found the malaria carriers. One afternoon Malakai held out his bare arm and showed me a probing little insect. "She stands on her head when she feeds," he said, "and she has spotted wings." *Anopheles punctulatus*, sure little poisoner, conveying disease from the sick to the well. It was impossible to get anything like an adequate supply of quinine from Tulagi.

Lautaua in his own way described the symptoms and testified that malaria was an old inhabitant. Did the sickness begin with a chill? "Oh, master, plenty too much." Realistically he acted out a malaria chill. Had it been here long? "Yes, master, fader belong me, fader belong him, all same." Did the children have it too? "Small fellow, my wort! Him shake too much all same dis." More synthetic chills. "Behind (after) him he hot too much; now water he come out all same rain."

Their light contact with trading ships and their habit of using the tidewater for toilet purposes had saved them from hookworm. There were only two cases of yaws, secondary and in children. The people called it *matona* instead of *tona*, the usual Polynesian name. They said that *tona* was an old-timer, but had died down. I saw no evidences of it among the adults.

In lighter vein let me tell you about Black Daniel's other boil, for he had developed a lusty carbuncle on his hip. I opened it with the cleverest instrument at hand, a razor blade; and with no anesthetic, of course. Daniel had no ambition to be a Christian martyr. It took four of his disciples to hold him down while I drained out the pus, and he called on his Saviour in the voice of a wounded lion.

His Sikiana flock was a contrast in stoicism. Their beautiful teeth were going — ill-balanced diet, probably — and in one afternoon Malakai and I extracted thirty teeth. We had only straight forceps, and it was a pretty mangling job; but we didn't hear a moan during the whole ordeal.

Like all primitives, the people of Sikiana confused the diagnosis with the cure; remember how the Cook Islanders had thought I could make them well by putting a stethoscope on their chests? Tuberculin injections are merely given for negative or positive reactions. But to them the needle was a sovereign remedy, and they always went away smiling. Only the very young children objected when the point was jabbed under their skin. As to the others their faith was rather heart-rending. It was the same all over the Solomons.

After the boil operation Black Daniel so far relented as to let his congregation dance for us, with the beautiful old-fashioned abandon — but with plenty of clothes on. It was the first time in three years that they had been allowed to revert to this pretty, jolly paganism. Before our otter boat pulled us back to the *Zaca*, Daniel and his three dusky assistants occupied four chairs and consented to be photographed. Gathered around them a group of Sikiana girls in white pinafores and white capes looked for all the world like tropical Girl Scouts. Templeton Crocker, suffering from a lame foot and feeling satirical, watched the photographic group, a drift of snow with a bucket of coal in the middle. "The Four Black Crows," he said, thinking of a popular vaudeville team. But the holy dictator and his followers were speeding us on our way with "God be with you till we meet again."

God be with Sikiana, I thought glumly. For twelve years that little place had been one of the pets of my memory. I decided that it would need a hustling Native Medical Practitioner, if anything was to be accomplished.

We interrupted our work and turned back to Tulagi. Dr. Hynes had reported that Toschio, our Japanese photographer, was so ill that he needed hospital attention. Crocker's sore foot had caused a friendly disagreement between Hynes and me. Before he reached Suva, the Zaca's owner had scratched his foot on some submerged coral. He had pluckily said nothing about it until the infection had begun heating up. As a young graduate of New York's Presbyterian Hospital, Dr. Hynes might have been a bit more interested in major operations than in minor bruises. But I had seen many coral scratches and knew that they could, if neglected, prove as stubbornly hard to cure as a gastric ulcer.

At Tulagi — in the humble little capital, very neat and British — we ran into a mess of colonial politics. My very good friend J. C. Barley, who had won the general approval of the High Commission and had aided the natives in so many kindly ways that they thought of him as "Government," had been sidetracked again. Captain Ashley had come back as Resident Commissioner, and that had left Barley, the obvious choice, out in his small post on Auki; Barley, who knew more about the customs, language and social traditions of the people than any white man who had ever lived on the Solomons; Barley, whose affection for the natives was fatherly, and who had devoted his splendid life to them.

At last I got around to see Captain Ashley, who had been so kind about helping me on my first Rennell trip and had sent out a relief boat to find me. What I wanted to talk about more than anything else was Solomon Island candidates for our Central Medical School. We had two native practitioners working on the group. Dr. Hetherington, the C.M.O., had only one white physician whom he could put in the field. There were a few medical missionaries, some of them very good — especially those of the Melanesian Mission, which had a leper asylum of sorts on Malaita.

How about getting some more Solomon Island students into our school at Suva? Well, the Protectorate was about broke — stony truth — and even our small tuition would be burdensome. Norman Wheatley of New Georgia had sent his two sons, Trader Kuper of Santa Ana was educating his older boy, Geoffrey, in a New Zealand school. Geoffrey seemed especially bright, and ought to make a fine N.M.P.

I reminded Captain Ashley of how I had first looked those boys over, back in 1921. Norman Wheatley, retired blackbirder, had settled sedately on Roviana Lagoon, where he had married a native woman. His early adventures should have made him rich, but a ruling vice had reduced his surplus to near the vanishing point. His vice was collecting prize-winning small craft in Sydney. All around the lagoon were his ancient yachts, racing schooners and launches, rotting away for lack of use and attention. Wheatley's sons were pretty small then, but he had listened to me when I said that he ought to make doctors out of them.

Trader Kuper was then living on Santa Ana with his native wife, a fine woman who had posed for my camera in her tribal costume. Her two boys, the older not more than four, were running wild on the beach, absolutely naked. The mother was bare from the top of her head to the waistband of her *lavalava;* around her neck were shark's teeth, and a long pencil of polished shell ran through the septum of her nose. Tenderly she picked the children up and told me that they were nice boys, but not strong. I had found that they had hookworm, and I delayed my departure to dose them with chenopodium. When I left I had given Mrs. Kuper instructions as to further treatment. I saw Mr. Kuper a few years later and he told me that they had grown to be fine husky kids, and he was grateful because we had saved their lives. I had reminded him, as I had Norman Wheatley, that his sons ought to go to Suva and study medicine.

Well, so young Geoffrey Kuper was studying in New Zealand. Certainly he would be an ideal candidate for the Medical School, Ashley said.

Again I heard the old story of benevolent Dr. Fox of the Melanesian Mission. Earnestly wishing to help the natives and to understand them, Fox specialized in ethnology. In order to put himself in closer touch with native family ways, he offered to change lives with Joni, one of his dark parishioners. Joni agreed to change his name to Dr. Fox; Dr. Fox to become Joni. The real Dr. Fox handed the real Joni his bankbook and so on, while the metamorphosed clergyman moved into the native house and took over all the family with all the duties, except the intimate matrimonial ones. He didn't learn much, because the natives remained secretive. The French farce situation became intolerable when the simon-pure Fox discovered that his counterfeit had been strutting all over the island using Dr. Fox's name and prestige so successfully that there were many newborn infants being called "Dr. Fox." So *lavalava* was immediately exchanged for clerical garb, and all bets were off. That was a classic yarn around Tulagi, but still good for a wicked smile.

We coasted down the shore of Malaita, a great hulk of mountainous woods 110 miles long, beautiful and forbidding. When I had covered the Solomons in 1921 a convenient hurricane had beaten us away from the shore. This island held a horrid fascination. Twelve years ago no white man had dared the interior jungles, and there was still little knowledge of its wild hill tribes. The splendid black Malaitamen were good workers, when you could get them. Recruiters, there to pick up field hands for the plantations, always worked in pairs; wise laws of the Protectorate compelled them to do so, for bloody experience had proved the necessity of armed caution.

The luxurious *Zaca* skirted the savagery of Malaita, which the Spaniards called "Mala" for short; and it was "Bad" to them, as ghastly stories reveal. Over there lay Sinarango where Tax Collector Bell with Cadet Lilies and fourteen native police had been butchered in 1927. There were some missionaries, planters and traders scattered along the coastline. The spread of disease was diminishing the Malaitamen, and my object in visiting them would be to learn, if possible, the role played by tuberculosis. Also I was keen to look over the Melanesian Mission's leper establishment, for I had been told that about one per cent of Malaita's population was afflicted.

Around Malaita are many artificial islands, time-old and mysterious as the people who inhabit them. A long native canoe, with no outrigger, landed us on one of them, about three acres built of huge coral-chunks that had been planted on the reef and filled in with soil and rubble. Dr. Macgregor pointed out children with bright yellow hair; no, it hadn't been sunburned to that color, or bleached with lime to destroy lice. This was natural hair. When we examined a grown girl's hair down at the roots, where the sun could never reach it, the color was almost as yellow as straw. There were gray eyes, too, flashing out of dark brown faces. Gray eyes are often found among Polynesians who have had no intimate contact with Europeans. But these were no Polynesians. They were almost as dark as the other Solomon Islanders.

White and Malakai and I had all day ashore at Tai Harbor, lining up hundreds for tuberculin tests. I was aboard ship again when I learned that my much-admired friend J. C. Barley was at Tai on inspection. When I told Crocker about Barley my host suggested that I go ashore and ask him to dinner on the *Zaca*. That was a pleasant assignment, for I must have a talk with the man who knew his natives inside and out.

He came around the side of a leaf-house, cool, clean and physically fit. Shaking hands, I knew that he was glad to see me again, as I was to see him. Yes, the Solomons were in a bit of a jam and all that, he said, and a jolly good thing, Lambert, that you're looking over our tuberculosis. He spoke with gratitude, as though I had been treating him personally. That was Barley all over, responsible for every man, woman and child under his care. He had been District Commissioner for Malaita — splendid job. There were over 50,000 natives on Malaita, and we must have treated nearly 40,000 of them for prevalent diseases. Not that they wouldn't stand a lot more of it. Naturally those wild fellows up in the hills weren't so tubercular as the coast dwellers, he said, but they'd bear looking over. The news had spread to them that the white doctors jabbed them with a needle. They were all crazy for the treatment.

Barley was going to be married; nice Australian girl — he hoped she wouldn't be lonely out here. (As if anybody could be lonely with him.) He had just gotten back from Rennell Island, he said, and had brought Buia with him. Buia! Sure enough, there was Buia, somewhat disguised in a pair of shorts, but the same muscular hunky figure. We didn't rub noses this time, but shook hands, European style. Buia was becoming a man of the world.

And how was Rennell? Well, said Barley, what had happened there might have sounded funny, only it was rather terrible. Too many visiting ships, of course, with Tahua's charming girls to lure them into the White Sands. But there was something much worse. The Seventh Day Adventist outfit had gotten at them, rather. Pastor Borgas landed on the White Sands and informed the Big Masters that they had come to "teach" them. "You know," said Barley, "how crazy the Rennellese are to learn English. They thought teaching meant just that. When the Adventists taught them to say 'Me want skula' — meaning 'We want a school' — they didn't know that school was the Adventist word for batches of Old Testament and vegetarian diet. Old Testament for a people living in an age that's older than Isaac and Rebecca; vegetarian diet for a race that's starving for meaty proteins! Well, before Mr. Borgas went home he gave strips of white cloth for Tahua and Taupangi to wear; white arm bands with 'M.V.' marked on them in big black letters."

"What's 'M.V.'?" I asked.

"Mission Volunteer," said Barley with a wry smile.

I let out a whoop. Imagine those archaic and bearded kings strutting around with Mission Volunteer on their arms!

But Barley couldn't see the comic side. Neither could I after he told me the rest. "When Taupangi and Tahua found out what those cranks had been up to, they flew into a rage and vowed that no missionary should ever again come within bow-shot of their island. I say, this thing is breeding trouble. Next thing you know they'll be killing off another parcel of Christian teachers. Then there'll be hell to pay. I don't want to see a punitive expedition go into Rennell Island and hang a lot of them."

Barley seemed to be reading my thoughts when he said: "If I had my way I'd put a reliable N.M.P. or two on that island, with plenty of medicine. And I'd keep everybody else out, except scientists, maybe. You won't find the people in as good condition as they were when you saw them last. Sea-changes are very sudden in the Pacific."

So Barley went back with me to the *Zaca*. It was one of Crocker's company dinners — grilled steak which had come frosted from Montana, and 1922 Perrier–Jouët. Barley was answering a shower of questions. The Malaita warriors, he said, were Proper Men, and took no nonsense from anybody. They didn't know how to lie. When you asked them how many they had killed they either told you that it was none of your business, or candidly counted over the murders to their credit. . . .

Under softly shaded table lamps our stewards were delicately pouring vintage wine. Right over there, blacker than the darkness, lay
Malaita. . . .

With Gordon White and Malakai I went to the leper colony at
Quaibaita. I knew that leprosy, of comparatively recent importation,
ran about one per cent on Malaita. Whenever colonists mentioned the
Melanesian Mission doctors, they usually said, "Wonderful work!" I
was not disappointed when I saw the mission colony, order in the
midst of green chaos: a hospital and church built of concrete, and the
leper institution set a little too near for safety. The Empire Leper Association subsidized them for drugs, the Protectorate furnished some
medical supplies and a tiny dole for food. I was astonished at first when
I found that two of their orderlies were arrested cases of leprosy;
then I realized the stringent economy under which these devoted men
and women must work in order to keep their mission enterprise on its
feet. Educated and gently reared, they slaved out their lives in genuine
Christian cheerfulness. Some of them, I fancied, had not had a square
meal for years.

I had lunch with them. If they had been French priests they would
have gathered a delicious meal somewhere out of the jungle, for
that's French genius. Here the missioners chatted gaily over the poor
things that came on the table. I knew it was the very best they had,
for we were their guests.

The doctors and the nursing sisters told me that it was hard to suit
Malaitamen, when they got a notion in their heads — which was most
of the time. The mission here was treating 73 lepers, but they had
had as high as 147. Many of them were out-patients; that is to say
they preferred to live in their own village, about a mile away.
They dropped in for treatment about when they felt like it; or else
just wandered away. The Melanesian Mission was trying to get a law
passed that would compel lepers to stay put. Natives loved everything
that was treated with the "needle," but they couldn't be cured with
two or three injections, as they could for yaws. The leprosy treatment
took a great deal of time, and after a couple of injections the Malaitaman would say to his brothers, "What the hell? This fellow's magic
isn't working."

All this was uphill for the brave medical missionaries. My only suggestion was that the leper establishment was too near the "clean" hospital, where they were treating a little of everything else. And it looked tricky to me, having a leper acting as head warder. The obvious thing to say was: Round them up and send them to Mokogai. But that would have been out of the question for a government whose finances were already strained. Without going into figures, it would have cost the Protectorate a large share of its revenue, if they had gone to the expense of shipping away an estimated 950 lepers. Add to that the physical impossibility of taking the sick away from regions so wild that the Government itself did not dare to penetrate; regions where fierce savages were warring, tribe against tribe, and the white man an hereditary enemy. It was just another tragedy of European rule over a native race.

Around the Quaibaita Mission Station I wish to put a bright red mark of approval. Striving against heavy odds, it has done the Lord's work in a practical way, and every year it has shown improvement. Its workers, keeping body and soul together on forty pounds a year, reveal the missionary at his classic best: a civilizer, a healer and a defender of the helpless.

We had been injecting around Tai Harbor, and our technique was so popular that it drew wild men from the hills many miles away. Our needles wore out and our fingers grew stiff from puncturing the skin of hundreds who applied, clamoring for "neela" (needle). A tuberculin test, to prove anything, required two applications and two inspections, five days in all. The difficulty was to get the people back for the second injection and the last inspection, and I was fascinated by Gordon White's orations in lively pidgin. "This big fellow doctor along Fiji, him he come dis time for giving nother kind neela. Now dis nother kind neela, him for stop dis sick along coughie where some fellow he spit blut. . . ." And in the elaborate roundabouts he was telling them that they'd had their two injections, but must be back at the "house takis" (tax house) for the third inspection on Tuesday. The heavy rate of tuberculosis, shown in fierce reactions, made it quite obvious that Malaita needed a tuberculosis sanitarium. That, considering the Protectorate's finances, would have been no more available than a general roundup of lepers.

Our investigations, I hope, threw some light on the prevalence of tuberculosis. Those we examined on Tai Lagoon ran over 77 per cent

infection. Those we were able to get from the bush village showed
60 per cent. The very unpopular officials who had gone out to collect
the head tax reported that taxpayers on Malaita had fallen from 14,000
to 10,000 in a decade. Since the Solomon Islands plantations relied on
Malaita for nearly three quarters of their plantation labor, this falling off
was disastrous. Run the gamut of diseases, from tuberculosis to ringworm, and you have the medical problem that faced the land-poor
Protectorate. The only salvation — I must repeat myself — would be
to send the largest possible number of native students to study medicine
in Suva. That time was coming, I felt sure, for my School was beginning to draw a deep breath.

While we worked ashore Templeton Crocker remained a true sportsman, enjoying himself as best a temporary cripple could. For weeks
he sat on deck, his sore foot propped up on a chair, and had the vicari-
ous pleasure of hearing what the doctors and anthropologists and
other -ologists had been doing on their expeditions. For an active and
adventurous man it must have been torment. The foot was improving,
very slowly as a neglected infection must in a damp, hot climate. Now
and then, when British residents invited us for tea or cocktails, Crocker
would get himself into the sedan chair Dr. Hetherington had given him,
and be carried ashore. Sitting aloft with four black men lifting the
poles, Crocker looked for all the world like a Roman proconsul on his
way to a banquet or a temple, or wherever proconsuls went.

For hours he would sit on deck, listening to Buia's descriptions of
Rennell Island and his reasons for not liking Adventist missionaries.
"Fish he tabu; meat he tabu; walk about he tabu; tobacco he tabu; altogether along dis fellow he tabu." Crocker, a confirmed hater of tabus,
was sympathetic, and liked to hear Buia declare that Mr. Borgas, who
had tacked "M.V." on the arms of Tahua and Taupangi, might have
fooled those old men, but he hadn't fooled Buia for a second. He well
remembered what Mr. Hamlin and Dr. Lambert had said about them:
"That mission he altogether no good along Mungava."

Templeton Crocker had gone to the greatest pains and expense to
organize this expedition. All along the way he had been annoyed by a
quaint turn in customs regulations, which suddenly whimmed to charge
duties on a little of everything. Never before had the *Zaca* been bothered that way by a British Colony. We were out serving the High Com-

mission by invitation and deserved the freedom of the port. However, you never can tell which way island politics are going to turn.

Those of us working ashore had our basket of troubles also, and trouble on Malaita means that you'd better run for your life.

As I have said, tuberculin tests take five days. We inject one day, then skip a day, and on the third inject the cases found negative with a stronger solution; then we skip another day and on the fifth get our final negative cases — those thought not to have an infection and never to have had one. A positive reaction, showing that a person has, or has had, tuberculosis, is revealed by a small and slightly raised pink circle around the site of infection. The confused natives thought that the pink circle was the desirable thing, and they would strut proudly away to show their friends. It was very difficult to make the final negatives understand that they had had the full works — for where was the pink spot they were after?

Well, we had been at it four days, and the course was almost over. Then who should show up but several native teachers with a note from the Seventh Day Adventist white missionary, asking us to inject his people. We knew that we wouldn't have time to finish the five-day job, but a single injection to the new lot might prove something. Also one always wants to sustain a white man's authority before the natives, and it wouldn't do to refuse this request. Remember, the Malaitamen thought that our tests were a cure, for God knows what — tuberculosis or leprosy or yaws, it was all about the same, so long as they got the magic "neela." No, one jab wouldn't do them any harm; it might buck them up spiritually. So on that sophistry, we decided to inject the Adventist's choice.

To complicate matters, we had been obliged to refuse injections to the multitude of natives who had come after the first day, and they were pretty sullen about it. Who could blame them, considering their long trudge over mountaintops, probably without food? They gathered around us with black scowls, inwardly wondering why if five days did a lot of good, four or three wouldn't do *some* good, anyhow. Then the word got around that we were making an exception in favor of the Adventist crowd — and things started to boil.

Newcomers had been flocking in daily, and in front of our "house takis" there was a jam almost as far as one could see: black, ugly faces, determined to have their share of injections, if we started another lot.

We had already tested about 1,500, and eight native policemen had guarded us every minute of the time. They changed guard every hour, with impressive swinging of rifles, always with fixed bayonets. I was soon to realize good old Barley's common sense in sending them along under John White's direction, for John knew his job.

But here we were on a tough spot. I had promised to inject the Adventist's natives. Looking around at the angry black men, crowding in on us, I changed my mind. Not only did we have to save our own skins, but if the mob set on us the Adventist converts would be the first to go. I had thought that the native police were a joke, until I saw them spring into line. I yelled to an interpreter, "Tell the Adventists that we haven't got time!"

He told them. Arms flourished and waved and there was a deafening racket from a thousand husky throats. "Neela! Neela! Me want im neela!" The noise was so great that John White had to shout in my ear, "Better give it to them. Just jab them any way, never mind if it doesn't mean anything. If you don't treat them all, and the mission natives especially, they'll certainly kill the lot of us." I stood my ground with nothing more defensive than a hypodermic syringe. Maybe it was long medical discipline that made me shake my head; I wasn't going to waste a batch of expensive tuberculin on any wholesale fake. "What have we got an armed guard for?" I asked.

Much to my surprise the native police began doing their duty. With bayonets leveled they formed a rough cordon between us and the mass of howling hill-fellows. Then we stood not upon the manner of our beating, but beat it at once, an undignified scramble into the otter boat and a frantic paddling back to the ship. A bedlam of threatening yells followed us out to sea.

When I found Crocker resting his foot on deck he asked me what sort of mob scene we had been pulling over there. I told him that it was the kind of melodrama most explorers were looking for, but I didn't care for it. I was sweating freely, very cold sweat for so warm a day. It reminded me, I said, of what Winston Churchill once told a certain Commissioner from a certain Pacific island group, who came back to London to explain a lot of things. Churchill was Colonial Secretary then and the Commissioner was an old friend. "Winston," said the Commissioner, "they accuse me of keeping women." "But Charles, my dear boy," said Winston, "why shouldn't you?"

I was in trouble with Malaita, but why I shouldn't be was an open question.

Too often on that voyage I was forced to say "I told you so," comparing what I saw with what I had seen twelve years before. Stevenson's "Drink and the devil had done for the rest" might have been transposed into "Disease and the traders." Casual islands, where casual ships dropped in and the people had no moral barriers against strangers, were obviously on the downgrade. In 1921, when we had made an overnight survey around Star Harbour, my medical mind had worried over the carefree sex-generosity of the women there. It was none of my business that, according to native custom, young men hired their fiancées out long enough to earn a marriage dowry. That was the fashion, and there seemed to be no ill results — so long as they confined their promiscuity to their own tribesmen. Their freedom with visiting sailors, black, white or yellow, caused me to foresee what I found there in 1933. That horrid visitor, venereal granuloma, had come to play and stayed to kill. A Chinaman, they said, had brought it there. Life was shortening, the birth rate was almost nil. The abundant missionaries were doing what they could to curb immorality. What they could do wasn't much. Star Harbour was too good a trading station to keep away from.

When the Zaca lay at anchor in the colored waters of Mohawk Bay I came upon the end of a short story which had taken twelve years to tell. It was here, you remember, that back in 1921 I had given a midnight hookworm lecture, in what I thought was a mission village; after the lecture I was resting in a whaleboat near the beach when a naked man, darker than the darkness, had waded out to me and told me that he was Sam, a mission teacher; and his lively pidgin had informed me of my mistake — that I had gone to a heathen village; his was the Christian community, where I should have lectured in the name of the Lord. So I had given him a number of tins, told him what to say in his lecture, and asked him to bring me the specimens in the morning, and he had obeyed. Poor devil, like so many others, he had thought his people would be cured merely by filling the tins. He was foolish, but a true Christian.

Well, as Templeton Crocker's luxury yacht now idled in this bay a missionary came aboard with a number of natives. One of them kept crouching close to my chair, and I recognized him. He was Sam the Christian. "So you're still the mission teacher here," I said. "No, master," — softly, — "you talk along me that night in whaleboat, but me no mission." I liked the old rascal, and spent a day with him, looking over his village and getting at the truth of his story, which was just this: When he had waded out to my boat with the Christian yarn, he had been a pagan, living among pagans; he had come to me with his pious line of talk because, he explained, the heathens never got any plums from the whites; plums all went to the missionized ones. His people had hookworm, and he didn't care what he said so long as he got the cure.

Sam was goodfellow too much, so I gave him some more lessons in hookworm treatment and some drugs to help out. He was still a heathen, he told me, although the native teacher had marked him for an extremely hot Eternity. . . .

So much for scenes revisited, and all not happy ones. We had weighed anchor and were churning out to sea, heading now once more toward Rennell Island. I had seen the mischief done in gentle Sikiana and in other unprotected places. What had happened to Rennell? Buia, coming home with us, said some disturbing things.

CHAPTER IV

THE FATE OF A RACE

Again the great coral wall with its skimpy crown of trees; again the mysterious crack in the cliffs that marked Kungava Bay. Buia, who had acquired malaria on his trip, had been running a temperature all night. He was quite normal now, but excited. His eyes glistened, his white teeth shone as he pointed out familiar landmarks. Over there was Ungu Ungu (Head Head) point. He had a place there, but no house; the piece of land he had inherited from his father's line. On Kanava he had three pieces of land and a fine, big house. Yes, Buia had improved a lot since last night, when he had mourned, "Belly belong me he no good kaikai belong white man. Now me no look him Kanava again." Part of that depression was malaria, the rest seasickness, for the ship had rolled heavily.

Canoes began pulling out toward us. Friends were coming aboard, and the foremost among them was Buia the Bastard, full of news, because the Big Master of Mengehenua was dead. God, who was "Master along Sky," had cursed the chief for neglecting to send him gifts of food. Another Big Master had also forgotten his God, and was pretty sick. "Sick belong wind, him he too cold." Whether he was describing influenza or tuberculosis it was hard to say.

After we had anchored inside the reef and come ashore we were permitted to approach Tahua, whom we found seated in state on a soapbox. On behalf of Mr. Crocker I made a presentation speech and laid an adze, a string of red beads, two razor blades and a butcher knife before the Presence. Tahua said simply, "Thank you." The men of Rennell have no taste for the echo-ringing oratory of Samoa and Tonga.

Because it was raining, Tahua took us to his "house," merely a tiny shelter, open at one end. "House him all bugger up," he apologized, and showed a pile of beams cleverly hewn with the axes we had left on our former trip; all ready for the grand new architectural effect he was planning, to be Rennell's show place, and to Tahua the largest building in the world. There was a ridgepole thirty-five feet long and several curved ribs to support the sloping pandanus-leaf roof. Tahua was getting to be a very rich man.

He was nobody's fool. When I told him about the needles we wanted to use for the good of the people he understood and said that he would summon many for the stick-medicine. Shrewdly he added that when so many came around he could put them to work building his new house. He obliged Macgregor, there to inquire into racial origins, by reciting twenty-four generations of his ancestors and scraps of mouth-to-mouth history which, I think, had been garbled by European recorders. He told us that all the people of his district were blood kin, related to him. A common ancestor had come from Uvea (Wallis Island, directly to the west) and had crossed Rotumah and the Solomons. Tahua's history, liberally salted with myth and demonology, might have been partly authentic. Undoubtedly all the Rennellese were first or second cousins; a picture of an inbred people who were far from physically degenerate. Their tabu against incestuous unions was so strict that brother and sister were not allowed to take medicine out of the same glass.

Macgregor, who talked with Tahua whenever he could, told me that the Big Master had named a great many of the islands where his ancestor had touched on his long voyage to Rennell. This was interesting, but threw no light on the racial origin. Their language was so nearly Polynesian that Macgregor could piece out whole sentences; his Polynesian was so like their own tongue that the people thought that he must have come from Rotumah, and took it for granted that he knew much more than he did of their customs and theogony. For this reason they showed him many sacred places hidden in the bush, forbidden to all but the initiate.

Tahua was grimly silent about Mr. Borgas, the missionary who had tagged him "M.V.," but when the inhabitants came crowding into our ship we soon found that the missionary scandal was the biggest news that had broken on Rennell since the day of the famous murder. Superficially these natives had not changed much, except that they spoke more pidgin and had somehow lost their light-fingered habit of carrying away every little thing they happened to fancy. Already the girls were approaching the personable members of our crew, and by their clamorous "Me want knifie" and "Me want akis (axe)" it was plain to see that the price of love had gone up. Razor blades were coming in, so empty beer bottles had lost their market value.

In all his wide travel Crocker had never seen anything like the Rennellese. Aside from their racial oddity, he said, they were the friendliest people he had yet encountered. I mentioned a doctor I once knew who was so darned sociable — always poking me with a toothbrush — that I learned to dislike him. Crocker didn't understand my simile — then. Later on he did.

One big man, kneeling beside my table, talked volubly about missionary Borgas. He called him "Bawgus" as in the tone in which you'd mention some unmentionable disease. Bawgus had baited the hook by asking them aboard ship — "You like lookim along shippie?" So they looked along shippie. "Then he go ashore he putim tabu along shippie." Mr. Borgas hadn't offered any tribute to Tahua, either in the way of food or tobacco. The only thing he had to offer gratis was Salvation — and "M.V." armbands. . . . My faith in Rennell was somewhat renewed when the kneeling man beside me said, "Mission he come, Master he finish. Big Master along Sky he finish too." Meaning, in plain English, that if Rennell became missionized its past would vanish; and they were on the alert.

I hope I haven't satirized the friendliness of these people. Their generosity surpassed anything I have seen anywhere, the Cook Islands not excepted. They may have seemed overeager in grasping for the things they wanted — mostly things of steel; but in their trades they gave away the best they had, and with the faith of little children. I was fairly sickened by the sight of their carefree swapping with some of our crew — precious heirlooms for a few cigarettes or a tin rattle. I saw one beautifully carved and polished ebony "Big Master's stick" — a royal scepter to them — go to a sailor for a penny stick of rank twist. The sailor wanted the stick, and the owner just couldn't refuse. There were many fine museum pieces frittered away like that. Why argue about the price, when visitors were so pleasant?

From a doctor's point of view, the traffic in women was still more discouraging. Tahua, as a mark of extreme favor, offered me his daughter, although, he explained, she was promised to Buia the Bastard. When I informed him that I was married and had a "mary" of my own, he listened respectfully; I'm sure he didn't know what that had to do with it.

For several nights the parties in the forecastle went on at a furious pace; they kept it up until Crocker showed the sailors that he was boss of the *Zaca* and would allow no visitors aboard after six o'clock. In the riotous period that led up to the ultimatum I found one deck hand solemnly scrubbing a native beauty with a piece of brown soap and rinsing her at the end of a hose. It was probably the first real bath she ever had; I was surprised at the lightness of her skin, which would match that of the purest Polynesian.

When I had come there on the *France*, we jaunty explorers were all so dirty that we had somewhat deadened our sense of smell. But fresh from the luxurious cleanliness of the *Zaca*, I was conscious of the prevalent B.O. of Rennell. It took some tact for me to remind Buia that what he needed was a bath. He received the news amiably, dived into the bay and swam like a fish. Even without soap he lightened at least two shades, and was vain about it when I held up a mirror.

Panio, the political strong-arm, was especially aromatic; I was quite overcome by his meekness when I suggested that he follow Buia's example. When he came out of the water, a paler and a better man, he told me that he had had some experience with talk-marks, the kind I made on the typewriter. But his words hadn't been any good. He handed me a piece of paper which a visiting skipper had given him by way of introduction to passing ships. But when Panio had shown it to other skippers they had been cross too much. I read his paper and quite understood. It said, "To whom it may concern. Don't have anything to do with this bloody bastard. He is a proper wrong un." The skipper who wrote that reference was a student of human nature.

I had thought that Templeton Crocker's firm stand against midnight visitors might have dangerous repercussions. Or at least the effect wouldn't be very lasting. It was good for about twenty-four hours, I found; the people were kind but insinuating, and they all came back. The only way to shorten visiting hours, we learned, was to see the Big Masters; and when we managed that, the scene grew quieter — Or did it? One evening after dinner, a number of native beauties were draping their pretty figures over about everything on the ship, animate or inanimate. "Maury" Willowes, who was serving as a human coat-hanger for about six of the clinging ladies, did not attempt to brush them off as he made his *bon mot:* "Just another quiet evening at home." And our host, who had at first declared the Rennellese among the most beautiful works of nature, sniffed a little at the prevalent native bouquet.

Next day I wrote in my diary: —

> Mr. Crocker is working on the deck astern, or trying to; Panio is summoning some friends at a half-mile distance, in a voice that might blow a hole in the ship; a girl and two boys are playing mouth organs steadily in my right ear; Maury, heaven help us, is trading out baby rattles, the kind with bells on them; a man is bouncing a rubber ball, and is so awkward about catching it that my little Sara Celia could show him how. Older men are clamoring for knives and hatchets, but the ones of military age have gone crazy about musical tops. . . . Where was I, anyhow? Oh, yes, this morning on the beach I gave a cigarette to Teina, and he said, "You pickaninny belong me." I suppose he was trying to say that I was his father. . . .

Rennell Island was advancing, but in her march of progress she had taken the wrong fork in the road. A great many of the men had discarded native costume and were taking a fancy to *lavalavas*. To impress us, perhaps, they would pull *lavalavas* over the time-honored breachclouts they called *kongoa*. Or they'd take off the *kongoa* altogether and substitute "calicoes" for them. On Barley's recent trip his crew had brought in several thousand cigarettes, salvaged from a wrecked Japanese vessel, and the Rennellese had taken to them like so many ducks to water. New tastes, new ways. . . . The growing craze for European costume was illustrated in the behavior of Mua, son of Taupangi, who followed me around the ship, archly suggesting that I give him a pair of trousers and a shirt. I tried to tell him that it would curse Rennell, if he started such nonsense.

What had happened to the fierce tabu on feces examinations, which had embarrassed us on our former trip? Old Tahua, in whose presence we had not dared to whisper the forbidden thing, was now strangely approachable. Perhaps an extra box of fishhooks tickled his overdeveloped acquisitiveness. At any rate, he permitted Malakai, aided by Buia, to give him our stock hookworm lecture with chart and all the fixings.

Immediately he commanded that a number of young boys should report to the tent we had set up on the beach, and be properly examined. Later on he ordered out a number of women for the same inspection.

This concession was obliging to us and convenient to our work. But underneath the courtesy I felt a certain loosening of the old religious ties which had held Rennell's proud racial identity. World without end, they had worshiped with a single-mindedness which was like that of Medieval Europe when the Church was all in all and the Pope its interpreter. Religion had come first with the Rennell folk, and had entered into every duty of their practical lives.

Outwardly they were still religious. But what undercurrents of doubt were entering the new desires and ambitions? They still seemed unquestioningly obedient to the Big Masters, who spoke with the voice of God. Did the Divine One and his lesser divinities still listen to their inner thoughts, as they had three short years ago? Their code of sins and virtues had been different from ours, but just as strict. What would happen to them when all their traditions went to the junk-pile?

As I worked in my tent on the beach, many things that I had not known before came filtering in. Dr. Macgregor told me more, for he was there to study the past and present of a strange people. Through Buia, loyal to the White Sands, I learned why I had better not go to the Lake this time. Tahua and Taupangi were in a jealous quarrel again over property rights. In the past year or so Taupangi had had an inspiration: If Tahua got iron through his possession of the White Sands, then Taupangi would have an anchorage of his own. Therefore he had made a three-mile shortcut to a place in the cliffs where it was just possible to get up and down. Here he could launch canoes and invite the crews of passing ships to come to the Lake by the shortest way; something like our road-signs, "Shortest Route to Atlantic City." Roughhewn as the idea was, it fetched some trade to Taupangi's district. Tahua was in a boiling rage, and the people of the White Sands well knew that the two lesser Masters who had aided in Taupangi's forbidden trail had been afflicted with a fatal sickness which only Tahua's God could inflict.

An embassy from the Lake visited my tent with Taupangi's cordial invitation to come to his district with my treatments. Buia gave me a warning look, so I was obliged to decline. We were indebted to the White Sands for our anchorage and headquarters. No telling what

Tahua might do if the white witch doctor should desert him for a hated rival. So I let Gordon White go to the Lake with some of the *Zaca*'s scientists. Tahua granted them that favor, after I had offered a practical idea for his benefit. Why not join forces with the Lake people and cut a good trail across that awful eight miles of vines and coral? Make communications easy, and Taupangi would forget about his rival anchorage. . . . It was like asking a blue Republican to junk a tariff barrier for the benefit of mutual trade. But Tahua thought it over. . . .

They were pouring in from every district to be lined up in our tent. While we worked at our trade Macgregor, at the other end, worked at his, and Dr. Hynes, our surgeon, studied the blood groupings of 100 people in hopes of throwing some light on their racial origin. They were almost equally divided between Group O and Group B, with almost no A's or AB's, a quite different finding than European grouping, which furnishes data for specialist study in anthropology; and they did not seem to check up with other Polynesian typing.

Dr. Macgregor, who was a Harvard Ph.D. in anthropology and had had the superlative advantages offered by the Bishop Museum, was a young scientist with the proper equipment of learning and enthusiasm. As the line of natives passed through our tent he took head measurements and found a cephalic index of 74–75, about the same as that of the so-called Nordics. He reached the conclusion that they were not usual Polynesians in the sense that Hawaiians, Samoans, Cook Islanders, and others are Polynesians. They had many elements of Melanesian culture, such as certain points in their god-worship, and their habit of betel-chewing. They knew nothing of that Polynesian favorite, kava; and many of their words were not Polynesian at all. But physically they were not Melanesian, nor were they of the Micronesian race that I myself had seen in the Gilberts and the western Bismarks. It was no wild conjecture to call them pre-Polynesian, of which there is still a small element in Tonga.

Somewhere in their first long voyage from Nowhere to Nowhere they had picked up certain Polynesian arts and habits: like the making of tapa cloth and the smearing of their bodies with sacred turmeric. History records that the Tongafiti, conquering fathers of Polynesia, had fallen upon Rennell Island some 400 years before; but not to conquer. The Rennellese warriors had slain all but one man. That man finally built a canoe and started for his home. The Rennellese had some knowledge of invaders very like the Tongafiti. As we saw them there were no mixed bloods — with the exception of two half-castes, probably the issue of visiting sailors.

Malakai and I, representing the medical end of the enterprise, were busy with a count of native diseases. We were saving hookworm examinations for the last and were winning popular confidence through less objectionable tests. If I had been pessimistic when I came back to Rennell, I was glad to find many of my fears groundless. There was no filariasis, nor was any evidence to be found of the anopheline mosquito; and there were no diagnostic signs of malaria. Buia actually had malaria; I knew, because I treated him for it. But he had been with Barley on Malaita, where he undoubtedly picked it up. As to tuberculosis, I found less on Rennell than anywhere else I had visited. Yaws was no menace; the local habit of isolating sufferers until the sores were healed had reduced the disease to a few tertiary cases — Buia told me that I would find much yaws on Bellona, where they did not practise the ancient quarantine custom. There was still plenty of itch on Rennell, but that too seemed to be wearing itself out.

I have described the technique of getting hookworm, but because the question was most important to me on Rennell, I hope to be forgiven for describing it again.

Little tins are given out for feces specimens, and their contents examined. If you want worms you choose the people who have been found positive through examination; positive because hookworm eggs have been found in their specimens. You dose them with the drug, say tetrachloride, then you give them a "jerry," which is usually a five-gallon benzine tin, and tell them that all their bowel motions for the day must be deposited in the big container. A purge has been given after the tetrachloride, to hurry things up. At the end of twenty-four hours the whole stool is washed through several thicknesses of surgical gauze until only a sediment remains. This sediment is taken by tablespoonful and floated with a little water in a photograph tray, where the worms can be seen with difficulty, especially if the patient has been eating fibrous vegetables. Then he is given another saline purge and he deposits his bowel motion for another twenty-four hours. Then the same procedure is repeated. To do a good job another day's collection should be made. This is difficult in a hospital, and much more difficult among savages. In New Guinea we had to put them behind barbed wire, in Fiji we often locked them up.

On Rennell we were not given permission to do this work until the last few days, and we only got Tahua's consent by paying him liberally in fishhooks. The examinations were on the beach, and the subjects all girls; they had been forced to submit by the Big Master, who cannily believed that if some magic curse should fall on a few girls it wouldn't matter. Malakai and Gordon were supposed to keep guard over these patients; but with new ones coming all the time, they were probably not very well watched. The infection was very light, and probably many of the stools missed. Later on, when we examined the material, we found no worms. The trouble was that the Big Master's permission had come so late that a technique suited to such bizarre circumstances was impossible. The delay resulted in our frustration.

They had no conception of disease. When it came to tuberculin tests we had immense difficulty in getting them to report for more than one injection, for the Big Parade was always going on and they didn't want to miss any of it. Time, of course, was nothing to them. That mental quirk, as well as those above noted, worked dead against us. Remember, it was a land of savages, a stark beach, no houses to speak of and an almost constant rain. Add to this the native's superstitious shyness. Once, when I caught Buia in a very personal occupation, he almost died of fear.

I had done my best to inquire into the prevalence of gonorrhea, the old enemy of racial fertility. Examinations were, of course, out of the question — you could examine a Rennellese man only by felling him with an ax. I suspected that this venereal germ had revisited Rennell, and when I looked over our crew after departure my suspicions were justified. I could learn little from a people who in no way associated the infection with promiscuity; they regarded all disease as merely a curse following the violation of a tabu, even an unconscious violation. But what I found that our sailors had picked up from Rennell alarmed me as to the island's future. The barriers were down, the White Sands were offering the most generous hospitality to visiting sailors. I had seen other island populations sink for similar reasons.

A nightly chore was counting the sick aboard ship. Templeton Crocker's foot was about well; however we had persuaded him not to bruise it again in that awful overland walk to the Lake. Stuart, our botanical collector, was in bed with a severe leg ulcer. He had tramped all over Java and Borneo in the Chancellor–Stuart expedition, and now he chafed because his legs were not taking him along. Toschio seemed to have recovered from the sickness that took us to Tulagi, and other- wise we seemed fit to carry on. Except that I was suffering from a boil on my leg.

One night Buia came aboard and asked Malakai to intervene with Mr. Crocker for more food for the people who had come down to be treated. Malakai, always a sympathetic observer of the natives, said that he had watched them and they had gone all day without a thing to eat. These people were nomads, really — nomads on an island fifty miles long. When they traveled they never thought of carrying pro- visions. I went to Crocker, and found him generous again. In free feeds for Rennell he had already dipped pretty deep into our stock of eatables, but he managed to dig up another banquet and send it ashore. I asked Buia why the people went hungry when they could fish in the bay, and he said it was tabu to eat fish from the bay while our sewage was emptying there.

I caught Buia off his guard and told him that I had learned the names of the two Gods who ruled his island: they were the old Tetanosanga, whose girth measured ten fathoms, and his grandson Teaitutabu. Listening to the sacred words, Buia stood aghast and begged me never, never to say those names again. Only the Big Masters could speak them, and that only in a whisper. I liked Buia for his reverence, when he prayed away my rash impiety. While he prayed I felt that faith had not departed from his people, and might strengthen them to stand against the white invader, as they had stood against the Tongafiti.

Prayer was a part of their daily lives. Gordon Macgregor on his visit to the Lake saw a sacred and secret ceremony never before shown to a white man. He had asked a question, and old Taupangi went into a "sweating trance," seeking divine guidance. His two compan- ions held the chief's heavily perspiring body while his eyes rolled and his head fell. They were afraid he would die. At last his assistant took a strip of tapa and bound it tightly around his waist to squeeze out the possessing spirit. Then he recovered from his trance and delivered a somewhat confused message: Possibly it would be all right, he said, for his son to go on a trip with Macgregor.

Taupangi was the only one of the five Big Masters who could speak

directly to God. The others had to communicate through an intermediary. Tahua lacked the mystic power. With receptive soul he had
waited all his life for God to enter him and show favor, but he died
with his wish unanswered.

Religion was an everyday, every hour affair with these simple, de-
vout people, and the way to Heaven was marked out for them. When
a soul entered Paradise it was a very small soul, but it grew as a child
grows, and attained magnificent size among the immortals. It was a
man's Heaven, for earth-women were hardly worth sending there,
especially since Eternity was supplied with many beautiful creatures,
superior in every way to the merely human female. When a Big
Master died a heavy club was buried with him to protect him against
devil-devils on the way to his Valhalla. The "Big Master's stick," his
wand of office, was stuck on the top of his grave, and this marked his
term of office as a spiritual interpreter; for as long as the stick lasted
his earthly successor might use it as a mouthpiece to Heaven and con-
sult with the late Big Master, and with the supreme Ngenggo, the
Grandson God. When the stick rotted in the ground the deceased
was no longer the heavenly interpreter, and the next in line assumed
the office.

Macgregor was at last keen enough to see that my pidgin was a
valuable means of communication. He found that the sacred name for
their god was Ngenggo, the same as Rengo in Rotumah.* Rengo was
another name for turmeric, sacred to the bodies of high personages.
Between us we found that the Big Masters spoke indirectly to the
gods, through their ancestors. As if to throw up a defense across the
sacred names, they had two names at least for the two principal
gods. On my first trip a Master told me that the principal god was
called Tainatua, as I understood it — really Taiinggatua. Then Barley,
a little later, learned that the two were Tetanosanga and Teaitutabu
(the Sacred God). At the Lake, Macgregor found that Teaitutabu
and Ngenggo were one and the same. He collected some wonderful
material there, especially concerning religion and ceremonies, and
was able to improve on it through his wide experience in Rotumah
and the Tokelaus. Incidentally Macgregor saw a two-headed stick
used as an object of worship.

As we worked out the puzzling pantheon, Tetanosanga (another

* Rotumah is one of the steppingstones of the ancient Polynesian Invasion,
over 1,000 miles from Rennell. See Part Two, Chapter II.

name for Taiinggatua) was grandfather to the god Teaitutabu (otherwise Ngenggo). They presided over the world, as Rennell knew it, and Ngenggo never left his home in the skies. His grandfather, however, roamed the earth and reported happenings to Ngenggo. The Grandson God was the most powerful of the Sky Masters, and Buia said, "Suppose him he talk-talk he sabe make you die quick." While Ngenggo stayed at home the Old One went everywhere, saw and heard everything, and if there were those who ignored divine laws, Ngenggo punished them. Not only could he kill men, but he could demolish trees, islands, anything. There were prayers to the gods before every simple meal. There were ceremonies of food presentation to the gods, too involved to describe in anything but a book on anthropology. But if the regular tribute of food to a god was neglected, the offender would surely sicken and die.

Buia told me of Charley Cowan's ship which had anchored at Taupangi's Lake anchorage. Charley, Buia said, gave the ship to Taupangi, and Taupangi in turn gave it to the Big Master along Skies. Then the divinity replied that Cowan might go on using his vessel, provided that he came back at intervals to Taupangi's anchorage. The Big Master warned him not to take it to Tahua's beach, but Cowan on his next trip went to the White Sands. As a result of this disobedience, Buia said, Taupangi "talked along" the watchful Grandson God, and as a result both Cowan and his partner died. (As a matter of fact, these men did die, to my knowledge.) It was *post hoc* rather than *propter hoc;* but try to make a Rennellese believe that Taupangi didn't pray them to death! Buia was afraid for the *Zaca* if it called at Taupangi's anchorage for Macgregor and White. . . .

Nothing was attempted and few thoughts conceived without first seeking the advice of the gods. The people even consulted their ancestors through a bamboo stick dug into a grave. I once caught the tough Panio using this sort of spirit-telephone.

Gordon White, coming back from Tenggano with the usual tatters and coral scratches, reported that the Lake People had not depreciated much in health. He said that my old chum Taupangi grieved that I had not come up to live with him for the balance of my life. The *Zaca's* party at the Lake had dined with the Big Master every day, and were interested to find that somebody had taught him to eat with a fork and drink tea out of a china cup. He liked plenty of sugar in his tea and stirred it for five minutes, with his fork. They took movies of the harvest festival, and Gordon noticed what a change had come over the scene since last we saw it. There was no high fence around the grounds, and women were allowed to look on. Another old tabu was fading out.

Not to be outdone by his hated rival, Taupangi had loosened up on the hookworm tabu; but his people were still so queer about being examined that our party got no good specimens. There was an epidemic of head colds, so frequent that our outfit was now catching the germ from Rennell — a reversal of our first experience there.

When Macgregor came back to the White Sands the majority of the Lake population followed him, crazy to see the *Zaca*. Gordon White tried to bribe them to stay home, offering toy balloons and tin trumpets, but these things bored them. They were out for iron, and intended to get it. Taupangi overcame his grouch against Tahua (who would allow him nothing better than a leaky leaf-shelter when he was on the beach) and joined the exodus. So did Tekita and Tamata. Only Mua remained as intermediary; although he was the Big Master's son and heir he hadn't had enough of God's authority to coax the people up to Gordon's tent, so it had become a matter of visiting every leaf-shelter in the place and giving tests. Tuberculosis didn't seem alarming. Wanderlust was the prevailing ailment. Mua, Tekita, Tamata, everybody who could get a word in edgewise, had tried to wheedle Gordon into taking them away on the boat. If Buia had traveled and learned about the great world, why shouldn't they? These simple folk, to whom Rennell had been all in all, were growing restless, discontented with this frugal island which had once satisfied their every want — because they had never learned to want the unnecessary. A self-containing social structure, an unquestioning faith in divinities who could give and who could take away, scanty food which they gained by wholesome labor and gratefully thanked God for . . . That was their plenty. But to human nature, plenty is too often not enough. Perhaps that is the real Martyrdom of Man.

Little Bellona Island (Mungiki) lay twenty-five miles over there, and I was anxious to survey it again, and to show it to Crocker's expedition. The Big Masters of Rennell had explained carefully why Mungiki had a richer soil than theirs. In days of old, the semi-mythical

Ko Fiti had been driven out of Rennell, but before they left they had done a spiteful thing; they had scraped the good topsoil off Rennell and dumped it on Mungiki.

Our *Zaca* moved across the short stretch of sea. In sight of Bellona's forbidding cliffs I sent a short radio message to Eloisa; a demonstration of science in the midst of savagery.

A man came out in a canoe and gave his name as Samoana, which was pure Samoan for Guardian of the Sea. He guided us to a beach which had changed so in three years that I hardly knew it. Great storms had washed it clean of sand; now it was a forest of sharp coral points. When I sat down on the softest lump I could find, I was immediately surrounded by a half-hundred fierce faces; threatening fists were full of bows, arrows and spears. A man who came out of a cave seemed to own the beach, and I asked him if we might pitch our tent there. No, he said archly, if we set up a tent ("big calico") we might take a notion to stay. A poor start, but with the help of Buia I managed to persuade him that we were moving on in four days. When I asked for the chiefs to come to me — a policy I adopted on Bellona — Samoana went away, then came back to report that Ponge, the Big Master, sat with three lesser Masters, presiding at a great festival. He couldn't possibly come, as he was very tabu; his face was blackened, which was the deepest of all tabus.

Buia brought in the three lesser Masters, who surprised me with their willingness to have the people inspected. And of course it would be all right to have the big calico on the shore — if we didn't stay too long. When I told them that I had left much of my equipment in a big calico on the White Sands, with the assurance that nothing would be stolen, the three Masters promised me that my goods would be respected. And they kept their word. Even on Rennell I had found that the people were learning the difference between *meum* and *teum*. Sleeping on that beach would be about as comfortable as a Hindu fakir's bed of nails, and Bellona's geological freaks made water available only by catching it in coconut shells or the funny wooden bowls they used for that purpose. The Bellonese, who were the gentlest people in the world in spite of their savage look, seemed to subsist almost without water. A little coconut juice satisfied bodies that had adjusted themselves to conditions.

I loaded the three Masters on the small boat and we presented them with candy and tinned meat. Crocker turned on the phonograph, with startling effect. They all began to shake and shiver; Buia's cousin Takeika rose nervously and tried to take the machine down to his canoe. We had to tell him that it was very tabu for anybody but Crocker, who was Captain to them — the highest title they could understand. We didn't turn the record on again. They were very curious about the two little fishes which Buia had tattooed on my left ankle. They didn't know that my ankle was still sore where a needle (made from a sliver of human bone) had gone in, or that my leg was sensitive from a couple of buried boils, which I had carried with me from Suva and hadn't given a chance to cure. They smacked their lips and rolled their eyes, marveling at the tattooed fishes, symbols of Rennell.

They seemed to think that the Rennell people put on airs. Macgregor found that Bellona gave a soft sound to *ng*, as in "sing," where Rennell hardened it to *ngg*, as in "finger." Probably considered an affectation, like the English broad *a* . . .

Malakai and I, setting up a tent on the beach, found that the petting habit on Bellona was slightly worse than that of Rennell. People surrounded us like sticky flies. Two or three would run their hands down my shirt collar, to see if my worshipful belly was real or just padding; two or three more would be lifting up my trousers to marvel at my white ankles, and the tattooed fishes. That massage, with inquisitive and dirty hands, went on for four days. It went hardest with Crocker, who had more respect for his personal dignity than some of us. He was getting used to being called Captain — on Rennell he had tried to insist that his name was Owner, but that hadn't made sense to the native. Captain meant Boss, and you couldn't go any higher than that.

At last we went to Big Master Ponge, since he was too sacred to move from his seat of dignity. Every time my sore leg came down I suppressed a moan, and wondered why I had ever left Suva in such condition. Whenever the choking scrub along the way opened up a little I had pleasant views of the neat, thatched houses. They looked very pretty at a distance, but when I went into some of them I found only dirt floors, with hardly a mat to squat on — and all the time dirty natives were patting my hands, pawing my shoes, stockings, every inch of me.

Big Master Ponge had invited us to a dance, and that was the reason for those weary three miles. As we had done in Rennell, we crawled on our stomachs under the low eaves and faced the Presence on all fours. And there was the great Ponge, seated on his dais and looking for all the world, as Maury said, like a Chinese mandarin. But a mandarin doing a black-face act, for his cheeks, nose and forehead were thick with tabu soot. He shook hands all round and listened carefully when I told him why we had come, and how Crocker had invited him to visit the *Zaca*. Macgregor talked, and presented him with a cane-knife — and I hoped he'd use it to clear a path through that awful scrub. In behalf of his Master Tahua, Buia gave him an American ax. By way of ecclesiastical blessing Ponge pronounced us "good fellow too much." I didn't wait for the dance, but limped back over the terrible trail. I had business awaiting me on the beach.

I looked over the people that filed through my tent and was surprised to see how much clearer skinned and robust they were than the inhabitants of the White Sands. They appeared cleaner, but they smelled a little worse than the Rennellese. I saw some hideous cases of yaws, and remembered what Buia had said: The Bellona folk did not quarantine it. In fact the Rennellese quarantine was the only one I ever saw among primitive people.

Bellona called it *caho*, and when I asked in the presence of the crowd where *caho* came from, they answered to a man that Dr. Deck's missionaries had brought it. Dr. Deck had botched his expeditions sufficiently, without this. Even though Deck's excursions might have brought some of it, it was just a case of yaws meet yaws, I thought. If the people of Bellona were Polynesian, this was the only Polynesian spot on the Pacific where the disease was not called *tona* or some name much like it. Their ignorance of the word suggested that they had been pushed out of some Western Polynesian group before they had had a chance to come in contact with the Tongans; for yaws is a curse that does not die out of itself, and if they had come to Bellona after meeting Tongans, they would have carried the Tongan name *tona*.

Macgregor, taking anthropological measurements, found them physically identical with the Rennellese — probably the relics of a pre-Polynesian race. I found that they needed a doctor for yaws, and not much more; otherwise they would be a thousand times better off if no white man's foot ever again touched their coral-scragged beach. Isolation had made them happier than the Rennellese, I thought. Five ships had touched at Rennell Island in three years, and more were coming. Bellona had only seen two in that time, and those two had been given a cool reception. An object lesson in self-preservation.

It seemed strange that they had more iron tools per capita than the Rennellese, until I heard that Bellona was arrow-maker for Rennell, and demanded her pay in iron. The chiefs might have been sharp traders, but one of the Masters was pretty dull when he gave Crocker a royal treasure out of respect to his rank as "Captain." The gift might take rank with Charlemagne's scepter for its antiquarian value and its rare material. It was a king's mace, a shaft of wood with a knob of stone on the end. To Rennell and Bellona real stone was worth its weight in diamonds, for there was absolutely none of it between the beetling coral cliffs. The piece that tipped this relic might have come from Tucopia in olden times, or from undreamed-of distances. It was the last king's mace on either island, and there are only four in the world. The other three are in museums: at Brisbane, Cambridge University, and the British Museum.

Macgregor had tried sleeping in the tent on the beach, but had given it up for uncanny reasons. He had set up an army cot, got into it — and found that two local chiefs had decided to sleep on the coral floor right under him. In the middle of the night his cot began to shake, and he found the worried chiefs rousing him. "Master," they said, "you must go at once. In our dreams God spoke in our heads asking, 'Who is this that dares sleep above me?'" Macgregor didn't argue the point, but went.

On Bellona there was one big native who seemed to double for Panio as local nuisance. He had bothered me a great deal when we were there on the *France* expedition. Now he was on and off the *Zaca*, strutting like a magpie and yelling his slogan in my ear: "Gimme, thank you! Gimme, thank you!" I called him Mr. Gimme and tried to laugh him off, which was pretty hard to do when I was giving injections on the beach with him clinging to my elbow. Our last afternoon at Bellona I told Maury Willowes how I should love to plant my foot on Mr. Gimme's sciatic nerve, and Maury grinned, "Why don't you?"

We were safely near sailing time when Mr. Gimme came at me

again and had hardly opened his mouth for the familiar slogan when I put my walking stick against his mid-section and firmly poked him halfway down the accommodation ladder. He plunked into his canoe and his look was demoniacal as he yelled his farewell curse: "Gimme, thank you!"

There were no reprisals. Peaceably the three kings came aboard to shake hands all around and receive their final gift of hardware. They were very cordial, glad that we were going so soon. I admired their self-protective attitude, and hoped that they wouldn't weaken, as Rennell was weakening. They were fine people, and I didn't hold Mr. Gimme against them. There is at least one Panio in every neighborhood that I know of.

Before the *Zaca* pulled away from the White Sands and headed toward Tulagi I had a farewell glimpse of a people who were turning too soon towards ideals which could never work anything but harm for them. Over on the beach Tahua was bossing a construction gang. They were putting up the frame of his house, a big house, a fine house, a house that would make Taupangi feel pretty small. Keeping up with the Joneses, and a lap ahead of them. . . . When Taupangi came aboard to rub noses and wish us all back soon, he reminded Gordon White that he had given him a present of fine mats — but he was keeping them for him up at the Lake, so that Gordon would be sure and return there with more medicine. Competition was making old Taupangi canny as a Scot. Many of the natives, who stayed with us until the ship's propeller turned, came in fashionable *lavalavas*.

Buia remained aboard until we were rounding Unga Unga, then a canoe picked him up. Buia, I am afraid, was getting a touch of bighead. He was too intelligent to become another Panio, but his reputation as a cruise conductor had done him no good. Crocker had been annoyed with his way of walking in on every party and taking possession. I was more relenting, for I had a real affection for this heir to a Big Mastership, and knew that he might rule with wisdom, if only he were let alone to serve his native God. To him we were something to be admired and imitated, and he had sought to adjust himself as best he knew how. Hadn't they all?

He paddled away in his canoe. The *Zaca* turned out to sea; Rennell

Island became a faint blue shadow in the distance. I wondered what could be done about these unique people, infinitely valuable to scientific study. It was something like an emergency case; but in the wide Pacific you can't send a fast ambulance to emergency cases. Relief comes slowly, biding its time for the Government to make up its mind, for competent medical men to take over the work, for boats to sail, for treasuries to cover the necessary expenses. Sometimes years pass between visit and visit — especially to a small world like Rennell Island, which needed protection far more than it needed medicine.

At last, graduate N.M.P.'s were sent to Rennell Island; they went one at a time for a six months' service, fully equipped, but alone. An outstanding one was Eroni, a full-blood Fijian who gained a nickname: "the only white man on Mungava." Patient and responsible as only a Fijian can be, he went barefoot over every coral snag and bog on the island. Conscientiously he treated everything they had. Once he saw the natives catch a shark according to custom; they wrestled with it in the water, bound it with ropes and hauled it in. One man had his hand bitten off, and Eroni saved him with a tourniquet. He was surprised to find that the Rennellese themselves had always known how to apply a tourniquet. Eroni was ever ready for emergency calls as well as methodical mass treatments.

But one medical man, work as he might, could not enforce that ounce of prevention which, on Rennell, would have been worth many pounds of cure.

Before the High Commission in Suva I tried to drive home the necessity of government protection for these defenseless people. The waters should be patrolled and mischievous ships kept away. Medical authority should be carefully admitted, and a properly hand-picked anthropologist. At the very mention of the latter profession I met opposition. A number of vicious playboys who masked as "scientific investigators" had put anthropology in bad odor. It used to be that everybody's hat was off to every wandering bluffer who claimed to hold a key to the mystery of man's origin. Too many of these fellows had overstayed their time — usually on islands where women were the prettiest. One "anthropologist" had just been ordered off the Pacific; he had been charged with violating two little girls. So the High Commission, although they quite understood my attitude, rather thought that I should take the matter up in London. The snag was somewhere in the Colonial Office, they said.

Here are a few lines from a letter I wrote His Excellency, the High Commissioner; just an item in the literature that passed back and forth in my long plea for the Rennell Islanders: —

> Spiritually they have a gentle religion in which there is no skepticism and no cruelty. Socially it would be hard to convince me that these savages are not more highly advanced than we are. There is almost a complete absence of crime. Morally they have a code which suits them, and to which they adhere exactly. They themselves say that they do not want government, missions or doctors . . .

The High Commissioner's reply, in part: —

> The Bishop of Melanesia has suggested that he should be allowed to select young men from Rennell, train them as preachers, and send them back. What is your view of this proposal?

My answer in brief: —

> . . . Unfortunately, when anyone's ideas on any subject differ from those of a missionary, he is immediately put down as anti-missionary, if not anti-Christian. The only question on which all of the Mission Societies will unite is opposition to any attempt to limit in the least degree, for any purpose whatsoever, the extension of mission work. On all other questions they are drawn up in armed camps against each other. I am not anti-mission in any particular, and any reasonable man must be pro-mission, if he is acquainted with the history of mission efforts in the Pacific, where they have been the great humanizers and educators of the native races. However . . .

In 1936 the Foundation's business took me to London, where I told my story to three famous anthropologists: Elliot-Smith, Haddon and Malinowski; their sympathy was all with my plan to protect the two islands, Rennell and Bellona. The important man to see was Sir Thomas Stanton, Briton's Chief Medical Officer. Sir Thomas was easy to meet and to talk to. He was one of the Central Medical School's enthusiasts. When I had finished my work in Fiji, he suggested, why couldn't I go to the West Indies and organize an institution on the Suva plan? And I was delighted to hear that he had about decided to promote my friend, Dr. McGusty, to the post of the High Commission's C.M.O. Nothing could be better luck for the Pacific, and I am proud if I put in a good word for a good man. I hope I had a share in his appoint‧ ment.

My main proposal, aside from a plan to protect Rennell from mischievous influences, was to have a thorough anthropological survey made there. I suggested that the Bishop Museum of Honolulu take charge of this, for it had been founded in memory of a high-born Hawaiian lady, and her husband's wealth had made it pre-eminent in Polynesian culture. Dr. Peter Buck, a Maori, was curator; the Museum could furnish just the talent we needed.

I was referred to the Colonial Office, where I struck the mysterious snag. Possibly the British objected because the Bishop Museum was an American institution; if so, they were stretching a point, for its leader was (and still is) a New Zealand Maori.

More likely it was the Church that stood in our way. When the news spread that I thought the old-time religion of Rennell was good enough for the people, and that the missionaries had only brought murder, disease and discontent to the little island, the Bishop of Melanesia sent a thundering message, declaring that he could "permit no boundaries to the Empire of Christ." Possibly the Adventists were putting in an oar, too; for I had heard one of them say in objection to the exclusion of his faith: "For we bring to the Rennellese God's greatest gift, the Bible." And there was another who said, "I would feel that I must go, even if I knew that as a result every one of them would die."

Governments and missions have been too often slandered, I think, because they have failed to accomplish miracles. In the Pacific they have been called upon to face hell and high water, literally, and my hat is off to their many achievements for the good of humanity. But I left London with the bitter knowledge that I had encountered the blind side of Christian officialdom — the sort of bigotry which means lack of understanding.

Perhaps I carried my message a year too late. As Barley said, "Sea-changes are very sudden on the Pacific."

Four years after the *Zaca* cruise I received reports from Eroni, saying that gonorrhea had spread from the White Sands to remoter districts where white men had never gone. Malaria was everywhere —

and I had found no trace of it when I surveyed the island in 1930 and 1933.

Outwardly the natives were prospering. The chiefs were building more and better houses with the handy tools for which they had traded their racial integrity. In 1920 when George Fulton's ship went there to recruit, he had seen no houses at all; a healthy, contented people were sleeping in caves or in the open. Now Rennell Island was having a building boom, and her population was going steadily downhill at the beck and call of every trading stranger.

About 1937 Dr. Crichlow made a survey there, and his worried findings came to me roundabout, in a letter from the Solomons. Everything that I had feared had come to pass. Gonorrhea had increased so that not a child had been born on Rennell Island in the past eighteen months.

I lost all desire to go back. I didn't care to see a splendid and unique race dying on its feet.

CHAPTER V

SUCH A LITTLE SCHOOL

I don't think that I am a sentimental man. I shouldn't be, for my work has not been along sentimental lines, and daily routine should have tried all the sugar out of my system. But when the *Mariposa* pulled out to sea I seemed to be pulling against it, every inch of the way. The races I had worked among for twenty-one years were not mine. Yet I had a foolish feeling that they were my people. I had been with them so constantly; even during my short leaves in the States they had seldom left my thoughts. A public health physician is no missionary. He does not starve for a 'Cause. He is well paid for his services, and if he is honest he does his level best to earn his wages. Looking back toward the last dot among the outlying Fijis, I hoped that I had earned my pay.

My older daughter Harriette, who was born in Mexico and whom Eloisa had carried as a baby into every tropical port where we could make another temporary home, was now grown. Sara Celia, born in Fiji, would be nine pretty soon. After all Eloisa had gone through — and she had gone through a great deal, practically and cheerfully — she didn't look her age, they told me. I was too near-sighted to tell very accurately, but somehow I knew that she didn't look her age.

My sight had very definitely failed, and that was what caused my retirement in June, 1939. The faulty vision which had bothered me in my student days was now far beyond a point where it could be corrected. I should have retired a year before I did, but one all-important thing held me in Suva — the Central Medical School.

"Such a tiny little school!" a very great lady had said, wasting a patronizing glance on the small buildings and a knot of students going into class. I had had no time to tell her that this little school had cost one man seventeen years of ambitious planning. Webb Waldron, when he was all too kind to me in his write-up in *Harper's Magazine*, had called it "unique in the world's educational institutions." He had done me honor overmuch, as Robert Emmet would have put it; but I was vain enough to believe that he had come nearer the truth than the very great lady.

As my days in Suva were coming toward an end my trusted champion the *Times and Herald* also did me honor overmuch in obituary tones. "Dr. Lambert brought to his work in Fiji, and in other adjacent groups, a personal enthusiasm that seemed to grow the longer he stayed. . . . He appeared to accept all the health problems of the Pacific as a personal challenge to S. M. Lambert. Many of these problems have either been solved or are in process of solution, and we . . . have been given strong reason to hope that the natural problems arising through the contact of white civilization with native races need not necessarily mean the gradual decay of these native races. . . ."

Well, I wasn't dead yet. Although I had caught some of the diseases I treated, I had recovered. No crocodile had eaten me, no snake or cannibal had done me harm. In all my years down there I had had but one accident: a Ford door closed on one of my fingers, and I lost a nail.

I was still sufficiently alive to wish that I could stay longer and drive home other nails which I had been hammering at for many years. The day before I left, Sir Maynard Hedstrom, who had supported me in everything, pointed to the School and said, "Next you know, Lambert, they'll be putting up a statue to you." I said, "I don't like statues. But if I rate one, I hope it will be of solid brass and show me wearing a pair of wrinkled shorts and carrying an armful of specimen tins. No, in a year or so if anybody says 'Lambert' they'll be asking 'Who?' I'm not worrying about a sculptor. What does worry me is the chance of some political thimblerigger coming along to undo everything we've done."

I spoke with healthy pessimism, and only half-believed my warning. The Central Medical School had been going for a little over ten years, and seemed to have stemmed the tide. It was one of the three pet ideas which Montague and I had hatched back in 1922: a model leper colony at Mokogai, an advanced Medical School for natives, and a Unified Medical Service to cover every island group in the Pacific. Two of these pets thrived and grew to maturity. The Mokogai colony came in with a rush of enthusiasm in 1923, and building began almost at once. The School required seven years of wire-pulling before it began to operate at the beginning of 1929. Up to then there had been but a poor little makeshift, backed by the only funds the Fiji Government could afford.

I have told you of my disappointment in the buildings when the school first opened. The Principal had to run his office in the physiological and chemistry laboratory, which we also used for a classroom; lectures on pathology were about ruined by the horrible overcrowding in the postmortem room, which was a little death trap. The dormitory for men was so inadequate that we had to limit students and hold the scholastic course down to three years.

Then came more ambitious planning, and a long tussle with Bacteriologist John Campbell, who insisted on a pathological laboratory that would cost £5,500 and upward. Dr. Heiser visited us in 1934 and saw our plans for the structure, 70′ × 33′ with floor space for a postmortem theater that would seat the whole student body; this building would be adequate for research work all over the South Pacific, and serve as a teaching institution for our N.M.P.'s. In 1934 the Foundation granted the money for this improvement. On my return from a three weeks survey in New Zealand I had brought back plans, drawn up by their experts, so that we could include a biochemical laboratory in the plant. Dr. Macpherson, our newly acquired bacteriologist, had meanwhile decided with Mr. Campbell that another building must be added and that most of our old equipment must be junked — these items would come to around £2,500 more.

Dr. Heiser had stipulated that the Colony should bear the cost of equipment. Fiji's wisely economical Chief Medical Officer, Dr. McGusty, thought that £500 would cover everything. Campbell and Macpherson finally convinced him that four times that amount would be needed, and they were right, I thought. I was more or less a referee in this argument between one Irishman and two Scotchmen. But we finally got our beautiful laboratory for research and for practical instruction in preventive medicine.

These facts and figures are just to show, in brief, the time and the effort it cost us all to bring things to anything like a satisfactory conclusion. In 1935 Mr. E. J. Theodore, an Australian mining man, gave £5,000 for a children's ward in the Hospital. That was a generous gift. But in my absence somebody decided to place the addition right next to our Central Medical School, so near that the noise would interrupt lectures; the idea behind it was to create a nuisance that would compel us to move the School off the Memorial Hospital grounds. . . . The politicos had been playing with our plan ever since we began building.

It required the long arm of Sir Murchison Fletcher, Fiji's fair-minded and progressive Governor, to scotch the plot. In 1936, when I went to London to confer with Sir Thomas Stanton, Britain's Chief Medical Officer, Stanton must have heard from Fletcher, for he asked me if I was satisfied with the location of the children's ward. I said, "No!" explosively, and Stanton cabled Fletcher not to do anything about that building until I got back and talked to him. Fletcher, aside from being my good friend, was an excellent bridge player and one of the best losers I have ever sat against — a rare virtue in the Colonies where winning any game from the Governor "isn't done," or is done at the risk of his friendship. It didn't take long for Fletcher to settle the matter of that spite-building, and in our favor.

The third of the schemes which Montague and I had formulated succeeded "in effect" in 1927. That was the Unified Medical Service for the South Pacific. We got another half-loaf there; the other half was lost through Montague's sense of honor, combined with the hen-minded jealousy of Fiji's very little Colonial Secretary.

My ruling ambition, all the time I was down there, was to tighten up the loose and scattered medical authority on all the island groups. The only hope was to centralize power, or nothing would ever get done. We had centralized it in the Mokogai leper colony, an unqualified success. We had centralized it more and more in the Medical School, where the same professional education was being given to natives from the four corners of Oceania. Suva had grown to be the South Pacific's medical center, and the one logical thing was to vest the whole public health authority in Fiji's Chief Medical Officer.

That seemed simple, for the Colonial Governors were behind us. Then politics came in through the door and common sense flew out of the window. My plan was to put Fiji's medical chief at the head of this wide service as Central Medical Authority with additional pay of £300 — little enough, especially when you take into consideration his increased duties, which would involve personal visits of inspection to all the island groups. The Foundation agreed to pay fifty per cent of this sum for a period of four years.

All set to go. But were we? Dr. Montague's honor chided him to a decision that he would accept no money that was not paid to him by the Empire that he served. Sir Eyre Hutson, then Governor, agreed that the High Commission Group would pay it all; but Montague objected that he did not deserve the extra stipend, as I would be doing practically all the work. We were stuck on that point. The annual pay of £300, added to Montague's salary of £1,100, would have been an inducement sufficient to attract an excellent man. But to ask anything like a first-class physician to devote all his time and energy to the Unified Service for £1,000 a year was simply out of the question.

When Montague retired, I raised the question again, and struck an obstacle no larger than a gallstone, and quite as tormenting. It was the little bureaucratic mind of Fiji's Colonial Secretary, who sat around all day worrying for fear that somebody in the Government would be making a halfpenny more than he did. You know the type. There's one — at least — in every American county courthouse. Mr. Colonial Secretary sat brooding, "Ha! If that rule goes through, the C.M.O. will be topping my salary!"

Well, it didn't go through. During my London visit in 1936, I discussed the deadlock with Sir Thomas Stanton. He said, "It's a splendid idea, and it would take hardly any new machinery to put it over. It has my hearty approval." But Fiji's Colonial Secretary belonged to another branch of the service, over which Stanton had no power. Suva's petty politician held a strategic corner where he could pop a pinch of sand into the wheel. Unfortunately all my suggestions have been pigeonholed.

In 1927 the Unified Medical Service had been voted in — on a small scale. It was devised to control the High Commission groups only; five in all. New Zealand, who had endorsed the idea from the first, was clamoring to come in. But our Colonial Secretary couldn't see it that way. Somebody would be getting too much power, with the run of all those islands. Therefore New Zealand was out. . . . All so like a chapter from the history of New York's Republican Party — or Democratic.

In spite of this I found myself appointed to the sonorous position of Deputy Central Medical Authority, under the Chief Medical

Officer as Central Medical Authority, who controlled the health work of the five groups. As he had never visited all these groups, and I had, I was kept quite busy as his adviser. In 1934 the Medical Authority went into fuller effect, so that the Chief could make the rounds and study conditions at first hand. The other day Dr. McGusty, now Chief Medical Officer, wrote me that these visits had become a part of his routine.

Here is something from my files. It is headlined "Memorandum for Dr. McGusty."

> Based on personal experience with administrations in the South Seas since 1916, I regret to record that nowhere in the world have I found so large a percentage of doctors who discredited the medical profession and the various governments that employed them. Poor organization is another important factor. . . . I have been greatly interested in the efforts of (Governor) Sir Murchison Fletcher to bring about more effective aid. The plan to amalgamate the medical services of Tonga, Gilbert and Ellices, Samoa and other groups with Fiji is an important step to make the service more attractive and draw to it the type of man and woman who may be counted upon to bring about a vast improvement. . . .

This document, in its original, was signed, "Victor G. Heiser." When last heard of, however, the local Colonial Secretary was still pouring sand into the dynamo.

Facts, figures, politics — those were all long rows to hoe. Now back to my School — I still call it mine, although it has passed into other hands. When you watch young people grow in body and intelligence you seem to grow with them. Despite my work in other fields, I was very close to them all for ten years, marking their improvement and their deficiencies. We had to make allowances for the first batch that came to us when we opened for business; they had been sent rather helter-skelter, but did surprisingly well under the circumstances. Because there were far more applicants than we could handle, we stiffened the entrance examinations all along the line. No more sentimentality in the choosing, and no political favoritism. We opened with forty boys, but with increased accommodations we soon had fifty. When we considered taking care of sixty there was a nervous murmur in

Suva: "Pretty soon we'll be overrun with N.M.P.'s and not need the School any more." That was ridiculous, for the increase in graduates was far behind Fiji's increase in population. Not to mention the needs of other island groups, clamoring for more places. I was always afraid that the School would be voted out of existence, for some unreasonable reason like the one I have mentioned.

Australia never sent any students from Papua or New Guinea; they still maintained that these natives were too "backward." I had worked in the jungle with Papuan and New Guinea boys, and I knew that they were no more backward than the inhabitants of the Solomon Islands and New Hebrides, who were represented with us from the first. I still feel that Australia, with her tremendous problem, will never make any progress with native health until she establishes some institution similar to the one in Suva — which is out of the question now, because they haven't the proper set-up. Sydney has an admirable school of tropical medicine and hygiene — for whites. It lacks both the clinical material and the stuff to cope with natives, and native conditions. Once in a great while this school will take in a black boy, merely to exhibit him as a curiosity.

Perhaps I am a co-educationalist; I have never settled that point with myself. But I feel very sure that no race advances very far unless its women advance with it. On the strength of that theory I made every effort to improve the condition of native student nurses. When the European nurses of the War Memorial moved to larger quarters I was glad to see the native girls housed in the abandoned building, a great improvement on what they had had.

Steps had been taken toward their advanced education. Before admission the young girls were given a course in the Methodist mission school, largely to teach them the rudiments of English. A Rockefeller Foundation fellowship sent a European nurse to the States to educate her in the modern theory and practice of training nurses. She returned in 1940 to open a school for native nurses, which would synchronize theoretical instruction with practical work in the hospital. Thus they would attain as high a rating in their profession as the N.M.P.'s in theirs. In outlying Fijian districts it was the policy to send out two native nurses with each N.M.P., to take care of two very important items: infant welfare and obstetrical cases.

I was pleased by the many marriages of these young women and our practitioners; they were usually happy. I fondly believed that two equal minds, mated in a common interest, would have all the advantages from the start. I was seldom disappointed. In the field the young wife was her husband's busy partner. If she retired to her village to settle down and have babies, she brought modern methods into her neighborhood.

For many of the boys the English language was a stumbling block, especially at first. The Polynesian students both spoke and wrote it well; New Zealand had taken care of that. But the Melanesians were another matter; during the first years of the School they came to us with nothing better than a smattering of English. We corrected that in time by requiring a preliminary course in English for all candidates. Even then they were handicapped, and it was interesting to see the Melanesian patience with which they slowly struggled through the mystery of our grammar, until they could rival their Polynesian classmates.

As underclassmen the boys from the Cooks and Samoa, to whom English was a second language, worked on the inferiority complex of Fijians and Solomon Islanders. Then as years went on, we watched the Melanesian lads begin to pull up. No, sir, they weren't going to let a lot of blithering Polynesians beat them at any game. They pored over books, they wrote reams, they spoke English among themselves and corrected one another's compositions. Sir Maynard Hedstrom was offering a senior year gold medal for excellence in Public Health studies. The Polynesians were bright enough to win it more often than not, but as upperclassmen they had to put up a lively fight to outdo the Melanesians. The earnest and industrious black fellows clawed their way to the top, every hour of that four-year course.

Here's a classroom scene, picturing the competitive spirit: —

[*Numa, a Cook Islander, is pointing at a skeleton and asking questions. He addresses Daniele, from the New Hebrides. Daniele is blue black, but not negroid. His eyes are circled with white and his white teeth glisten as he tries to concentrate on something he knows perfectly well, but can't express in English. Or if he can express it, it will come hard. He has to mine it out. Daniele is the one I liked to put on the front seat and rag, knowing that he would agonize over the answer, but would finally get it right.*
NUMA: How many bones in the human hand?]

DANIELE: Eight. (*After an inner struggle.*)

NUMA: Right! (*Daniele shows a thousand dollars' worth of per-fect teeth.*)

[*Numa turns to Mu, who is not very bright for a Samoan.*

NUMA: What bones are affected by a Colles's fracture?

[*Mu groans and hesitates. He won't give up, but Numa is tired of waiting, so he passes it to Tatoa, a dark, chunky Gilbertese who usually knows the answer.*

TATOA: The radius ulna.

[*Sounds of approval from the whole class, and a rather shocked expression because Mu knows so little.*

As an example of the steady, capable Fijian mind I think I should select Sowani, born a chief and mentally so well endowed that he became probably the outstanding one of the old School's graduates. He served in the Gilbert and Ellices for some thirty years, and had been stationed there for a long time when I first met him. European doctors might come and go, but most of the Europeans wanted Sowani when they were sick. During the First World War he was made Acting Senior Medical Officer, the highest medical position in the Group. The Government appreciated his services by giving him a salary and allowance which permitted him a European standard of living. About the time I left Fiji he retired on a pension and was decorated by the King, quite a distinction for a native boy. When I made my survey he had completed his 20,000th operation for glands in the neck; his surgery was beautiful. Incoming Senior Medical Officers in the G. & E. were squeamish about being successors to the dark-skinned Practitioner. When patients called for him in preference to the white doctors, poor Sowani would remain the pattern of etiquette. "Mr. So-and-So had called for you, Doctor," he would say; but when the white physician called, the patient was disappointed. One candid and sick Australian said, "Get out, you Son of Something! It's Sowani I want." Sowani was always to be counted on. He was a Fijian.

When I looked over the classes in our growing school, with no intent to play favorites — for I think I know the contrasting virtues of these two fine races — I could not help but see that in practical application the Fijian was far superior to the Samoan and the Cook Islander. The latter were brilliant in theory, but set a Fijian to reasoning a thing out for himself and his conclusions were more apt to be right, for the slow logic of his mind was almost Scottish. Principal Clunie and I watched the work of one plum-colored Fijian named Ravuki. Ravuki wasn't worth his salt, at first, and was too lazy to put on his own *lavalava*. But in his senior year he developed a burst of speed that was quite astonishing. He fairly shone in the preventive medicine course. He blazed his way forward at such a pace that he threatened the performance of Alo, a Tongan boy who had been the School's wonder and had walked away with all the prizes. In the final examination Ravuki seemed to have the edge on Alo. I was afraid that my affection for Fiji had biased my judgment, so I ordered a second examination and called in two European physicians to sit with me as referees. This time the Fiji boy was so good that he was still talking when the two other judges made up their minds that he had won hands down.

Ravuki became one of our most successful N.M.P.'s, and like most Fijians, almost tragically conscientious. Right after graduation he was sent out to the jungle to control a typhoid epidemic. In his work our prize pupil picked up a typhoid germ — and was so ashamed of it that he refused to visit the School, all the time I was there.

His upper-class rival, Alo, had a much more romantic story when he went into practice. Principal Clunie — and a "damn good man" as we say unofficially — was something of a prize winner himself. He started with the rank of tutor, and before he was through with it Australia gave him a gold medal for his work among native races. Well, if I unconsciously played favorites with Ravuki, Clunie was much inclined toward Alo, and had such faith in his ability that he gave him special favors in surgery. Alo got to be as good a surgeon as you could ask for anywhere.

He was so capable that the C.M.O. of Tonga let him do surgery there. When Alo was put in charge of the Haapai group, the medico of the Vavau group was much annoyed, for all his surgical work began going to Haapai. The young Practitioner had set eyes on a pretty girl of a noble Haapai family, and was in despair because his sweetheart's parents objected to his humble lineage. All the traders and other Europeans were in sympathy with the Romeo and Juliet situation, and from one of the sympathizers Alo borrowed a sea-going launch and filled it with gas. This was on Sunday night when all good Christians were at church. Very conveniently the girl stepped out of church and into the boat. When her family came out to give chase they found that all the launches in the dock were out of commission. Somebody had drained off the gas and crippled the engines.

The job of selecting boys for our School was never an easy one. Different races and different environment had to be taken into consideration. In Fiji we advertised for candidates, and the competitive examinations included the three R's, plus a certain knowledge of English. We had to compromise between the over-young and the over-old. Boys from fifteen to sixteen would graduate too young. Those of twenty had been out of school too long. In the matter of sending incompetents, I had to visit several island groups and lecture the Europeans on their duty to keep up the standard. This brought about the rigid tests we required, and with satisfactory results. Two visiting English medical professors pleased me by saying that our boys in daily recitation compared favorably with students of the same grade in the University of London's Medical School.

The matter of habit and custom had to be attended to. We had to treat them all as equals, and strike some common denominator. The lads from the Solomon Islands and New Hebrides — before well educated half-castes came to us — had never eaten off a table or sat in a chair. Their *milieu* was the floor. To give them credit in the eyes of the sophisticated Polynesians we must teach them certain rudimentary table manners. The Samoan and Cook Island boys, on the other hand, often showed up at the Grand Pacific Hotel's dances in tail coats and stiff shirts.

This was something of a situation, in the School's first years. Our Polynesians weren't quite at ease with their low-browed associates. Then, to their credit, they began to see what it was all about, and things straightened out to a generally loyal corps spirit. We saw the danger of over-Europeanizing them; for they must not return to their homes and be discontented with island ways. We always put more stress on cleanly, sanitary habits than "fussy fixin's" like tablecloths. Some of our students who had been too Europeanized by New Zealand before they came did not turn out so well. They knew so much already that they saw no necessity to work for what they got. It was another case of the hare and the tortoise; or, more properly, the hare became the tortoise and loafed on the job.

There was one of our Cook Islanders whose scholastic record was so unusual that the Administration there wanted to send him to London to complete his education, until I seriously objected. Such a precedent would fill the School with jealous discontent. The Cook Islands, I found later, had spoiled the boy so badly that he acquired vicious habits. He had enough character to reform himself, but not until his Practitionership was taken away from him.

His was an exceptional case.

My volunteer marriage bureau for Practitioners and native nurses became an unqualified success. In Fiji the quality of nurses was improving all the time, and before long an especially pretty one was a marked girl the minute she got her diploma. There have been many such marriages, and there would be still more if it were not for the native missionaries, who are cutting ahead of our boys. In Samoa, where the New Zealand system turns out Polynesian nurses who are sweet as sugar and smart as chain lightning, it is almost taken for granted that an N.M.P. will lead one to the altar, or make a brave try at it.

A cross-eyed Samoan named Tongamau, one of our brightest and best, married a native nurse. Both he and his young wife had specialized on infant feeding, so after the baby was born and had attained a few months' growth Tongamau took him off breast-feeding and decided to bring him up entirely on native food. On that basis the Tongamaus worked out a whole formula of infant diet and composed careful instructions for preparing the ingredients, the change and weight of meals from week to week, and so on. Tongamau's account of this successful experiment was first printed in our school publication *The Native Medical Practitioner* and was widely reviewed in standard medical journals.

N.M.P. Okeseni also married a native nurse, and his article in the same publication reveals another Practitioner's cleverness in the use of materials at hand. (Okeseni, by the way, is the Samoan pronunciation of "oxygen.") Okeseni's essay is entitled "Coconut Fiber Used in Ligatures," and says, ". . . I was thinking . . . that the fibers of the husk could be used instead of silkworm gut; for they are protected from any outside contamination. . . ." He employed them successfully in many operations.

Any copy of the *Practitioner* is worth looking over for interesting articles, written in businesslike professional English. "General Practice in Native Villages of Fiji," by N.M.P. Ieni; "Foodstuffs in the Gilbert Islands," by Third-Year Student Arobati Hicking; and there's one called "Medical Work on Rennell Island" by N.M.P. Hughie Wheatley which I especially remember. He is the half-caste son of Norman Wheatley, the yacht-collector; and Hughie's article tells how he adopted a four-months-old Rennellese baby whose mother was too feeble to nurse it; he saved the child with a diet of native food, somewhat after Tongamau's formula.

I have watched the lives of all my boys, going out into the world. There was Tau Cowan, a half-British Cook Islander who married out of his profession. The girl he picked was a daughter of the King of Rarotonga; she had been beautifully educated in New Zealand, and has made him a good wife; Tau has become one of our outstanding graduates.

John Numa, on the other hand, found his wife in an insane asylum. She was far from crazy; in fact she was the native warder's daughter. It was the warder's reason that was endangered, for John's courtship was so hot and heavy that I was called in, and a minister was immediately summoned. Some of the whites wanted to make a scandal out of John's behavior — which was not scandalous according to the native code — but the couple went to the Cooks, where Mrs. Numa was a great social hit and became the successful rival of a lady who had long ruled the roost, a half-caste official wife. John Numa made an outstanding survey of the leper situation on Penrhyn.

We went in for athletics, of course, and a school band. Ielu Kuresa, a Samoan, organized the band, and as he conducted the popular tunes his pale scholar's face was filled with the spiritual earnestness that finally led him to his death. Mesalume, the husky Fijian, was a Lau boy, and a contrast in character. We taught him to box, and when he was matched with Helu, a Tongan about twice his size, Mesalume put him out in the third round with a stiff one on the chin. This Fijian was a natural athlete, and the mainstay of our football team.

Ielu and Mesalume — contrasting types of contrasting races, they met the same end in the line of duty.

I have a sort of father's affection for the natives of all the groups, but my admiration always turns back to the Fijian, a tower of strength, who never lets you down when you need him. I have seen so many of them go out into the field and do far more than their share, far better than their competitors, — dignified, ethical medical men.

Mesalume had great force of character, and an intellectual independence. Once I had to intervene when he got into an argument with an Australian nurse in the War Memorial. The delicate point was that Mesalume was right, but a colored boy was not supposed to have an opinion of his own. It took diplomacy to get him out of that mess. His reaction was very Scottish. "I still think so," he told me in confidence.

Early in the School's career we organized their teams, intramural affairs. True, it was not American football, but the more open Rugby. With the gusto of old gridiron experience, I saw that their play could be just as rough as ours. Men like Mesalume played for the glory of Fiji, for the Fijian is "unco' proud" of his strength and skill. The only disharmony that ever arose in the Medical School was when the boys were choosing players; the Polynesians all ganged up against the Fijians, and vice versa, most definitely. When we crystallized into a unit we played against the Police Team, the Agricultural Department and about six other organizations. The pick of our boys got the "shield," and some were chosen for the much coveted All Fiji Team. The chosen ones were Fijians, with no exception. And Mesalume, of course, was one of them.

In a series of inter-island battles the All Fijis met the famous New Zealand Maoris, who had bowled over about everything they had met, wherever Rugby was played. When Fiji met Maori it was a different story, "all blood and guts," as an Australian critic expressed it. Our native boys had the advantage because they could kick barefoot — wonderful, how they could do it. They would come on the field in the regulation Rugby uniform, but after the first scrimmage the air would be full of shoes and stockings — the Fijians were rushing into battle as their cannibal grandsires did, with naked toes and tiger hearts. Then larger objects would come soaring out of the huddle; the bodies of Maoris, falling with a deadly plunk. In reprisal the flying Maoris would come back with a thud that was like a convulsion of nature. Their convulsion was more deadly in the last game of one series. We of Fiji were small-minded enough to say, "Well, let 'em have it this time. The officials were all New Zealanders, and they couldn't let their champions go home again with nothing to show for it."

Pride of race takes some queer turns. The one Negro in Fiji was a coal-black American who said, "Yassa, I was de first white man on the Mba River." Pride of race was rampant in Peti, one of our Samoans, who never failed to boast of his American blood. His grandfather was a Negro sailor. On the strength of this distinction he won the hand of a well-born Fijian half-caste and took her back to Samoa. He was another one who did great credit to the School.

Our Fijian N.M.P. Eroni came from Lau, where the people are fair-skinned as Polynesians. When he worked alone on Rennell it was quite understandable that he should have gained the reputation of being the first "white man" who had penetrated half the island. Eroni's success among white residents of the Solomons was so great that one lady wrote to a Sydney paper to thank him for saving her life and her sister's. Such achievements are a commonplace in Fiji; Britishers in the back country argue about the attainments of an N.M.P. as we people at home discuss the family doctor.

One of these days, a Fijian basso will sing Otello's role in the Metropolitan Opera House. If you have ever heard their deep, true voices you will agree with me. And if you have ever watched the action of their mighty thews on the playing field, you may well believe that a world's heavyweight champion will also emerge from one of these dark islands. So far, however, they have much to learn. I read of one who went to London to meet a middleweight; but since the sports columns are not featuring him, I think he may not have done so well.

There is a gigantic fellow named Ratu Mbola who has degenerated into a half-Europeanized show-off, and throws out his chest when the boats come in in hopes that somebody will buy him a drink. To distinguish himself from the common herd he wears golf socks, and tennis shoes, and carries a fly-brush over his shoulder. "Bar Fly" is the name both he and his brush have earned.

In days gone by when Jack Johnson became champion of the world by defeating Tommy Burns in Australia there was rejoicing in every Fijian village. "One of our race has conquered!" was the cry. At that time Ratu Mbola was in his prime, a muscular chief of Mbau. On the way home from his defeat Tommy Burns stopped off at Suva and the hushed word went through the villages, "He's running away from the black man who beat him!" So Ratu Mbola came forth as a local black hope, and challenged Mr. Burns. The evening of the fight the arena was packed with natives who thronged in to see a white man crumple under a volley of Fijian blows. But somehow Tommy didn't crumple. He played cat and mouse for two rounds, pretending to be groggy from Mbola's blows. In the first minute of the third he got tired of making false passes and floored Mbola with one heartbreaking upper-cut. The referee did not render a decision. He didn't have a chance. Mbola went through the ropes on all fours, and when next seen was running down the street, waving his boxing gloves.

All of this was quite unfair to the Fijian. It was like taking him to the piano and asking him to play a Bach fugue. Mesalume, as an athlete and professional man, was of a quite different pattern. We sent him to the New Hebrides, a field that would try the soul of any man. His reports came in; he was administering medicine in feverish jungles that had been beyond the reach of government officials. He was treating thousands for every disease under the tropical sun. Mr. Paton, always the stanch friend of my N.M.P.'s, took him in when he could and worried because the boy was so overworked.

Suddenly Mesalume's reports stopped coming in. What had happened to him? Then a letter from Mr. Paton: —

. . . Mr. Siller, an Austrian, at South West Bay, Malekula, had blackwater fever. Dr. Mesalume treated him, and thought that he was on the mend. But Mr. Siller died next day. Dr. Mesalume contracted blackwater fever. Mr. Corlette was most kindly and attentive, but Dr. M. died. We are all deeply grieved. He was always so willing and keen to help. . . . I remember what pride he had in his Medical College, and I think that he would have increased its usefulness. . . . He earned the respect of the natives, so that the nearest village of Tatau had made a yam garden for him, without pay. . . .

I went to the New Hebrides and found the place where he had died on duty, in a remote corner of the jungle. Mesalume, like all the men of Lau, had a passionate love of home, and this was so far away, so completely lonely . . . Wild black faces had stared in at the window, wondering what he was saying in his delirious ramblings. Blackwater fever might have killed him; nobody really knew. I did the sentimental thing, I suppose, when I asked the Condominium Government to mark his grave. They put up a handsome concrete block with some of his history on it and the epitaph, "He Died in a Foreign Country." Yes, he had given the best he had to save life, and when his time came he had died the death of a lonely dog. I had always thought that something like that would happen to me. But, God, here I am!

After this death we could have got a dozen to go up there and take his place. That's the Fijian for you.

Ielu, his Samoan classmate, was another story, just as tragic. When he died on duty Dr. Heiser said it was one of the greatest losses imaginable for the Pacific. Ielu had worked for his own people with the fiery zeal of a priest. Through all his training in the Medical School he sweated his way upward with one ambition: to go home and bring help to his own Samoans. His tall, slender figure was forever bending over books, his luminous brown eyes drinking in the useful facts that would contribute to his future. He was monastic in his self-effacement. He should have been a lonely type, but underneath his detachment there was a warmth which made him popular with his classmates, and he became a leader in student activities.

Well, he went back to Samoa, and I was a bit nervous about what might happen to him. The Mau Rebellion was in full swing, and with his zealous temperament I was afraid that he would be in it up to the ears. Instead of that, he became the bellwether that kept the sane ones in line. He was there as a doctor, and never for a moment did he forget his duty to the Medical Administration. I have one vivid memory of Ielu in action. It was on a Samoan back porch, none too roomy at best, and the patient's relatives were crowded around the table with the usual prayers and palaver. Dr. Hunt, the C.M.O., was with me to watch the operation, which was for an elephantoid scrotum. With people threatening to jog his elbow, with relatives yammering in his ear, Ielu handled his instruments with concentrated exactitude. When it was over and Ielu was washing up, Dr. Hunt said softly, "I wish I could get as good a job as that in the Apia Hospital."

In March, 1936, an epidemic of influenza broke out in Upolu and Ielu came down with it. He was always working on the hairline of his strength; and with the emergency of the epidemic he was called from his sickbed to give aid. He put in days of long hours before his exhausted heart gave out. He died in Dr. Pat Monaghan's arms. The Samoan obituaries did not need to tell me that they had lost a surgeon who was on his way to greatness. A Samoan student, writing about him in our *Native Medical Practitioner*, told the simple truth when he said, "He died in harness. . . . He was kind to the human race and all loved him." The Samoan Administration established the Ielu Kuresa Gold Medal in his memory, and generously marked it *For the best Fijian of the year*. That was their gratitude to us for giving them Ielu.

The passing of these brave and devoted men still touches me so deeply that I seldom speak of them. Another one who died is still more tragic to me, for that death was not so long ago. Last summer a letter from Fiji came to me at my California home. It was from Malakai and told me that Vakatawa, who had been my assistant, had committed suicide. I couldn't understand it. Vakatawa had stood like a rock and worked like a hero in every assignment I had given him. An expert on tuberculosis, he had examined all the chests in the Colos, and his reports were works of art in their scientific accuracy. He had his sense of humor, too. Once I sent him on a survey over a far corner of Viti Levu, and he came back with nothing but a tattered *lavalava* and his boxes of equipment. It turned out that a fishing party from Mbengga had met him on the coast and stripped him of every rag he had on; they gutted his suitcases, relieved him of five pounds cash, left him naked on the beach. Pretty rough work, but it was an old-time custom when the people of Mbengga met the people of Lau, and vice versa. Vakatawa had fought so hard for his microscope and other scientific items that they decided to let him keep them. Quite unembittered, he had borrowed a *lavalava* and come home smiling. When I said, "I guess I'll go out and survey Mbengga myself," Vakatawa chuckled, "Better not, Doctor. They'll strip you too, because you're with me."

Those who knew him well said of Vakatawa, "He has the mind of a first-class white man." That remark was a bit patronizing, but it expressed the general confidence in him. He had gone very deeply into the study of magic, and to his reports I owe a great deal of what I learned about *draunikau* and the ritual of the seven curses.*

* Described in Part II, Chapter I.

Did Vakatawa end his life as the result of some magic wish? That was out of the question. Time and again, he had outfaced the witch doctors with practical lessons in modern medicine, and he was too well-loved among the villages for anybody to put a curse on him. I have looked into Vakatawa's case as best I could from where I sit and where he lies, and I think I know the reason why he locked himself in his room and put a razor blade across his wrists. Always a sensitive man, he had a sensitive man's high temper, which his racial courtesy seldom allowed to get the better of him. But that hot temper got him into some sort of brawl, and after it was over he felt that he had disgraced himself and had not lived up to his responsibilities as a Practitioner. He was inordinately proud of his profession, and when his brooding mind told him that he had let the School down, he decided that there was no use living any longer.

I give Vakatawa an honored place among those who died in the line of duty.

Our little School has grown, and is growing. My constant hope is that its roots have gone so deep into the soil of Fiji that no political whim or Anglo-Saxon prejudice shall ever blast it in some clumsy attempt at transplanting. Already we have sent out well over a hundred competent medical men; not many, perhaps, in the millions of ocean miles which their work must cover. But their efficiency shows in the general improvement in health wherever they have operated.

To the outsider it may seem a bit incredible that the descendants of cannibals — and the majority of them are just that — should be devoting their young talents to saving life, where their ancestors were bent on destroying it. But to me the protean change is a very logical thing. The cannibals were anatomists, and their gruesome habits made them familiar with the set-up of the human body. Just as Roman surgeons studied the victims dragged from the arena, so the wiser of the anthropophagi observed and learned. Neither ways were pretty roads to knowledge, but strange things have happened in the Martyrdom of Man.

As I lectured the students in the postmortem theater I often paused in interest at the skill of this one and that, plying the knife. No one of them had ever seen cannibalism in practice; but ancestral voices, turned friendly and benevolent, seemed to be telling them what to do.

I have a photograph which I took down in Santa Ana, Solomon Islands. It is of a brown woman, practically nude, with shark's teeth around her neck and a long clam-hinge sticking through her nose. I think I've told you how I took this picture of Mrs. Kuper, the trader's wife. She was holding up one small, naked boy, and another stood at her side. I have another picture; it is of a good-looking boy, very collegiate in a tweed suit and striped necktie. He would be hard to recognize as the naked child in the first picture.

Geoffrey Kuper's father was sufficiently well-to-do to send him for study in New Zealand. He graduated from our Central Medical, class of '38, and Sydney gave him a prize "for the most distinguished scholar of the year." Before he took up his duties as N.M.P. in the Solomons, he dropped in on his old school-friends in Auckland. A reporter got hold of him and Geoffrey told of the first scholastic prize he ever received, an honorary belt which his mother's tribe gave him as an introduction to manhood. It was a hard initiation. For six months he had stayed in the ceremonial house, among the ancestral canoes and family skulls. Priests came to his pagan retreat to instruct him in tribal duties, which included house-building and the preparing of a yam and dalo garden.

Then he was put in a fishing canoe where the priests angled until they caught a great bonito. It was the boy's task to wrestle with the fish and hold it until it ceased to flap. Boy and fish were taken to the pagan altar where priests squeezed the bonito's gills and let drops of blood fall into the initiate's mouth. At the end of the long ceremony Geoffrey was taken to a high tower and allowed to throw food down to the admiring populace. "That part was fun," he said.

A graduate Practitioner, Geoffrey had been away from his mother's tribe so long that he had forgotten her inherited language. But his father, a very progressive European, wanted his son to have the best of our civilization. He was right, I think, for Geoffrey is doing fine work in the Solomons.

CHAPTER VI

IN RETROSPECT

As the Pacific's halfway house, Suva has become more and more of a stopping-off place for the great and the near-great. Royalty, inquiring novelists and scientific bigwigs have come in the regular way, by sea. The first visitor from the sky was Kingsford-Smith, and because he must have trees cut down from the parade ground to make a safe landing, Suva was in a dither. The residents loved those trees so fondly that they didn't start to fell them until after they learned that the aviator's plane was well on its way from Hawaii. Then down they came, and when the giant bird roared in it was probably the high moment in Fijian history.

English princes and royal dukes weren't exactly a commonplace. Their comings and goings threw the colony into a patriotic frenzy. Before the then Prince of Wales decided on "the woman I love" Suva all but gave him a coronation. The Duke of Gloucester's visit in 1935 caused a social upheaval among the natives, who were preparing a colossal dance in his honor. Many of the boys, in imitation of European styles, had been cutting off their great bundles of hair. The master of ceremonies gave it out that no dancer would be eligible unless he wore the high, round hairdress of classic Fiji. One of the high chiefs of Mbau, whose hereditary privilege it was to act as cup-bearer in the kava ceremony, defied the rule and came to the dance in his college cut. He was incontinently rejected. The Duke had two Scotland Yard men with him, but that didn't interfere with his efforts to be democratic. He was especially fond of the bacon-and-egg parties common in young Suva society after the ball; these were at about dawn, when the Duke's watch-dog equerry was sound asleep. After many stiff-collar affairs in the larger colonies Gloucester found his release, I think, in Suva's simple, kindly hospitality.

His voyage was bothered, however, by people who were less considerate of royal democracy. As *H.M.S. Australia* was leaving Samoa, the little yacht *Seth Parker,* owned by an enterprising radio star, sent out an S O S. When the *Australia* came about for rescue work the yacht announced: "Open your wireless set and you can hear a broadcast all over the U. S., saying that the Duke of Gloucester has come to the rescue of the *Seth Parker.*" Another coy one followed: "Won't the Duke come up on the bridge so that we can take his picture?" Gloucester's sulphuric words must have raised a storm, for an hour or so after the royal cruiser went her way a hurricane blew up, and the battered *Seth Parker* sent out another S O S, a real one this time. Dutifully the *Australia* turned back again, and stood by for two days until a vessel from Pago Pago came and picked up the offensive little yacht.

Before the present King and Queen of England even dreamed of wearing crowns they paid us a visit as Duke and Duchess of York. We met them on two occasions, an official ball at Government House and a more informal affair in the Grand Pacific's ballroom. The Duke of York said that his father had visited Fiji and had drunk the kava which they "spit in the bowl." So that party with old Thakombau was family history. The Duchess was what we Americans call a "nice girl," and her poise never seemed to get in the way of her good humor. I liked the way she handled a young cadet, whom the occasion and the champagne had somewhat exhilarated. It was contrary to custom, but he wanted to win a bet when he asked her for a dance. She said, "Sorry, my card's full." Well, so was the young cadet; he took another drink and asked her again. Again she was sorry. Next afternoon he woke with a headache and moaned, "Lord, what did I do?" His pals were all too ready to tell him, and with flights of imagination. He prepared himself to be cashiered, but nothing happened. It would be romantic to say that the Duchess intervened in his behalf. I doubt if she remembered his name.

When the School was well started and I could spend more of my time in Suva's civilized environment I occupied a crossroads position where I met many, going and coming. Earl and Lady Beatty were guests at Sir Harry Luke's dinner party, and I was much flattered when I found that the Earl knew quite a lot about the School. This contact was more impressive, perhaps, but less engaging than the one I made when the yacht *Caroline* came in and her owner asked me to come aboard with some medical advice. The owner was Douglas Fairbanks, and the tall, blond lady with arched eyebrows was his

When I first saw the Solomon Islands they served as a type example. In the northwest islands near New Guinea, where shipping, trading, recruiting and missionizing were plentiful, the disease rate was high. As we traveled to the southeast into areas less accessible to visitors the so-called "native diseases" steadily diminished. Twelve years later showed me the change: The Southeast was sick from tuberculosis, dysentery, pneumonia and venereal, which strangers had carried there and spread among non-immune natives. I have mentioned the incidence of these seemingly unaccountable plagues, burning like fire in dry grass. The old-time voyagers, who did their share to spread infection, have noted the evil effects. These things are still going on in the remote corners of the Pacific.

The recruiting of contract labor was once a curse, but more enlightened government has turned it into something of a blessing; wise labor laws have made it so that a worker usually leaves the plantation with his health better than when he came. The New Hebrides, where French planters serve drink, drugs and firearms to their native helpers, is an exception.

There is a school of thought which points to the "decay of custom" as depopulation's main cause. The native has ceased to take interest in a warrior's physical well-being. The missions have discouraged those picturesque ancient ceremonials which were the background of tribal life. The Rivers Theory argues that boredom creates a psychic depression which actually decreases reproductive power; that it also encourages abortion and infanticide amidst the cry, "Why grow slaves for another race?" Undoubtedly this theory works out in some regions I have seen, where Christianity has been an ineffective substitute for the war club and the tribal dance. The warrior grows flabby. His wife, a squaw, slaves on.

But the main cause of depopulation in the Pacific, let me repeat, *is the introduction of diseases to which the natives have no immunity*. Even in the heart of Papua, where the Fathers of the Sacred Heart performed practical miracles among ferocious mountain cannibals a hundred miles from the coastline, working a non-malarious soil that produced bountiful nourishment, I heard the death-knell. I can't forget how I heard Father Fastre's bemused voice speaking under the moon: "Doctor, when I first came here I could stand at my doorway and see ten thousand people." Where had they gone? The nearest village was four hours away, and from where he gazed the good priest saw only moonlit ghosts.

Cannibalism and head-hunting were rough blessings, because they quarantined tribe against tribe. Cannibalism is a shocking habit, as Herman Melville, if I remember correctly, pointed out, adding, "I ask whether the mere eating of human flesh so far exceeds in barbarity that custom [hanging, drawing and quartering, perhaps] which only a few years since was practiced in enlightened England?" I am not pro-cannibal, but medically speaking I can see how well it worked to keep the other fellow in his place.

And what of it? asks Mr. Homebody as he walks toward the old parking lot off Main Street. How in the world will it affect me or the boys around American Legion Hall if those sun-kissed yahoos on the Isle of Gumbo do happen to curl up and die? Head-hunters are all right in side-shows, but they don't affect business on Main Street.

Main Street is the very point, Mr. Homebody. I once told you how far-off contagions might someday travel to your front door and disturb your parochial calm. But here's another side of it — something which might upset your business, because you're a partner in world business, whether you know it or not.

The European seized the Pacific, and that's an old story. In spite of the horrible example of bombing and burning which European civilization is showing today to the uncivilized, the settled holdings of various national governments over a quarter of the globe's surface, the Pacific, must remain *in statu quo*. Unless it does, you will hear something you will not like, Mr. Homebody. The *status quo* over that vast empire is all-important, and it cannot be maintained unless the white man takes up his burden and carries it through.

Why? Because tropical products have become world business. The lands down there, including immense Australia, vast New Guinea and big New Zealand, make up a territory comparable in size to our Western Hemisphere. The failure of mines, plantations and fisheries on one side of our quarrelsome Earth cannot fail to react banefully on the other side. Copra, hemp, cotton, sugar, gold, spices, fruits, pearls, innumerable varieties of oils and drugs which have been discovered, or will be, are only items among the tropical products which have entered the international market. They are burdening ships in enormous quantities, and the tonnage will grow greater, unless . . .

If native labor fails, Oceania's production will fail. Healthy, contented native labor is indispensable to the producer. The importation of Asiatics will not answer the question. Regard the Fiji Government's experiment with East Indians, who are today outbreeding the Fijian, and have brought him no benefits. Observe Japan's taking-over of the Marshall Islands, and the subsequent infiltration of yellow men all over the Pacific. These strangers came because the native was too sick to work the land. The oriental's peaceful penetration is already doing mischief down there; he brought with him a set of political and social ideas which inevitably hook up with his homeland prejudices, and extend into every intrigue of *Weltpolitik*. He has nothing in common with the simple islander whom he is pushing aside.

What will come of it all? Supply and demand are cruel partners. The planter must work his plantation, the shipper fill his ships; and if there is not enough healthy native labor to do the work, then send away to Shanghai or Bombay for what you can get. These fellows may not last long, either, but they will stay long enough to disturb the economic balance. South Sea industry will grow anemic, an easy prey to whatever Axis happens to be grinding blood out of the human race.

That, Mr. Homebody, will mean another war; and even if you are a year or two too old for military service, your Main Street will rumble with the jar of an economic balance overthrown. Before that breaks right in front of your office building, maybe you will agree with the Rockefeller Foundation's theory of economics. Keep the native alive, restore his health, give him enough European knowledge to fend him against the evils of Europe, then he will go happily ahead cultivating the soil for the world and himself.

Perhaps in these pages I have dwelt too much on the savagery of certain backward tribes. Have I said enough about the self-sufficing social pattern which these so-called barbarians had built around themselves before the pale invader came to fuddle them? Have I said enough of the ideal family life and wise social laws that prevailed over old Polynesia? It needed no British or American schoolmaster to teach them the kindness and neighborly generosity that are the aim of higher civilization. They had these things, which are at the heart of social happiness.

Definitely, I am not a Cassandra. The islander, I feel, will survive to achieve great things in a brave new world. Already he has contributed to science and statecraft, and in some cases has dominated in a business world which yesterday was a closed book to him. He will make his way in the arts, literature, music, painting. He had been misled and fooled for generations, but his intellect is overcoming an inferiority complex which the pale overlord once foisted on him. Island governments have become humane and understanding, more missionaries are letting fanaticism yield to common sense. Utopia is always a long way off, but I'll risk a prophecy. Guide the native with sympathetic intelligence, and the time will come when he will cease to be our pupil. He will become our teacher. Not in the science of war, God deliver us, but in the more difficult art of living together in harmony and peace.

So the Lamberts have bought a house in California. Eloisa tells me that she will soon have the best rose garden in Walnut Creek. We are a bit too far inland to see the Pacific; but I can feel it, over in the west. Fiji doesn't seem so far away.

THE END

INDEX

INDEX

The South Pacific Islands, where Dr. S. M. Lar[...]

since 1918. Equatorial scale 0 — 500 Nautical mil[...]

140 150 160 170

0

AUSTRALIAN MANDATE

Nauru
Ocean

ADMIRALTY IS.
Mussau
N. Hanover
Aitape
N. Ireland
BISMARCK
ARCHIP.

DUTCH
NEW
GUINEA
Sepik R.
N.E. NEW GUINEA
Austr. mandate
Madang
New Britain
PAPUA
to Austr.
FLY R.

Bougainville
Choiseul
Sta. Isabel
SOLOMON
N. Georgia
Sikiana
Malaita
Guadalcanal
S. Cristobal

G   E

TAMAZ
FACES

Buna
Tufi
Murua
LOUISIADE IS.

Port
Moresby
Abau
Misima
Rossel
Tagula

SANTA CRUZ IS.
Fat[...]
Tukop[...]

Torres St.
C. York

Bellona
Rennel
Is.

NEW HEBRIDES

BANKS IS.
Espiritu Santo
Malekula
Efate
Erom[...]
Tann[...]
Fu[...]

10

Great Barrier Reef

CHESTERFIELD IS.

Island of lost race

Belep
LOYALTY IS.
New Caledonia

F R A N

20

Tropic of Capricorn

Brisbane

AUSTRALIA

Norfolk

30

Sydney

Adelaide
Canberra

W   E

Melbourne

S

40

140 150 160 170